Lecture Notes in Computer Science 9609

Commenced Publication in 1973
Founding and Former Series Editors:
Gerhard Goos, Juris Hartmanis, and Jan van Leeuwen

More information about this series at http://www.springer.com/series/7407

Manuel Mazzara · Andrei Voronkov (Eds.)

Perspectives of System Informatics

10th International Andrei Ershov Informatics Conference, PSI 2015
in Memory of Helmut Veith
Kazan and Innopolis, Russia, August 24–27, 2015
Revised Selected Papers

 Springer

Editors
Manuel Mazzara
Innopolis University
Innopolis
Russia

Andrei Voronkov
The University of Manchester
Manchester
UK

ISSN 0302-9743 ISSN 1611-3349 (electronic)
Lecture Notes in Computer Science
ISBN 978-3-319-41578-9 ISBN 978-3-319-41579-6 (eBook)
DOI 10.1007/978-3-319-41579-6

Library of Congress Control Number: 2016942778

LNCS Sublibrary: SL1 – Theoretical Computer Science and General Issues

Printed on acid-free paper

This Springer imprint is published by Springer Nature
The registered company is Springer International Publishing AG Switzerland

Preface

To the memory of Helmut Veith

The Ershov Informatics Conference (the PSI Conference Series) is the premier international forum in Russia for research and applications in computer, software, and information sciences. The conference brings together academic and industrial researchers, developers, and users to discuss the most recent topics in the field. PSI provides an ideal venue for setting up research collaborations between the rapidly growing Russian informatics community and its international counterparts, as well as between established scientists and younger researchers.

The 10th edition of the conference was held during August 24–25, 2015, in Kazan and Innopolis City, in Tatarstan (Russian Federation). In particular, the first and last day of the conference were hosted in the new ultramodern complex of Innopolis City (http://www.innopolis.com/main/) while the core days were held at the Korston Conference Center, in downtown Kazan.

This volume contains a selection of papers presented at PSI 2015. It includes two invited papers and 23 papers selected out of 56 submissions. We wish to thank all those involved in the organization as well as the Program Committee members and the anonymous reviewers. Without them and all their hard work, the realization of such an ambitious project would not have been possible.

During the preparation of this volume, a dramatic event stunned us and the members of the international scientific community, in Austria and worldwide. Helmut Veith, whose invited paper is published in this volume, died tragically on March 12, 2016. This volume is dedicated to the memory of a bright colleague and dear friend.

April 2016

Manuel Mazzara
Andrei Voronkov

Organization

Program Committee

Farhad Arbab	CWI and Leiden University, The Netherlands
David Aspinall	University of Edinburgh, UK
Marcello M. Bersani	Politecnico di Milano, Italy
Eike Best	Universität Oldenburg, Germany
Nikolaj Bjørner	Microsoft Research, USA
Nail Bukharaev	Kazan Federal University, Russia
Andrea Calì	University of London, Birkbeck College, UK
Mauro Caporuscio	Politecnico di Milano, Italy
Néstor Cataño	Madeira Interactive Technologies Institute, Portugal
Gabriel Ciobanu	Romanian Academy, Iasi, Romania
Volker Diekert	University of Stuttgart, Germany
Salvatore Distefano	University of Messina, Italy
Nicola Dragoni	Technical University of Denmark, Denmark
Schahram Dustdar	TU Wien, Austria
Dieter Fensel	University of Innsbruck, Austria
Carlo A. Furia	ETH Zurich, Switzerland
Carlo Ghezzi	Politecnico di Milano, Italy
Sergei Gorlatch	University of Münster, Germany
Jan Friso Groote	Eindhoven University of Technology, The Netherlands
Arie Gurfinkel	Carnegie Mellon University, USA
Cliff Jones	Newcastle University, UK
Joost-Pieter Katoen	RWTH Aachen University, Germany
Konstantin Korovin	The University of Manchester, UK
Maciej Koutny	Newcastle University, UK
Laura Kovacs	Chalmers University of Technology, Sweden
Gregory Kucherov	CNRS/LIGM, France
Johan Lilius	A bo Akademi University, Finland
Anthony Widjaja Lin	Yale-NUS College, USA
Zhiming Liu	Birmingham City University, UK
Jan Madsen	Technical University of Denmark
Rupak Majumdar	MPI-SWS, Germany
Manuel Mazzara	Innopolis University, Russia
Klaus Meer	TU Cottbus, Germany
Hernan Melgratti	Universidad de Buenos Aires, Argentina
Bertrand Meyer	ETH Zurich, Switzerland
Torben Mogensen	DIKU, Denmark
Peter Mosses	Swansea University, UK

Martin Nordio	ETH Zurich, Switzerland
Jose R. Parama	University of A Coruna, Spain
Wojciech Penczek	ICS PAS and Siedlce University, Poland
Peter Pepper	Technische Universität Berlin, Germany
Alexander K. Petrenko	Russian Academy of Sciences, Russia
Paul Pettersson	Mälardalen University, Sweden
Nadia Polikarpova	ETH Zürich, Switzerland
Qiang Qu	Innopolis University, Russia
Wolfgang Reisig	Humboldt-Universität zu Berlin, Germany
Andrey Rybalchenko	Microsoft Research, UK
Davide Sangiorgi	University of Bologna, Italy
Klaus-Dieter Schewe	Software Competence Center Hagenberg, Germany
Natalia Sidorova	Technische Universiteit Eindhoven, The Netherlands
Giancarlo Succi	Free University of Bozen-Bolzano, Italy
Max Talanov	Kazan Federal University, Russsia
Alexander Tormasov	Innopolis University, Russia
Mark Trakhtenbrot	Holon Institute of Technology, Israel
Kishor Trivedi	Duke University, USA
Andrei Voronkov	The University of Manchester, Chalmers University of Technology, and EasyChair, UK/Sweden
Domagoj Vrgoc	Center for Semantic Web Research, Chile
Sergey Zykov	Higher School of Economics, Russia

Additional Reviewers

Akbar, Zaenal	Kahsai, Temesghen	Prüfer, Robert
Barylska, Kamila	Keshishzadeh, Sarmen	Rasch, Ari
Dan, Li	Lorenzen, Florian	Seghir, Mohamed Nassim
Enoiu, Eduard Paul	Marinescu, Raluca	Steggles, Jason
Fensel, Anna	Mezzetti, Nicola	Szreter, Maciej
Fleischhack, Hans	Moelle, Andre	Veselov, Alexander
Freitas, Leo	Noll, Thomas	
Haidl, Michael	Penabad, Miguel R.	

Contents

Quantitative Analysis of Collective Adaptive Systems

Jane Hillston[✉]

LFCS, School of Informatics, University of Edinburgh, Edinburgh, Scotland, UK
jane.hillston@ed.ac.uk
http://www.quanticol.eu

1 Introduction

Quantitative formal methods, such as stochastic process algebras, have been used for the last twenty years to support modelling of dynamic systems in order to investigate their performance. Application domains have ranged from computer and communication systems [1,2], to intracellular signalling pathways in biological cells [3,4]. Nevertheless this modelling approach is challenged by the demands of modelling modern collective adaptive systems, many of which have a strong spatial aspect, adding to the complexity of both the modelling and the analysis tasks.

In this talk I gave an introduction to formal quantitative analysis and the challenges of modelling collective adaptive systems, together with recent developments to address those challenges using the modelling language CARMA.

2 Quantitative Analysis

Performance analysis has a long tradition in computer and communication engineering dating back to the 1960s, as the dynamic behaviour of systems can sometimes be counter-intuitive and hard to predict without detailed mathematical models. Since many aspects of the system must be abstracted in order to construct tractable models, probability distributions are used to represent the variability within the timing characteristics of the system, for example, due to different data characteristics. Specifically continuous time Markov chains (CTMCs) were found to offer a good compromise between faithfulness and tractability. Initially queueing networks [5] were the dominant approach to capturing the conflict for resources which is often at the root of performance problems. From such descriptions it is easy to build a CTMC, typically with a simple birth-death process for each queue, but in many cases this is not even necessary as analytical solutions are known, circumventing the need for the explicit construction and analysis of the CTMC [6].

However, the advent of large distributed systems, in which multiple resources may be needed by processes simultaneously, led to the use of more flexible modelling frameworks such as stochastic Petri nets [7] and stochastic process algebras [8]. Stochastic process algebras are small textual description languages

© Springer International Publishing Switzerland 2016
M. Mazzara and A. Voronkov (Eds.): PSI 2015, LNCS 9609, pp. 1–5, 2016.
DOI: 10.1007/978-3-319-41579-6_1

which represent a system as a number of interacting processes. At the basic level each process is a small CTMC capturing the ordering and (stochastic) timing of activities that the process may undertake. The construction of the model specifies how these processes are constrained to interact through shared activities. A large CTMC capturing the complete behaviour of the system can be automatically constructed from the stochastic process algebra description, allowing the modeller to focus on the higher level behaviour of the system rather than the underlying state space. Prime examples of stochastic process algebras include PEPA [8], EMPA [9] and IMC [10]. Note, however, that the system description and the underlying mathematical model (CTMC) are inherently discrete and this can pose significant challenges for representing large scale systems due to the problem of *state space explosion*. In particular, numerical solution to find the probability distribution over the state space becomes intractable, and stochastic simulation becomes computationally expensive, as the size of the system grows.

3 Challenges in Modelling Collective Adaptive Systems

Recent years have seen increasing interest in collective adaptive systems. Such systems, which appear in many natural scenarios such as the behaviour of social insects, are increasingly forming a paradigm for the construction of the software systems of the future. Collective adaptive systems (CAS) are seen to be comprised of a large number of interacting entities whose behaviour is based on their local perception, without access to global control or knowledge. Moreover entities are typically replicated to establish robustness to failure of individual entities whilst adaptivity provides robustness to changes at a higher level.

The global or emergent behaviour of such systems can be difficult to predict making it paramount that we develop adequate modelling formalisms to capture and reason about the behaviour at both local and global levels. The compositional nature of stochastic process algebras make them strong candidates for developing models at the local level, but the state space explosion problem places severe challenges on their analysis.

In the last decade there have been efforts to alleviate the problems of state space explosion for very large systems by the use of *fluid approximations* [11]. In this approach an approximation of the underlying discrete CTMC is constructed as a set of ordinary differential equations that capture the average behaviour of the system when a large population of entities is involved. Analysis techniques, such as stochastic model checking, have been adapted to work with this approximation [12].

Other significant challenges for stochastic process algebras when modelling CAS stem from the spatially distributed nature of the entities and the adaptation. The spatial aspect is important because entities are restricted to interact and communicate locally so capturing the relative positions of entities is crucial. Similarly, the ability of an entity to have a goal which guides changes in behaviour based on the information that it receives has not previously been considered in stochastic process algebras. To address these challenges we have developed a new process algebra-based language CARMA [13].

4 CARMA

CARMA has been designed specifically to represent systems developed according to the CAS paradigm [14]. The language offers a rich set of communication primitives, and permits exploiting attributes, captured in a store associated with each component, to enable attribute-based communication. For most CAS systems we anticipate that one of the attributes could be the location of the agent. Thus it is straightforward to model those systems in which, for example, there is a limited scope of communication or there is the restriction to only interact with components that are co-located, or where there is spatial heterogeneity in the behaviour of agents. The use of a store to explicitly capture a limited set of data associated with an entity is a compromise between full agent-based modelling and the approach of data abstraction that has previously been adopted in stochastic process algebra-based languages.

The rich set of communication primitives is one of the distinctive features of CARMA. Specifically, CARMA supports both unicast and broadcast communication, and permits locally synchronous, but globally asynchronous communication. This richness is important to take into account the spatially distributed nature of CAS, where agents may have only local awareness of the system, yet the design objectives and adaptation goals are often expressed in terms of global behaviour. Representing these patterns of communication in classical process algebras or traditional stochastic process algebras would be difficult, and would require the introduction of additional model components to represent buffers, queues and other communication structures.

Another key feature of CARMA is its distinct treatment of the *environment*. It should be stressed that although this is an entity explicitly introduced within our models, it is intended to represent something more pervasive and diffusive of the real system, which is abstracted within the modelling to be an entity which exercises influence and imposes constraints on the different agents in the system. For example, in a model of a smart transport system, the environment may have responsibility for determining the rate at which entities (buses, bikes, taxis etc.) move through the city. However this should be recognised as an abstraction of the presence of other vehicles causing congestion which may impede the progress of the focus entities to a greater or lesser extent at different times of the day. The presence of an environment in the model does not imply the existence of centralised control in the system. The role of the environment is also related to the spatially distributed nature of CAS — we expect that the location *where* an agent is will have an effect on *what* an agent can do.

To summarise, in CARMA a system is composed of a *collective* of components that exist in an *environment*. Each component consists of a *process* and a *store* where the process captures the possible behaviours of the component in a similar manner to previous process algebras, whereas the store records the state of the component with respect to a number of *attributes*. These attributes, which can be thought of as enumerated types, allow the behaviour, including the communication partners, of a component to be dependent on its current state.

5   Future Perspectives

CAS present an interesting and challenging class of systems to design and construct, with many exciting prospects for future software systems as well as socio-technical systems, in which users themselves become entities in the system. Example areas of application include smart urban transport systems, smart energy networks and swarm robotics. The role of CAS within infrastructure systems, such as within smart cities, make it essential that quantitative aspects of behaviour, in addition to functional correctness, are taken into consideration during design, but the scale and complexity of these systems pose challenges both for model construction and model analysis. CARMA aims to address many of these challenges, supporting rich forms of interaction, using attributes to capture explicit locations and the environment to allow adaptivity. Moreover analysis techniques based on fluid approximation offer hope for scalable quantitative analysis techniques. However, to tackle the full range of behaviours which can occur within CAS extensions to classical fluid approximation techniques are needed. For example, recent work by Bortolussi [15] proves convergence results in terms of hybrid systems which take into account multi-scale behaviour with respect to time and/or populations.

Acknowledgement. This work is partially supported by the EU project QUANTI-COL, 600708.

References

1. Hermanns, H., Herzog, U., Katoen, J.: Process algebra for performance evaluation. Theor. Comput. Sci. **274**(1–2), 43–87 (2002)
2. De Nicola, R., Latella, D., Massink, M.: Formal modeling and quantitative analysis of klaim-based mobile systems. In: Proceedings of the 2005 ACM Symposium on Applied Computing (SAC), Santa Fe, New Mexico, USA, 13–17 March 2005, pp. 428–435. ACM (2005)
3. Priami, C.: Algorithmic systems biology. Commun. ACM **52**(5), 80–88 (2009)
4. Ciocchetta, F., Hillston, J.: Bio-PEPA: a framework for the modelling and analysis of biological systems. Theor. Comput. Sci. **410**(33), 3065–3084 (2009)
5. Kleinrock, L.: Sequential processing machines (S.P.M) analyzed with a queuing theory model. J. ACM **13**(2), 179–193 (1966)
6. Baskett, F., Chandy, K.M., Muntz, R.R., Palacios, F.G.: Open, closed, and mixed networks of queues with different classes of customers. J. ACM **22**(2), 248–260 (1975)
7. Marsan, M.A., Conte, G., Balbo, G.: A class of generalized stochastic petri nets for the performance evaluation of multiprocessor systems. ACM Trans. Comput. Syst. **2**(2), 93–122 (1984)
8. Hillston, J.: A Compositional Approach to Performance Modelling. CUP, Cambridge (1995)
9. Bernardo, M., Gorrieri, R.: A tutorial on EMPA: a theory of concurrent processes with nondeterminism, priorities probabilities and time. Theor. Comput. Sci. **202**(1–2), 1–54 (1998)

10. Hermanns, H.: Interactive Markov Chains: The Quest for Quantified Quality. LNCS. Springer, Heidelberg (2002)
11. Hillston, J.: The benefits of sometimes not being discrete. In: Baldan, P., Gorla, D. (eds.) CONCUR 2014. LNCS, vol. 8704, pp. 7–22. Springer, Heidelberg (2014)
12. Bortolussi, L., Hillston, J.: Model checking single agent behaviours by fluid approximation. Inf. Comput. **242**, 183–226 (2015)
13. Hillston, J., Loreti, M.: Specification and analysis of open-ended systems with CARMA. In: Weyns, D., Michel, F. (eds.) E4MAS 2014. LNCS, vol. 9068, pp. 95–116. Springer, Heidelberg (2015)
14. Bortolussi, L., De Nicola, R., Galpin, V., Gilmore, S., Hillston, J., Latella, D., Loreti, M., Massink, M.: CARMA: collective adaptive resource-sharing Markovian agents. In: Bertrand, N., Tribastone, M. (eds.) Proceedings Thirteenth Workshop on Quantitative Aspects of Programming Languages and Systems, QAPL 2015. EPTCS, London, UK, 11th–12th April 2015, vol. 194, pp. 16–31 (2015)
15. Bortolussi, L.: Hybrid behaviour of markov population models. Inf. Comput. **247**, 37–86 (2016). CoRR abs/1211.1643 (2012)

What You Always Wanted to Know About Model Checking of Fault-Tolerant Distributed Algorithms

Igor Konnov[✉], Helmut Veith, and Josef Widder

TU Wien (Vienna University of Technology), Vienna, Austria
konnov@forsyte.tuwien.ac.at

Abstract. Distributed algorithms have numerous mission-critical applications in embedded avionic and automotive systems, cloud computing, computer networks, hardware design, and the internet of things. Although distributed algorithms exhibit complex interactions with their computing environment and are difficult to understand for human engineers, computer science has developed only very limited tool support to catch logical errors in distributed algorithms at design time.

In the last two decades we have witnessed a revolutionary progress in software model checking due to the development of powerful techniques such as abstract model checking, SMT solving, and partial order reduction. Still, model checking of fault-tolerant distributed algorithms poses multiple research challenges, most notably parameterized verification: verifying an algorithm for all system sizes and different combinations of faults. In this paper, we survey our recent results in this area which extend and combine abstraction, partial orders, and bounded model checking. Our results demonstrate that model checking has acquired sufficient critical mass to build the theory and the practical tools for the formal verification of large classes of distributed algorithms.

1 Introduction

Fault-tolerant distributed algorithms (FTDA) are a central research area in distributed computing theory [2,28]. While such algorithms typically have been used in safety critical applications in the automotive or avionic industries, new application domains such as cloud computing provide additional motivation to study fault-tolerant algorithms: with the huge number of computers involved in a cloud, faults are the norm [30] rather than an exception. Together, this motivates our research on automated verification techniques for fault-tolerant distributed algorithms. We need to automatically verify such mechanisms for several hundreds or even thousands of components. However, a straightforward application of model checking to systems of such a scale suffers from combinatorial state space explosion.

Supported by the Austrian Science Fund (FWF) through the National Research Network RiSE (S11403 and S11405) and project P27722 (PRAVDA), and by the Vienna Science and Technology Fund (WWTF) through project ICT15-103 (APALACHE).

M. Mazzara and A. Voronkov (Eds.): PSI 2015, LNCS 9609, pp. 6–21, 2016.
DOI: 10.1007/978-3-319-41579-6_2

A paradigmatic approach to verify very large systems is *parameterized model checking*: if $M(n)$ is a distributed or concurrent system consisting of n identical components, and ϕ is a temporal logic formula, parameterized model checking requires us to check whether $\forall n. M(n) \models \phi$. Already for quite restricted classes of concurrent systems the problem is undecidable, cf. our recent survey [4]. For fault-tolerant distributed algorithms there are (at least) two more challenges that we shall discuss below: (i) multiple parameters with arithmetic constraints and (ii) parameterized code. Let us describe these challenges more precisely. First, in addition to n there is a parameter t that expresses the assumed number of faulty components, and algorithms are typically correct only under a *resilience condition*. A typical resilience condition in the case of Byzantine fault tolerance [14,31] is $n > 3t$. Second, while the parameterized model checking problems discussed in [4] assume that the process code and state space are independent of the parameters, FTDAs often count messages: Due to faults, processes cannot wait for messages from specific (possibly faulty) senders. Therefore, most FTDAs use counters, e.g., if a process receives a certain message from more than t distinct senders, then it concludes that one of the senders must be non-faulty. We call such conditions on counters *threshold guards*.

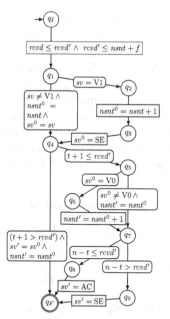

Algorithm 1. Core logic of the broadcasting algorithm from [35].

Code for processes i if it is correct:
Variables

1: $v_i \in \{\text{FALSE}, \text{TRUE}\}$
2: $\text{accept}_i \in \{\text{FALSE}, \text{TRUE}\} \leftarrow \text{FALSE}$

Rules

3: **if** v_i **and** not sent $\langle\text{echo}\rangle$ before **then**
4:     *send* $\langle\text{echo}\rangle$ to all;
5: **if** *received* $\langle\text{echo}\rangle$
        from at least $t + 1$ *distinct* processes
        and not sent $\langle\text{echo}\rangle$ before **then**
6:     *send* $\langle\text{echo}\rangle$ to all;
7: **if** *received* $\langle\text{echo}\rangle$ from at least $n - t$ *distinct* processes **then**
8:     $\text{accept}_i \leftarrow \text{TRUE}$;

Fig. 1. A control flow automaton of the Algorithm 1 for Byzantine faults.

Algorithm 1 presents a threshold-based FTDA in pseudo code, as is typical for the distributed algorithms literature. It uses threshold guards in lines 5 and 7. In Fig. 1, we give a graphical representation of a control-flow automaton that serves as a formal representation of the algorithm. For instance, the local variable *rcvd* represents the number of received messages, which is implicitly assumed in the pseudo code, while the global variable *nsnt* represents the number of messages sent by the correct processes. Moreover, the local variable *sv* represents the local control state of a process, which is implicit in the pseudo code in the phrases "not sent $<echo>$ before" and "$accept_i \leftarrow$ TRUE". Note that the expressions over the parameters are compared to the value of variable $rcvd'$, which contains the number of received messages, including the messages received at the current step. A system is then composed of $n - f$ instances of the control-flow automaton that run concurrently and represent the correct processes. The formal definition and the semantics of control-flow automata can be found in [21].

We observe that the process code and state space depend on the parameters (in our example on n and t). In addition to the parameterized number of processes and faults, automatic verification of FTDAs has to deal with process code which refers to parameters in a non-trivial way. We address this problem by stacking different techniques that we will survey in the following section.

2   Verification Techniques

Figure 2 gives an overview of our techniques that we introduced in a series of papers on parametrized model checking of FTDAs [21,23,24]. In Sect. 3, we discuss how these techniques interact with each other in the framework of our tool ByMC. We deal with the parametrized code and state space by a parametrized interval data abstraction [21] in Sect. 2.1. After that step, we have obtained a more classic parametrized model checking problem where all processes are uniform [4] and the system is thus *symmetric*. Symmetry allows us to change representation into a counter representation (Sect. 2.2) which gives rise to different techniques, namely, counter abstraction (Sects. 2.3 and 2.4), and offline partial order reduction with acceleration (Sects. 2.5 to 2.7).

2.1   Parametric Interval Data Abstraction (PIA Data)

In [21] we formalized threshold-guarded statements (e.g., the one from line 5 in the pseudocode example given in Algorithm 1) using a special form of control flow automata, e.g.:

$$ q_4 \longrightarrow \boxed{t + 1 \leq rcvd'} \longrightarrow q_5 $$

The above edge from q_4 to q_5 can be executed only if the number of received messages $rcvd'$ is greater than or equal to $t + 1$. The central insight is that for evaluating this condition, the precise value of $rcvd'$ is not important, it suffices to know whether $rcvd'$ is above the threshold. Our case study in [21] contained an additional threshold guard of $n - t$. This motivated an *abstract domain* of four intervals $I_0 = [0, 1[$ and $I_1 = [1, t + 1[$ and $I_2 = [t + 1, n - t[$ and $I_3 = [n - t, n]$. In our approach, the abstract domain is extracted from the guards automatically.

Recall that we want to get rid of parameterized process code. To this end, we can now replace the guards that refer to unbounded variables and parameters by

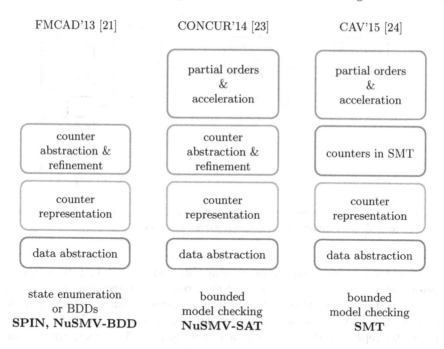

Fig. 2. Stacks of techniques

their *abstraction*. In our abstract domain, if the guard "$t + 1 \leq rcvd'$" evaluates to true, this means that $rcvd'$ is in the interval $[t + 1, n - t[$ or $[n - t, n]$. These intervals correspond to the abstract values I_2 and I_3, respectively. Thus, we can replace the guard by:

$$q_4 \longrightarrow \boxed{rcvd' = I_2 \vee rcvd' = I_3} \longrightarrow q_5$$

In this way we obtain a finite-state abstract process. Still, the resulting system is a parallel composition of a parametric number of such processes.

2.2 Counter Representation

A system that consists of concurrent anonymous (identical) processes can be modeled as a counter system by exploiting the symmetry of the system: *Instead of recording which process is in which local state, we record for each local state, how many processes are in this state.* Thus, we need one counter per local state ℓ, which we denote by $\kappa[\ell]$. After the PIA data abstraction, abstract processes have a fixed finite number of local states, hence we have a fixed number of counters. A step by a process that goes from local state ℓ to local state ℓ' is modeled by decrementing $\kappa[\ell]$ and incrementing $\kappa[\ell']$. When we fix the number of processes, e.g., by giving a concrete value to n, each counter is bounded by the number of processes n.

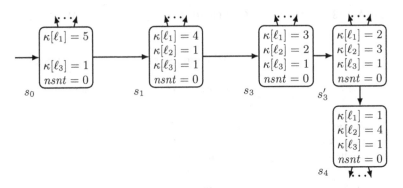

Fig. 3. An illustration of a counter representation for a system with $n = 7, t = 1, f = 1$. States s_3 and s_3' correspond to the single abstract state $\hat{s}_3$ in Fig. 4.

Figure 3 illustrates a transition system obtained by switching to a counter representation of a system of six correct processes (hence, the sum of counters is six in each state). Note that each transition decrements one counter and increments another one. As one can see, if the original system does not have self-loops, the counter representation does not have them either. This is in sharp contrast to counter abstraction, which is presented in Sect. 2.3.

However, as we are interested in the parametrized problem, we have to consider systems for all values of n. That is, after changing the representation, we have not reached a finite state representation. Thus another abstraction is needed.

Remark. In the literature, "counter representation" is sometimes referred to as "counter abstraction," partly because such a system can be viewed as more abstract due to absence of process identifiers. As the specifications of FTDAs do not single out processes but refer to process states only using quantification over the individual processes, for us this "counter representation" maintains all information which is present in the parallel composition of processes. Thus, in our setting, the counter representation is precise for the specifications of FTDAs that quantify over all correct processes.

2.3   Parametric Interval Counter Abstraction (PIA Counter)

In the counter representation of Sect. 2.2, the unbounded counter values are the only source of an unbounded state space. To get rid of this, the natural idea is to replace integer counters by counters over a finite abstract domain. In our work, we use the same domain as in the PIA data abstraction in Sect. 2.1, e.g., for Algorithm 1, we use the domain of four intervals $I_0 = [0, 1[$ and $I_1 = [1, t + 1[$ and $I_2 = [t + 1, n - t[$ and $I_3 = [n - t; n]$. Figure 4 illustrates counter abstraction of counter representations for all parameter values. For instance, the abstract states $\hat{s}_0, \hat{s}_1, \hat{s}_3, \hat{s}_4$ represent the concrete states s_0, s_1, s_3, s_3', s_4 from Fig. 3. The

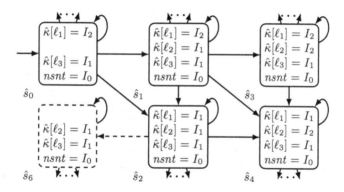

Fig. 4. A small part of the transition system obtained by counter abstraction of counter representations for all parameters.

abstract state $\hat{s}_2$ represents states that do not appear for the parameter values in Fig. 3, but occur, e.g., for $n = 4, t = 1, f = 1$.

For decrementing and incrementing counters, a counter abstraction introduces abstract operations. For instance, an increment of abstract value I_1 should overapproximate that a concrete value from the interval $[1, t + 1[$ is incremented. Note that increment can result in the same interval I_1 or in the next interval I_2. Similarly, decrement either maintains or changes its abstract value. When decrement and increment maintain the counter values, the abstract transitions form self-loops, as one can see in Fig. 4. Hence, abstract increment is not deterministic. In particular, applying an abstract increment to a counter does not have to change the counter value ever, which introduces spurious behavior, i.e., abstract paths that do not correspond to real paths.

Our PIA counter abstraction uses many ideas developed by Pnueli et al. [32]. Regarding the abstract domain, they focused on mutual exclusion and thus used the well-known "(0, 1, more)" abstract domain, whereas we focus on FTDAs and use intervals with parametric boundaries.

In this way, we arrive at a system of a fixed number of counters that range over a finite domain, that is, a finite-state model checking problem. We have used this in [21] (cf. [16] for technical details) to check *safety and liveness* of classic fault-tolerant broadcasting algorithms under a number of fault models. As in [32], abstraction makes liveness verification more challenging as it requires to add *justice* constraints. Moreover, for liveness we had to deal with spurious counterexamples, cf. Sect. 2.4.

2.4 Parametrized Abstraction Refinement

Our PIA abstraction maintains the relevant properties of threshold guards and counters, so that the classic CEGAR approach [10], which consists of refining the state space, is not suitable. However, the non-determinism due to abstract

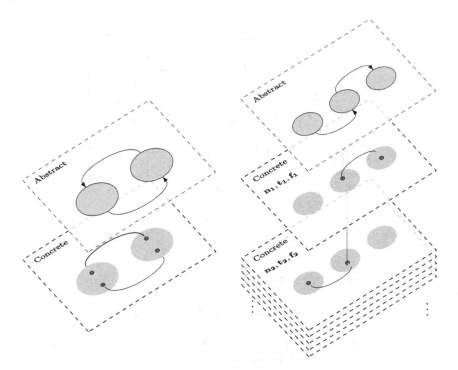

Fig. 5. Spurious loop due to coarse abstraction in classic CEGAR [10] on the left, and a spurious path due to many concrete systems that are mapped to one abstract systems in parametrized model checking on the right.

operations on counters leads to *spurious transitions* that lead to spurious counterexamples. Hence our abstraction refinement approach deals with removing transitions.

Our main problem stems from the non-determinism due to abstract counters. If a process moves from local state ℓ to ℓ' we have to decrease the counter $\kappa(\ell)$ and increase $\kappa(\ell')$. However, abstract decrease may lead to a smaller abstract value, while abstract increase maintains the counter value. Overall, processes may be lost. As we use global variables to record the number of message sent, we have the same effect there and messages "may be lost" due to abstraction. As messages may be required to make progress, this generates challenges for the verification of liveness properties.

Our current approach is to use an SMT solver to check whether abstract transitions correspond to concrete ones. If this is not the case, we explicitly remove these transitions from the transition relation of the counter abstraction. See [16] for implementation details, where we also discuss how we refine unfair loops that occur in some case studies.

We would like to mention that abstraction refinement in parametrized model checking generates challenges different from classic CEGAR. As shown in Fig. 5, abstract transitions that build a path in the abstract system may stem from different concrete systems for different parameter values. Currently, we deal with such counterexamples by user-provided invariant candidates that our tool checks to be invariants and which are then used for verification. To achieve more automation, one has to detect spurious paths instead of individual spurious transitions. However, this is challenging in the parameterized case, as infinitely many concrete systems are involved.

2.5   Threshold Automata

In Sects. 2.1–2.4, we used control-flow automata (CFA) as an input to our model checking techniques (cf. Fig. 1). A CFA is a formal presentation that is close to pseudo code and symbolically captures the transition relation of a single process as a formula over input, output (primed), and temporary variables. A path through the control-flow automaton (non-deterministically) computes a single transition in the transition relation of the algorithm. For instance, the leftmost path of the CFA shown in Fig. 1 computes the local transition from the local state with the assignment $sv \mapsto \text{V0}$, $rcvd \mapsto 0$, and $nsnt \mapsto 0$ to the local state with the assignment $sv \mapsto \text{V0}$, $rcvd \mapsto f$, and $nsnt \mapsto 0$ (once the target state of the transition is computed, the primes are dropped). If we apply data abstraction (see Sect. 2.1) to the *local variables*, we obtain an abstract control-flow automaton. Likewise, a path through the abstract control-flow automaton computes a single transition in the abstract transition relation. There is, however, an important difference between the input CFA and the CFA that is created by data abstraction: the domain of the local variables, e.g., $rcvd$, in the abstract CFA is finite, and hence the local state space of each process is finite. This observation allows us to use another representation of the abstract transition relation, which we call a *threshold automaton* [23].

In a nutshell, a threshold automaton is a graph, whose nodes correspond to the abstract local states of a process, and the edges correspond to the local transitions. The edges are annotated with linear arithmetic constraints over the parameters and the shared variables, e.g., $nsnt \geq (n-t)-f$, as well as with increments of the shared variables, e.g., $nsnt' = nsnt + 1$. Note the three important differences of a threshold automaton from a CFA:

1. The nodes of a threshold automaton correspond to the local states, whereas the nodes of a CFA correspond to the locations in the control flow of the code computing the next state of the algorithm;
2. An atomic step of the algorithm is represented by an edge of a threshold automaton, as opposite to a path of a CFA;
3. The edges of a threshold automaton are annotated only with shared variables and parameters, whereas the values of the local variables are implicit in the automata nodes.

Figure 6 illustrates a threshold automaton that is constructed automatically from the CFA shown in Fig. 1 by our tool. For instance, if a process is in local state 00 and $nsnt \geq (n - t) - f$, then the process may go to the local state 22. In doing so, it increases $nsnt$.

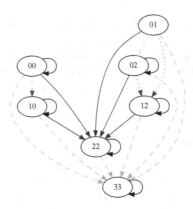

Fig. 6. A threshold automaton for the CFA shown in Fig. 1. The nodes correspond to the local states of the processes, while the edges correspond to the guarded transitions. The edges are annotated with guards as follows: the bold gray edge is guarded with *true*; the dotted edges are guarded with $nsnt \geq 1 - f$; the solid edges are guarded with $nsnt \geq (t + 1) - f$; the dashed edges are guarded with $nsnt \geq (n - t) - f$. Finally, $nsnt$ is incremented by the edges from the local states 00, 10, and 01 to the local states 12, 22, and 33, whereas all other edges do not change $nsnt$.

In our case studies, all increments of shared variables in threshold automata are outside of loops. This is a consequence of the class of FTDAs under consideration: each correct process sends a message of each type at most once, and thus increases each shared variable at most once. The partial order reduction techniques in Sects. 2.6 and 2.7 exploit this property to guarantee completeness of bounded model checking.

2.6 Checking Reachability by Bounded Model Checking Using Offline Partial Order Reduction and Acceleration

In [23], we apply SAT-based bounded model checking to verify reachability properties of the finite model obtained by counter abstraction of FTDAs (see Sect. 2.3). It is well-known that to make bounded model checking complete for reachability properties, one has to analyze executions of length up to the diameter of the transition system [3].

To this end, we first compute an upper bound on the diameter of the counter representation, that is, an upper bound on the minimal number of steps required to reach any configuration σ' from a configuration σ. From the bound on the counter representation we obtain a diameter bound on the counter abstraction. In the following we discuss why, surprisingly, the diameter is bounded.

Assume σ' is reached from σ by steps of two processes where each process transitions from local state ℓ to local state ℓ'. In classic interleaving semantics, this run has length 2. However, we might also model this as a single update on the counters, that is we may decrease the counter $\kappa(\ell)$ and increase $\kappa(\ell')$ by two, respectively. This idea is illustrated in Fig. 7. In general, we may move arbitrarily

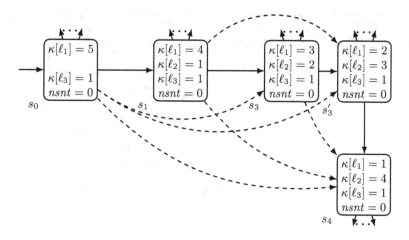

Fig. 7. A counter system in Fig. 3 extended with accelerated transitions (dashed)

many process at once, and call such runs of counter systems *accelerated*. In this example, 2 would be the *acceleration factor*. In the context of parametrized model checking, the important property is that because we may move arbitrarily many process at a time, there is potential to bound the diameter *independently* of the value of the parameters!

Exploiting commutativity arguments not given in detail here, by swapping two neighboring transitions in a run, we obtain the same final state. To combine this with acceleration, one would like to swap transitions in such a way that many neighboring transitions can be accelerated. Importantly, one has to ensure that after swapping the guard of a transition still evaluates to true. Ensuring this has great influence on the actual bound and is the key technical argument from [23], where we also show that the resulting bounds are sufficiently small to check several case studies. Note that our method can be seen as a form of partial order reduction that is applied before model checking, i.e., an offline partial order reduction.

2.7   Bounded Model Checking Using SMT

Our final method avoids counter abstraction and directly encodes runs of the counter representation in SMT. A global system state, which contains basically one counter per local state, can be represented as a vector of integer variables (one for each local state). As in SAT-based bounded model checking, one can then encode the transition relation, and the subsequent global state using a fresh vector of integer variables (or fresh integer variables for the counters that have actually been updated).

While the technique of Sect. 2.6 conceptually enumerates all runs of length up to the diameter, in [24] we only encode a small set of "schemas", and show that the (representative) runs generated from the schemas span the reachable state

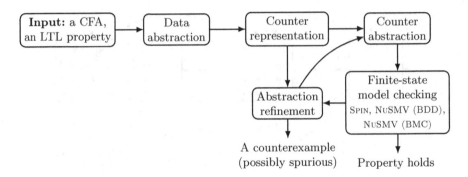

Fig. 8. Parameterized verification of FTDAs with data and counter abstractions [16, 21, 23]

space. A schema is essentially a sequence of scheduling constraints containing guards. The schemas are obtained by an improvement of the partial order ideas that we used in [23] to bound the diameter. Thus, we obtain a more aggressive offline partial order reduction, and significantly better experimental results that are discussed in Sect. 4.

To illustrate schemas, consider the threshold automaton depicted in Fig. 6. The automaton has three guards: $\varphi_1 \equiv nsnt \geq 1 - f$, $\varphi_2 \equiv nsnt \geq t + 1 - f$, and $\varphi_3 \equiv nsnt \geq n - t - f$. Consider the following transitions of the threshold automaton: the transition r_1 from 01 to 02; the transition r_2 from 02 to 22, the transition r_3 from 22 to 33. Then, a schema $\{\}r_1\{\varphi_1, \varphi_2\}r_1r_2r_3\{\varphi_1, \varphi_2, \varphi_3\}$ generates runs for various parameter values, where the transition r_1 is executed by several processes first and makes the guards φ_1 and φ_2 true; after that the transitions r_1, r_2, and r_3 are executed by several processes one after the other and make the guard φ_3 true.

The number of different threshold guards in the typical distributed algorithms in the literature varies from one to ten, which results in a reasonably large number of schemas that have to be checked, typically several thousand schemas [24]. Note that the schemas can be verified independently, and thus, in parallel.

3   Implementation: Byzantine Model Checker

We have implemented the techniques described in Sect. 2 in our tool ByMC: Byzantine Model Checker[1]. Figures 8 and 9 illustrate two different workflows that combine our techniques within ByMC.

In the first workflow depicted in Fig. 8, our tool computes data and counter abstractions and invokes a model checker to verify a finite-state abstract system. Depending on the choice of the model checker, ByMC can verify either safety properties, or both safety and liveness: the explicit-state model checker

---

[1] http://forsyte.at/software/bymc/.

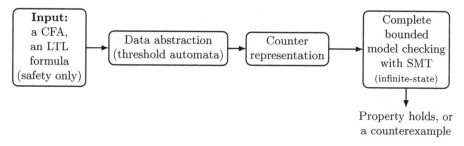

Fig. 9. Parameterized verification of FTDAs with data abstraction and SMT-based bounded model checking [24]

Spin [18] or the BDD-based symbolic algorithms in NuSMV/nuXmv [7] allow us to verify safety and liveness as described in [21]; the SAT-based bounded model checker implemented in NuSMV/nuXmv allows us to verify safety properties[2] as described in [23]. When a model checker reports a counterexample, ByMC checks whether the counterexample is spurious, and when it finds spurious behavior, ByMC refines the counter abstraction.

In the second workflow depicted in Fig. 9, our tool computes only data abstraction (Sect. 2.1), constructs a threshold automaton (Sect. 2.5) and computes a complete set of schemas (Sect. 2.7) as described in [24]. Each schema is encoded as an SMT formula in linear integer arithmetic and checked with an SMT solver, e.g., Z3 [11] or MathSAT [9]. As this technique maintains precise process counters, it does not produce spurious counterexamples that are caused by counter abstraction in the first workflow. Thus, the refinement loop is not required in our experiments.

4   Evaluation and Case Studies

In Figs. 10 and 11 we show how our techniques allowed us to check more and more involved distributed algorithms.

We are currently able to verify FTDAs that use threshold guards and work in asynchronous systems:

Broadcast. Reliable broadcast is a problem that can be solved in asynchronous systems, and we have verified the core of several such algorithms: Folklore reliable broadcast ("first forward to all then accept", e.g., given in [8]), Consistent Broadcast [35], Asynchronous Byzantine agreement [5]. Also the problem called "Condition-based consensus" can be solved in asynchronous systems and bears some similarities to broadcasting. We verified the condition-based consensus algorithm from [29]. After we published our verification results, a broadcasting algorithm very similar to [35] but with a different threshold was published in [19], and our tool easily checked its correctness.

---

[2] Although NuSMV implements bounded model checking for LTL, our present results guarantee completeness only for safety properties.

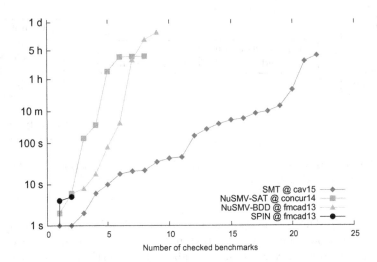

Fig. 10. Time to verify instances of fault-tolerant distributed algorithms (Color figure online)

FTDAs using Failure Detectors. The impossibility of solving non-blocking atomic commitment in asynchronous systems can be circumvented by using oracular mechanisms like failure detectors. They can be easily encoded in linear temporal logic. Thus, we verified such atomic commitment algorithms from [17,33].

Fast Consensus Algorithms. The idea of this class of algorithms is to have a quick (cheap) distributed preprocessing to a more expensive consensus algorithm: the algorithm terminates quickly in average runs, e.g., if there are no faults, if the system is not "too asynchronous", or if all processes have the same initial value. In case the preprocessing does not lead to a conclusive result, a "more-expensive" fall-back consensus algorithm is started with specific initial values. Our tool can check the correctness of this preprocessing of the algorithms BOSCO [34], C1CS [6], and CF1S [12].

Our techniques are currently limited to the class of asynchronous FTDAs that use only threshold guards. In particular, as consensus cannot be solved in asynchronous systems [15], we cannot completely verify algorithms for consensus, atomic broadcast, state machine replication, non-blocking atomic commitment, and similar hard problems. For that we need to restrict the interleavings and move from asynchronous systems to partially synchronous systems [14]. Only then, famous FTDAs like in [14] or Paxos [25] can be verified automatically in their entirety.

Our tool uses an extension of PROMELA as a front-end for CFA [16,22]. Their source code and the code of the threshold automata are freely available.[3]

---

[3] https://github.com/konnov/fault-tolerant-benchmarks/.

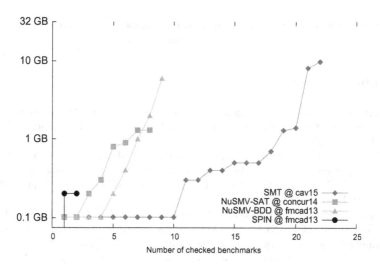

Fig. 11. Memory to verify instances of fault-tolerant distributed algorithms (Color figure online)

5   Conclusions and Future Work

Automatic verification of fault-tolerant distributed algorithms is a challenging task. To the best of our knowledge, besides our own work, there are only few papers that deal with parameterized verification of FTDAs [1,13]. The main complications stem from multiple parameters, that are related by resilience conditions, as well as the fact that not only the number of processes, but also the code of each process is parameterized.

To make progress in automatic verification, our first steps have focused on domain-specific abstractions for a large class of fault-tolerant distributed algorithms with threshold guards. These guards are quite natural constructs in the distributed algorithms literature: for instance, majority voting on a value is a natural technique to achieve agreement. The algorithms we address with our technique operate in the standard interleaving semantics (with fairness constraints). In terms of distributed algorithms literature, they are asynchronous. In the future, we will address also other computational models such as completely synchronous, partially synchronous, timed systems, and round-based systems.

Further, we want to develop more domain-specific techniques for increasingly larger classes of FTDAs. We are currently developing a tool[4] that implements these techniques and applies them to the popular TLA$^+$ specification language [27]. This will give us a framework and a toolset for verification of complex distributed algorithms such as Paxos [26].

---

[4] http://forsyte.at/apalache/.

Acknowledgements. We are grateful to Annu Gmeiner and Ulrich Schmid for their contributions to several papers [16,20–22] of our research agenda.

References

1. Alberti, F., Ghilardi, S., Pagani, E., Ranise, S., Rossi, G.P.: Universal guards, relativization of quantifiers, and failure models in model checking modulo theories. JSAT **8**(1/2), 29–61 (2012)
2. Attiya, H., Welch, J.: Distributed Computing, 2nd edn. Wiley, New York (2004)
3. Biere, A., Cimatti, A., Clarke, E., Zhu, Y.: Symbolic model checking without BDDs. In: Cleaveland, W.R. (ed.) TACAS 1999. LNCS, vol. 1579, pp. 193–207. Springer, Heidelberg (1999)
4. Bloem, R., Jacobs, S., Khalimov, A., Konnov, I., Rubin, S., Veith, H., Widder, J.: Decidability of Parameterized Verification. Synthesis Lectures on Distributed Computing Theory. Morgan & Claypool Publishers, San Rafael (2015)
5. Bracha, G., Toueg, S.: Asynchronous consensus and broadcast protocols. J. ACM **32**(4), 824–840 (1985)
6. Brasileiro, F., Greve, F.G.P., Mostéfaoui, A., Raynal, M.: Consensus in one communication step. In: Malyshkin, V.E. (ed.) PaCT 2001. LNCS, vol. 2127, pp. 42–50. Springer, Heidelberg (2001)
7. Cavada, R., Cimatti, A., Dorigatti, M., Griggio, A., Mariotti, A., Micheli, A., Mover, S., Roveri, M., Tonetta, S.: The NUXMV symbolic model checker. In: Biere, A., Bloem, R. (eds.) CAV 2014. LNCS, vol. 8559, pp. 334–342. Springer, heidelberg (2014)
8. Chandra, T.D., Toueg, S.: Unreliable failure detectors for reliable distributed systems. JACM **43**(2), 225–267 (1996)
9. Cimatti, A., Griggio, A., Schaafsma, B.J., Sebastiani, R.: The MathSAT5 SMT Solver. In: Piterman, N., Smolka, S.A. (eds.) TACAS 2013 (ETAPS 2013). LNCS, vol. 7795, pp. 93–107. Springer, Heidelberg (2013)
10. Clarke, E., Grumberg, O., Jha, S., Lu, Y., Veith, H.: Counterexample-guided abstraction refinement for symbolic model checking. J. ACM **50**(5), 752–794 (2003)
11. de Moura, L., Bjørner, N.S.: Z3: an efficient SMT solver. In: Ramakrishnan, C.R., Rehof, J. (eds.) TACAS 2008. LNCS, vol. 4963, pp. 337–340. Springer, Heidelberg (2008)
12. Dobre, D., Suri, N.: One-step consensus with zero-degradation. In: DSN, pp. 137–146 (2006)
13. Drăgoi, C., Henzinger, T.A., Veith, H., Widder, J., Zufferey, D.: A logic-based framework for verifying consensus algorithms. In: McMillan, K.L., Rival, X. (eds.) VMCAI 2014. LNCS, vol. 8318, pp. 161–181. Springer, Heidelberg (2014)
14. Dwork, C., Lynch, N., Stockmeyer, L.: Consensus in the presence of partial synchrony. J. ACM **35**(2), 288–323 (1988)
15. Fischer, M.J., Lynch, N.A., Paterson, M.S.: Impossibility of distributed consensus with one faulty process. J. ACM **32**(2), 374–382 (1985)
16. Gmeiner, A., Konnov, I., Schmid, U., Veith, H., Widder, J.: Tutorial on parameterized model checking of fault-tolerant distributed algorithms. In: Bernardo, M., Damiani, F., Hähnle, R., Johnsen, E.B., Schaefer, I. (eds.) SFM 2014. LNCS, vol. 8483, pp. 122–171. Springer, Heidelberg (2014)
17. Guerraoui, R.: Non-blocking atomic commit in asynchronous distributed systems with failure detectors. Distrib. Comput. **15**(1), 17–25 (2002)

18. Holzmann, G.: The SPIN Model Checker. Addison-Wesley, Boston (2003)
19. Imbs, D., Raynal, M.: Simple and efficient reliable broadcast in the presence of Byzantine processes. CoRR abs/1510.06882 (2015). http://arxiv.org/abs/1510.06882
20. John, A., Konnov, I., Schmid, U., Veith, H., Widder, J.: Brief announcement: parameterized model checking of fault-tolerant distributed algorithms by abstraction. In: PODC, pp. 119–121 (2013)
21. John, A., Konnov, I., Schmid, U., Veith, H., Widder, J.: Parameterized model checking of fault-tolerant distributed algorithms by abstraction. In: FMCAD, pp. 201–209 (2013)
22. John, A., Konnov, I., Schmid, U., Veith, H., Widder, J.: Towards modeling and model checking fault-tolerant distributed algorithms. In: Bartocci, E., Ramakrishnan, C.R. (eds.) SPIN 2013. LNCS, vol. 7976, pp. 209–226. Springer, Heidelberg (2013)
23. Konnov, I., Veith, H., Widder, J.: On the completeness of bounded model checking for threshold-based distributed algorithms: reachability. In: Baldan, P., Gorla, D. (eds.) CONCUR 2014. LNCS, vol. 8704, pp. 125–140. Springer, Heidelberg (2014)
24. Konnov, I., Veith, H., Widder, J.: SMT and POR beat counter abstraction: parameterized model checking of threshold-based distributed algorithms. In: Kroening, D., Păsăreanu, C.S. (eds.) CAV 2015. LNCS, vol. 9206, pp. 85–102. Springer, Heidelberg (2015)
25. Lamport, L.: The part-time parliament. ACM Trans. Comput. Syst. 16(2), 133–169 (1998)
26. Lamport, L.: Paxos made simple. ACM SIGACT News 32(4), 18–25 (2001)
27. Lamport, L.: Specifying Systems: The TLA+ Language and Tools for Hardware and Software Engineers. Addison-Wesley Longman Publishing Co., Inc., Boston (2002)
28. Lynch, N.: Distributed Algorithms. Morgan Kaufman, San Francisco (1996)
29. Mostéfaoui, A., Mourgaya, E., Parvédy, P.R., Raynal, M.: Evaluating the condition-based approach to solve consensus. In: DSN, pp. 541–550 (2003)
30. Netflix: 5 lessons we have learned using AWS (2010). http://techblog.netflix.com/2010/12/5-lessons-weve-learned-using-aws.html
31. Pease, M., Shostak, R., Lamport, L.: Reaching agreement in the presence of faults. J. ACM 27(2), 228–234 (1980)
32. Pnueli, A., Xu, J., Zuck, L.D.: Liveness with $(0, 1, \infty)$-counter abstraction. In: Brinksma, E., Larsen, K.G. (eds.) CAV 2002. LNCS, vol. 2404, pp. 107–122. Springer, Heidelberg (2002)
33. Raynal, M.: A case study of agreement problems in distributed systems: non-blocking atomic commitment. In: HASE, pp. 209–214 (1997)
34. Song, Y.J., van Renesse, R.: Bosco: one-step byzantine asynchronous consensus. In: Taubenfeld, G. (ed.) DISC 2008. LNCS, vol. 5218, pp. 438–450. Springer, Heidelberg (2008)
35. Srikanth, T., Toueg, S.: Simulating authenticated broadcasts to derive simple fault-tolerant algorithms. Dist. Comp. 2, 80–94 (1987)

Applying MDA to Generate Hadoop Based Scientific Computing Applications

Darkhan Akhmed-Zaki, Madina Mansurova$^{(\boxtimes)}$, Bazargul Matkerim,
Ekateryna Dadykina, and Bolatzhan Kumalakov

Faculty of Mechanics and Mathematics, Al-Farabi Kazakh National University,
Al-Farabi 71, Almaty, Republic of Kazakhstan
`mansurova01@mail.ru`

Abstract. The paper presents an attempt to develop and deploy a functioning MDA (Model-Driven Architecture) model of a distributed scientific application. The main focus is a problem of modeling high performance computing processes in a visual notation and automatic generation of an executable code using the resulting diagrams. The article describes the efforts to create a platform independent model of process execution, transformation it into a platform specific model and, finally, automatic generation an application code. The research novelty includes a platform independent model of the classic hydrodynamics problem, equivalent Hadoop based platform specific model and the testing results that confirm feasibility of the research.

Keywords: Model-Driven Architecture · Hadoop · Scientific computing

1 Introduction

Model Driven Development (MDD) is a software engineering methodology that treats "formal specification of the function, structure and actions of the system" as the main object of development [1]. Other objects, such as program codes, are generated at a later stage from these specifications also called models. Models are usually developed using standard or extended Unified modeling language (UML) diagrams, which make one more level of abstraction in the object-oriented design paradigm. In this case, the increased level of abstraction facilitates development of platform independent application templates that are easily converted to an executable code for any platform. In other words, one may build a template application (set of diagrams) that may be used by an automated code generator to produce an executable code for any known software platform.

In the early 2000s, OMG consortium [2] defined the conceptual infrastructure of Model driven architecture (MDA) that serves as the basis for MDD methods and defines standard specification, model description and transformation languages. Figure 1 presents a generic MDA development cycle.

First, user requirements are processed and formalized in a form of Platform-independent-model (PIM). Despite being presented as a set of UML diagrams,

© Springer International Publishing Switzerland 2016
M. Mazzara and A. Voronkov (Eds.): PSI 2015, LNCS 9609, pp. 22–35, 2016.
DOI: 10.1007/978-3-319-41579-6_3

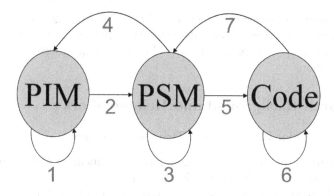

Fig. 1. An MDA application development cycle.

PIM has to take into account how the automated interpreter would further transform the model with the final goal of building a working solution. There is rich discussion on MDD modeling techniques in academic literature, which is out of the scope of this article. In this section, let us point out that an initial prototype of the model may contain inaccuracies or discrepancies, therefore, it goes through repetitive validation and introduction of changes before it proceeds to the second stage (Fig. 1, step 1).

Platform-specific-model (PSM) is the same system specification as PIM, but with the elements of the target platform. For instance, if the system has to run under particular environment (target environment) such elements would include environment components, interfaces, data storage, etc. Thus, every time when it is necessary to adapt the system to new technology only PSM should be reconsidered (Fig. 1, step 3). In the cases when it is necessary to introduce changes to the functioning system, for example, to start it with the help of other technology, PIM and PSM models should be reconsidered (Fig. 1, steps 4 and 7). Steps 2 and 5 are the steps of model transformations.

Code stage in the figure represents automated executable generation (Fig. 1, step 6). It involves special software that interprets PSM and produces final output. Such tools are available in different varieties and their properties vary depending on vendor and employment proposals. Academic literature provides some brief introduction to such tools, but this discussion is out of the scope of this article.

At this stage it should be noted that MDA and MDD have been successfully applied in several domains of software engineering including high performance scientific computing (HPSC). This article presents an attempt to construct and evaluate all levels of HPSC MDA models, define their transformation rules and generate an executable code.

The remaining part of the article is structured as follows: Sect. 2 presents an extensive literature review and puts the article results on the body of knowledge landscape. Section 3 provides a detailed description of the solution including the main components overview (Subsect. 3.1), PIM (Subsect. 3.2) and PSM (Subsect. 3.3) descriptions. Next, Sect. 4 describes the experiment design and evaluation results. Finally, the article is completed by a relevant discussion and further research directions.

2   Research Background and Related Work

2.1   HPSC Model Development Process Overview

Figure 2 vizualizes the process of designing and implementing HPSC application using UML 2.0 activity diagram. The process is divided into 5 stages. Each stage is performed by a specialist indicated on the left and its result is the corresponding MDA model shown on the right.

HPSC application design and development is carried out by a group of specialists as presented in Fig. 3. A specialist in oil-gas industry defines the problem statement. Next, a mathematician creates a mathematical model that is passed on to a specialist in the field of the numerical methods. He/she finds a corresponding explicit or implicit numerical method and defines an application algorithm. Next, a MDD modeler constructs HPSC application architecture, and, finally, a programmer implements the solution.

Throughout the complex application development errors may appear at different stages. Causes include ambiguity in interpretation of models, complexity of a program code, upgrade from one parallel architecture to another, modification of software, documentation updates, etc. Investigations show that MDD gives good results, when developing HPSC applications.

2.2   Related Work Review

In order to develop scientific computing applications using MDD methodologies, several contributions have been proposed. The paper of Lugato [3] is one of the early works that proposed MDE for high performance computing applications. Later in [4], he presented the idea in detail. The papers of [5–9] proposed MDE approach by creating a domain specific modeling language. Palyart et al. [7] proposed an approach called MDE4HPC using their own domain specific modeling language - High Performance Computing Modeling Language to describe abstract views of the software. Implementation of the approach using the tool ArchiMDE is integrated with Paprika studio and Arcane framework. Palyart et al. [6] introduced a DSVL to help in specifying and modeling high performance computing (HPC) applications. They focus on specification of solution parallelism. However, they did not show how their language could be used to generate HPC code. Brual et al. [8] reported the needs for leveraging on knowledge and expertise by focusing on Domain-Specific Modeling Languages (DSML) application. Similarly, Almorsy et al. [10] proposed their prototype of scientific Domain Specific Visual Languages (DSVLs)-based toolset. However, they did not consider the distributed scientific computing. In [11], the authors developed an approach to interoperation of high performance, scientific computing applications based upon math-oriented data modeling principles. In [12], the authors

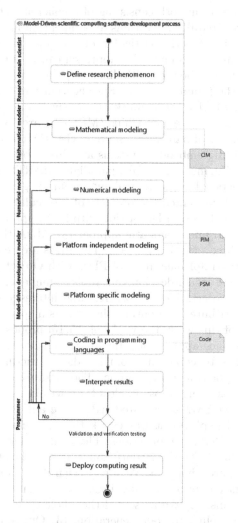

Fig. 2. MDD process of HPSC software.

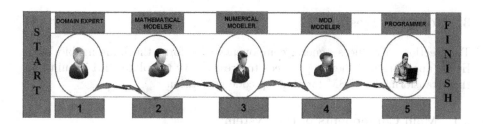

Fig. 3. Relay race of specialists in HPSC application development.

define the architecture framework consisting of a coherent set of viewpoints to support the mapping of parallel algorithms to parallel computing platforms. The feature of the approach [12] is the particular focus on optimization at the design level using architecture viewpoints. This approach can be adopted for different parallel algorithms and can be used with different parallel technologies. Gamatie et al. [13] represent the Graphical Array Specification for Parallel and Distributed Computing (GASPARD) framework for massively parallel embedded systems on Multi-Processor System-on-Chips (MPSoCs) architectures to support optimization of the usage of hardware resources. GASPARD uses MARTE standard profile for modeling embedded systems at a high abstraction level. Based on the Model-Driven Engineering (MDE) paradigm, MARTE models are refined towards lower abstraction levels, this making automatic generation of the code possible. Danniluk [14] presented the problem of Molecular Beam Epitaxy and Reflection High-Energy Electron Diffraction with MDA approach. In the paper, he described a practical and pragmatic approach to MDA that had been used during the work at three scientific projects. The PIMs are described with UML and PSMs that specify implementation of PIMs with Object Pascal and C++. They applied MDD and visual-development tools to numerical simulation problems. Each of these projects has its own research interests and none of them considers Hadoop distributed computing platform as a specific platform. Similarly to the authors of this work, the works of [15,16] proposed MDD approach in developing MapReduce applications. In [15], the authors apply Map/Reduce to EMF-based models to cope with complex data structures in the familiar an easy-to-use and type-safe EMF fashion. They store large EMF models in Hadoop's HBase and then use those models from within the Map/Reduce programming model using EMF's generated APIs. The authors of [16] developed an MDE-based cloud deployment framework that automates the deployment and execution of MapReduce applications. The model-driven approach is used to predict the performance of MapReduce application in the cloud environment. The features of our approach are: (1) We create scientific computing components for modeling scientific computing applications. Application modeling is achieved by using UML diagrams. (2) We presented the whole cycle of MDA process of development from modeling to code generation. (3) Our approach is oriented to the MapReduce application development for one of oil extraction problems. (4) The presented work is the continuation of earlier works [17,18].

3   Solution Design

This section introduces generic components that form the building blocks of HPSC applications. Then it proceeds to present how template PIM is built and then transformed to PSM for Hadoop code generation.

3.1   Main Components of the System

In order to design models, we implement four generic components that will serve as basic building blocks for HPSC applications. The developed components are divided and named depending on the peculiarities of HPC applications. At this stage, we assume that a scientific computing problem is of no importance for the solution, because the model can be constructed from these components in any case (for discussion on components functions see [19]).

For any application one has to determine input and output parameters, class of equations, explicit or inexplicit methods of computation and instruments (tools) for performing parallel computations. Therefore, we presented these 4 invariable independent parts in the form of 4 basic components. They are: an input-output component InOutPut, a component of equations of numerical methods NumerMethods and a component of organization of a high performance computing environment PEOrganize. Every component consists of several classes. Description of the components - as applied to MapReduce application - is presented below:

1. Component PEOrganize is used for creation of the topology on Hadoop platform.
2. Component NumerMethods is used for determination of a numerical model with different types of grid and numerical methods.
3. Component SciEquations is used for determination of a mathematical model with the number of final differential equations and conditions for these equations.
4. Component InOutPut consists of classes of reading from the file and writing into the file with the help of which input and output data of HPSC application are prescribed (set).

As is shown in Fig. 4, in the process of designing and development of applications there takes place transformation of models starting from the upper level to the lower level.

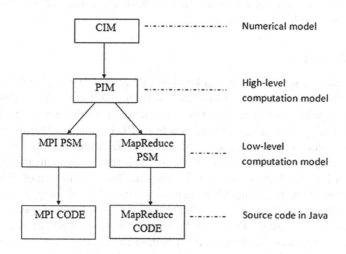

Fig. 4. MDA modeling.

As it was mentioned above, MDD specialist receivers a computationally independent model CIM from the specialist in numerical methods. In case of solution of the problem, CIM contains the algorithm of a numerical solution of the problem by the explicit method. In his turn, MDD-specialist creates an independent on the platform and the programming language PIM model for the given numerical CIM model using HPSC components. Model CIM can be described by the components of input-output-InOutPut, the component of equation of a scientific computing problem SciEquations, the component of numerical methods NumerMethods.

But in CIM model there is no information for the component of organization of high performance computational environment PEOrganize as the environment of development in the computational models is not considered.

The work resulted in the development of the MDA model and realization using the Hadoop technology.

3.2 PIM Model

In our case, computations are performed in MapReduce Hadoop environment. The algorithm with the use of MapReduce consists of the stage of initialization and iteration stage, a separate MapReduce work being fulfilled at each iteration.

Computations are performed on Hadoop platform, a MapReduce problem receives a cube of data, Mappers perform 1D decomposition, each Reducer receives its block of data and performs computations. After computations are completed, boundary data are entered into a distributed file system HDFS, the values of inside points are written into a local file system. Then a new cycle begins. The process continues until the condition is satisfied.

Thus, we have developed a PIM model for HPSC applications for the problem with the help of UML diagram of classes (Fig. 5) indicating relations between the classes. On account of retrieving calling methods of each other, the classes of components are in associative relations.

3.3 PSM Model

Models of transformation of PIM to PSM can be classified by several categories: improving the quality of transformation, with perfection of the development, with refining, with specialization, translation, abstraction, generalization and forms of designing. In our case, transition from PIM model to MapReduce Java PSM model refers to the category with refining. Refining means redetermination in the course of transition from CIM to PIM, transition from PIM to PSM. Refining can be added at one level of abstraction. Transformation of PIM model to MapReduce Java PSM model is transformation of UML-diagram of classes Java to the diagram of classes Java with addition of MapReduce specification to PSM. When transforming PIM model to MapReduce Java PSM model, multiple succession, associations of classes and qualified associations must be removed. In PSM model, the relations between components shown in Fig. 6 are preserved, but specification of the programming language Java is added. The Hadoop PSM

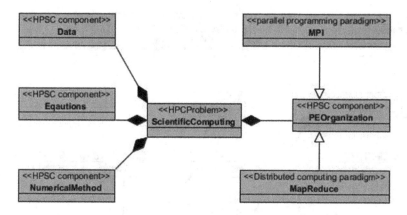

Fig. 5. PIM model.

model in Fig. 6 shows specification of the HPSC component - PEOrganization. The MapReduce distributed programming paradigm which consists of initialization and iteration stages of computation is modeled with the help of Map class and Reduce class.

4 Experiment Design and Evaluation

4.1 Hydrodynamics Problem Definition

Let us consider a hypercube in anisotropic elastic porous medium $\Omega = [0,T] \times K\{0 \leq x \leq 1, 0 \leq y \leq 1, 0 \leq z \leq 1\}$.

Let Eq. (1) describe the fluid dynamics in hypercube Ω under initial conditions (2) and boundary conditions:

$$\frac{\partial P}{\partial t} = \frac{\partial}{\partial x}(\phi(x,y,z)\frac{\partial P}{\partial x}) + \frac{\partial}{\partial y}(\phi(x,y,z)\frac{\partial P}{\partial y}) + \frac{\partial}{\partial z}(\phi(x,y,z)\frac{\partial P}{\partial z}). \quad (1)$$

$$P(0, x, y, z) = \varphi(0, x, y, z). \quad (2)$$

$$\frac{\partial P}{\partial n}|_\Gamma = 0. \quad (3)$$

Here, (3) is the surface of cube Ω. In Eq. (1) the solution function $P(t, x, y, z)$ is seam pressure in point (x, y, z) at the moment t; $\phi(x, y, z)$ is diffusion coefficient in the reservoir; $f(x, y, z)$ is density of sources. To solve (1)–(3) Jacobi's numerical method was used. In order to implement a test solution, we employ a mathematical problem for a particular case with functions from [17].

First, the original domain is divided into sub-domains (Fig. 7). Every sub-domain consists of three main parts: ghost slab, boundary slab and interior slab.

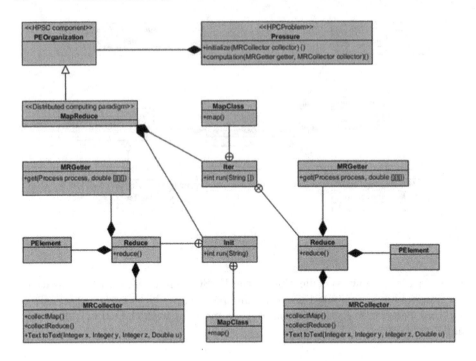

Fig. 6. Hadoop based PSM model.

Data transformations (defined by the algorithm) can proceed independently only in the interior slab. The boundary slab of the sub-domain, when being computed, requires boundary slab values of its neighbors and those are stored in the ghost slab. In other words, the ghost slab stores copies of neighbors boundary slab values.

The algorithm of numerical solution of the problem with the help of MapReduce Hadoop technology consists of two stages: the stage of initialization at which MapReduce work of the first level is performed only once and the iteration stage at which a cycle of MapReduce works of the second level is performed. Mapper of the first level loads data from the file system HDFS. Then, Mapper distributes the data between Reducer processes on slabs, thus realizing 1D decomposition of the data.

Reducer, in its turn, performs computations, duplications of boundary slabs into the ghost slabs of the neighbors and stores the obtained results. The data used by Reducer for computations are divided into two kinds: local data, i.e. the data which refer to the interior slab and shared boundary data (boundary slab). Reducer enters local computed data directly into a local file system and enters the shared boundary data into the output file of the distributed file system HDFS, which will be an input file for Mapper of the second level at the next iteration. At each iteration Mapper of the second level distributes the updated boundary data among Reducers, thus providing the exchange of boundary values

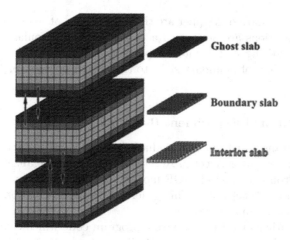

Fig. 7. 1D-decomposition of computational domain. (Color figure online)

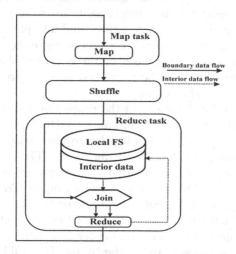

Fig. 8. Iterative MapReduce framework scheme.

between slabs. The flow of data corresponding to the description is presented in Fig. 8.

The distributed algorithm consists of two stages:

1. The stage of initialization;
2. The iteration stage.

The stage of initialization is a MapReduce task Initial in which there takes place initialization and writing of files necessary for computations in the process of iterations.

The iteration stage is a MapReduce task Iterations. At each iteration in Mapper, points of the field with the same keys, i.e. numbers of subcubes, are grouped. The input data of Mapper are the output data of Reducer. In Reducer, the main computations are performed according to the formulae of the explicit method. Then, writing of the interior parts of files into the local file system and transfer of values of boundary slabs to the output of Reducer Iterations are performed.

4.2 Computational Experiment Results

An automatic transition from MapReduce Java PSM to Java code is realized with the help of generator Acceleo. Acceleo is a pragmatic realization of Object Management Group (OMG) of MOF model. Acceleo UML2 for Java is a code generator based on Acceleo 3.2. This generator supports creation of the initial code Java for classes and interfaces.

After automatic generation we have a program code which contains description of classes and methods as well as relations between methods corresponding to PSM model (Fig. 6). Then, the methods of each class of HPSC components are written down according to their functionality or called from class libraries. According to Fig. 2 the process of code writing and interpretation of the results goes on till the program gives the results corresponding to the results of a sequential program. The computing experiments on the generated MapReduce program and the sequential program must be performed at equal pre-determined parameters of the computational problem.

We have performed all the stages of the process of MapReduce application development for problem (1)–(3) according to MDD methodology and have obtained the same computing results for the problem solution of the sequential program code and generated MapReduce code. The experimental design and the results of the generated MapReduce program execution on a special deployed Apache Hadoop Mini-Cluster of Laboratory of Computer Science of al-Farabi Kazakh National University are presented below.

Apache Hadoop 2.6.0 Mini-Cluster consists of 1 master node and 7 slaves. All slave nodes have Ubuntu 14.04 on board, master node has Ubuntu Server 14.04. Master node hardware characteristics: Hardware: HP ProLiant-BL460c-Gen8, Architecture: x86-64, CPU(s): 4, Model name: Intel(R) Xeon(R) CPU E5-2609 0 @ 2.40 GHz. Slaves hardware characteristics: Architecture: x86-64, CPU(s): 4, Model name: Intel(R) Core(TM) i5-2500 CPU @ 3.30 GHz. NFS server is configured on master node. Slaves have the same folder mounted with read/write access rights. Nodes are connected using Ethernet devices, this providing up to 1000 Mbps, Intel(R) PRO/1000 Network Connection. 3D problem sizes are chosen by the possibility of the memory of computing nodes: $256 \times 128 \times 128$, $1024 \times 128 \times 128$, $4096 \times 128 \times 128$, $8192 \times 128 \times 128$.

The results obtained for the dependence of the speedup and efficiency are presented in Figs. 9 and 10. We can see that only the problem size of $8192 \times 128 \times 128$ has got the four times of speedup, it means that, according to the features of Hadoop platform, with the increase of MapReduce application data size the speedup increases. Figure 10 also shows that when we choose a big problem size the computing nodes are more effectively used.

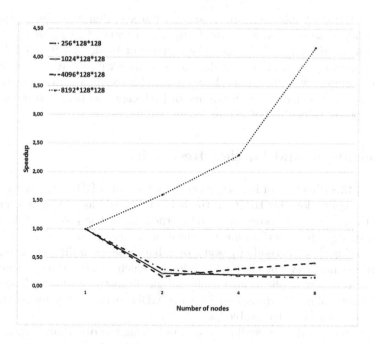

Fig. 9. The speedup versus the number of nodes for different meshes.

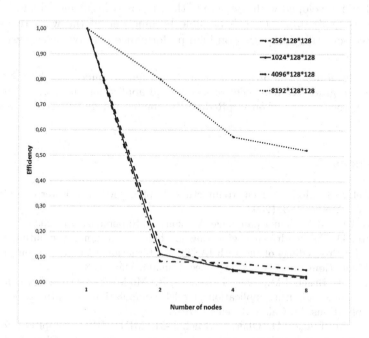

Fig. 10. The efficiency versus the number of nodes for different meshes.

To test the fault tolerance appearance of IOException with the probability of 33 % is added to the Reducer code. In the experiment, 3 jobs have taken part each of which initiates 8 Reducers. The number of broken Reducers is 25 out of 97. The average time of the problem performance without IOException and with IOException was the same. Thus, it can be concluded that the time of performance does not depend on failures of Reducers and their restarting. The computations obtained in both cases have equal values.

5   Conclusion and Further Research

The aim of this direction of investigations is the use of MDD methods for development of applications for HPSC in the field of oil and gas production. For the work, MDA standard is chosen as MDD methodology. The process of designing and developing a high performance application is described on the example of MDA modeling. The method of passing on a baton between different specialists of oil and gas industry, the close interaction of which can facilitate the work on creation of complex applications for oil and gas industry, is shown. The investigation results show the prospects of using MDD methodology for solution of complex resource intensive problems.

The experimental results allow to conclude that the distributed application works well and with the increase in the volume of the data being processed the performance of Hadoop implementation increases. HPSC applications can be designed and developed with the help of the proposed MDA model and its basic components. This approach will possible become one of the ways to perform distributed scientific computing on high performance heterogeneous systems.

Acknowledgments. The presented research was funded under Kazakhstan government research grant "Development of models and applications for high performance distributed processing based on MapReduce-Hadoop technology for oil extraction problems".

References

1. Frankel, D.S.: Model Driven Architecture: Applying MDA to Enterprise Computing. Wiley, New York (2003)
2. OMG. Unified Modeling Language, Version 2.2. Superstructure (2009)
3. Lugato, D.: Model-driven engineering for high-performance computing applications. In: Proceedings of the 19th IASTED International Conference on Modeling and Simulations, Quebec City, Quebec, Canada, May 2008
4. Lugato, D., Bruel, J.M., Ober, I., Venelle, B.: Model-driven engineering for high-performance computing applications, modeling simulation and optimization - focus on applications. In: Cakaj, S. (ed.) (2010)
5. Palyart, M., Lugato, D., Ober, I., Bruel, J.-M.: MDE4HPC: an approach for using model-driven engineering in high-performance computing. In: Ober, I., Ober, I. (eds.) SDL 2011. LNCS, vol. 7083, pp. 247–261. Springer, Heidelberg (2011)

6. Palyart, M., Lugato, D., Ober, I., Bruel, J.: A modeling language dedicated to high-performance scientific computing. In: Proceedings of the 1st International Workshop on Model-Driven Engineering for High Performance and CLoud computing, MDHPCL 2012. Article No. 6 (2012)
7. Palyart, M., Lugato, D., Ober, I., Bruel, J.-M.: Improving scalability and maintenance of software for high-performance scientific computing by combining MDE and frameworks. In: Whittle, J., Clark, T., Kühne, T. (eds.) MODELS 2011. LNCS, vol. 6981, pp. 213–227. Springer, Heidelberg (2011)
8. Bruel, J.M., Combemale, B., Ober, I., Raynal., H.: MDE in practice for computational science. In: ICCS 2015, pp. 660–669 (2015)
9. Arkin, E., Tekinerdogan, B.: Domain specific language for deployment of parallel applications on parallel computing platforms. In: Proceedings of the ECSAW 2014. Article No. 16 (2014)
10. Almorsy, M., Grundy, J., Sadus, R.J., van Straten, W., Barnes, D.G., Kaluza, O.: A suite of domain-specific visual languages for scientific software application modelling. In: VL/HCC, pp. 91–94 (2013)
11. Miller, M.C., Reus, J.F., Matzke, R.P., Arrighi, W.J., Schoof, L.A., Hitt, R.T., Espen, P.K.: Enabling interoperation of high performance, scientific computing applications: modeling scientific data with the sets and fields (SAF) modeling system. In: Alexandrov, V.N., Dongarra, J.J., Juliano, B.A., Renner, R.S., Tan, C.J.K. (eds.) Computational Science - ICCS 2001. LNCS, vol. 2074, pp. 158–167. Springer, Heidelberg (2001)
12. Tekinerdogan, B., Arkin, E.: Architecture framework for mapping parallel algorithms to parallel computing platforms. In: Proceedings of the 2nd International Workshop on Model-Driven Engineering for High Performance and CLoud computing, MDHPCL 2013, pp. 53–63 (2013)
13. Gamatie, A., Le Beux, S., Piel, E., Ben Atitallah, R., Etien, A., Marquet, P., Dekeyser, J.-L.: A model-driven design framework for massively parallel embedded systems. ACM Trans. Embed. Comput. Syst. **10**(4), 39 (2011)
14. Daniluk, A.: Visual modeling for scientific software architecture design. A practical approach. Comput. Phys. Commun. **183**, 213 (2012)
15. Scheidgen, M., Zubow, A.: Map/reduce on EMF models. In: Proceedings of the 1st International Workshop on Model-Driven Engineering for High Performance and CLoud computing, MDHPCL 2012. Article No. 7 (2012)
16. Shekhar, S., Caglar, F., An, K., Kuroda, T., Gokhale, A., Gokhale, S.: A model-driven approach for price/performance tradeoffs in cloud-based mapreduce application deployment. In: Proceedings of the 2nd International Workshop on Model-Driven Engineering for High Performance and CLoud computing, MDHPCL 2013, pp. 37–43 (2013)
17. Mansurova, M., Akhmed-Zaki, D., Matkerim, B., Kumalakov, B.: Distributed parallel algorithm for numerical solving of 3D problem of fluid dynamics in anisotropic elastic porous medium using MapReduce and MPI technologies. In: Proceedings of 9th International Joint Conference on Software Technologies ICSOFT 2014, Vienna, Austria, pp. 525–528 (2014)
18. Matkerim, B., Akhmed-Zaki, D., Barata, M.: Development high performance scientific computing application using model-driven architecture. Appl. Math. Sci. **7**(100), 4961–4974 (2013)
19. Bezivin, J.: Object to Model Paradigm Change with the OMG/MDA Initiative, presentation of Summer School on MDA for Embedded System Development, pp. 16–20, Leon, France (2002)

Site-Level Web Template Extraction
Based on DOM Analysis

Julián Alarte[1], David Insa[1], Josep Silva[1(✉)], and Salvador Tamarit[2]

[1] Universitat Politècnica de València, Camino de Vera s/n, 46022 Valencia, Spain
{jalarte,dinsa,jsilva}@dsic.upv.es
[2] IMDEA Software, Universidad Politécnica de Madrid,
Campus Montegancedo UPM, 28223 Pozuelo de Alarcón, Madrid, Spain
stamarit@software.imdea.org

Abstract. One of the main development resources for website engineers are Web templates. Templates allow them to increase productivity by plugin content into already formatted and prepared pagelets. For the final user templates are also useful, because they provide uniformity and a common look and feel for all webpages. However, from the point of view of crawlers and indexers, templates are an important problem, because templates usually contain irrelevant information such as advertisements, menus, and banners. Processing and storing this information leads to a waste of resources (storage space, bandwidth, etc.). It has been measured that templates represent between 40 % and 50 % of data on the Web. Therefore, identifying templates is essential for indexing tasks. In this work we propose a novel method for automatic web template extraction that is based on similarity analysis between the DOM trees of a collection of webpages that are detected using an hyperlink analysis. Our implementation and experiments demonstrate the usefulness of the technique.

Keywords: Information retrieval · Content extraction · Template extraction

1 Introduction

A web template (in the following just template) is a prepared HTML page where formatting is already implemented and visual components are ready to insert content into them. Templates are an essential component of nowadays websites, and they are important for web developers, users, and also for indexers and crawlers:

This work has been partially supported by the EU (FEDER) and the Spanish *Ministerio de Economía y Competitividad (Secretaría de Estado de Investigación, Desarrollo e Innovación)* under grant TIN2013-44742-C4-1-R and by the *Generalitat Valenciana* under grant PROMETEOII/2015/013. David Insa was partially supported by the Spanish Ministerio de Eduación under FPU grant AP2010-4415.

M. Mazzara and A. Voronkov (Eds.): PSI 2015, LNCS 9609, pp. 36–49, 2016.
DOI: 10.1007/978-3-319-41579-6_4

– Web developers use templates as a basis for composing new webpages that share a common look and feel. This also allows them to automate many tasks thanks to the reuse of components. In fact, many websites are maintained automatically by code generators that generate webpages using templates.
– Users can benefit from intuitive and uniform designs with a common vocabulary of colored and formatted visual elements.
– Crawlers and indexers usually judge the relevance of a webpage according to the frequency and distribution of terms and hyperlinks. Since templates contain a considerable number of common terms and hyperlinks that are replicated in a large number of webpages, relevance may turn out to be inaccurate, leading to incorrect results (see, e.g., [3,19,21]). Moreover, in general, templates do not contain relevant content, they usually contain one or more pagelets [3,7] (i.e., self-contained logical regions with a well defined topic or functionality) where the main content must be inserted. Therefore, detecting templates helps indexers to identify the main content of the webpage. Gibson et al. [10] determined that templates represent between 40 % and 50 % of data on the Web and that around 30 % of the visible terms and hyperlinks appear in templates. This justifies the importance of template removal [19,21] for web mining and search.

Our approach to template extraction is based on the DOM [8] structures that represent webpages. Roughly, given a webpage in a website, (1) we first identify a set of webpages that are likely to share a template with it, and then, (2) we analyze these webpages to identify the part of their DOM trees that is common with the original webpage. (3) This slice of the DOM tree is returned as the template.

Some of the ideas in this paper were previously discussed in their earlier version in [1,2]. Herein we further develop them, we put them all together, we add new technical results and algorithms, and finally, we describe our implementation of the whole system.

The rest of the paper has been structured as follows: In Sect. 2 we discuss the state of the art and show some problems of current techniques that can be solved with our approach. In Sect. 3, we present our technique with examples and explain the algorithms used. In Sect. 4 we give some details about the implementation and show the results obtained from a collection of benchmarks. Finally, Sect. 5 concludes.

2 Related Work

Template detection and extraction are hot topics due to their direct application to web mining, searching, indexing, and web development. For this reason, there are many approaches that try to face this problem. Some of them have been presented in the CleanEval competition [4], which periodically proposes a collection of examples to be analyzed with a gold standard. The examples proposed are especially thought for boilerplate removal and content extraction.

Content Extraction is a discipline very close to template extraction. Content extraction tries to isolate the pagelet with the main content of the webpage. It is an instance of a more general discipline called *Block Detection* that tries to isolate every pagelet in a webpage. There are many works in these fields (see, e.g., [6,11,12,20]), and all of them are directly related to template extraction.

In the area of template extraction, there are three main different ways to solve the problem, namely, (i) using the textual information of the webpage (i.e., the HTML code), (ii) using the rendered image of the webpage in the browser, and (iii) using the DOM tree of the webpage.

The first approach is based on the idea that the main content of the webpage has more density of text with less labels. For instance, the main content can be identified selecting the largest contiguous text area with the least amount of HTML tags [9]. This has been measured directly on the HTML code by counting the number of characters inside text and the number of labels. This measure produces a ratio called CETR [20] used to discriminate the main content. Other approaches exploit densitometric features based on the observation that some specific terms are more common in templates [14,16]. The distribution of the code between the lines of a webpage is not necessarily the one expected by the user. The format of the HTML code can be completely unbalanced (i.e., without tabulations, spaces or even carriage returns), specially when it is generated by a non-human directed system. As a common example, the reader can see the source code of the main Google's webpage. At the time of writing these lines, all the code of the webpage is distributed in only a few lines without any legible structure. In this kind of webpages CETR is useless.

The second approach assumes that the main content of a webpage is often located in the central part and (at least partially) visible without scrolling [5]. This approach has been less studied because rendering webpages for classification is a computational expensive operation [15].

The third approach is where our technique falls. While some works try to identify pagelets analyzing the DOM tree with heuristics [3], others try to find common subtrees in the DOM trees of a collection of webpages in the website [19,21]. Our technique is similar to these last two works.

Even though [21] uses a method for template extraction, its main goal is to remove redundant parts of a website. For this, they use the Site Style Tree (SST), a data structure that is constructed by analyzing a set of DOM trees and recording every node found, so that repeated nodes are identified by using counters in the SST nodes. Hence, an SST summarizes a set of DOM trees. After the SST is built, they have information about the repetition of nodes. The most repeated nodes are more likely to belong to a noisy part that is removed from the webpages.

In [19], the approach is based on discovering optimal mappings between DOM trees. This mapping relates nodes that are considered redundant. Their technique uses the RTDM-TD algorithm to compute a special kind of mapping called *restricted top-down mapping* [18]. Their objective, as ours, is template extraction, but there are two important differences. First, we compute another kind of mapping to identify redundant nodes. Our mapping is more restrictive because it forces all nodes that form pairs in the mapping to be equal. Second, in order to select the webpages of the website that should be mapped to identify the template, they pick random webpages until a threshold is reached. In their experiments, they approximated this threshold as a few dozens of webpages. In our technique, we do not select the webpages randomly, we use a new method to identify the webpages linked by the main menu of the website. We only need to explore a few webpages to identify the webpages that implement the template. Moreover, contrarily to us, they assume that all webpages in the website share the same template, and this is a strong limitation for many websites.

3   Template Extraction

Our technique inputs a webpage (called key page) and it outputs its template. To infer the template, we identify what concrete other webpages in the same website should be analyzed. Our approach introduces three new ideas to solve the following three problems:

1. Minimize the number of webpages to be analyzed from the (usually huge) universe of directly or indirectly linked webpages. For this, starting from the key page, we identify a *complete subdigraph* in the website topology.
2. Solve conflicts between those webpages that implement different templates. For this, we establish a *voting system* between the webpages.
3. Extract the template by comparing the set of webpages analyzed. For this, we calculate a new mapping called *equal top-down mapping* (ETDM) between the DOM tree of the key page and the DOM trees of the webpages in the complete subdigraph.

The three processes are explained in the following sections.

3.1   Finding Webpage Candidates to Extract the Template

The first phase of our technique identifies a set of webpages that share their template with the key page. This phase was proposed and described in [1] as an independent process that can be used by any template extraction technique. In fact, this phase is orthogonal to the other phases that extract the template. Roughly, we detect the template's menu and analyze the hyperlinks of the menu to identify a set of mutually linked webpages. One of the main functions of a template is in aiding navigation, thus almost all templates provide a large number of hyperlinks, shared by all webpages implementing the template. Locating the menu allows us to identify in the topology of the website the main webpages of each category or section. These webpages very likely share the same template.

Given a website topology, a *complete subdigraph* (CS) represents a collection of webpages that are pairwise mutually linked. A n-complete subdigraph (n-CS) is formed by n nodes. Our interest in complete subdigraphs comes from the observation that the webpages linked by the items in a menu usually form a CS.

Fig. 1. Webpages of Innopolis University sharing a template

This is a new way of identifying the webpages that contain the menu. At the same time, these webpages are the roots of the sections linked by the menu, and thus they very likely share a common template.

Example 1. In Fig. 1, we see two webpages of Innopolis University that share the same template. The left webpage is reached from the menu option "Education". The right webpage is reached from the menu option "Research". In both pages the main content is at the bottom right. They both share the same header, menu, and general structure, and they form a 2-CS. Similarly, the 6 webpages linked by the menu at the top form a 6-CS, and they all implement the whole template. Our technique uses these webpages as candidates.

This simple idea is so powerful that it significantly increases the quality of the webpage candidates (main webpages of a category normally maximize the amount of template implemented), and at the same time it increases performance: contrarily to other approaches, we only need to investigate a reduced set of webpages linked by the key page, because they will for sure contain a CS that represents the menu. Contrarily to our approach, with independence of the approach followed to compare the candidates, the most extended way of selecting them is manually. For instance, the *ContentExtractor* algorithm and its improved version, the *FastContentExtractor* algorithm [17], take as input a set of webpages that are given by the programmer. The same happens in the methodology proposed in [13].

Other approaches select the candidates randomly. For instance, in [21], SSTs are built from a collection of webpages. They do not have a methodology to select the webpages, and they do not propose a number of webpages needed. In their experiments, they randomly sample 500 webpages, and the time taken to build a SST is always below 20 s. Similarly, in [19], in order to select the webpages of the website that should be mapped to identify the template, they pick random webpages until a threshold is reached. In their experiments, they approximated this threshold as a few dozen of webpages. They need 25 webpages to reach a 0.95 F1 measure using a collection of product description webpages that share the same template. Therefore, contrarily to us, they assume that all webpages in the website share the same template, and this is too restrictive for many websites.

By analyzing the hyperlinks (in the following, links) in the key page, it is possible to select those links that most likely produce a CS. This is essential to avoid analyzing all links and thus significantly increasing the performance. Our strategy to identify the links that should be analyzed is based on the structure of the website, and the structure of the website can be inferred from the own links. In particular, by analyzing the links in the key page, we can establish an order of relevance (i.e., an order that states what links should be analyzed first). For this, we use the hyperlink distance and the DOM distance:

Hyperlink Distance. It represents the distance in the file system between the directories pointed by two links. This can be observed in Fig. 2 (left), which represents a tree of directories that contain webpages. There, we can see the distance of the webpage in the gray directory to the rest of webpages. Note that the hyperlink distance can be negative and it is asymmetric. This can be also observed in Fig. 2 (right) where hyperlink distance is represented with *hDistance*.

DOM Distance. It is just the standard tree nodes distance in the DOM tree between two link nodes. Hence, two hyperlink nodes have zero DOM distance if and only if they are exactly the same node. Contrarily, two different hyperlink nodes (even if they have the same URL, and thus the same hyperlink distance) necessarily have a positive DOM distance. An example of DOM distance can be observed in Fig. 2 (right) where DOM distance is represented with *dDistance*.

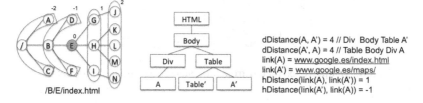

Fig. 2. Hyperlink distance (left). A DOM tree T (center) with its information (right).

There exists a clear relation between hyperlink distance and the probability of the linked webpages to share the template. Another observation is that we want the candidates that share the template to be as different as possible to ensure representativity of the website (e.g., avoiding to select all webpages about the same sport in a sports website). Therefore, the process of obtaining webpages that share the same template tries to identify webpages with an hyperlink distance as close to zero as possible, but at the same time maximizing the DOM distance (to ensure that the webpages are as different as possible), and giving priority to the hyperlink distance.

Concretely, to compute the n-CS, we sort the links of the key page, and iteratively explore them until they form a n-CS. The order of the links is created using both the hyperlink distance and the DOM distance. The order is the following: First, those links with zero hyperlink distance, then, those links that are closer to the key page with a positive distance, and finally those links that are closer to the key page with a negative distance. In the three cases, if a draw occurs, then, the draw is broken using the DOM distance: those links that are farer to the already selected links are collected. A formalization together with the algorithms used to compute a n-CS can be found in [1].

3.2   Solving Conflicts Between Webpages with Different Templates

One problem that we detected in previous techniques is the general assumption that the website has a unique template. Contrarily, a single webpage can implement various templates, or even subsets of different templates. This is illustrated in the following example.

Example 2. In Fig. 3 we see the key page and two webpages used to extract its template. The two webpages implement a different template, and they are disjoint except for the root node. If we assume that all webpages implement the same template, then, the template extracted would be only the root node (it is the only one shared by the three webpages). Contrarily, it is possible that the key page implements a part of the template of one webpage, and a part of the other webpage, being the template the gray nodes. Thus, even if the webpage candidates are disjoint, they can contribute to the template.

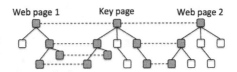

Fig. 3. Template extracted from webpages with different template

Example 2 shows that not all webpages must share a node to consider this node as template. But, how many of them are necessary? The answer is: it depends on the size of the CS. We experimented with a benchmark suite and measured the recall and precision obtained with all combinations of CS size and number of votes needed. The results are summarized in the first two columns of Table 2. For instance, with a CS of size 6, 3 votes are enough to get the best F1. As a result, our algorithm implements a voting system to extract the template from a set of candidates, and it uses a parameter that represents the number of votes needed for a node to be considered template. This algorithm is presented in the next section in such a way that it is parametric so that it can be used for any size of the CS and for any number of votes needed.

3.3   Template Extraction from a Complete Subdigraph

In the following, given a DOM tree $T = (N, E)$, $parent(n)$ represents node $n' \in N$ such that $(n', n) \in E$. Similarly, $subtree(n)$ denotes the subtree of T whose root is $n \in N$.

In order to identify the part of the DOM tree that is common in a set of webpages, our technique uses an algorithm that is based on the notion of mapping. A mapping establishes a correspondence between the nodes of two trees. In order to identify templates, we define a very specific kind of mapping that we call *equal top-down mapping* (ETDM) (see Fig. 4).

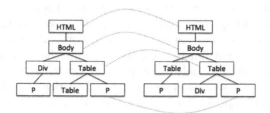

Fig. 4. Equal top-down mapping between DOM trees

Definition 1 (Equal Top-Down Mapping). *A* mapping *from a tree* $T = (N, E)$ *to a tree* $T' = (N', E')$ *is any set* M *of pairs of nodes* $(n, n') \in M$, $n \in N, n' \in N'$ *such that, for any two pairs* (n_1, n_1') *and* (n_2, n_2') *in* M, $n_1 = n_2$ *iff* $n_1' = n_2'$. *Given an equality relation* $\triangleq$ *between tree nodes, a mapping* M *between two trees* T *and* T' *is said to be* equal top-down *if and only if*

- *equal: for every pair* $(n, n') \in M$, $n \triangleq n'$.
- *top-down: for every pair* $(n, n') \in M$, *with* $n \neq root(T)$ *and* $n' \neq root(T')$, *there is also a pair* $(parent(n), parent(n')) \in M$.

Note that this definition is parametric with respect to the equality relation $\triangleq$. We could simply use the standard equality ($=$), but we left this relation open, to be general enough as to cover any possible implementation. In particular, other techniques consider that two nodes n_1 and n_2 are equal if they have the same label. However, in our implementation we use a notion of node equality much more complex that compares two nodes considering their HTML *id*, CSS classes, their number of children, their relative position in the DOM tree, and their HTML attributes. We refer the interested reader to our open and free implementation (http://www.dsic.upv.es/~jsilva/retrieval/templates/) where relation $\triangleq$ is specified.

This definition of mapping allows us to be more restrictive than other mappings such as, e.g., the *restricted top-down mapping* (RTDM) introduced in [18]. While RTDM permits the mapping of different nodes (e.g., a node labelled with *table* with a node labelled with *div*), ETDM can force all pairwise mapped nodes to have the same label. Figure 4 shows an example of an ETDM using: $n \triangleq n'$ if and only if n and n' have the same label.

After we have found the webpage candidates (the CS), we identify an ETDM between the key page and a set of webpages in the CS. For this, initially, the template is considered to be empty. Then, we iteratively compute an ETDM between the template and v webpages in the set, being v the number of votes needed for a node to be considered template. The result is a template with all those nodes of the key page appearing in at least v other webpages of the CS. This process is formalized in Algorithm 1, which uses function $ETDM$ to compute the biggest ETDM between a set of trees. Algorithm 1 uses a loop (foreach $(\{p_1 \ldots p_v\}$ in $P)$) that iterates over all possible partitions of P formed with v pages (because v votes are needed). Then, an ETDM is computed between these webpages and the key page. Observe that function $ETDM$ is recursive. It traverses the trees top-down collecting all those nodes that are equal modulo $\triangleq$. Note that function $ETDM$ assumes that, given two webpages $p_1 = (N_1, E_1), p_2 = (N_2, E_2)$, only one node $n_1 \in N_1$ satisfies $n_1 \triangleq n_2$ for a given $n_2 \in N_2$. Of course, this strictly depends on the definition of $\triangleq$. In the case that $\exists\, n_1, n'_1 \in N_1,\ n_2 \in N_2\,.\, n_1 \triangleq n_2 \,\wedge\, n'_1 \triangleq n_2$, then, the algorithm should be augmented with a mechanism to select only one node (either n_1 or n'_1).

Algorithm 1. Extract a template from a set of webpages

Input: A key page $p_k = (N, E)$, a set P of n webpages, and the number of votes v needed for a node to be considered template.
Output: A template for p_k with respect to P and v.

```
begin
    template = (N_t, E_t) = (∅, ∅);
    foreach ({p_1 ... p_v} in P)
        if root(p_k) ≜ root(p_1) ≜ ... ≜ root(p_v)
            (N', E') = ETDM(p_k, p_1, ..., p_v);
            (N_t, E_t) = (N_t ∪ N', E_t ∪ E');
            template = (N_t, E_t);
    return template;
end

function ETDM(tree T_0 = (N_0, E_0), tree T_1 = (N_1, E_1), ..., tree T_v = (N_v, E_v))
    r_0 = root(T_0); r_1 = root(T_1); ...; r_v = root(T_v);
    nodes = {r_0};
    edges = ∅;
    foreach n_0 ∈ N_0, ..., n_v ∈ N_v . n_0 ≜ ... ≜ n_v, (r_0, n_0) ∈ E_0, ..., (r_v, n_v) ∈ E_v
        (nodes_st, edges_st) = ETDM(subtree(n_0), ..., subtree(n_v));
        nodes = nodes ∪ nodes_st;
        edges = edges ∪ edges_st ∪ {(r_0, n_0)};
    return (nodes, edges);
end function
```

As in Definition 1, we left the algorithm parametric with respect to equality relation $\triangleq$. This is done on purpose, because this relation is the only parameter that is subjective and thus, it is a good design decision to leave it open. For instance, a researcher can decide that two DOM nodes are equal if they have the same label and attributes. Another researcher can relax this restriction ignoring some attributes (i.e., the template can be the same, even if there are differences in colors, sizes, or even positions of elements. It usually depends on the particular use of the extracted template). Additionally, this design decision gives us control over the recall and precision of the technique. Because the more restrictive $\triangleq$ is, the more precision (and less recall).

4   Implementation

The technique presented in this paper, including all the algorithms, has been implemented as a Firefox's extension accepted by Mozilla as an official add-on (https://addons.mozilla.org/en-US/firefox/addon/template-extractor/). In this tool, the user can browse on the Internet as usual. Then, when he/she wants to extract the template of a webpage, he/she only needs to press the "Extract Template" button and the tool automatically (internally) loads the appropriate linked webpages to form a CS, analyzes them, and extracts the template. The template is then displayed in the browser as any other webpage.

4.1   Empirical Evaluation

Initially, we wanted to use a public standard collection of benchmarks to evaluate our tool, but we are not aware of any public dataset for template extraction. In particular, the standard CleanEval suite [4] contains a gold standard prepared for content extraction (each part of the webpages is labelled as *main-content* or *non-content*), but it is not prepared for template extraction. We tried to use the same benchmark set as the authors of other template extraction papers. However, due to privacy restrictions, copyright, or unavailability[1] of the benchmarks we could not use a previous dataset. It is surprising, and quite disappointing, to see how few systems are open-source, or even otherwise (freely) available. In many papers, it is stated that a prototype was developed but we were not able to find the tool. In some cases, a system might be mentioned to be open source but you need to contact the authors to get it. This is the cause why we are reinventing the wheel, implementing similar systems once and again. Moreover, not providing the dataset makes impossible to validate or replicate experiments. For this reason, we made our system, open-source and publicly available, so that other researchers can reuse it or join efforts to further developing it. And we decided to create a new suite of benchmarks that is also publicly accessible, both the dataset and the gold standard. This is one of the main contributions of our work. Any interested researcher can freely access and download our dataset from: http://www.dsic.upv.es/~jsilva/retrieval/teco/.

The dataset is composed of a collection of web domains with different layouts and page structures. This allows us to study the performance of the techniques in different contexts (e.g., company websites, news articles, forums, etc.).

---

[1] Some authors answered that their benchmarks were not stored for future use, or that they did not save the gold standard.

Table 1. Results of the experimental evaluation

Benchmark	DOM	Template	Retrieved	Recall	Precision	F1	Time
www.water.org	948	711	668	93, 95 %	100 %	96, 88 %	5661
www.jdi.org.za	626	305	305	100 %	100 %	100 %	2928
www.stackoverflow.com	6450	447	461	100 %	96, 96 %	98, 46 %	18348
www.eclipse.org	256	156	160	97, 44 %	95 %	96, 20 %	3382
www.history.com	1246	669	593	88, 19 %	99, 49 %	93, 50 %	16946
www.landcoalition.org	1247	393	433	98, 47 %	89, 38 %	93, 70 %	4901
www.es.fifa.com	1324	276	239	84, 78 %	97, 91 %	90, 87 %	8171
www.cordis.europa.eu	959	335	327	97, 01 %	99, 39 %	98, 19 %	5115
www.clotheshor.se	459	231	225	97, 40 %	100 %	98, 68 %	2176
www.emmaclothes.com	1080	374	368	98, 40 %	100 %	99, 19 %	8641
www.cleanclothes.org	1335	266	288	100 %	92, 36 %	96, 03 %	7725
www.mediamarkt.es	805	337	329	97, 63 %	100 %	98, 80 %	5903
www.ikea.com	1545	407	565	99, 75 %	71, 86 %	83, 54 %	7326
www.swimmingpool.com	607	499	349	69, 94 %	100 %	82, 31 %	2514
www.skipallars.cat	1466	842	828	98, 34 %	100 %	99, 16 %	10042
www.tennis.com	1300	463	419	90, 50 %	100 %	95, 01 %	7312
www.tennischannel.com	661	303	236	77, 89 %	100 %	87, 57 %	3520
www.turfparadise.com	1057	726	818	99, 72 %	88, 51 %	93, 78 %	6756
www.riotimesonline.com	2063	879	861	97, 96 %	100 %	98, 97 %	50528
www.beaches.com	1928	1306	1172	89, 74 %	100 %	94, 59 %	11201
http://users.dsic.upv.es/~jsilva	197	163	163	100 %	100 %	100 %	7419
http://users.dsic.upv.es/~dinsa	241	74	88	100 %	84, 09 %	91, 36 %	1457
www.engadget.com	1818	768	767	99, 09 %	99, 22 %	99, 15 %	19116
www.bbc.co.uk/news	2991	364	355	97, 53 %	100 %	98, 75 %	13806
www.vidaextra.com	2331	1137	992	87, 25 %	100 %	93, 19 %	17787
www.ox.ac.uk/staff	948	525	533	99, 43 %	97, 94 %	98, 68 %	59599
www.clinicaltrials.gov	543	389	394	97, 17 %	95, 94 %	96, 55 %	4746
www.en.citizendium.org	1083	414	447	100 %	92, 62 %	96, 17 %	13414
www.filmaffinity.com	1333	351	355	100 %	98, 87 %	99, 43 %	5279
www.edition.cnn.com	3934	192	180	93, 75 %	100 %	96, 77 %	31076
www.lashorasperdidas.com	1822	553	536	96, 93 %	100 %	98, 44 %	19379
www.labakeryshop.com	1368	218	193	80, 73 %	91, 19 %	85, 64 %	7893
www.felicity.co.uk	300	232	232	100 %	100 %	100 %	2217
www.thelawyer.com	3349	1293	1443	93, 81 %	84, 06 %	88, 67 %	19998
www.us-nails.com	250	18	215	100 %	85, 58 %	92, 23 %	3386
www.informatik.uni-trier.de	3085	64	63	98, 44 %	100 %	99, 21 %	10174
www.wayfair.co.uk	1950	702	700	99, 29 %	99, 57 %	99, 43 %	30990
www.catalog.atsfurniture.com	340	301	304	100 %	99, 01 %	99, 50 %	2862
www.glassesusa.com	1952	1708	1656	96, 96 %	100 %	98, 45 %	19462
www.mysmokingshop.co.uk	575	407	428	100 %	95, 09 %	97, 49 %	89887
Average	1444, 3	499, 1	492, 2	95, 44 %	96, 35 %	95, 61 %	14226, 08

To measure our technique, we randomly selected an evaluation subset. Table 1 summarizes the results of the performed experiments. First column contains the URLs of the evaluated website domains. For each benchmark, column DOM shows the number of nodes in the key page's DOM tree; column Template shows the number of nodes in the gold standard template; column Retrieved shows the number of nodes that were identified by the tool as the template; column Recall shows the number of correctly retrieved nodes divided by the number of nodes in the gold standard; column `Precision` shows the number of correctly retrieved nodes divided by the number of retrieved nodes; column `F1` shows the F1 metric that is computed as $(2 * P * R)/(P + R)$ being P the precision and R the recall; finally, column `Time` shows the total milliseconds used to obtain the template.

Experiments reveal an average precision of more than 96 %, and an average recall of more than 95 % which, from the best of our knowledge, produce the highest F1 in the state of the art. To produce this result, we have performed more than half a million experiments to tune our definition of $\triangleq$ combining different DOM parameters such as label, class, id, children, position, etc. See http://www.dsic.upv.es/~jsilva/retrieval/templates/ for details.

Table 2. Determining the ideal size of the complete subdigraph

Size	Votes	Recall	Precision	F1	Loads
1	1	88,56 %	94,89 %	88,69 %	2
2	1	96,34 %	90,32 %	91,93 %	5, 6
3	2	95,44 %	96,35 %	95,61 %	10, 13
4	3	94,61 %	96,88 %	95,27 %	16, 52
5	3	94,69 %	96,96 %	95,40 %	18, 68
6	3	95,21 %	96,82 %	95,69 %	23, 68
7	3	95,46 %	96,31 %	95,57 %	30
8	4	95,14 %	96,57 %	95,54 %	32, 08

In the experiments, we also evaluated empirically what is the ideal size of the CS computed. Results are shown in Table 2. This table summarizes many experiments. Each row is the average of repeating all the experiments in Table 1 with a different value for n in the n-CS searched by the algorithm and for a different value for all $v < n$. All possible combinations were evaluated. Column `Size` represents the size of the CS that the algorithm tried to find in the websites. And column `Votes` represents the best v value obtained for each CS size. In the case that there did not exist a CS of the searched size, then the algorithm used the biggest CS with a size under the specified size. Column `Loads` represents the average number of webpages loaded to extract the template.

We determined that a subdigraph of size 3 is the best option because it keeps almost the best F1 value, while being very efficient (only 10 webpages must be loaded to extract the template). Therefore, the results shown in Table 1 have been computed with a 3-CS.

5   Conclusions

This work presents a new technique for template extraction. It uses a hyperlink analysis to identify the menu of a given webpage. With this menu, the technique collects a set of webpages that form a CS and, thus, they probably share the same template. The DOM structures of these webpages are then compared with a new mapping called ETDM to identify the blocks that are common to some of them. The exact number has been approximated empirically. Our best values considering both F1 and performance are a size of the CS of 3, and 2 votes needed to be considered template. To the best of our knowledge, the idea of using the menus to locate the template is new, and it allows us to quickly find a set of webpages from which we can extract the template. This is especially interesting for performance, because loading webpages to be analyzed is expensive, and this part of the process is minimized in our technique. As an average, our technique only loads 10 pages to extract the template (a mean of less than 15 s for the overall template extraction process).

References

1. Alarte, J., Insa, D., Silva, J., Tamarit, S.: Automatic detection of webpages that share the same web template. In: ter Beek, M.H., Ravara, A. (eds.) Proceedings of the 10th International Workshop on Automated Specification and Verification of Web Systems (WWV 2014). Electronic Proceedings in Theoretical Computer Science, vol. 163, pp. 2–15. Open Publishing Association, July 2014
2. Alarte, J., Insa, D., Silva, J., Tamarit, S.: Web template extraction based on hyperlink analysis. In: Escobar, S. (ed.) Proceedings of the XIV Jornadas sobre Programación y Lenguajes (PROLE 2015). Electronic Proceedings in Theoretical Computer Science, vol. 173, pp. 16–26. Open Publishing Association, September 2015
3. Bar-Yossef, Z., Rajagopalan, S.: Template detection via data mining and its applications. In: Proceedings of the 11th International Conference on World Wide Web (WWW 2002), pp. 580–591. ACM, New York (2002)
4. Baroni, M., Chantree, F., Kilgarriff, A., Sharoff, S.: Cleaneval: a competition for cleaning web pages. In: Proceedings of the International Conference on Language Resources and Evaluation (LREC 2008), pp. 638–643. European Language Resources Association, May 2008
5. Burget, R., Rudolfova, I.: Web page element classification based on visual features. In: Proceedings of the 1st Asian Conference on Intelligent Information and Database Systems (ACIIDS 2009), pp. 67–72. IEEE Computer Society, Washington, DC (2009)
6. Cardoso, E., Jabour, I., Laber, E., Rodrigues, R., Cardoso, P.: An efficient language-independent method to extract content from news webpages. In: Proceedings of the 11th ACM Symposium on Document Engineering (DocEng 2011), pp. 121–128. ACM, New York (2011)
7. Chakrabarti, S.: Integrating the Document Object Model with hyperlinks for enhanced topic distillation and information extraction. In: Proceedings of the 10th International Conference on World Wide Web (WWW 2001), pp. 211–220. ACM, New York (2001)
8. W3C Consortium. Document Object Model (DOM) (1997). http://www.w3.org/DOM/
9. Ferraresi, A., Zanchetta, E., Baroni, M., Bernardini, S.: Introducing and evaluating ukWaC, a very large web-derived corpus of English. In: Proceedings of the 4th Web as Corpus Workshop (WAC-4), pp. 47–54 (2008)

10. Gibson, D., Punera, K., Tomkins, A.: The volume and evolution of web page templates. In: Ellis, A., Hagino, T. (eds.) Proceedings of the 14th International Conference on World Wide Web (WWW 2005), pp. 830–839. ACM, May 2005
11. Gottron, T.: Content code blurring: a new approach to content extraction. In: Tjoa, A.M., Wagner, R.R. (eds.) Proceedings of the 19th International Workshop on Database and Expert Systems Applications (DEXA 2008), pp. 29–33. IEEE Computer Society, September 2008
12. Insa, D., Silva, J., Tamarit, S.: Using the words/leafs ratio in the DOM tree for content extraction. J. Logic Algebraic Program. **82**(8), 311–325 (2013)
13. Kadam, V., Devale, P.R.: A methodology for template extraction from heterogeneous web pages. Indian J. Comput. Sci. Eng. (IJCSE) **3**(3), 449–452 (2012)
14. Kohlschütter, C.: A densitometric analysis of web template content. In: Quemada, J., León, G., Maarek, Y.S., Nejdl, W. (eds.) Proceedings of the 18th International Conference on World Wide Web (WWW 2009), pp. 1165–1166. ACM, April 2009
15. Kohlschütter, C., Fankhauser, P., Nejdl, W.: Boilerplate detection using shallow text features. In: Davison, B.D., Suel, T., Craswell, N., Liu, B. (eds.) Proceedings of the 3th International Conference on Web Search and Web Data Mining (WSDM 2010), pp. 441–450. ACM, February 2010
16. Kohlschütter, C., Nejdl, W.: A densitometric approach to web page segmentation. In: Shanahan, J.G., Amer-Yahia, S., Manolescu, I., Zhang, Y., Evans, D.A., Kolcz, A., Choi, K.-S., Chowdhury, A. (eds.) Proceedings of the 17th ACM Conference on Information and Knowledge Management (CIKM 2008), pp. 1173–1182. ACM, October 2008
17. Nguyen, D.Q., Nguyen, D.Q., Pham, S.B., Bui, T.D.: A fast template-based approach to automatically identify primary text content of a web page. In: Proceedings of the 2009 International Conference on Knowledge and Systems Engineering, KSE 2009, pp. 232–236. IEEE Computer Society (2009)
18. de Castro Reis, D., Golgher, P.B., Silva, A.S., Laender, A.H.F.: Automatic web news extraction using tree edit distance. In: Proceedings of the 13th International Conference on World Wide Web (WWW 2004), pp. 502–511. ACM, New York (2004)
19. Vieira, K., da Silva, A.S., Pinto, N., de Moura, E.S., Cavalcanti, J.M.B., Freire, J.: A fast and robust method for web page template detection and removal. In: Proceedings of the 15th ACM International Conference on Information and Knowledge Management (CIKM 2006), pp. 258–267. ACM, New York (2006)
20. Weninger, T., Hsu, W.H., Han, J.: CETR: content extraction via tag ratios. In: Rappa, M., Jones, P., Freire, J., Chakrabarti, S. (eds.) Proceedings of the 19th International Conference on World Wide Web (WWW 2010), pp. 971–980. ACM, April 2010
21. Yi, L., Liu, B., Li, X.: Eliminating noisy information in web pages for data mining. In: Proceedings of the 9th ACM SIGKDD International Conference on Knowledge Discovery and Data Mining (KDD 2003), pp. 296–305. ACM, New York (2003)

Verification Support for a State-Transition-DSL Defined with Xtext

Thomas Baar[✉]

Hochschule für Technik und Wirtschaft (HTW) Berlin,
Wilhelminenhofstraße 75A, 12459 Berlin, Germany
thomas.baar@htw-berlin.de

Abstract. A Domain-Specific Language (DSL) allows the succinct modeling of phenomena in a problem domain. Modern DSL-tools make it easy for a language designer to define the syntax of a new DSL, to specify code generators or to build a new DSL on top of existing DSLs. Based on the language specification, the DSL-tool then generates rich editors. Often, these editors support features such as syntax highlighting, code completion or automatic refactoring.

In this paper, we describe an approach of adding verification support for DSLs defined within the Eclipse-framework Xtext. Xtext provides good support for checking the well-formedness rules of the DSL's syntax. In contrast, support for specifying the language's semantics as well as verification support have been rather neglected so far. Our approach of incorporating semantic verification techniques is illustrated by a very simple State-Transition-DSL, which has been fully implemented in Xtext. The DSL's editor verifies on the fly that the current model holds some semantic properties such as deterministic execution and invariant preservation. The verification services for this DSL are based on the theorem prover PRINCESS.

Keywords: DSL · Model verification · Proof obligation · State machine

1 Motivation

20 years ago, the three amigos of the UML were proud to win the war of notation. They have successfully extracted the main modelling concepts of the predecessors of the UML, such as OMG, Booch, Shlaer-Mellor, and created a graphical language with 9 diagrams at the beginning. This language was supposed to be applicable in many domains.

The nice thing about UML was (and still is) that, while being an open standard, it triggered many research activities, e.g. research groups mainly from academia reported at the UML conference series (which was 2005 renamed into MoDELS) on progress when working with models, i.e. their efficient creation, understanding, reuse, and semantic analysis. These efforts enjoyed great interest in the scientific community due to the large user base of UML.

© Springer International Publishing Switzerland 2016
M. Mazzara and A. Voronkov (Eds.): PSI 2015, LNCS 9609, pp. 50–60, 2016.
DOI: 10.1007/978-3-319-41579-6_5

However, not only the general purpose modelling languages made progress, but also Domain-specific languages (DSLs). Tool support for DSLs has concentrated so far in the easy definition of abstract and concrete syntax, and how to define code generators that take a model as input (see [1] for an overview).

Tools for the semantic analysis of the model formulated in such a DSL have been rather neglected. A typical example is the tool Yakindu [2], which implements a statechart DSL and provides an editor for editing and even simulating statecharts. Internally, Yakindu is based on Xtext.

When editing a statechart, Yakindu's editor gives very valuable feedback if the user constructs a *syntactically ill-formed* model, e.g., if she adds a transition ending in the start state or refers to a non-existing variable or event. However, Yakindu's editor does not offer any support if the model is semantically incorrect. For example, it does not issue a warning if the model contains dead transitions. In the simplest case, a transition is dead if it is annotated with a guard [false], but any other unsatisfiable guard (e.g. [3 > 7]) would also lead to a dead transition.

The detection of dead transitions goes beyond syntactic checks. It requires to interpret guards and - for example - to reduce a guard [3 > 7] to [false] due to the standard interpretation of mathematical symbols 3, 7, >.

In this paper, we develop a DSL for describing simple state machines using Xtext. The editor for this DSL offers semantic model checks, e.g. the detection of dead transitions. Our semantic model checks are internally based on the theorem prover PRINCESS, which supports reasoning on integer arithmetic and first-order logic. PRINCESS works very fast and discards each proof obligation from the example discussed in this paper within less than 10 ms. Thus, semantic checks are not more expensive than ordinary syntactic checks and can be executed on-the-fly by the DSL's editor while the user enters the model.

2   The Framework Xtext

Xtext is a framework for the development of textual DSLs. It is implemented in Java and is available in form of a plugin for the popular IDE *Eclipse*. Illustrative examples on what can be achieved via Xtext can be found on its homepage [3].

In order to define a DSL, the user first has to define a grammar in an EBNF-like syntax. Based on the grammar, the Eclipse plugin will then generate the so-called *language infrastructure*, consisting of a textual editor, the Ecore-metamodel, and the Java API for easy model access. This generation process as well as the resulting tools can be customized by the user in numerous ways, e.g. by implementing classes for presenting the syntax tree differently (so-called *label providers*) or by defining additional constraints on the syntax tree (implemented by a so-called *validator*).

The implementation of customization classes is done in Xtend, a Java-based language developed by the creators of Xtext. Using Xtend, many typical programming tasks such as traversing a syntax tree, creating a net of objects, or template-based string generation can be solved very elegantly.

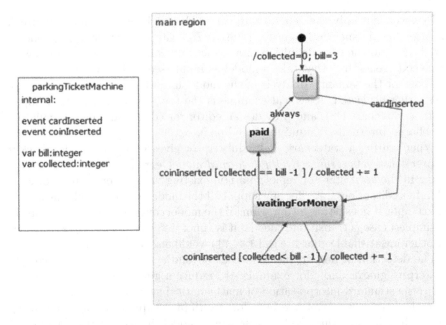

Fig. 1. ParkingTicketMachine (PTM) specified with Yakindu

2.1 Yakindu

Yakindu [2] is an open-source tool for the specification of statecharts [4]. It allows the user to *draw* states, nested states, and transitions; in this respect Yakindu is a tool for a graphical modelling language.

Since Yakindu is heavily based on Xtext, it is developed and maintained mainly by software engineers from *Itemis*, the company also standing behind Xtext. Yakindu allows the user to add to a transition an annotation consisting of a *guard*, an *event*, and an *action*. The formalism to express the annotation is internally defined as an Xtext-language.

An action can be a *named action* or an *update* of *state variables* with new values. Events, named actions, and state variables have to be declared separately. When specifying guards or updates, the user can take advantage of a pre-defined language for arithmetical and logical expressions.

Yakindu checks the type rules for expressions and sub-expressions instantly while a guard is typed in. Yakindu also executes additional *syntax checks* automatically, for example to ensure that each statechart has a start-state.

Yakindu does not offer *semantic checks*, which could help to prevent non-intended behaviour when executing the statechart. The only possibility for the user to analyze the run-time behaviour of the specified system is to execute the statechart in Yakindu's simulator.

2.2   Running Example ParkingTicketMachine (PTM)

In Fig. 1 we see a screenshot from Yakindu when editing a small statechart, which models a ticket machine in a parking deck (called *ParkingTicketMachine (PTM)*). The machine is waiting (state `idle`) for a customer inserting her park ticketing card (event `cardInserted`). Now, the ticket machine changes its state (to `waitingForMoney`) and the customer has to pay a certain amount of money (variable `bill`). The machine now expects coins to be inserted (event `coinInserted`) until the amount to be paid has been reached. For the sake of simplicity, we assume all coins to have the same value and that the amount to be paid is exactly the value of N many coins ($N > 0$). Once enough coins have been inserted, the machine changes its state first to `paid` and then immediately to `idle` (due to the pseudo-event `always`).

Unfortunately, the statechart has a semantic error: The machine collects the money correctly only from the first customer! After the machine has walked through the states `idle` - `waitingForMoney` - `paid` - `idle`, the state variable `collected` has the same value as `bill`. So, after the next customer has inserted her card, she can insert as many coins as she wants, but she will never reach the state `paid`!

3   Adding Verification Support for DSLs

In this section, we will demonstrate how one can implement verification support for DSLs implemented with Xtext. The verification support targets semantic properties of model written in the DSL. For the sake of illustration, we explain the verification techniques using the simple statechart introduced in Sect. 2.2.

Since our verification approach should serve as a blueprint for adding verification support to any textual DSL created with Xtext, we will start with the development of a DSL, which is able to denote simple forms of Yakindu's statecharts, but in a purely textual notation. Our language is called *SMINV* and models expressed in this language are called *state machines* in order to distinguish them easily from Yakindu's *statecharts*.

3.1   SMINV– A Textual DSL for Encoding Simple State Machines

A language to denote state machines can be basically subdivided into two parts: (1) The sublanguage for defining the 'infrastructure' of a state machine using concepts like *state, transition, event, state variable* and (2) the expression language for defining *guards* and *updates* of state variables.

Sublanguage for Infrastructure. The grammar definition for SMINV starts[1] with the start rule:

---

[1] Due to the paper's page limit, only the important parts of the grammar are presented here. The full grammar is available from [5].

```
SminvModel:
    vd=VarDecl
    sd=StateDecl
    ed=EventDecl
    td=TransDecl
```

A state machine is a sequence of declarations for variables, states, events, and transitions. While a variable, state or event is just declared by its name (which must be unique), the definition of a transition is a little bit more complex:

```
Transition:
    pre=[State] '=>' post=[State]
    (ev=[Event])? ('[' g=Term ']')? ('/' act+=Update+)? ';'
```

A transition connects two states (pre, post) and has optional annotations for event, guard, and updates.

Sublanguage for Expressions. The sublanguage for expressions is defined as usual in Xtext (see, for example, [6] for enlightening tutorial examples). Compared to the language supported by Yakindu, our expressions are simpler. We decided to allow only INT and BOOL as expression types. Thus, an expression is either a formula (boolean) or a term of type INT. Note that variables always have the type INT.

Running Example Formulated in SMINV. Despite its simplicity, our language allows to formulate many interesting models, including the running example PTM:

```
vars   collected bill
states  start idle waitingForMoney paid
events  cardInserted coinInserted

transitions
start => idle / collected = 0 bill = 3;

idle => waitingForMoney cardInserted;

waitingForMoney => waitingForMoney  coinInserted
        [collected < bill - 1 ] / collected += 1;

waitingForMoney => paid coinInserted
        [collected == bill - 1] / collected += 1;

paid => idle;
```

Adding Invariants. The semantic problem of the *PTM* was due to the fact, that it has been forgotten to set the value of collected to 0 when the transition from **paid** to **idle** is fired. In other words, the PTM only works correctly, if the variable **collected** has the value 0 when the system is in the state **idle**.

The statechart language of Yakindu does not offer the possibility to formulate invariants. In SMINV, the specification of state invariants is made possible by adding an additional element to the start rule of our grammar. The complete start rule of SMINV looks as follows:

```
SminvModel:
    vd=VarDecl
    sd=StateDecl
    ed=EventDecl
    td=TransDecl
    (id=InvDecl)?;
```

The definition of invariants is enabled by the following rules of the grammar:

```
InvDecl:
    {InvDecl} 'invariants' invs+=Inv*;

Inv:    state=[State] ':' inv=Term ';';
```

An invariant is an arbitrary term that has been attached to a state. However, this term must of type boolean, what is checked by an ordinary syntax check in SMINV's validator class.

Finally, we can now formulate the invariant for state **idle** formally.

invariants
idle : collected == 0;

However, in order to be able to prove the invariant, we should first fix the bug in PTM and add an update to the transition from **paid** to **idle**:

paid ⇒ idle / collected = 0;

3.2   Semantic properties to be verified

The verification of statecharts and related formalisms has been and still is a research topic for many authors [7,8]. The goal for this paper is to demonstrate how a language designer can implement verification support according to her needs for her user-defined DSL. For the language SMINV, we consider the following semantic model properties worth to be checked.

Invariant-Preserving Transitions. An state invariant is a boolean term expressing a constraint on the values of state variables (e.g. $v1 > 4$). By attaching a state invariant to a single state one claims, that a running state machine will satisfy the constraint on the values of state variables, whenever the machine is in the corresponding state. States without an attached invariant have always the implicit invariant **true**. The start state must not have any invariant attached.

By a simple induction argument, one can prove that all invariants are satisfied in all reachable states, if each transition establishes the invariant of the post-state.

Deterministic Transitions. It is also important to know whether the specified state machine works *deterministically* (recall that generation of implementation code from a state machine is in most cases meaningless when a specified state machine can behave non-deterministically). A non-determinism occurs when the system could change its state to more than one post-state upon receiving an event. This could happen, if a state exists that has at least two outgoing transitions that are triggered by the same event and whose guards overlap.

Alive Transitions. A state machine should have only *alive* transitions, because *dead* transitions are never executed. A transition is dead, if the constraints expressed by the transition's guard and the invariant of its pre-state are disjoint. In other words, it is not possible to find such values for the state variables that both the invariant of the pre-state and the guard are evaluated to *true*.

3.3   Proof Obligations

All semantic model properties described above can be formulated in form of proof obligations for model elements (for SMINV, either states or transitions). A proof obligation is a first-order formula with interpreted symbols for arithmetic operators. In the following, we formulate the proof obligation for each of the above described semantic model properties formally.

Invariant-Preserving Transitions. In order to prove that an invariant I_S for state S holds, one has to show that for all transitions t, which are incoming in state S, the update annotated on t is sufficient to establish the invariant I_S. Note that the start-state of the state machine must not be annotated by any invariant (start-states always have *implicitly* the invariant `true` annotated).

One can assume that the invariant annotated to the pre-state of t holds as well as the guard annotated to t. More formally:

Let Σ be the set of all states and S an element from Σ. For any such S, I_S denotes the invariant annotated to state S and $I_S[v \leftarrow update(t)]$ denotes the substitution of all variables in I_S according to the update annotated on transition t. Furthermore, $guard(t)$ denotes the guard annotated to t (*true* is taken when no guard is specified). By $pre(t), post(t)$ the pre/post-state of transition t is denoted and $\forall \vec{v}$ means the all-quantification of all state variables $v1, v2, \ldots$.

Then, one has to prove the following *proof obligation* for all transitions t:

$$\forall \vec{v} \ (I_{pre(t)} \wedge guard(t)) \longrightarrow I_{post(t)}[v \leftarrow update(t)] \tag{1}$$

Deterministic Transitions. In order to prove a state machine being deterministic, one has to show for all transitions t_1, t_2 that have the same pre-state and that are triggered by the same event:

$$\forall \vec{v} \ I_{pre(t_1)} \longrightarrow \neg(guard(t_1) \wedge guard(t_2)) \tag{2}$$

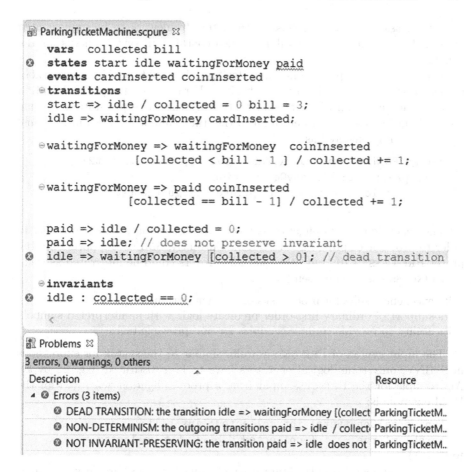

Fig. 2. Semantic error messages in editor for SMINV

Alive Transitions. In order to prove a transition t being alive, one has to show the satisfiability of its guard together with the invariant of the pre-state. More formally:

$$\exists \vec{v} \; I_{pre(t)} \wedge guard(t) \tag{3}$$

3.4   Implementation

The language SMINV as well as the corresponding toolset is free software, the sources of this software are made available on GitHub and can be downloaded from [5]. Figure 2 shows the editor running on the PTM-example, with some additional faulty transitions to cause some validation errors (note the error markers in the text as well as in the view *Problems*).

The semantic proof obligations discussed above have been implemented by @Check-annotated methods in the validator class of the language SMINV. The validator class is a standard class in the Xtext-framework to be implemented by each DSL separately. The validator also contains all syntax checks for the language.

The generation of proof obligations itself is delegated to another class, whose implementation in Xtend is surprisingly short. For example, the proof obligation for checking that transitions *t1* and *t2* (having the same pre-state and same event) do not cause an non-determinism (i.e. they cannot fire both in the same situation) is implemented as:

```
def getPO_NonDeterminism(Transition t1, Transition t2) {
    t1.pre.invariantsCopyConjunction
       .implies(neg(t1.guardCopy.and (t2.guardCopy)))
}
```

The generated proof obligation is passed to an automatic theorem prover in order to prove or disprove the obligation. Currently, SMINV supports only the prover PRINCESS [9,10], but other suitable provers could be integrated as well.

PRINCESS has been chosen for

- its excellent results for proof tasks on integer arithmetic
- its support of ordinary first-order predicate logic with uninterpreted symbols
- its ability to provide counterexamples for non-provable tasks

The input syntax of PRINCESS is quite similar to the syntax for expressions in SMINV, only some logical operators have to be substituted (e.g. && by &). An example for the PRINCESS input from a proof obligation generated for the PTM-example is:

```
\universalConstants{ int collected; int bill;}
\problem{true -> ! ( collected < bill-1 & collected =
bill-1)}
```

The experimental results obtained when using PRINCESS are very encouraging. All proof obligations generated for the PTM example could be proved/disproved within 2 ms – 8 ms on a Windows8 notebook (1.8 GHz, 8 GB RAM). Thus, the DSL editor can give instant feedback to the user also for semantic checks.

4 Discussion and Related Work

In the past, providing verification support for modelling languages was rather a task for either research groups or for companies selling tools for general purpose languages. The effort of implementing verification techniques only pays off when a language has a broad user base. In contrast, DSLs developed in industry for a very specific purpose often have very few users. One cannot expect tool builders to offer any dedicated support for single DSLs. Consequently, tool support has to be provided by the creator of the language herself.

There is another reason why verification support is less common for DSLs than for general purpose languages. It is not always clear what a (formal) semantics of a DSL could look like, though some DSLs has been recently made available, whose purpose is to define the semantics of other DSLs formally. For Xtext, such a DSL is Xsemantics [11]; the corresponding DSL for Spoofax [12] is called DynSem [13]). For general purpose languages, a common understanding of the language is evolving over time. This process eventually results in commonly accepted documents describing an informal or even formal semantics [14]. During this process, bugs, mistakes, and inconsistencies might be found by the broad user community. The semantics evolves over time. For DSLs, writing up the semantics might result in similar inconsistencies as in case of writing up the semantics of general purpose languages.

5   Conclusion and Future Work

DSLs allow to model succinctly for a certain purpose, but this flexibility also often means to abandon classical semantics for modelling languages. Consequently, semantic checks are currently neglected by DSL-definition frameworks such as Xtext, while syntax checks are very common and widely used.

The goal of this paper is to demonstrate that Xtext allows to implement DSL-specific semantic checks with moderate effort. Technically, semantic checks are realized analogously to syntax checks within the DSL's validator class. Thanks to the speed of the used theorem prover PRINCESS, also semantic checks can give instant feedback to the user. From the user's perspective, semantic checks make an editor much more intelligent, since they can detect *semantic errors* the user has made.

In future, we plan to address the following issues. Firstly, an integration into the tool Yakindu would make this tool much more usable. One challenge here is to extend the verification support to the expression language used by Yakindu, which is more expressive than those of SMINV. Secondly, we plan to extend SMINV and to include other language constructs, e.g. nested states and **else**-guards for transitions. This will result in a more user-friendly DSL to describe state machines. Finally, besides PRINCESS, other theorem provers supporting arithmetics and first-order logic should be integrated.

References

1. Aßmann, U., Bartho, A., Bürger, C., Cech, S., Demuth, B., Heidenreich, F., Johannes, J., Karol, S., Polowinski, J., Reimann, J., Schroeter, J., Seifert, M., Thiele, M., Wende, C., Wilke, C.: Dropsbox: the Dresden open software toolbox - domain-specific modelling tools beyond metamodels and transformations. Softw. Syst. Model. **13**(1), 133–169 (2014)
2. Yakindu: Homepage. http://statecharts.org/
3. Xtext: Homepage. http://www.eclipse.org/Xtext/
4. Harel, D.: Statecharts: a visual formalism for complex systems. Sci. Comput. Program. **8**(3), 231–274 (1987)
5. Baar, T.: SSMA - Simple State Machine Analyzer. https://github.com/thomas-baar/simplesma
6. Bettini, L.: Implementing Domain-Specific Languages with Xtext and Xtend. Packt Publishing, Birmingham (2013)

7. Ghezzi, C., Menghi, C., Sharifloo, A.M., Spoletini, P.: On requirement verification for evolving statecharts specifications. Requir. Eng. **19**(3), 231–255 (2014)

8. Prashanth, C.M., Shet, K.C.: Efficient algorithms for verification of UML statechart models. JSW **4**(3), 175–182 (2009)

9. Rümmer, P.: Princess homepage. http://www.philipp.ruemmer.org/princess.shtml

10. Rümmer, P.: A constraint sequent calculus for first-order logic with linear integer arithmetic. In: Cervesato, I., Veith, H., Voronkov, A. (eds.) LPAR 2008. LNCS (LNAI), vol. 5330, pp. 274–289. Springer, Heidelberg (2008)

11. Bettini, L.: Xsemantics Documentation (2015). http://xsemantics.sourceforge.net/documentation/

12. Wachsmuth, G., Konat, G.D.P., Visser, E.: Language design with the Spoofax language workbench. IEEE Softw. **31**(5), 35–43 (2014)

13. Vergu, V.A., Neron, P., Visser, E.: Dynsem: a DSL for dynamic semantics specification. In: Fernández, M., (ed.) 26th International Conference on Rewriting Techniques and Applications, RTA 29 to 1 July 2015, Warsaw, Poland, vol. 36 of LIPIcs, Schloss Dagstuhl - Leibniz-Zentrum fuer Informatik, pp. 365–378, June 2015

14. Object Management Group: Unified Modeling Language (UML), version 2.5, June 2015. http://www.omg.org/spec/UML/2.5/

Towards Using Exact Real Arithmetic
for Initial Value Problems

Franz Brauße[1], Margarita Korovina[2], and Norbert Th. Müller[1(✉)]

[1] Abteilung Informatikwissenschaften, Universität Trier, Trier, Germany
mueller@uni-trier.de
[2] A.P. Ershov Institute of Informatics Systems, Novosibirsk, Russia

Abstract. In the paper we report on recent developments of the iRRAM software [7] for exact real computations. We incorporate novel methods and tools to generate solutions of initial value problems for ODE systems with polynomial right hand sides (PIVP). The algorithm allows the evaluation of the solutions with an arbitrary precision on their complete open intervals of existence. In consequence, the set of operators implemented in the iRRAM software (like function composition, computation of limits, or evaluation of Taylor series) is expanded by PIVP solving.

Keywords: Computable analysis · Taylor models · Ordinary differential equations · Exact real arithmetic

1 Introduction

The field of 'exact real arithmetic' (ERA) aims to combine the elegance and correctness of mathematical theories for real numbers with optimized algorithms. The theoretical background for ERA is called 'computable analysis' or 'type-2-theory of effectivity' (TTE), see e.g. [13]. In TTE, a real number x is usually represented as a sequence $(r_n)_{n \in \mathbb{N}}$ of rational numbers r_n with a known rate of convergence. Computability on $\mathbb{R}$ is defined via Type-2 Turing machines. Usually the rate of convergence is expressed as a constraint '$\forall n : |x - r_n| \leq 2^{-n}$' (leading to the 'Cauchy representation' in [13, p. 88]). Formulated with notations from interval arithmetic, x is represented as a converging sequence $(I_n)_{n \in \mathbb{N}}$ of intervals.

ERA now uses similar concepts to implement real numbers on real-world computers. Pioneering in this direction was the iRRAM library [7] the initial version of which was presented already in 1996. Since then it has been continuously enhanced and improved. A big advantage of this package is a simple user

The research leading to these results has received funding from the People Programme (Marie Curie Actions) of the European Union's Seventh Framework Programme FP7/2007-2013/ under REA grant agreement n° PIRSES-GA-2011-294962-COMPUTAL and from the DFG/RFBR grant CAVER BE 1267/14-1 and 14-01-91334.

M. Mazzara and A. Voronkov (Eds.): PSI 2015, LNCS 9609, pp. 61–74, 2016.
DOI: 10.1007/978-3-319-41579-6_6

interface, as it uses internal book keeping of approximation accuracies and precisions. Therefore the user can concentrate on the mathematics behind algorithms.

Main aspects of this paper are enhancements for the iRRAM package originating from optimizing an implementation for the arbitrary precision evaluation of the solution to initial value problems (IVPs) presented in [3]. Many ODEs may be transformed into systems with polynomial right hand sides [10], therefore solving IVPs for this class is of great importance. For this purpose we constructed and implemented the new iRRAM-operator PIVPSOLVE: $\mathrm{Poly}^d \times \mathbb{R}^d \times \mathbb{R} \to C(\mathbb{R}^d)$. Applying PIVPSOLVE to the input values $\boldsymbol{f}$, $\boldsymbol{w}_0$ and t_0 (denoting an IVP) results in (a representation of) the solution $\boldsymbol{y}$. Evaluating $\boldsymbol{y}$ at some point t_{end} works in steps $(t_i, \boldsymbol{w}_i)$ such that $t_0 < \cdots < t_s \leq t_{\mathrm{end}} \leq t_{s+1}$. On every step i the Taylor series $\sum_{n \in \mathbb{N}} \boldsymbol{a}_n (t - t_i)^n$ of $\boldsymbol{y}$ around t_i is constructed and evaluated at t_{i+1} to get the initial value $\boldsymbol{w}_{i+1}$ for the next step.

It is worth noting that a key to evaluating power series is additional information about a pair $(R, M) \in \mathbb{R}^2$ with $|\boldsymbol{a}_n| \leq M \cdot R^{-n}$ [4]. This allows reliable bounds for the truncation error. Computing 'good' (R, M) is of great importance for computability and for efficiency. Larger R allow increased step sizes $t_{i+1} - t_i$ as well as reduced numbers of Taylor coefficients in each step.

A common problem of interval algorithms is that they suffer from wrapping effects, i.e. unnecessary growth of approximation intervals. Reducing such wrapping effects is an important issue in interval arithmetic [9, p. 15ff]. We discuss two methods to deal with this effect: (a) applying appropriate local Lipschitz bounds and (b) using Taylor Models [2] as primary data type.

The paper is organized as follows: In Sect. 2 we detail basic ideas of iRRAM and discuss how its tools can be applied to control error propagation. In Sect. 3 we present methods for computing the parameters (R, M) and local Lipschitz bounds. We then present the main algorithm in Sect. 4 and conclude with experimental results in Sect. 5 and future work.

We will use the following notations throughout the paper: $\mathbb{N}$, $\mathbb{Z}$, $\mathbb{R}$, $\mathbb{C}$ denote the natural, integer, real and complex numbers. The set of dyadic numbers is $\mathbb{D} := \{z \cdot 2^p : z, p \in \mathbb{Z}\}$, $\mathbb{U}$ is the closed interval $\mathbb{U} := [-1, 1]$. Vectors $\boldsymbol{w}$ of any kind are written in bold and $\|\boldsymbol{w}\|$ denotes the maximum norm $\|\boldsymbol{w}\|_\infty$. For closed real intervals $[a, b]$ we use the notation $c + e\mathbb{U}$, with $c = \frac{a+b}{2}$ as center and $e = \frac{b-a}{2}$ as radius of the interval. In the case of vectors $\boldsymbol{w}_0$ of complex numbers and for real $\mu \geq 0$ we will use $[\boldsymbol{w}_0 \pm \mu] := \{\boldsymbol{w} : \|\boldsymbol{w} - \boldsymbol{w}_0\| \leq \mu\}$.

2   Exact Real Arithmetic Using iRRAM

The iRRAM [7] is a software library implemented in C++. It is licensed under LGPL and is freely available at https://github.com/norbert-mueller/iRRAM. The central structure is a class **REAL**, whose objects behave like real numbers in TTE [13]. An important feature of the iRRAM is the ability to compute limits of certain user-defined sequences of real numbers.

The basic idea of the implementation is simple: Essentially, all operations on real numbers are being replaced by corresponding interval versions. The main difference to ordinary interval arithmetic is as follows: If errors grow too big, e.g. to compare two numbers x and y (i.e. the intervals corresponding to x and y overlap), the whole computation is repeated with a higher precision.

The iRRAM uses a simplified interval arithmetic based on the dyadic numbers $\mathbb{D}$. Intervals take the form $I := d + e\mathbb{U}$ for $d, e \in \mathbb{D}$. The center d is implemented as an arbitrarily long multiple-precision floating-point number using the MPFR library [14] while two 32-bit integers are used to represent the mantissa and the exponent of e. In consequence, computations with these intervals are only slightly more expensive than with isolated multiple-precision numbers.

Of course, long computations suffer from the usual wrappings in interval arithmetic. This may be addressed using additional knowledge about the computed numerical functions. To this end we discuss two methods recently implemented in the iRRAM: exploiting Lipschitz bounds [6,7] and Taylor models [2].

Lipschitz Bounds: The iRRAM library is based on intervals although this is hidden to the user. Suppose the user wants to compute a value $g(x)$ for a function $g : \mathbb{R} \to \mathbb{R}$ (we will only consider the one-dimensional case here). On the internal level x is given as an interval X with $x \in X$, also the computation of $g(x)$ is implemented using interval arithmetic. So instead of g an interval extension G of g will be used. As the exact value of x is unknown, G must have the property $g(X) \subseteq G(X)$. Quite often $G(X)$ is much larger than $g(X)$.

If we have access to a Lipschitz bound L valid for g on X, it is possible to reduce this overestimation. Suppose $X = c + e\mathbb{U}$ with center c and radius e. Instead of computing G on X we can compute G on the point interval $\{c\} = c + 0\mathbb{U}$, leading to some interval $c' + e'\mathbb{U} := G(\{c\})$. Of course, $c' + e'\mathbb{U}$ will be an overestimation of the point interval $\{g(c)\}$. Now using that L is a Lipschitz bound for g, we see $g(X) \subseteq c' + e'\mathbb{U} + L \cdot e\mathbb{U}$. So all we need is to add $L \cdot e$ to the radius e' of the interval $c' + e'\mathbb{U}$. If L is small and the overestimation in $c' + e'\mathbb{U}$ is not too bad, then $c' + e'\mathbb{U} + L \cdot e\mathbb{U}$ will be better than $G(X)$ as an approximation of $g(X)$.

If L were minimal, the resulting interval $c' + (e' + Le)\mathbb{U}$ would be nearly identical to $g(X)$, almost without any influence from wrapping. However, in practice it is very hard to find the minimal possible value for L.

Taylor Models: Taylor models (see papers by Kyoko Makino and Martin Berz, e.g. [2]) can be interpreted as a sophisticated version of the basic idea from the previous section. Instead of depending on an externally given Lipschitz bound L, the computation on the center c of the interval $c + e\mathbb{U}$ is performed in parallel to the computation of certain approximations connected to first (or even higher) derivatives on $c + e\mathbb{U}$ of the function under consideration.

Usually Taylor models are defined as sums $T + I$. Here $T(\boldsymbol{\lambda}) = \sum_{\mathbf{n} \neq 0} c_{\mathbf{n}} \boldsymbol{\lambda}^{\mathbf{n}}$ is a polynomial in a vector $\boldsymbol{\lambda} = (\lambda_1, \ldots, \lambda_k)$ of 'error symbols' and I is an interval enclosing any approximation errors (called *interval remainder* of the Taylor model). Most implementations restrict the coefficients $c_{\mathbf{n}}$ in T to be in double precision, but they could also be arbitrary real numbers. The error symbols λ_i denote unknown values within the interval $\mathbb{U}$ and allow to express functional dependencies between Taylor models that share those error symbols.

A very important manipulation on Taylor models is called *sweeping*: whenever appropriate, a monomial $c_n \lambda^n$ from T can be replaced by the interval $c_n \mathbb{U}$, thus enlarging the interval I. Every sweeping removes information about functional dependencies to some extent and thus adds some wrapping effect to the Taylor model, but it also helps to control the size of the Taylor model.

We use the following modification of Taylor models: Our Taylor models are polynomials $\sum c_n' \cdot \lambda^n$, where λ is the vector of error symbols and *each* coefficient c_n' is an interval. Sweeping can then be implemented by replacing an interval monomial $c_n' \cdot \lambda^n$ by an interval monomial $c_n' \cdot \lambda^k \cdot \mathbb{U}$ for arbitrary $k < n$.

The original Taylor model with a single interval remainder is included here, if sweeping always uses $k = 0$. However we propose to use $k \neq 0$ when sweeping to retain at least linear functional dependencies.

In the iRRAM, where each REAL is already stored as an interval, such Taylor models can be implemented quite easily based on vectors of REAL. The IVP solver described in this paper starts with an initial set of error symbols for w_0 at t_0 and heuristically selects time instances t_i to revise this set in order to recompress the representation of w_i and to improve the subsequent computations. For our purpose, restricting the degrees of monomials to ≤ 1 achieved the highest performance, i.e. we use Taylor models of order ≤ 1 but with interval coefficients in the form $T(\lambda) = c_0' + \sum c_i' \lambda_i$.

The Lipschitz approach considers a worst case scenario and the Lipschitz bound has to be provided externally, while a computation with Taylor models computes similar dependencies on the fly. However, the Lipschitz approach is independent from the length of a computation and from the precision used in the computation whereas the coefficients in the Taylor models might suffer from wrapping effects themselves. So at least for the purpose of proving the soundness and termination of algorithms, the Lipschitz approach is very useful.

3   Theoretical Background

A d-dimensional *polynomial* ODE system is defined by a vector of polynomials $f : \mathbb{R}^{d+1} \to \mathbb{R}^d$ and an initial value problem has the form

$$\dot{y}(t) = f(t, y(t)), \tag{3.1}$$
$$y(t_0) = w_0$$

for some $t_0 \in \mathbb{R}$ and $w_0 \in \mathbb{R}^d$. For simplicity, we assume that $t_0 = 0$.

The Picard-Lindelöf theorem guarantees the existence of a unique holomorphic solution y on some interval containing 0. In this region around zero y can be written in the form of d Taylor series $y_\nu(t) = \sum_{n \in \mathbb{N}} a_{\nu,n} t^n$ for $\nu = 1, \ldots, d$.

Solving the initial value problem can be divided into three components:

(a) the computation of the coefficients $a_{\nu,n}$ of these series (see [3]),
(b) the evaluation of the sum function $\sum_{n=0}^{\infty} a_{\nu,n} t^n$ (e.g. based on [4]) and
(c) the retrieval of a pair $(R, M) \in \mathbb{R}^2$ with $|a_{\nu,n}| \leq M \cdot R^{-n}$.

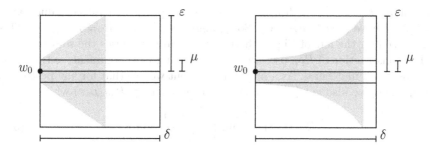

Fig. 1. Existence of solutions according to Picard-Lindelf (left) and improved (right).

The component (c) is necessary for (b) [5] and allows to use the simple formula $\sum_{n=k+1}^{\infty} |a_{\nu,n} t^n| \leq \frac{M \cdot R}{R - |t|} \cdot \frac{|t|^{k+1}}{R^{k+1}}$ for the truncation error for $|t| < R$.

In this section we mainly address two aspects: (i) we show how to derive (R, M) in the case of IVPs, i.e. component (c), and (ii) the dependency on perturbations of the initial value. Therefore we consider the family of solutions $\boldsymbol{y}(t, \boldsymbol{w})$ parameterized by initial values $\boldsymbol{w}$ from the complex interval $[\boldsymbol{w}_0 \pm \mu]$ for arbitrary positive $\mu \in \mathbb{R}$. This dependency can be characterized by a local Lipschitz bound L_μ with $\|\boldsymbol{y}(t, \boldsymbol{w}) - \boldsymbol{y}(t, \boldsymbol{w}_0)\| \leq L_\mu \|\boldsymbol{w} - \boldsymbol{w}_0\|$ for $t \in \mathbb{R}$, $|t| < R$. One of the options in our algorithm in Sect. 4 is to use this bound L_μ.

(i) Computing Truncation Error Parameters (R, M): Let us consider positive values δ (for time intervals) and $\mu \in \mathbb{R}$ (for perturbations of initial values). For any $\varepsilon \geq \mu$ let $C_\varepsilon = C_\varepsilon(\boldsymbol{w}_0, \delta)$ be the complex region

$$C_\varepsilon := \{(t, \boldsymbol{v}) \in \mathbb{C}^{d+1} : \|\boldsymbol{v} - \boldsymbol{w}_0\| \leq \varepsilon, |t| \leq \delta\}.$$

Figure 1 visualizes the usual relation of the values within C_ε.

Let $M := \|\boldsymbol{w}_0\| + \varepsilon$; for simplicity we will hide the dependancy of M on $\boldsymbol{w}_0$ and ε. Then M trivially is a bound for $\boldsymbol{y}(t, \boldsymbol{v})$ whenever $(t, \boldsymbol{y}(t, \boldsymbol{v})) \in C_\varepsilon$. To find a matching R we only need to ensure that $(t, \boldsymbol{y}(t, \boldsymbol{v})) \in C_\varepsilon$ for any $t \in \mathbb{C}$ with $|t| \leq R$. Then R is a lower bound for the radii of convergence of the series and $|a_{\nu,n}| \leq M \cdot R^{-n}$ follows from the Cauchy integral formula.

Since $\boldsymbol{f}$ is continuous on C_ε, there is a monotonic function $p(\varepsilon)$ bounding $\|\boldsymbol{f}(C_\varepsilon)\|$. On the one hand, since $\boldsymbol{f}$ is a vector of polynomials, it is easy to derive a polynomial p_1 that bounds $\|\boldsymbol{f}(C_\varepsilon)\|$ essentially by taking absolute values of the coefficients, as it has been done in [3,11]. On the other hand, using complex interval arithmetic to evaluate $p_2(\varepsilon) = \|\boldsymbol{f}(C_\varepsilon)\|$ often results in smaller values due to cancellation effects. A combination of both methods, i.e. $p(\varepsilon) = \min\{p_1(\varepsilon), p_2(\varepsilon)\}$, can be used. Please keep in mind that $p(\varepsilon)$ is still implicitly depending on the parameters δ and $\boldsymbol{w}_0$.

A first formula for R immediately follows from the theorems of Picard-Lindelöf and of Cauchy-Peano on the existence of solutions of ODEs, see [12],

$$R_{\mathrm{PL}}(\mu, \varepsilon) := \min\left\{\delta, \frac{\varepsilon - \mu}{p(\varepsilon)}\right\}. \tag{3.2}$$

Here for all $t \in \mathbb{C}$, $|t| \leq R_{\mathrm{PL}}(\mu, \varepsilon)$, and for all perturbed initial values $\boldsymbol{w} \in [\boldsymbol{w}_0 \pm \mu]$ we have $(t, \boldsymbol{y}(t, \boldsymbol{w})) \in C_\varepsilon$. So we might define R as $R := R_{\mathrm{PL}}(\mu, \varepsilon)$. This is visualized on the left of Fig. 1 where the grey area encloses the solution.

The construction of R_{PL} uses a very simple worst case argument, so the result is far too small in general. As a first improvement we use that for any perturbed $\boldsymbol{w} \in [\boldsymbol{w}_0 \pm \mu]$ we also get $(t, \boldsymbol{y}(t, \boldsymbol{w})) \in C_\varepsilon$ even for $|t| \leq R_{\mathrm{int}}(\mu, \varepsilon)$ where

$$R_{\mathrm{int}}(\mu, \varepsilon) := \min \left\{ \delta, \int_\mu^\varepsilon \frac{1}{p(s)} \, \mathrm{d}s \right\} \tag{3.3}$$

so $R := R_{\mathrm{int}}(\mu, \varepsilon)$ can be used as well. A visualization of this idea can be found on the right of Fig. 1, where the grey area enclosing the solution is now extended to a bigger part of the time axis.

We do not need the exact value of the integral in 3.3, lower bounds would suffice. So we may use approximations $R_{\mathrm{sum}}(\mu, \varepsilon)$ determined as a lower Riemann sum of this integral. This is much easier to evaluate and can be based on a suitable sequence $\varepsilon_0 := \mu$, $\varepsilon_i < \varepsilon_{i+1}$ and $\varepsilon_k := \varepsilon$ as follows

$$R_{\mathrm{sum}}(\mu, \varepsilon) := \sum_{i=0}^{k-1} \frac{\varepsilon_{i+1} - \varepsilon_i}{p(\varepsilon_{i+1})}. \tag{3.4}$$

All three choices for R above are based on a worst case analysis, so usually the actual solution will stay in C_ε even longer. To exploit this, we use that for any already known R and any $|t| < R$ the solution $\boldsymbol{y}(t)$ exists and can be computed. Now choose $r < R$ and let $m(r) := \max\{\|\boldsymbol{y}(t, \boldsymbol{w}) - \boldsymbol{w}_0\| : |t| \leq r\}$ be the maximal distance to the initial value $\boldsymbol{w}_0$ that actually arises up to r. By definition, for any $|t| \leq r$ the values $(t, \boldsymbol{y}(t))$ must stay within the region $C_{m(r)}$.

Choosing $m(r)$ as the perturbation μ in Eq. (3.3) we get $(t, \boldsymbol{y}(t)) \in C_\varepsilon$ even for $t \leq R' := \min\{\delta, r + R_{\mathrm{int}}(m(r), \varepsilon)\}$. So from the initial R we now get a new and larger lower bound R' for inclusion in C_ε. This enlargement $R \mapsto R'$ can be repeated as in Algorithm 1.

We would like to give some short remarks on the actual implementation: (i) The bound ε is heuristically adapted between steps. (ii) For $\int_\mu^\varepsilon 1/p(s) \, \mathrm{d}s$ a table of lower bounds is maintained. (iii) For $m(r)$ we evaluate the Taylor series with complex interval arithmetic on $[0 \pm r]$. This is possible as $r < R$ allows to compute a bound on the truncation error.

Algorithm 1. Pushing the Radius
---
function IMPROVERADIUS(R)
  repeat
    Choose r with $r < R$
    $R \leftarrow \min\{\delta, r + R_{\mathrm{int}}(m(r), \varepsilon)\}$
  until no significant improvement
  return R
end function

(ii) Obtaining Lipschitz Bounds on Solutions: Using any of the above formulae $R(\mu, \varepsilon)$ we are already able to compute bounds on the truncation error for the Taylor series of $\boldsymbol{y}(t, \boldsymbol{w})$ for any t with $|t| \leq R(\mu, \varepsilon)$ and any $\boldsymbol{w} \in [\boldsymbol{w}_0 \pm \mu]$. However, any interval implementation will additionally suffer from the wrapping effect mentioned before, so the precision of the result would also drastically

depend on the error propagation properties of the computation of the coefficients of the series. As mentioned in Sect. 2, we can use Lipschitz bounds or Taylor models to improve on the error propagation.

In the following we derive a Lipschitz bound $L_\mu^C(t)$ valid for $\boldsymbol{w} \in [\boldsymbol{w}_0 \pm \mu]$ from the behaviour of the solution in C_ε, so $\|\boldsymbol{y}(t, \boldsymbol{w}) - \boldsymbol{y}(t, \boldsymbol{w}_0)\| \le L_\mu^C(t) \cdot \|\boldsymbol{w} - \boldsymbol{w}_0\|$.

One way [11] to derive such a Lipschitz bound uses the generalized Gronwall's Lemma yielding $L_\mu^T(t) := e^{L|t|}$, where L is a Lipschitz bound valid on $\boldsymbol{w}$ in $\boldsymbol{f}(t', \boldsymbol{w})$ for all $t' \in [0, t]$, c.f. [12]. $L_\mu^T(t)$ is valid even for t beyond $R(\mu, \varepsilon)$.

We propose another way based on the Cauchy integral formula on polydiscs, $\forall \boldsymbol{w} \in U : D^{\boldsymbol{k}} y_\nu(t, \boldsymbol{w}) = \frac{k!}{(2\pi i)^I} \int_{\partial U} \frac{y_\nu(t, \boldsymbol{\xi})}{(\boldsymbol{\xi} - \boldsymbol{w})^{\boldsymbol{k}+1}} \, d\boldsymbol{\xi}$, where U is the open polydisc with common radius η centered at $\boldsymbol{w}_0$ for some value η. If for all $\boldsymbol{\xi} \in \partial U$ we have $(t, \boldsymbol{y}(t, \boldsymbol{\xi})) \in C_\varepsilon$, then the numerator $y_\nu(t, \boldsymbol{\xi})$ in the integrand is bounded by M. By definition of $R(\cdot, \varepsilon)$ we see that this is true if $|t| \le R(\eta, \varepsilon)$. In the following fix t, $0 < |t| < R(\mu, \varepsilon)$, and let η be as large as possible such that $|t| \le R(\eta, \varepsilon)$.

Therefore if $\eta > \sqrt{2} \cdot \mu$, then a lower bound for the denominator in the integrand is $(\eta - \sqrt{2} \cdot \mu)^{d+1}$. Hence for any $\boldsymbol{w} \in [\boldsymbol{w}_0 \pm \mu]$ we get

$$\|D^{\boldsymbol{e}_i} y_\nu(t, \boldsymbol{w})\| = \left\| \frac{1}{(2\pi i)^I} \int_{\partial U} \frac{y_\nu(t, \boldsymbol{\xi})}{(\boldsymbol{\xi} - \boldsymbol{w})^{\boldsymbol{e}_i+1}} \, d\boldsymbol{\xi} \right\| \le \frac{M \cdot \eta^d}{(\eta - \sqrt{2} \cdot \mu)^{d+1}} =: L_\mu^C(t) .$$

(3.5)

Please note that η depends on ε and on t. Furthermore, if η is large compared to μ, $L_\mu^C(t) \approx M/\eta$ will be quite small. In an interval implementation exploiting Lipschitz bounds, this already helps to reduce the wrapping effects significantly.

Obviously there is a tradeoff between (a) choosing t close to $R(\mu, \varepsilon)$ to get a large step size and (b) choosing t small to have good bounds on the truncation error as well as to get a small $L_\mu^C(t)$. In our implementation this is currently reflected by the restriction $t \le R_{\text{scale}} \cdot R_{\text{sum}}(\mu, \varepsilon)$ for a heuristically chosen value $R_{\text{scale}} \in (0, 1)$. The necessary η is computed using the lower Riemann sum (3.4).

4   PIVP Algorithm

We now describe our main Algorithm 2 to solve a PIVP system. Its basic structure is as follows: While trying to evaluate the power series with a truncation error bound below the intended precision, the needed Taylor coefficients of the solution are computed recursively. Dynamic programming is used to avoid reevaluations in this recursion. To that end four operators have been introduced to iRRAM. We now shortly describe the respective mappings. Let $k \in \mathbb{N}$.

- TAYLORCOEFFICIENTS: $\mathbb{R}^d \to (\mathbb{N} \to \mathbb{R}^d)$, $\boldsymbol{w}_0 \mapsto (\boldsymbol{a}_n)_n$ where $\boldsymbol{a}_n = (a_{\nu,n})_\nu$ using a recursion on the coefficients.
- POWERSERIES: $(\mathbb{N} \to \mathbb{R}^k) \times \mathbb{R}^2 \to (\mathbb{R} \to \mathbb{R}^k)$, $((\boldsymbol{a}_n)_{n \in \mathbb{N}}, R, M) \mapsto \boldsymbol{g}$ analytic with the expansion $\boldsymbol{g}(t) = \sum_{n \in \mathbb{N}} \boldsymbol{a}_n t^n$ centered in 0 iff $\forall n : \|\boldsymbol{a}_n\| \le MR^{-n}$.
- LIPSCHITZIFY: $(\mathbb{R} \to \mathbb{R}^k) \times \mathbb{R} \to (\mathbb{R} \to \mathbb{R}^k)$, $(\boldsymbol{g}, L) \mapsto \tilde{\boldsymbol{g}}$, where $\boldsymbol{g}$ is a computable function, $\tilde{\boldsymbol{g}} = \boldsymbol{g}$, but the interval extensions $\tilde{G}$ of $\tilde{\boldsymbol{g}}$ and G of $\boldsymbol{g}$ satisfy $\tilde{G}(c + e\mathbb{U}) = G(\{c\}) + eL\mathbb{U}$. For details see Sect. 2.

Algorithm 2. PIVP-Solver

function PIVPSOLVESINGLE($\boldsymbol{f}, \boldsymbol{w}_0, t_0, t_{\text{end}}, \delta, \varepsilon, R_{\text{scale}}$)

   $i \leftarrow 0, h_0 \leftarrow t_0$

   loop

      recenter $\boldsymbol{f}$ at h_i in case $\boldsymbol{f}$ is non-autonomous

      $(R_i, M_i, L_i, \varepsilon) \leftarrow$ TAYLORBOUNDS$\boldsymbol{w}_i, \boldsymbol{f}, \delta, \varepsilon, R_{\text{scale}}$ ▷ see Sect. 3

      $(a_n)_n \leftarrow$ TAYLORCOEFFICIENTS$\boldsymbol{w}_i$

      $\boldsymbol{y} \leftarrow$ POWERSERIES$(a_n)_n, R_i, M_i$ ▷ recentered solution via Taylor series

      $\boldsymbol{y} \leftarrow$ LIPSCHITZIFY$\boldsymbol{y}, L_i$ ▷ optional, see Sect. 2

      $h_{i+1} \leftarrow R_{\text{scale}} \cdot R_i$ ▷ step size

      if $t_{\text{end}} \in (t_i \pm h_{i+1})$ **then**   ▷ multi-valued test whether target is in range

         return $\boldsymbol{y}(t_{\text{end}} - t_i)$ ▷ evaluate solution at t_{end}, initiating recursion

      end if

      $t_{i+1} \leftarrow t_i + h_{i+1}$

      $\boldsymbol{w}_{i+1} \leftarrow \boldsymbol{y}(h_{i+1})$ ▷ evaluate solution at t_{i+1} to get new initial value

      reconsider Taylor model for $\boldsymbol{w}_{i+1}$ ▷ optional, see Sect. 2

      $i \leftarrow i + 1$

   end loop

end function

– PIVPSOLVE: Poly$^k \times \mathbb{R}^k \times \mathbb{R} \to (\mathbb{R} \to \mathbb{R}^k)$, $(\boldsymbol{f}, \boldsymbol{w}_0, t_0) \mapsto \boldsymbol{y}$ with the property $\dot{\boldsymbol{y}}(t) = \boldsymbol{f}(t, \boldsymbol{y}(t))$ for $[t_0, t] \subset \text{Dom}(\boldsymbol{y})$ and $\boldsymbol{y}(t_0) = \boldsymbol{w}_0$. It is implemented by calling PIVPSOLVESINGLE (see Algorithm 2) with appropriate choices for the control parameters $R_{\text{scale}} < 1$, δ and initial ε which strongly influence the step size and speed of the algorithm as detailed in Sect. 3.

Generation of Taylor Polynomial Coefficients and Evaluation: In the settings of iRRAM, we represent a vector $\boldsymbol{f}$ of polynomials $f_\nu : \mathbb{R}^{d+1} \to \mathbb{R}$, $\nu = 1, \ldots, d$, as d finite index sets $E_\nu \subset \mathbb{N}^{d+1}$ together with coefficients $c_{\nu,k,i} \in \mathbb{R}$ indexed by E_ν as follows:

$$f_\nu(t, \boldsymbol{w}) = \sum_{(k,i) \in E_\nu} c_{\nu,k,i} \cdot t^k \cdot \boldsymbol{w}^i$$

It is not necessary that all coefficients given in that way are non-zero, but by definition all coefficients not in this finite set are zero: $(k, \boldsymbol{i}) \notin E_\nu \implies c_{\nu,k,i} = 0$. A few examples for such index sets E_ν can be found below.

1. Consider the following linear and autonomous system $\boldsymbol{x}$ of dimension $d = 4$ and corresponding index sets E_ν, $\nu = 1, \ldots, 4$:

$$
\begin{aligned}
\dot{x}_1(t) &= x_2(t) & E_1 &= \{(0,0,1,0,0)\} \\
\dot{x}_2(t) &= x_3(t) & E_2 &= \{(0,0,0,1,0)\} \\
\dot{x}_3(t) &= x_4(t) & E_3 &= \{(0,0,0,0,1)\} \\
\dot{x}_4(t) &= x_1(t) & E_4 &= \{(0,1,0,0,0)\}.
\end{aligned}
$$

Here just 4 coefficients $c_{1,0,0,1,0,0} = c_{2,0,0,0,1,0} = c_{3,0,0,0,0,1} = c_{4,0,1,0,0,0} = 1$ are nonzero. For the initial value $\boldsymbol{w}_0 = (1, 0, -1, 0)$ at the time $t_0 = 0$, the solution of this system is $\boldsymbol{x} = (\cos, -\sin, -\cos, \sin)$.

2. Our second example is an autonomous Riccati equation:

$$\dot{x}(t) = 1 + x^2(t)$$

As index set for the nonzero coefficients we have

$$E = \{(0,0), (0,2)\}.$$

For initial value 0 at 0, the solution is $x(t) = \tan(t)$ exhibiting a singularity at $\pi/2$. In contrast to double precision algorithms, the approach proposed in this paper using exact real arithmetic is able to compute $x(t)$ beyond the limited range of double precision numbers, i.e. even for $t > \pi/2 - 10^{-17}$.

3. An example discussed many times in literature is the Van-der-Pol oscillator, which is a nonlinear and autonomous ODE:

$$\dot{x}(t) = y(t) \qquad\qquad\qquad E_1 = \{(0,0,1)\}$$
$$\dot{y}(t) = \alpha y(t) - x(t) - \alpha x^2(t) y(t) \qquad E_2 = \{(0,0,1), (0,1,0), (0,2,1)\}.$$

It is worth noting that there is no closed form solution for this ODE. We will consider this example again in Sect. 5.

In the following constructions we require $t_0 = 0$. There are two ways to meet this condition. One option is to alternatively solve the autonomous IVP

$$\dot{z}(t) = g(z(t)) = (1, f(z(t))), \qquad z(0) = (t_0, w_0)$$

that includes time as an additional component of the solution and then to project z on the d remaining components to get the desired solution y of (3.1).

Another approach is a recentering of the right hand side, i.e. to transform the right hand side f to $\bar{f}$ at each step in order to reposition the solution to 0 on the time axis. This involves formally expanding

$$\bar{f}_\nu(t, w) := f_\nu(t_0 + t, w) = \sum_{(k,i)\in E_\nu} c_{\nu,k,i} \cdot (t_0 + t)^k \cdot w^i \tag{4.1}$$

$$= \sum_{(j,i)\in \bar{E}_\nu} \underbrace{\left(\sum_{(k,i)\in E_\nu : k \geq j} c_{\nu,k,i} \binom{k}{j} t_0^{k-j} \right)}_{=: \bar{c}_{\nu,j,i}} \cdot t^j \cdot w^i,$$

thereby forming $\bar{E}_\nu := \{(j,i) : (k,i) \in E_\nu, 0 \leq j \leq k\}$, for all $\nu = 1, \ldots, d$. The new index sets $\bar{E}_\nu$ then contain all powers from 0 to k in the time variable, even if E_ν did not before. Therefore, from step 1 to step s, the size $|\bar{E}_\nu|$ of the discrete part of the representation of the RHS is bounded by $\max k \cdot |E_\nu|$ of the original RHS. After recentering, $\bar{y}(t) = y(t_0 + t)$ holds for $t_0 + t \in \text{Dom}(y)$. In the current version of the iRRAM library we chose to implement this second approach, however if the coefficients $\bar{c}_{\nu,k,i}$ grow too much, we can always take the first approach.

Therefore, without loss of generality we can assume $t_0 = 0$. Then, in a region around zero the solution $\boldsymbol{y}$ to (3.1) can be written as $y_\nu(t) = \sum_{n \in \mathbb{N}} a_{\nu,n} t^n$, $\nu = 1, \ldots, d$. To generate the coefficients $a_{\nu,n}$ we observe that $\dot{\boldsymbol{y}}$ can be written in two ways

$$\dot{y}_\nu(t) = \sum_{(k,i) \in E_\nu} c_{\nu,k,i} \cdot t^k \cdot (y_1(t))^{i_1} \cdot \ldots \cdot (y_d(t))^{i_d} = \sum_{n \in \mathbb{N}} (n+1) \cdot a_{\nu,n+1} \cdot t^n,$$

where the powers $(y_\nu(t))^i$ can be expressed as Taylor series $(y_\nu(t))^i = \sum_{n \in \mathbb{N}} a_{\nu,n}^{(i)} t^n$. Comparing coefficients leads to the following recursion scheme in $n, i \in \mathbb{N}$, $i \geq 2$.

$$a_{\nu,0}^{(0)} = 1, \tag{R1}$$

$$a_{\nu,n+1}^{(0)} = 0, \tag{R2}$$

$$a_{\nu,0}^{(1)} = w_{0,\nu}, \tag{R3}$$

$$a_{\nu,n+1}^{(1)} = \frac{1}{n+1} \sum_{(k,i) \in E_\nu} c_{\nu,k,i} \cdot \sum_{(j_l) \in \mathbb{N}^d : \sum j_l = n-k} a_{1,j_1}^{(i_1)} \cdot \ldots \cdot a_{d,j_d}^{(i_d)}, \tag{R4}$$

$$a_{\nu,n}^{(i)} = \sum_{j=0}^{n} a_{\nu,j}^{(\lceil i/2 \rceil)} \cdot a_{\nu,n-j}^{(\lfloor i/2 \rfloor)}. \tag{R5}$$

For details we refer to [3]. Now we discuss important optimizations of the implementation, especially of (R4). In examples above, the coefficient vectors are quite sparse with many zero values (that we already did exclude from the lists above).

From the recursion scheme we get $a_{\ell,j_\ell}^{(i_\ell)} = 0$ in case of $i_\ell = 0$ and $j_\ell > 0$. So often we do not have to consider all combinations that are suggested by the formula (R4), but we can omit combinations where $j_\ell > 0$ for a $i_\ell = 0$.

We then get the simpler version of (R4).

$$a_{\nu,n+1} = \frac{1}{n+1} \sum_{(k,i) \in E_\nu} c_{\nu,k,i} \cdot \sum_{\substack{j \in \mathbb{N}^d : j_1 + \ldots + j_d = n-k \, \wedge \\ (\forall 1 \leq \ell \leq d : j_\ell > 0 \implies i_\ell > 0)}} \left[a_{1,j_1}^{(i_1)} \cdot \ldots \cdot a_{d,j_d}^{(i_d)} \right] \tag{4.2}$$

This is equivalent to a sum just over combinations on reduced vectors of indices.

From the recursion scheme we further know $a_{\ell,j_\ell}^{(i_\ell)} = 1$ for $i_\ell = 0$ and $j_\ell = 0$. So, we only have to multiply those values $a_{\ell,j_\ell}^{(i_\ell)}$ where $i_\ell > 0$. For simplicity, in the following we fix a $\nu \in \{1, \ldots, d\}$, $n \in \mathbb{N}$ and $(k, \boldsymbol{i}) \in E_\nu$. Let $[\boldsymbol{i}] = \{\ell : i_\ell \neq 0, \ell = 1, \ldots, d\}$ denote the set of indices of non-zero components of $\boldsymbol{i} \in \mathbb{N}^d$ and let $[\boldsymbol{i}]_\ell$ be the ℓ-th smallest element in $[\boldsymbol{i}]$.

The inner sum over $\boldsymbol{j} \in \mathbb{N}^d$ in (4.2) can then be rewritten as

$$\sum_{\substack{(j_\ell)_{\ell \in [i]} \\ \sum j_\ell = n-k}} \prod_{\ell \in [i]} a_{\ell,j_\ell}^{(i_\ell)} \tag{4.3}$$

or equivalently – reducing the number of multiplications in a form similar to Horner's scheme

$$\sum_{\substack{j_1 \in \mathbb{N} \\ j_1 \leq n-k}} a_{[i]_1, j_1}^{(i_{[i]_1})} \cdot \sum_{\substack{j_2 \in \mathbb{N} \\ j_1 + j_2 \leq n-k}} a_{[i]_2, j_2}^{(i_{[i]_2})} \cdot \ldots \cdot \sum_{\substack{j_r \in \mathbb{N} \\ j_1 + \ldots + j_r = n-k}} a_{[i]_r, j_r}^{(i_{[i]_r})},$$

where $r = ||[i]||$. Please note that the innermost sum (including j_r) consists of just a single value. This formula is easy to implement as a recursion over $0 < r \in \mathbb{N}$,

$$A_i(n, 0) = \delta_{0,n}, \text{ where } \delta_{i,j} \text{ is the Kronecker symbol,}$$

$$A_i(n, r) = \sum_{l=0}^{n} a_{[i]_r, l}^{(i_{[i]_r})} \cdot A_i(l, r-1),$$

finally reducing (4.2) to

$$a_{\nu, n+1} = \frac{1}{n+1} \sum_{(k,i) \in E_\nu} c_{\nu,k,i} \cdot A_i(n-k, ||[i]||). \tag{R4$'$}$$

Formula (4.3) clearly indicates that the number of terms that have to be evaluated is usually much smaller than the number of all terms in the inner sum $\sum_{\substack{j_1, j_2, \ldots, j_d \in \mathbb{N} \\ j_1 + \ldots + j_d = n-k}} [\ldots]$ of the formula (R4) which is $\frac{(d+n-k-1)!}{(d-1)!(n-k)!} = \binom{d+n-k-1}{d-1}$.

Obviously the number of parameter components $||[i]||$ in the monomials of f_ν have more influence on the complexity than the dimension d of the ODE system. In our three examples, we had (1.) $||[i]|| = 1$, (2.) $||[i]|| \leq 1$ and (3.) $||[i]|| \leq 2$.

The evaluation of Taylor series and control of truncation errors are based on [4] and the refinements of Sect. 3.

Soundness: A big advantage of ERA is that soundness proofs are significantly easier than with ordinary double precision arithmetic. For any function f offered by an ERA implementation the following consistency property must hold, similar to interval arithmetic: the result of applying f to an argument x is consistent with the mathematically correct result $f(x)$. The argument x is represented internally as a sequence (I_n) of intervals converging to x, hence the result of applying f to x will internally be a sequence (J_n) of intervals all containing $f(x)$. In addition to this consistency of interval arithmetic, however, TTE promises that the resulting sequence (J_n) actually converges to $f(x)$. ERA implementations will never violate the consistency property and will deliver convergent results as far as time and the finite resources of real computers allow.

Our algorithm above just consists of applications of such basic functions: For the computation of the Taylor coefficients we only need basic arithmetic, implying that any such coefficent will eventually be computed arbitrarily precise. Also the computations of the pairs (R, M) only need basic functions. In addition, even evaluating the sum function of a Taylor sequence is a basic function in ERA [3,4]. We only had to make sure that the used pairs (R, M) fit to the Taylor sequences as mentioned at the beginning of Sect. 3.

In consequence it only remains to show termination in order to ensure soundness. Here termination means that the number of necessary 'exact' mathematical operations has to be finite. This boils down to proving that the number s of steps $(t_i, \boldsymbol{w}_i)$ necessary to reach a time instance t_{end} is finite.

The central argument here is that the number s of steps computed by the algorithm essentially depends on the size of the radii chosen per step, which are comparable to Picard-Lindelöf's, as detailed below. Therefore the number s of steps is finite.

More formally, for any closed and bounded interval $I = [t_0, t_{\text{end}}] \subset \text{Dom}(\boldsymbol{y})$ the set $\{(t, \boldsymbol{y}(t)) : t \in I\}$ is closed and bounded. With a standard compactness argument we conclude that there is a finite covering of I by intervals $(t_i \pm R_i)_i$ such that $t_{i+1} \in (t_i \pm R_i)$ for all i, where the R_i depend on t_i as follows. The vectors (t_i, μ_i, R_i, L_i) of time instances t_i, allowed perturbances μ_i of $\boldsymbol{w}_i$, corresponding radii R_i and Lipschitz bounds L_i are computed in every step i by Algorithm 2. From Sect. 3 we know that $R_i = R_{\text{sum}}(\mu_i, \varepsilon)$ in (3.4) is a lower bound on the radius of convergence of the Taylor series centered at t_i. To ensure that R_i is generally at least as large as the corresponding lower bound R_{PL} on the radius from the standard proof of the Picard-Lindelöf theorem, please note that in the construction e.g. $\varepsilon \geq k\mu$ and an equally-spaced partitioning $(\varepsilon_j)_{j=0}^k$ with $k \geq 2$ could be used. These radii are strictly positive on the complete compact interval I. As the step size h_i is chosen to be linear in R_i, the computed $(t_i \pm h_{i+1})_i$ cover I finitely. This shows that for any t_{end} within the interval of existence of the solution a finite number of steps is sufficient to compute the solution on the interval $[t_0, t_{\text{end}}]$. Please note that the above arguments are independent from any considerations on the precision.

The correctness of the presented method already follows from the construction in the previous sections without even using the Lipschitz approach or the Taylor models. However using the Lipschitz approach we can also get information on the speed of convergence. So for the rest of the section assume that we employ the (optional) LIPSCHITZIFY-operator in the algorithm.

Let L_i bound the dependency of solutions $\boldsymbol{y}(h_{i+1}, \boldsymbol{w})$ ($\boldsymbol{y}$ recentered at t_i) on perturbed initial values $\boldsymbol{w} \in [\boldsymbol{w}_i \pm \mu_i]$, i.e. $\|\boldsymbol{y}(h_{i+1}, [\boldsymbol{w}_i \pm \mu_i])\| \leq L_i \cdot \mu_i$. As has been detailed in Sect. 3, the computed $L_i = L_{\mu_i}^C$ even satisfies $\forall t \in [0, h_{i+1}]$: $\|\boldsymbol{y}(t, [\boldsymbol{w}_i \pm \mu_i])\| \leq L_i \cdot \mu_i$ and can therefore be applied to bound the error of $\boldsymbol{w}_{i+1}$.

So if we assume an initial condition $\boldsymbol{w}_0$ perturbed by at most μ, after an arbitrary number k of steps the sub-algorithm for the L_i ensures that $\mu L(0, k)$ with $L(i, k) := \prod_{j=i}^{k-1} L_j$ bounds the perturbation error on $\boldsymbol{w}_k$. This means to evaluate $\boldsymbol{w}_k$ with precision 2^{-n} at t_k, it is sufficient to compute each intermediate $\boldsymbol{w}_i$ up to a precision of $2^{-n - \lceil \log(\mu L(i,k)) \rceil}$. During the complete iteration process we lose only a constant number of bits that is independent on the required precision, if we apply the Lipschitz approach!

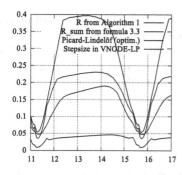

method	t_{end}	steps	time [s]	initial precision	final precision	bits / t_{end}
Lipschitz	10	139	131	2^{-601}	2^{-100}	51.1
	20	285	655	2^{-1151}	2^{-94}	52.8
Taylor model, org. sweep	10	139	30	2^{-207}	2^{-159}	4.8
	20	285	58	2^{-207}	2^{-115}	4.6
	50	711	277	2^{-207}	2^{-91}	2.3
Taylor model, our sweep	10	139	37	2^{-207}	2^{-190}	1.7
	20	285	71	2^{-207}	2^{-179}	1.4
	50	711	180	2^{-207}	2^{-174}	0.62
	100	1440	344	2^{-207}	2^{-156}	0.51

Fig. 2. Experimental results for Van-der-Pol with $\alpha = 3$, $w_0 = (1, 1)$.

5   Experimental Results

In this section we present some results of running our algorithm on the Van-der-Pol ODE with $\alpha = 3$ and initial value $(1, 1)$ at $t_0 = 0$. We compared the results from the three different methods for approximating the radius of convergence from Sect. 3 (R_{PL}, R_{sum}, Algorithm 1 on R_{sum}) as well as the effects from three different approaches to reduce wrapping effects (Lipschitz bound in Eq. (3.5), the original method of sweeping into c'_0, and the new method of sweeping into higher order monomials proposed in Sect. 2).

We compared our results with Nedialkov's package VNODE-LP [8], where we only had to change MU to α in his example vanderpol.cc. Computation times were significantly different, but the numbers of steps in both implementations were similar. The example vanderpol.cc used only 0.2 s to integrate this ODE up to $t_{end} = 100$, while our fastest version took about 344s on the same machine. A big part of the difference is due to the fact that VNODE-LP uses double precision hardware while the iRRAM uses a software multiple precision package instead.

The left part in Fig. 2 depicts the different lower bounds for the radii of convergence computed during a run of Algorithm 2 while $t_i \in [11, 17]$. The solution of the ODE is essentially periodic, the time interval $[11, 17]$ contains slightly more than a full circle of the solution. Additionally the corresponding stepsizes computed by vanderpol.cc from VNODE-LP are given. This shows that our approach gives competitive bounds for the radii of convergence.

The right part of Fig. 2 compares the three different methods to reduce wrapping effects. As expected, using a worst case analysis to compute Lipschitz bounds could not compete with Taylor models at all. However, our modified version of the Taylor models was superior compared to the version usually used.

6   Conclusion

Our implementation reliably computes results to arbitrary precision without the necessity for subsequent verification runs as in traditional numerical algorithms. Applying Taylor Models in the setting of ERA, using local Lipschitz bounds and improving validated upper bounds on intermediate step sizes substantially increase the efficiency of the solver as experimental results showed.

Further work is necessary to check whether this approach can also lead to refinements of the theoretical results from [1,11] on complexity of solving ODEs. We also plan to work on improvements of the core ODE solver to make it more competitive to double precision approaches.

References

1. Kawamura, A., Ota, H., Rösnick, C., Ziegler, M.: Computational complexity of smooth differential equations. Log. Meth. Comput. Sci. **10**(1), 1–15 (2014)
2. Makino, K., Berz, M.: Taylor models and other validated functional inclusion methods. Int. J. Pure Appl. Math. **4**(4), 379–456 (2003)
3. Müller, N., Korovina, M.: Making Big Steps in Trajectories. In: EPTCS (2010)
4. Müller, N.T.: Polynomial time computation of Taylor series. In: Proceedings of the 22th JAIIO - Panel 1993, Part 2, pp. 259–281, Buenos Aires (1993)
5. Müller, N.T.: Constructive aspects of analytic functions. In: Ko, K.I., Weihrauch, K. (eds.) Computability and Complexity in Analysis. Informatik Berichte, vol. 190, pp. 105–114. FernUniversität Hagen (September 1995), CCA Workshop, Hagen, 19–20 August 1995
6. Müller, N.T.: Towards a real real RAM: a prototype using C++. In: Ko, K.I., Mller, N., Weihrauch, K. (eds.) Computability and Complexity in Analysis, pp. 59–66. Universität Trier, Second CCA Workshop, Trier, 22–23 August 1996
7. Müller, N.T.: The iRRAM: exact arithmetic in C++. In: Blank, J., Brattka, V., Hertling, P. (eds.) CCA 2000. LNCS, vol. 2064, p. 222. Springer, Heidelberg (2001)
8. Nedialkov, N.S.: VNODE-LP — a validated solver for initial value problems inordinary differential equations. Technical report, CAS-06-06-NN, Department of Computingand Software, McMaster University, Hamilton, Ontario, L8S 4K1 (2006)
9. Nedialkov, N.S., Jackson, K.R., Corliss, G.F.: Validated solutions of initial value problems for ordinary differential equations. Appl. Math. Comput. **105**(1), 21–68 (1999)
10. Parker, G.E., Sochacki, J.S.: Implementing the Picard iteration. neural, parallel. Sci. Comput. **4**(1), 97–112 (1996)
11. Pouly, A., Graça, D.S.: Computational complexity of solving elementary differential equations over unbounded domains. CoRR abs/1409.0451 (2014)
12. Teschl, G.: Ordinary Differential Equations and Dynamical Systems. Graduate Studies in Mathematics. American Mathematical Society, Providence (2012)
13. Weihrauch, K.: Computable Analysis: An Introduction. Springer-Verlag New York, Inc., Secaucus (2000)
14. Zimmermann, P.: Reliable computing with GNU MPFR. In: Fukuda, K., Hoeven, J., Joswig, M., Takayama, N. (eds.) ICMS 2010. LNCS, vol. 6327, pp. 42–45. Springer, Heidelberg (2010)

Constraint Solving for Verifying Modal Specifications of Workflow Nets with Data

Hadrien Bride[1,2](✉), Olga Kouchnarenko[1,2], and Fabien Peureux[1]

[1] Institut FEMTO-ST – UMR CNRS 6174,
University of Bourgogne Franche-Comté, 16, route de Gray,
25030 Besançon, France
{hbride,okouchna,fpeureux}@femto-st.fr
[2] Inria Nancy Grand Est, CASSIS Project Campus Scientifique,
BP 239, 54506 Vandœuvre-lès-nancy Cedex, France
{hadrien.bride,olga.kouchnarenko}@inria.fr

Abstract. For improving efficiency and productivity companies are used to work with workflows that allow them to manage the tasks and steps of business processes. Furthermore, modalities have been designed to allow loose specifications by indicating whether activities are necessary or admissible. This paper aims at verifying modal specifications of coloured workflows with data assigned to the tokens and modified by transitions. To this end, executions of coloured workflow nets are modelled using constraint systems, and constraint solving is used to verify modal specifications specifying necessary or admissible behaviours. An implementation supporting the proposed approach and promising experimental results on an issue tracking system constitute a practical contribution.

Keywords: Workflows · Modalities · Coloured Petri nets · Constraint system

1 Introduction

To improve efficiency and productivity companies are used to work with workflows describing the set of possible runs of a particular system/process. The development of such workflows has become a crucial part of companies effort since they define the organisational core of these companies by increasing their business agility, flexibility and efficiency. Major Key Performance Indicators (compliance with respect to regulations and directives, end-user acceptance and confidence, etc.) are often directly determined by the quality of the workflows in use, and therefore much of the companies successes depends on them. From this, it requires workflow specifications to be properly designed and carefully verified to ensure they comply with the expected and needed workflows properties. However, the increasing complexity of such workflows makes them error-prone and the verification of the related models still remains a tough task [1].

© Springer International Publishing Switzerland 2016
M. Mazzara and A. Voronkov (Eds.): PSI 2015, LNCS 9609, pp. 75–90, 2016.
DOI: 10.1007/978-3-319-41579-6_7

Many modelling languages and related tooling to describe workflow systems have been proposed [2]. Among them, workflow Petri nets (WF-nets for short) [3] are well suited for modelling and analysing discrete event systems exhibiting behaviours such as concurrency, conflict, and causal dependency between events. They represent finite or infinite-state processes, and several important verification problems, such as reachability or soundness, are known to be decidable. However, due to the growing complexity of modeled processes, WF-nets describing them tend to be too complex and extremely large [4]. Moreover, WF-nets do not model the data often relevant to address realistic processes [5]. To handle data, workflows can be modelled by coloured Petri nets where data are assigned to the tokens and can be modified by transitions based on their contents [6].

Within refinement approaches for workflow development, modal specifications [7] have been designed to allow *loose* specifications by imposing restrictions on the possible refinements by indicating whether activities–transitions in the case of WF-nets–are *necessary* or *admissible*. Modalities provide a flexible tool for workflow development as decisions can be delayed to later steps of the development life cycle, when performing workflow refinements.

The paper first presents modal specifications with additional constraints on the initial state of the workflow as well as with conditions on coloured transitions and their causalities, i.e. on activities. Second, it defines a formal framework based on constraint systems to model executions of CWF-nets, which, in turn, enables the automated verification of modal specifications. Third, it reports on an implementation of the approach, which is successfully experimented on a concrete case study to validate an issue tracking system.

After providing preliminaries on Petri nets, coloured Petri nets and modal specifications in Sect. 2 and Sect. 3 introduces the *Questions and Answers Portal* motivating example and specifies it as a CWF-net. The main contribution in Sect. 4 consists of a formal framework based on constraint systems to model executions of CWF-nets and their structural properties, as well as to verify their modal specifications. An implementation supporting the proposed approach and promising experimental results constitute a practical contribution in Sect. 5. Finally, Sect. 6 concludes the paper by discussing related work and future work.

2   Background

This section presents preliminaries on Petri nets, coloured Petri nets [8] and introduces modal specifications based on proposals in [9,10].

2.1   Petri Nets

Petri nets are a basic model of parallel and distributed systems defined as follow.

Definition 1 (Petri net). *A Petri net is a tuple (P, T, F) where P is a finite set of places, T is a finite set of transitions ($P \cap T = \emptyset$), and $F \subseteq (P \times T) \cup (T \times P)$ is a set of arcs.*

A Petri net with arcs of weight 1 (i.e. every element of F is unique) is called an *ordinary* Petri net. Let $g \in P \cup T$ and $G \subseteq P \cup T$. We use the notations: $g^\bullet = \{g' | (g, g') \in F\}$, $^\bullet g = \{g' | (g', g) \in F\}$, $G^\bullet = \cup_{g \in G} g^\bullet$, and $^\bullet G = \cup_{g \in G} {}^\bullet g$. These definitions allow characterizing structural features such as siphons and traps.

Definition 2 (Siphon/Trap). *Let $N \subseteq P$ such that $N \neq \emptyset$: N is a trap if and only if $N^\bullet \subseteq {}^\bullet N$, and N is a siphon if and only if $^\bullet N \subseteq N^\bullet$.*

Lemma 1 [11]. *A marked trap cannot be unmarked, and an unmarked siphon cannot be marked.*

Theorem 1 [11]. *An ordinary Petri net without siphon is live.*

Coloured Petri nets [8] are high-level Petri nets where data assigned to the tokens can be modified by transitions based on their contents. Let Ξ be a non-empty set of *data-types* (called colours), where each *data-type* is a set of *data-values*. We denote here $\mathcal{L}(\mathcal{V}, \mathcal{W})$ the space of linear maps from $\mathcal{V}$ to $\mathcal{W}$, and $\mathcal{O}$ the zero map.

Definition 3 (Coloured Petri net). *A coloured Petri net (CPN) is a tuple (P, T, C, W) where:*

- *P is a finite set of places, T is a finite set of transitions, such that $P \cap T = \emptyset$,*
- *$C : P \cup T \rightarrow \Xi$ is the colour-function,*
- *$W^- : P \times T \rightarrow \mathcal{L}(\Xi, \Xi)$ is the pre-incidence function,*
- *$W^+ : P \times T \rightarrow \mathcal{L}(\Xi, \Xi)$ is the post-incidence function.*

A *marking* of a CPN is a function M defined on P, such that $\forall p \in P, M(p) \in C(p) \rightarrow \mathbb{N}$. Two markings M_a and M_b are in relation $M_a \geq M_b$ if and only if $\forall p \in P, \forall c \in C(p), M_a(p)(c) \geq M_b(p)(c)$.

A *weighted set of transitions* is a function x defined on T, such that $\forall t \in T, x(t) \in C(t) \rightarrow \mathbb{N}$. From now on, let $\circledast$ denote the generalized matrix-multiplication where each product is replaced by a function composition. With this notation, a transition defined by $x(t) \in C(t) \rightarrow \mathbb{N}$ is *enabled* in a marking M_a if and only if $M_a \geq W^-(t) \circledast x(t)$. When $x(t)$ is *enabled*, it may *fire*. If $x(t)$ *fires*, a new marking $M_b = M_a + (W^+ - W^-)(t) \circledast x(t)$ is reached. M_b is said to be *directly reachable* from M_a by transition $x(t)$, written $M_a \xrightarrow{x(t)} M_b$. Let *reachability* relation be the reflexive and transitive closure of the *direct reachability*.

Let $\sigma = x_1(t_1), .., x_n(t_n)$ be a sequence of transitions, i.e. $\forall i \in 1..n, x_i(t_i) \in C(t_i) \rightarrow \mathbb{N}$, we say that σ is a valid sequence of transitions with respect to the weighted set of transitions x, denoted $\sigma \models x$, if $\forall t \in T, x(t) = \sum_{i | t_i = t} x_i(t_i)$.

For example, let $\Xi = \{C_1, C_2\}$ where $C_1 = \{1, 2, 3, 4, 5, 6\}$ and $C_2 = \{1, 2, 3\}$. For the CPN_1 of Fig. 1, let $C(P_0) = C_1$ and $C(t_0) = C_2$. Let be $x \in C_2$ and $t_0(x)$ a transition such that $\forall e \in C_2 \setminus \{x\}, t_0(x)(e) = 0$ and $t_0(x)(x) = 1$. When transition $t_0(x)$ fires, it consumes a token x and produces

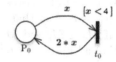

Fig. 1. Example of a CPN

a token $x * 2$ in P_0. Let $M_{CPN_1}(x)$ be the marking such that $\forall e \in C_1 \setminus \{x\}$, $M_{CPN_1}(x)(P_0)(e) = 0$ and $M_{CPN_1}(x)(P_0)(x) = 1$. For $\sigma = t_0(1), t_0(2)$, we have $M_{CPN_1}(1) \xrightarrow{t_0(1)} M_{CPN_1}(2) \xrightarrow{t_0(2)} M_{CPN_1}(4)$. Let wt be the weighted set of transitions such that $wt(t_0)(1) = wt(t_0)(2) = 1$ and $wt(t_0)(3) = 0$, we have $\sigma \models wt$.

2.2   Coloured Workflow Nets

From the framework of coloured Petri nets, we now define coloured workflow nets (CWF-nets for short).

Definition 4 (CWF-net). *A coloured Petri net (P, T, C, W) is a CWF-net if and only if: PN have two special places i and o where $^\bullet i = \emptyset$ and $o^\bullet = \emptyset$, and for each node $n \in (P \cup T)$ there exists a path from i to o passing through n.*

In the rest of the paper, the following notations are used:

- M_i: the set of initial markings of a CWF-net where $\forall M_a \in M_i, M_a(i) \neq \mathcal{O}$ and $\forall p \in P \setminus i, M_a(p) = \mathcal{O}$,
- M_o: the set of final markings of a CWF-net where $\forall M_a \in M_o, M_a(o) \neq \mathcal{O}$ and $\forall p \in P \setminus o, M_a(p) = \mathcal{O}$,
- $M_1 \xrightarrow{\sigma} M_n$: for $\sigma = x_1, x_2, ..., x_{n-1}$, there are markings such that $M_1 \xrightarrow{x_1} M_2 \xrightarrow{x_2} ... \xrightarrow{x_{n-1}} M_n$,
- $M_a \xrightarrow{*} M_b$: there exists σ such that $M_a \xrightarrow{\sigma} M_b$.

In our approach, constraints over markings and weighted sets of transitions are expressed using Presburger arithmetic [12] in order to remain within the realm of decidability. Let $M_a(p)$ be the marking of a place p, and f_p a first-order formula over Presburger arithmetic with free variables over $C(p)$. We denote by $M_a(p) \models f_p$ the fact that $M_a(p)$ satisfies f_p, i.e. $(\bigwedge_{d \in C(p)} d = M_a(p)(d)) \wedge f_p$ is satisfiable. Similarly, let $x_a(t)$ be the weighted set of transitions t, and f_t a first-order formula over Presburger arithmetic formulae with free variables over $C(t)$. We write $x_a(t) \models f_t$ when $x_a(t)$ satisfies f_t, i.e. $(\bigwedge_{d \in C(t)} d = x_a(t)(d)) \wedge f_t$ is satisfiable.

To illustrate this notation on CPN_1 of Fig. 1, let $f_{P_0} = (C_1(1) = 1)$ be a formula over Presburger arithmetic with free variables over $C(P_0)$. We have $M_{CPN_1}(1) \models f_{P_0}$, which expresses the fact that the marking $M_{CPN_1}(1)$ contains exactly 1 token of value 1. Likewise, let $f_{t_0} = (C_2(2) = 1)$ be a formula with free variables over $C(t_0)$, and wt the weighted set of transitions such that $t_0(2) \models wt$. We have $wt \models f_{t_0}$ expressing the fact that wt is valid with respect to a sequence of transitions containing a transition $x(t_0)$ where $x(t_0)(2) = 1$.

An execution between markings M_a and M_b of a CWF-net is a sequence of transitions σ such that $M_a \xrightarrow{\sigma} M_b$. An execution is a *correct* execution if and only if $M_a \in M_i$ and $M_b \in M_o$. The behaviour of a CWF-net is defined as the set Σ of all its *correct* executions.

2.3   CWF-nets with Modalities

Modal specifications permit specifiers to indicate that a transition is *necessary* or just *admissible*. In the context of CWF-nets, it usually means that there are two kinds of transitions: the *must*-transitions and the *may*-transitions. A *may*-transition (resp. *must*-transition) is a transition fired by at least one *correct* execution (resp. by all the *correct* executions) of a CWF-net.

We extend this concept to allow specifiers to indicate modal properties on several transitions and on their causalities. We also add the possibility to parameterize transitions as well as the initial marking, to permit a precise modal specification of desired behavior.

Definition 5 (Well-formed modal formula). *Let $CPN = (P,T,C,W)$ be a CWF-net. The language S of well-formed modal specification formulae is defined by the following grammar of axiom A, where $t \in T$ and p (resp. q) is a first-order formula over Presburger arithmetic formulae [12] with free variables over $C(t)$ (resp. $C(i)$):* $A \rightarrow [q]B$, $B \rightarrow (B \wedge B)|(B \vee B)|(\neg B)|t[p]$.

These formulae allow specifiers to express modal properties about CWF-nets' correct executions. Any modal specification formula $[q]m \in S$ can be interpreted as a *may*-formula or a *must*-formula. Given a CWF-net, a *may*-formula (resp. a *must*-formula) describes a behaviour constrained by m that has to be ensured by at least one (resp. all) correct execution of initial state satisfying q. Formally, the semantics of a formula m generated from B, where the semantics of $\neg, \vee$ and $\wedge$ is standard, is defined by:

- $wt \models_{may} t[p]$ iff $\exists \sigma = x_1, x_2, ..., x_{n-1} \in \Sigma. \ \sigma \models wt \wedge \exists k. \ x_k(t) \models p$,
- $wt \models_{must} t[p]$ iff $\forall \sigma = x_1, x_2, ..., x_{n-1} \in \Sigma. \ \sigma \models wt \wedge \exists k. \ x_k(t) \models p$.

Furthermore, given a *may*-formula (resp. *must*-formula) $[q]m \in S$, its semantics is inductively defined by:

- $CPN \models_{may} q[m]$ iff $\exists \sigma \in \Sigma, M_a \in M_i, M_b \in M_o. \ M_a \xrightarrow{\sigma} M_b \wedge M_a(i) \models q \wedge \sigma \models wt \wedge wt \models_{may} m$,
- $CPN \models_{must} q[m]$ iff $\forall \sigma \in \Sigma, M_a \in M_i.M_a(i) \models q.(\exists M_b \in M_o. \ M_a \xrightarrow{\sigma} M_b \Rightarrow (\sigma \models wt \wedge wt \models_{must} m))$.

Definition 6 (Modal Specification). *A modal specification is defined by a tuple (M_{may}, M_{must}) where*
  $M_{may} \subset S$ *is a finite set of may-formulae, and*
  $M_{must} \subset S$ *is a finite set of must-formulae.*

A CWF-net CPN satisfies a modal specification $MS = (M_{may}, M_{must})$, written $CPN \models MS$, iff $\forall m \in M_{may}. \ CPN \models_{may} m \wedge \forall m' \in M_{must}. \ CPN \models_{must} m'$.

2.4 Constraint System

A constraint system is defined by a set of constraints (properties), which must be satisfied by the solution of the problem it models. Such a system can be represented as a Constraint Satisfaction Problem (CSP) [13]. Formally, a CSP is a tuple $\Omega =< X, D, C >$ where X is a set of variables $\{x_1, \ldots, x_n\}$, D is a set of domains $\{d_1, \ldots, d_n\}$, where d_i is the domain associated with the variable x_i, and C is a set of constraints $\{c_1(X_1), \ldots, c_m(X_m)\}$, where a constraint c_j involves a subset X_j of the variables of X. It is such that each variable appearing in a constraint should take its value from its domain. Hence, a CSP models NP-complete problems as search problems where the corresponding search space is the Cartesian product space $d_1 \times \ldots \times d_n$.

The solution of a CSP Ω is computed by a labelling function $\mathcal{L}$, which provides a set v (called valuation function) of tuples assigning each variable x_i of X to one value from its domain d_i such that all the constraints of C are satisfied. More formally, v is consistent—or satisfies a constraint $c(X)$ of C—if the projection of v on X is in $c(X)$. If v satisfies all the constraints of C, then Ω is a consistent or satisfiable CSP. In the present paper, we propose to use Constraint Logic Programming over Finite Domains, written CLP(FD) [14], to solve the CSP representing the modal specifications to be verified.

3 Motivating Example

Let us consider a business process workflow of a *Question and Answer* portal, which is a part of a proprietary issue tracking system used to manage bugs and issues requested by the customers of a tool provider company[1]. It allows company's customers to ask questions that are then answered by the company's sellers. To use the system, users have to be registered. Three types of users can log-in: clients, sellers and administrators. Clients can ask questions that are then answered by sellers. Once the answer to a question has been validated by the client who asked it, the administrator archives the question. An execution of the workflow is complete once all users have been logged-out and unregistered. We present one of the several refinements of the workflow modelled by a CWF-net. For clarity, this CWF-net is described by several *sub*-CWF-nets where the places with the same name are the same, as, e.g., $HomeQA$ place in Figs. 2(a) and 3.

In this refinement, there are three colours. The first colour models a set $U = \{u_1, .., u_t\}$ of t user names representing the different users of the system. The second colour is used for a set $R = \{client, seller, admin\}$ of roles, which are assigned to users. Finally, to represent the question states, the third colour $Q = \{unanswered, answered, validated\}$ is a set of statuses. Table 1 shows the colours associated with places of the *Question and Answer* CWF-net, and Table 2 shows the colours, inputs, outputs and guards $(u, u_1, u_2 \in U, r \in R, q \in Q)$.

An execution of the *Question and Answer* CWF-net starts with at least three users (a client, a seller, and an administrator). To illustrate how this CWF-net works, let us consider the following execution with u_1, u_2 and u_3 as initial

---

[1] For confidentiality reasons, the details about this case study are not given.

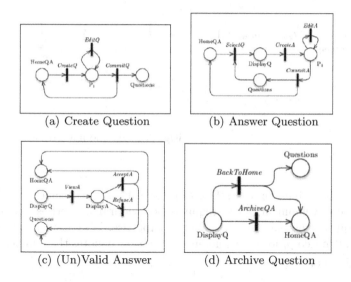

(a) Create Question   (b) Answer Question

(c) (Un)Valid Answer   (d) Archive Question

Fig. 2. *sub*-CWF-nets of the *Question and Answer* CWF-net

marking: each user is registered, then logs in and navigates to the QA's Home (Fig. 3):

- $Register(u_1, client)$, $Login(u_1, client)$, $HomeToQA(u_1, client)$
- $Register(u_2, seller)$, $Login(u_2, seller)$, $HomeToQA(u_2, seller)$
- $Register(u_3, admin)$, $Login(u_3, admin)$, $HomeToQA(u_3, admin)$

The client creates a new question (Fig. 2(a)):

- $CreateQ(u_1, client)$, $CommitQ(u_1, client, unanswered, u_1)$

The seller selects the question and the answer (Fig. 2(b)):

- $SelectQ(u_2, seller, unanswered, u_1)$, $CreateA(u_2, seller, unanswered, u_1)$
- $CommitA(u_2, seller, answered, u_1)$

The client selects the question, reads the answer and validates (Fig. 2(c)):

- $SelectQ(u_1, client, answered, u_1)$, $ViewA(u_1, client, answered, u_1)$
- $AcceptA(u_1, client, answered, u_1)$

The administrator selects the question and archives it (Fig. 2(d)):

- $SelectQ(u_3, admin, validated, u_1)$, $ArchiveQA(u_3, admin, validated, u_1)$

The users navigate to Home and then log-out and are unregistered (Fig. 3):

- $QAtoHome(u_1, client)$, $Logout(u_1, client)$ $UnRegister(u_1, client)$
- $QAtoHome(u_3, seller)$, $Logout(u_3, seller)$ $UnRegister(u_2, seller)$
- $QAtoHome(u_3, admin)$, $Logout(u_3, admin)$ $UnRegister(u_3, admin)$

Table 1. Colours of *Question and Answer* CWF-net's places

Colours	Places
U	i, o
$U \times R$	$P_0, Home, HomeQA, HomeSR$
$U \times R \times Q \times U$	$DisplayQ, DisplayA, P\_1, P\_3$
$Q \times U$	$Questions$

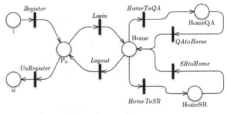

Fig. 3. Login and navigation *sub*-CWF-net

Regarding this business process, the goal is to verify, at the specification or design stage of the development, some required behavioural properties derived from textual requirements and business analyst expertise. We consider the following properties, denoted p_i for later references (*nbUsers* denotes the number of users in the initial marking: $nbUsers = \sum_{r=1}^{t} M_i(i)(r)$).

- p_1: $QA \models_{must} [true]Register[u = u_1] \wedge .. \wedge Register[u = u_t]$: all users must register;
- p_2: $QA \models_{may} [true]ViewA[r = admin]$: an admin may view an answer;
- p_3: $QA \models_{may} [true]CreateQ[r = client, u = u_x] \wedge RefuseA[r = client, u_1 = u_x]$: u_x client may create a question and refuse the answer;
- p_4: $QA \models_{must} [true]CommitQ[u_2 = u_x] \Rightarrow CommitA[u_2 = u_x] \wedge ArchiveQA[u_2 = u_x]$: when u_x asks a question it must be answered and archived;
- p_5: $QA \models_{must} [true]\neg CreateA[r = client]$: a client must not answer a question;
- p_6: $QA \models_{may} [nbUsers > 3]CreateQ[u = u_x] \wedge \neg CreateQ[u = u_y]$: there may be an user u_x who asks a question while another (i.e. u_y) does not;
- p_7: $QA \models_{must} [nbUsers < 3]\neg CreateQ[true]$: if there is less than three users, no question is asked;
- p_8: $QA \models_{must} [true]CreateQ[true] \Rightarrow (Register[r = client] \wedge Register[r = seller] \wedge Register[r = admin])$: if a question is asked then the system must have registered a client, a seller and an administrator.

Let us emphasize that these properties could not be expressed without taking colours into account because data are necessarily involved.

4   Modelling Executions of CWF-nets

This section aims to model the correct executions of a CWF-net by a constraint system, which is then solved to validate or invalidate properties of interest.

Theorem 2 (State equation [8]). *Let* $CPN = (P, T, C, W)$, *if a marking* M_b *is reachable from* M_a *then there exists* x *a weighted set of transitions such that:*

$$M_b = M_a + (W^+ - W^-) \circledast x. \tag{1}$$

Table 2. Colours, inputs, outputs, and guards of *Question and Answer* CWF-net's transitions

Transition	Colours	Inputs	Outputs	Guard
Register	$U \times R$	u	(u, r)	*True*
UnRegister	$U \times R$	(u, r)	u	*True*
Login, Logout	$U \times R$	(u, r)	(u, r)	*True*
HomeToQA	$U \times R$	(u, r)	(u, r)	*True*
QAtoHome	$U \times R$	(u, r)	(u, r)	*True*
HomeToSR	$U \times R$	(u, r)	(u, r)	*True*
SRtoHome	$U \times R$	(u, r)	(u, r)	*True*
CreateQ	$U \times R$	(u, r)	$(u, r,' unanswered', u)$	$r =' client'$
EditQ	$U \times R \times Q \times U$	(u_1, r, q, u_2)	(u_1, r, q, u_2)	*True*
CommitQ	$U \times R \times Q \times U$	(u_1, r, q, u_2)	(u_1, r) and (q, u_2)	*True*
SelectQ	$U \times R \times Q \times U$	(u_1, r) and (q, u_2)	(u, r, q, u)	*True*
CreateA	$U \times R \times Q \times U$	(u_1, r, q, u_2)	$(u_1, r,' answered', u_2)$	$r =' seller' \wedge q ='$ unanswered'
EditA	$U \times R \times Q \times U$	(u_1, r, q, u_2)	(u_1, r, q, u_2)	*True*
CommitA	$U \times R \times Q \times U$	(u_1, r, q, u_2)	(u_1, r) and (q, u_2)	*True*
ViewA	$U \times R \times Q \times U$	(u_1, r, q, u_2)	(u_1, r, q, u_2)	$u_1 = u_2 \wedge q ='$ answered'
AcceptA	$U \times R \times Q \times U$	(u_1, r, q, u_2)	(u_1, r) and $('validated', u_2)$	*True*
RefuseA	$U \times R \times Q \times U$	(u_1, r, q, u_2)	(u_1, r) and $('unanswered', u_2)$	*True*
ArchiveQA	$U \times R \times Q \times U$	(u_1, r, q, u_2)	(u_1, r)	$r =' admin' \wedge q ='$ validated'
BackToHome	$U \times R \times Q \times U$	(u_1, r, q, u_2)	(u_1, r) and (q, u_2)	*True*

To illustrate (1), let us consider the CWF-net described in Sect. 3. Let M_1 be a marking such that $M_1(i) = \{u_1\}, \forall p \in P \setminus \{i\}.M_1(p) = \mathcal{O}$, and M_2 be a marking such that $M_2(o) = \{u_1\}, \forall p \in P \setminus \{i\}.M_2(p) = \mathcal{O}$. The marking M_2 is reachable from M_1 by the transition sequence $\alpha = Register(u_1, client)$, $Unregister(u_1, client)$. Let x_1 denote the weighted set of transitions in α, then we have $M_2 = M_1 + (W^+ - W^-) \circledast x_1$.

The set of solutions of the state Eq. (1) of a CWF-net, where $M_a \in M_i$ and $M_b \in M_o$, defines an over-approximation of the set of its correct executions. A solution of the state Eq. (1) is called *spurious* if it does not correspond to an execution of the considered CWF-net. For example, let us now consider the weighted set x_2 of the transitions $Register(u_1, client)$, $Unregister(u_1, client)$, and $EditQ(u_1, client, unanswered, u_1)$. In this case we have $M_2 = M_1 + (W^+ - W^-) \circledast x_2$, however the weighted set of transitions x_2 does not correspond to any correct execution, i.e. x_2 is a spurious solution. This is because of the transition $EditQ$, which produces and consumes the same token in place P_1.

To dismiss spurious solutions, this over-approximation can be refined by considering structural properties of the places and transitions involved in the considered executions. To this end, we introduce the notion of the subnet of a CWF-net associated with a solution of its state Eq. (1).

Definition 7. *Let* $CPN = (P, T, C, W)$ *a CWF-net,* M_a, M_b *two markings of* CPN, *and* x *a weighted set of transitions such that* $M_b = M_a + (W^+ - W^-) \circledast x$. *We define the subnet* $sCPN(x) = (sP, sT, sF)$ *where:*

- $sP = \{p \in P \setminus \{p \in P | M_a(p) \neq \mathcal{O} \vee M_b(p) \neq \mathcal{O}\} \mid \exists t \in T, W^+(t, p) \circledast x(t) > 0 \vee W^-(p, t) \circledast x(t) > 0\}$
- $sT = \{t \in T \mid x(t) > 0\}$
- $sF = \{(a, b) \mid a \in (sP \cup sT) \wedge b \in (sP \cup sT) \wedge (W^+(a, b) \circledast x(a) > 0 \vee W^-(a, b) \circledast x(b) > 0)\}$

Among various structural properties of CWF-nets, the existence of a siphon and a trap in the subnet of a CWF-net, associated with a solution of its state Eq. (1), is relevant (Lemma 1). Moreover, any subnet of a solution of (1) that contains a siphon or a trap is a spurious solution. Theorem (3) defines a constraint system for determining the presence of a siphon in a Petri net.

Theorem 3 [10]. *Let* $\theta(PN)$ *be the following constraint system associated with a Petri net* $PN = (P, T, F)$: $\forall p \in P, \forall t \in {}^\bullet p. \sum_{p' \in {}^\bullet t} \xi(p') \geq \xi(p) \wedge \sum_{p \in P} \xi(p) > 0$ *where* $\xi : P \rightarrow \{0, 1\}$ *is a valuation function.* PN *contains a siphon if and only if there is a valuation satisfying* $\theta(PN)$.

In this way, checking the existence of traps and of siphons can be done simultaneously thanks to the following theorem.

Theorem 4. *Let* $CPN = (P, T, C, W)$ *a CWF-net,* M_a, M_b *two markings, and* x *a weighted set of transitions such that* $M_b = M_a + (W^+ - W^-) \circledast x$. *If* $sCPN(\nu)$ *contains a trap (resp. siphon)* N *then* N *is also a siphon (resp. trap).*

Structural properties (the siphon existence) can be exploited to refine the state Eq. (1) over-approximation. Let us consider the above-mentioned spurious solution x_2. The subnet of x_2 is shown in Fig. 4. We can see that in this subnet formed by the solution x_2, place P_1 is a siphon as the valuation ξ, such that $\xi(P_1) = 1$ and $\xi(P_0) = 0$, satisfies $\theta(sCPN(x_2))$.

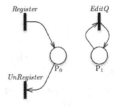

Fig. 4. Subnet of x_2

Theorem 5 uses the state Eq. (1) together with the constraint system of Theorem 4 to provide a constraint system for modeling executions of CWF-net without spurious solutions.

Theorem 5. *Let* $CPN = (P, T, C, W)$ *a CWF-net,* M_a, M_b *two markings of* CPN, x *a weighted set of transitions, and* $sCPN(x) = (sP, sT, sF)$ *the subnet associated to* CPN *and the weighted set of transitions* x. *Let* $\phi(CPN, M_a, M_b, x)$ *be the following constraint system:*

- $M_b = M_a + (W^+ - W^-) \circledast x$,
- *there is no valuation satisfying* $\theta(sCPN(x))$, *and*
- $\forall p \in sP, |{}^\bullet p| \leq 1 \wedge |p^\bullet| \leq 1$,

If $\phi(CPN, M_a, M_b, x)$ *is satisfiable then there exists* $\sigma \models x$ *such that* $M_a \xrightarrow{\sigma} M_b$.

Let $CPN = (P, T, C, W)$ be a CWF-net, M_a, M_b two markings of CPN, the set of solutions of $\phi(CPN, M_a, M_b, x)$ is an under-approximation of the set of correct executions reaching M_b from M_a in CPN. Any execution modelled by the constraint system ϕ is called a segment. Any correct execution of CPN can be modelled by a finite number of segments.

Theorem 6. *Let $CPN = (P, T, C, W)$ a CWF-net, M_a, M_b two markings of CPN. Let $\psi(CPN, M_a, M_b, X, K)$ be the following constraint system:*

- $\forall k \in 1..K, \phi(CPN, M_{k-1}, M_k, x_k)$,
- $M_0 = M_a \wedge M_K = M_b$, *and*
- $X = \{x_1, .., x_K\}$.

There exists $\sigma = \sigma_1, .., \sigma_K$ such that $\forall i \in 1..K, \sigma_i \models x_i$ and $M_a \xrightarrow{\sigma} M_b$ if and only if $\exists K \in \mathbb{N}$ such that $\psi(CPN, M_a, M_b, X, K)$ is satisfiable.

The constraint system of Theorem (6) allows modelling any correct execution of a CWF-net composed of at most K segments. This naturally leads us to consider two decision problems.

The first decision problem, called the *K-bounded validity of a modal formula*, only considers executions formed by K segments, at most. The second one, called the *unbounded validity of a modal formula*, generalizes the first problem by considering executions formed by an arbitrary number of segments.

To verify the *K-bounded* validity of a modal $[q]m$ *may*-formula determining the existence of a correct execution modelled by K segments starting from an initial marking satisfying q where the behaviour of m is satisfied, is enough. Similarly, determining the *K-bounded* validity of a modal $[q]m$ *must*-formula can be done by determining the non-existence of a correct execution modelled by K segments starting from an initial marking satisfying q where the behaviour of $\neg m$ is satisfied.

Let x be a weighted set of transitions, and $[q]m$ a modal formula. We denote $P(x, m)$ the constraint corresponding to the formula m. To construct this constraint, every terminal symbol $t[p]$ of the formula m is replaced by the corresponding constraint obtained by replacing every free variable of p in $C(t)$ by the corresponding variable over x. To illustrate this construction, let us consider $m = CreateQ[r = client, u = u_x] \wedge RefuseA[r = client, u_1 = u_x]$. The corresponding constraint $P(x, m)$ is $x(CreateQ)(r) = client \wedge x(CreateQ)(u) = u_x \wedge x(RefuseA)(r) = client \wedge x(RefuseA)(u) = u_x$. We say that $x \models m$ (i.e. x satisfies m) if and only if $x \wedge P(x, m)$ is satisfiable. Let $X = \{x_1, .., x_n\}$ be a set of weighted sets of transitions, $X \models m$ if and only if $x_1 \models m .. \vee x_n \models m$.

Theorem 7. *Let CPN be a CWF-net and $M = (M_{may}, M_{must})$ be a modal specification of CPN. CPN satisfies the modal specification M if and only if:*

- $\forall [q]m \in M_{may} \; \exists k \in \mathbb{N}, \; M_a \in M_i$ and $M_b \in M_o$ such that $M_a(i) \models q \wedge \psi(CPN, M_a, M_b, X, K) \wedge X \models m$ is satisfiable.
- $\forall [q]m \in M_{must} \; \exists k \in \mathbb{N}, \; M_a \in M_i$ and $M_b \in M_o$ such that $M_a(i) \models q \wedge \psi(CPN, M_a, M_b, X, K) \wedge X \models \neg m$ is not satisfiable.

Theorem (7), with $k \leq K$, defines a constraint system, which allows to determine the K-*bounded* validity of a modal specification.

Theorem 8. *Let CPN be a CWF-net where Ξ is composed of finite data-types, $\bar{R}_{must}$ the set of all well-formed must-formulae not satisfied by CPN, and R_{may} the set of all well-formed may-formulae satisfied by CPN. There exists K_{max} such that:*

- *$\forall [q]m \in \bar{R}_{must}\ \exists k \leq K_{max},\ M_a \in M_i$ and $M_b \in M_o$ such that*
$$M_a(i) \models q \wedge \psi(CPN, M_a, M_b, X, K) \wedge X \models \neg m \text{ is satisfiable.}$$
- *$\forall [q]m \in R_{may}\ \exists k \leq K_{max},\ M_a \in M_i$ and $M_b \in M_o$ such that*
$$M_a(i) \models q \wedge \psi(CPN, M_a, M_b, X, K) \wedge X \models m \text{ is satisfiable.}$$

Theorem (8) states that for any CWF-net where Ξ is composed of finite *data-types*, there exists K_{max} such that the K_{max}-*bounded* validity of a modal specification is equivalent to the *unbounded* validity of a modal specification. However this is not true for CWF-net where Ξ is composed of infinite *data-types*. This is consistent with the fact that *reachability* of CPN with infinite colours is undecidable as they can, for example, simulate a Minsky 2-counter machine [15].

5   Implementation and Experiments

This section describes the tool chain developed to experimentally validate this paper's proposals, and illustrates its use on the motivating example from Sect. 3.

5.1   Overview of the Prototype Architecture and Procedures

In order to assess our work, especially regarding its feasibility and efficiency, we have implemented our approach within the Eclipse platform on a trial basis. The process starts using a graphical CWF-net editor created within the Sirius framework[2], which is an EMF-based open source project to create customized graphical modeling workbench by leveraging Eclipse Modeling technologies. Basically, it provides a generic workbench for model-based architecture engineering that could be easily tailored to fit the specific needs of a given Domain Specific Language, e.g., CWF-nets in our context. Hence the developed CWF-net editor allows producing an XML file corresponding to the designed CWF-net model. It is completed by the modal specification, which is manually designed using a dedicated XML format. Once syntactically and semantically validated by a modal checker, these inputs are translated into constraint systems that are handled by the CLP(FD) library of Sicstus Prolog[3]. Finally, a report is generated.

To verify a *may*-formula (resp. a *must*-formula) $[q]m$, the tool first checks if there exists a solution x of the over-approximation, given by the state equation

---

[2] http://projects.eclipse.org/projects/modeling.sirius.
[3] https://sicstus.sics.se.

(Theorem (2)) for which the subnet (Theorem (7)) does not contain siphons, such that the modelled execution satisfies (resp. does not satisfy) $[q]m$ (we denote this constraint system φ). If such an execution exists, it then tries to find an execution modelled by K segments (Theorem (6)), which satisfies (resp. does not satisfy) $[q]m$ (we denote this constraint system $\phi(K)$). It then reports about the K-bounded validity of a given modal formula m. To cope with the complexity raised by K_{max}, K can be fixed to a manageable value. When fixing K to K_{max} (or greater than K_{max}), the algorithm enables deciding the unbounded validity of the *must*-formula m. The results given in Sect. 4 ensure its soundness and completeness. Finally, solving a CSP over a finite domain being an NP-complete problem with respect to the domain size, this algorithm inherits this complexity.

Modellers often use, in the context of workflow development, infinite colours (e.g., strings, integers) to represent data (e.g., usernames of a system, identifiers of files), even if these data are usually not directly manipulated by the control flow. However, CWF-nets with infinite colours cannot be directly handled due to the nature of the constraint solver over finite domains. Fortunately, abstraction techniques help to tackle the problem entailed by this restriction and can therefore cope with infinite colours. [16] proposes an algorithm to construct a finite state abstract program from a given, possibly infinite, state program (e.g., a CWF-net) by means of a syntactic program transformation starting with an initial set of predicates from a specification (e.g., modal specification).

This method is shown to be sound (the abstract program is always guaranteed to simulate the original one) and complete (the algorithm can produce a finite simulation-equivalent, resp. bisimulation-equivalent, abstract program if the concrete program has a finite abstraction with respect to simulation, resp. bisimulation, equivalence). On the one hand, in the case of a bisimulation-equivalent abstract program, the abstracted modal specification can be verified using our method, and the (in)validity of the modal specification can be directly inferred. On the other hand, for simulation-equivalent abstract program, only the validity of a *may*-formula and the invalidity of a *must*-formula can be inferred.

To handle infinite colours, another approach is to consider only a finite number of data of an infinite colour according to control-flow selection criteria (e.g., decision or condition coverage) [17]. However, this approach is not complete.

5.2 Experimental Results

The approach and the corresponding implementation have been applied to the industrial issue tracking system described in Sect. 3. Since the properties have initially been defined by the business analysts involved in the project, we assume that they are representative of properties that should be verified by engineers when they design and implement such business processes. Furthermore, the obtained verification results have been shared and discussed with them. Table 3 shows an extract of the experimental results focusing on the properties p_1 to p_8 from Sect. 3. In Table 3, the modal formula associated with each property is specified, and the computation result is given by its final verdict (valid or not) as well as the internal evaluation of φ. The input K and the corresponding

Table 3. Experimentation results

#	Formula	φ	K	$\phi(K)$	Result
p_1	$QA \models_{must} [true]Register[u = u_1] \wedge .. \wedge Register[u = u_t]$	TRUE	-	-	TRUE
p_2	$QA \models_{may} [true]ViewA[r = admin]$	FALSE	-	-	FALSE
p_3	$QA \models_{may} [true]CreateQ[r = client, u = u_x]$ $\wedge RefuseA[r = client, u_1 = u_x]$	TRUE	5	FALSE	-
			7	TRUE	TRUE
p_4	$QA \models_{must} [true]CommitQ[u_2 = u_x] \Rightarrow$ $CommitA[u_2 = u_x] \wedge ArchiveQA[u_2 = u_x]$	TRUE	-	-	TRUE
p_5	$QA \models_{must} [true]\neg CreateA[r = client]$	TRUE	-	-	TRUE
p_6	$QA \models_{may} [nbUsers > 3]CreateQ[u = u_x] \wedge \neg CreateQ[u = u_y]$	TRUE	12	TRUE	TRUE
p_7	$QA \models_{must} [nbUsers < 3]\neg CreateQ[true]$	TRUE	-	-	TRUE
p_8	$QA \models_{must} [true]CreateQ[true] \Rightarrow (Register[r = client]$ $\wedge Register[r = seller] \wedge Register[r = admin]$	TRUE	-	-	TRUE

computed value of $\phi(K)$ are also precised when it makes sense, i.e. when the algorithm cannot conclude without this bound.

On the one hand, we observe that when verifying *must*-formulae that are satisfied by the CWF-net (e.g., p_1, p_4), or *may*-formulae that are not satisfied by the WF-net (e.g., p_2), the over-approximation φ is usually enough to conclude. On the other hand, when verifying *may*-formulae that are satisfied by the CWF-net (e.g., p_3), or *must*-formulae that are not satisfied by the WF-net, the decomposition into K segments is needed. We empirically show that this decomposition is very effective since values of K_{max} are usually moderate ($K_{max} = 12$ for p_6, less than 30 on all the experiments conducted on this case study).

Thanks to the experiments conducted using this proof-of-concept prototype, we can conclude that the proposed method is suitable and efficient, and can therefore gain benefits within business process design and verification. Notably, these experiments highlighted that the approach is able to conclude about the (in)validity of the studied properties in a very short time (less than 5 s).

6   Conclusion and Related Work

This paper presents an approach based on constraint systems to model executions of CWF-nets in order to verify modal specifications. It allows managing realistic and complex specifications that manipulate and manage data types. This approach, supported by an Eclipse-based prototype, has been successfully experimented on a non-trivial case study to validate an issue tracking system. These promising results show the relevance and the effectiveness of the approach to validate complex business processes using modal specifications.

Modal specifications–originally introduced in [9]–allow loose or partial specifications in a process algebraic framework. Adapted to Petri nets, they allow defining relations between generated modal languages to decide specifications refinement and asynchronous composition [18]. In [10], modal specifications language over WF-nets expresses requirements on several activities and on their causalities. To handle CWF-nets, we extend modal specifications with additional conditions on initial state as well as on coloured transitions. Unlike [18], to verify modal specifications, our approach focuses on correct executions of CWF-nets.

A lot of results have been provided to model and to analyse Petri nets by using equational approaches [19]. Among popular resolution techniques, constraint programming has been successfully used to analyse properties of Petri nets. In [20], an SMT-based approach to the coverability problem using the state equation and traps is presented. Our CSP-based approach also takes advantage of trap and siphon properties in pursuance of modelling correct executions of CWF-nets. Furthermore, constraint programming makes it possible to tackle one of the major verification problems–the reachability problem, as shown in [21] where a decomposition into *step sequences*, i.e. segments, was modelled by constraints. Our approach is almost similar, but the constraints on step sequences are much stronger in our case because we address not only the reachability of a given marking, but also the transitions involved in the path reaching it.

As a future work, we plan extensive experiment to increase the scalability of our verification approach based on constraint systems. To improve its readiness level and to foster its use by business analysts, we plan to propose user-friendly modal properties patterns. On the theoretical side, investigating modal specifications preservation through refinements is a further research direction.

References

1. Cardoso, J., Mendling, J., Neumann, G., Reijers, H.A.: A discourse on complexity of process models. In: Eder, J., Dustdar, S. (eds.) BPM Workshops 2006. LNCS, vol. 4103, pp. 117–128. Springer, Heidelberg (2006)
2. Dumas, M., ter Hofstede, A.H.M.: UML activity diagrams as a workflow specification language. In: Gogolla, M., Kobryn, C. (eds.) UML 2001. LNCS, vol. 2185, pp. 76–90. Springer, Heidelberg (2001)
3. van der Aalst, W.M.P.: Three good reasons for using a petri-net-based workflow management system. J. Inf. Process Integr. Enterp. **428**, 161–182 (1997)
4. van der Aalst, W.M.P., Van Hee, K.M., Houben, G.J.: Modelling and analysing workflow using a Petri-net based approach. In: Workshop on Computer-Supported Cooperative Work, Petri nets and Related Formalisms, pp. 31–50, June 1994
5. Ellis, C.A., Nutt, G.J.: Modeling and enactment of workflow systems. In: Ajmone Marsan, M. (ed.) ICATPN 1993. LNCS, vol. 691. Springer, Heidelberg (1993)
6. Liu, D., Wang, J., Chan, S.C.F., Sun, J., Zhang, L.: Modeling workflow processes with colored Petri nets. Comput. Ind. **49**(3), 267–281 (2002)
7. Larsen, K.G.: Modal specifications. In: Sifakis, J. (ed.) Automatic Verification Methods for Finite State Systems. LNCS, vol. 407, pp. 232–246. Springer, Heidelberg (1989)

8. Jensen, K.: Coloured Petri nets. In: Brauer, W., Reisig, W., Rozenberg, G. (eds.) Petri Nets: Central Models and Their Properties. LNCS, pp. 248–299. Springer, Heidelberg (1987)

9. Larsen, K.G., Thomsen, B.: A modal process logic. In: 3rd Annual Symposium on Logic in Computer Science, LICS 1988, Edinburgh, UK, pp. 203–210. IEEE CSP, July 1988

10. Bride, H., Kouchnarenko, O., Peureux, F.: Verifying modal workflow specifications using constraint solving. In: Albert, E., Sekerinski, E. (eds.) IFM 2014. LNCS, vol. 8739, pp. 171–186. Springer, Heidelberg (2014)

11. Murata, T.: Petri nets: Properties, analysis and applications. IEEE **77**(4), 541–580 (1989)

12. Presburger, M.: Über die vollständigkeit eines gewissen systems der arithmetik ganzer zahlen, in welchem die addition als einzige operation hervortritt. In: Sprawozdanie z I Kongresu metematykw slowiaskich, Warszawa, Poland, pp. 92–101 (1929)

13. Macworth, A.K.: Consistency in networks of relations. J. Artif. Intell. **8**(1), 99–118 (1977)

14. van Hentenryck, P., Dincbas, M.: Domains in logic programming. In: National Conference on Artificial Intelligence, AAAI 1986, pp. 759–765, August 1986

15. Minsky, M.L.: Computation: Finite and Infinite Machines. Prentice-Hall Inc., Englewood Cliffs (1967)

16. Namjoshi, K.S., Kurshan, R.P.: Syntactic program transformations for automatic abstraction. In: Emerson, E.A., Sistla, A.P. (eds.) CAV 2000. LNCS, vol. 1855. Springer, Heidelberg (2000)

17. Vilkomir, S., Bowen, J.: Formalization of software testing criteria using the Z notation. In: 25th International Conference on Computer Software and Applications, COMPSAC 2001, Chicago, IL, USA, pp. 351–356. IEEE CSP, October 2001

18. Elhog-Benzina, D., Haddad, S., Hennicker, R.: Refinement and asynchronous composition of modal Petri nets. In: Jensen, K., Donatelli, S., Kleijn, J. (eds.) Transactions on Petri Nets and Other Models of Concurrency V. LNCS, vol. 6900, pp. 96–120. Springer, Heidelberg (2012)

19. Desel, J.: Basic linear algebraic techniques for place/transition nets. In: Reisig, W., Rozenberg, G. (eds.) APN 1998. LNCS, vol. 1491. Springer, Heidelberg (1998)

20. Esparza, J., Ledesma-Garza, R., Majumdar, R., Meyer, P., Niksic, F.: An SMT-based approach to coverability analysis. In: Biere, A., Bloem, R. (eds.) CAV 2014. LNCS, vol. 8559, pp. 603–619. Springer, Heidelberg (2014)

21. Bourdeaud'huy, T., Hanafi, S., Yim, P.: Incremental Integer Linear Programming Models for Petri Nets Reachability Problems. Petri Net: Theory and Applications. InTech, Rijeka (2008)

Behavioural Analysis of Sessions Using the Calculus of Structures

Gabriel Ciobanu[1] and Ross Horne[1,2,3(✉)]

[1] Institute of Computer Science, Romanian Academy, Iasi, Romania
gabriel@info.uaic.ro
[2] Faculty of Information Technology, Kazakh-British Technical University,
Almaty, Kazakhstan
[3] School of Computer Science and Engineering,
Nanyang Technological University, Singapore City, Singapore
rhorne@ntu.edu.sg

Abstract. This paper describes an approach to the behavioural analysis of sessions. The approach is made possible by the calculus of structures — a deep inference proof calculus, generalising the sequent calculus, where inference rules are applied in any context. The approach involves specifications of global and local sessions inspired by the Scribble language. The calculus features a novel operator that synchronises parts of a protocol that must be treated atomically. Firstly, the calculus can be used to determine whether local sessions can be compose in a type safe fashion such that sessions are capable of successfully completing. Secondly, the calculus defines a subtyping relation for sessions that allows causal dependencies to be weakened while retaining termination potential. Consistency and complexity results follow from proof theory.

1 Introduction

This work is the first to draw connections between a calculus that originates in proof theory, namely *the calculus of structures* [9], and the static analysis of sessions using *session types* [10,12].

In many systems, a protocol is initiated by opening a session between the parties involved. Participants in a protocol typically exchange a number of messages before closing the session. Each session can be characterised by the types of messages exchanged and also the order in which messages are sent. Such information can be captured in a session type. The session type declares a specification that can be used for both static and runtime analysis of the protocol concerned.

On the other hand, the calculus of structure is a proof calculus that was originally discovered by studying non-commutative operators, i.e. operators, say op, where A op B is not the same as B op A. Such operators are useful for expressing causal dependencies, such as the concept of A happening before B, which is clearly a non-commutative concept. There are simple and natural connections between the calculus of structures and session types that can be understood immediately:

© Springer International Publishing Switzerland 2016
M. Mazzara and A. Voronkov (Eds.): PSI 2015, LNCS 9609, pp. 91–106, 2016.
DOI: 10.1007/978-3-319-41579-6_8

– The calculus of structures is a *term rewriting system modulo an equational theory* [16]. Term rewriting systems modulo an equational theory are analogous to reduction systems modulo a structural congruence as typically used to express the operational semantics that govern the behaviour of session types.

– A *proof* in the calculus of structures is a special derivation that may *terminate successfully*. Session types can be used to analyse whether a family of participants in a session may together successfully complete the session, in which case they are multiparty compatible [5].

Further striking connections between session types and the calculus of structures are forthcoming. In the paper [10], which initiated interest in session types, Honda introduces the notion of a co-type, which respects the following properties resembling De Morgan dualities:

$$\sim(P \,\&\, Q) = \sim P \oplus \sim Q \qquad \sim(P \oplus Q) = \sim P \,\&\, \sim Q \qquad \sim(P \,;\, Q) = \sim P \,;\, \sim Q$$

It is no secret that the first two De Morgan dualities above were inspired by the additive operators *with* and *plus* (& and $\oplus$) of linear logic. Abramsky had already suggested [1] that & and $\oplus$ could be interpreted as a *external* choice and *internal* choice respectively.

More recently, proof theorists have independently devised proof calculi, by using the calculus of structures [9], that exhibit the De Morgan duality for sequential composition above. Because the De Morgan dual of sequential composition is also sequential composition, it is considered to be a *self-dual* operator. In this work, we argue that the self-dual non-commutative operator found in session types and the self-dual non-commutative operator found in the calculus of structures are essentially the same operator.

Section 2 introduces the running example of a simple two-phase commit protocol in a language inspired by the session type based language Scribble. The syntax of global and local types are defined as well as the projection from global types to local types. Section 3 defines the semantics of local types in the calculus of structures, and presents consistency and compatibility results. Section 4 compares our work to the body of work bridging session types and proof calculi, and highlights open problems.

2   A Core Calculus Inspired by Scribble

We begin with a concrete example of a ubiquitous protocol from distributed computing. Two-phase commit (2PC) ensures the atomicity of a transaction involving data persisted across distributed nodes. The language we introduce is heavily influenced by the Scribble language [11], which can be used to specify the global behaviour of the two-phase commit protocol. The Scribble language is an implementation of multiparty asynchronous session types [5,12], with a syntax deliberately chosen to appeal to software engineers that uses curly braces for disambiguation.

> **par** *p_begin* (*Payload*) **from** *Client* **to** *Participant*
> **and** *l_begin* (*Payload*) **from** *Client* **to** *Leader* ;
> *prepare* (*Timestamp*) **from** *Participant* **to** *Leader* ;
> **par** *c_commit* (*Timestamp*) **from** *Leader* **to** *Client*
> **and** *p_commit* (*Timestamp*) **from** *Leader* **to** *Participant*

Fig. 1. A global protocol for client driven two-phase commit.

The example protocol is presented in Fig. 1. The protocol describes interactions between three parties: a *Client* that initiates a transaction, a *Leader* that coordinates the transaction, and a *Participant* that must coordinate with the leader.

Global types of the form *prepare* (*Timestamp*) **from** *Participant* **to** *Leader* mean that role *Participant* sends a message of type *Timestamp* to the role *Leader*, using the channel *prepare*. A channel is assumed to be some messaging middleware that the sender passes a message to, and the receiver listens on. The type constructor **par** ... **and**... represents the parallel composition of two protocols. For example, in 2PC the leader sends commit timestamps to the *Client* and *Participant* in parallel. The semi-colon represents sequential composition. We assume that **par** takes higher operator precedence than semi-colon.

The variant of the Two Phase Commit protocol described in the global protocol is a client-driven two phase commit with one participant. The *Client* initiates the protocol by sending a payload to the *Leader* and *Participant*. The leader and the participant manage a disjoint range of keys associated with data. The payload for the leader and the client contains updates to apply at each respective node. When the participant receives the payload, the participant acquires locks for the relevant data, logs the transaction, picks a timestamp that is greater than the timestamp applied to any previous transaction, then sends the timestamp to the leader. Upon receiving the prepare timestamp from the *Participant* and the begin message from the *Client*, the leader locks its own data and picks a timestamp greater than the prepare timestamp from the *Participant* and greater than the timestamp applied to any transaction at the *Leader*. The leader then logs its own updates and the timestamp. Finally, the *Leader* notifies the *Client* and *Participant* about the timestamp chosen for the whole transaction, the *Participant* logs the timestamp and all locks are released.

Session types, such as Scribble, can be used for the design, implementation and verification of distributed systems. A methodology for using session types is as follows. Firstly, a systems analyst designs the global protocol, which describes the message exchanges between all parties in a distributed system. Secondly, the global protocol is automatically projected to local protocols, as presented in Fig. 2 for 2PC, where local protocols specify permitted patterns of sends and receives of messages for each role. Because the projection to local protocols is performed automatically such that a certain semantics is respected, the systems analyst knows that each local protocol is correct with respect to the global

Client: **Participant:**

par $\sim$*p_begin*(*Payload*) **to** *Participant*   *p_begin*(*Payload*) **from** *Client* ;

and $\sim$*L_begin*(*Payload*) **to** *Leader* ; $\sim$*prepare*(*Timestamp*) **to** *Leader* ;

commit(*Timestamp*) **from** *Leader*   *p_commit*(*Timestamp*) **from** *Leader*

Leader: *L_begin*(*Payload*) **from** *Client* ;

prepare(*Timestamp*) **from** *Participant* ;

par $\sim$*p_commit*(*Timestamp*) **to** *Participant*

and $\sim$*c_commit*(*Timestamp*) **to** *Client*

Fig. 2. Local types for roles *Client, Participant* and *Leader* projected from Fig. 1.

protocol. Verified automation eliminates human error that can be introduced when projection is performed manually using the intuition of the systems analyst.

A local protocol can fulfil several roles in the software engineering process. Firstly, a local protocol can be used as a reference for an engineer who is responsible for implementing the node that performs the role described in the protocol. Furthermore, the local protocol can be used to verify that the engineer's implementation does indeed conform to the given protocol. For some languages, there exist extensions [15,19] that enable the code itself to be statically analysed. For situations where there are either no static type checking tools or we do not have access to the code, runtime monitors can be automatically generated that observe the behaviour of nodes while they execute to detect whether a protocol violates its specification [14].

The syntax for global and local types is presented in Fig. 3. The syntax is heavily influenced by the global and local protocols of Scribble [11], but with some significant differences:

- We include a complementation operator over atoms, written as a tilde prefix, where atoms represent the separate send and receive events. Atoms and their complements interact to compose local protocols with channels.
- We also include a binary operator `sync`, which ensures that two events occur atomically. Types joined by `sync` "appear" to happen simultaneously, using separate resources, hence they cannot be interleaved. We use `sync` to capture synchrony in the transport mechanism, but we envision that it can form an extension to Scribble where complex atomic transactions are modelled.

Projection. The projection from global G to local types for a given role R is defined as follows, written $G \restriction_R$.

$$(G_0 \,; G_1) \restriction_R = (G_0 \restriction_R) \,; (G_1 \restriction_R)$$

$$(\text{par } G_0 \text{ and } G_1) \restriction_R = \text{par } (G_0 \restriction_R) \text{ and } (G_1 \restriction_R)$$

$$c\,(S) \text{ from } P \text{ to } Q \restriction_R = \begin{cases} \sim c\,(S) \text{ to } Q & if P = R \\ c\,(S) \text{ from } P & if Q = R \\ \{\} & otherwise \end{cases}$$

$$(\text{choice at } P \; G_0 \text{ or } G_1) \restriction_R = \begin{cases} (G_0 \restriction_R) \text{ or } (G_1 \restriction_R) & if P \neq R \\ (G_0 \restriction_R) \,\&\, (G_1 \restriction_R) & if P = R \end{cases}$$

$$S ::= int \mid string \mid S \times S \mid \dots \quad \text{sorts}$$

$$c \quad \text{channel} \qquad P \quad \text{role}$$

$$\begin{aligned}
A ::= &\; c(S) \text{ to } P &&\text{send to}\\
\mid &\; c(S) \text{ from } P &&\text{receive from}\\
\mid &\; {\sim}A &&\text{complementation}
\end{aligned}$$

$$\begin{aligned}
G ::= &\; c(S) \text{ from } P \text{ to } P &&\text{values}\\
\mid &\; G\,;G &&\text{seq}\\
\mid &\; \text{par } G \text{ and } G &&\text{par}\\
\mid &\; \text{choice at } P\; G \text{ or } G &&\text{choice}
\end{aligned}$$

$$\begin{aligned}
T ::= &\; \{\} &&\text{unit}\\
\mid &\; A &&\text{atom}\\
\mid &\; T\,;T &&\text{seq}\\
\mid &\; \text{par } T \text{ and } T &&\text{par}\\
\mid &\; \text{sync } T \text{ and } T &&\text{sync}\\
\mid &\; T \text{ or } T &&\text{internal choice}\\
\mid &\; T\,\&\,T &&\text{external choice}
\end{aligned}$$

Fig. 3. Syntax of global types (G), local types (T), atoms (A) and sorts (S).

The projection generates a local type for each role that appears in a global type. Notice that send events are prefixed with the complementation operator, which makes explicit the contravariant nature of sending on a channel [20] which we explain further when we introduce subtyping in the next section.

For simplicity, we assume synchronous communication where messages are received and delivered atomically. Channels are handled explicitly as special local types defined by the following projection from global types to local types. The projection below maps a message exchange to a send event synchronised with a receive event. Notice that polarities of atoms, indicated by the compliment operator, are opposite to atoms in the projection for roles.

$$d(S) \text{ from } P \text{ to } Q \lceil_c = \begin{cases} \text{sync } c(S) \text{ to } Q \text{ and } {\sim}c(S) \text{ from } P & \text{if } c = d\\ \{\} & \text{otherwise} \end{cases}$$

$$(\text{choice at } P\; T \text{ or } U) \lceil_c = (T \lceil_c) \text{ or } (U \lceil_c)$$
$$(G_0\,;G_1) \lceil_c = \text{par } (G_0 \lceil_c) \text{ and } (G_1 \lceil_c)$$
$$(\text{par } G_0 \text{ and } G_1) \lceil_c = \text{par } (G_0 \lceil_c) \text{ and } (G_1 \lceil_c)$$

Asynchronous channels and channels with queues of up to length two can also be handled by this framework. We refer to [12] for constraints restricting the order of events in asynchronous systems and avoiding races.

3   The Subtype System and Multiparty Compatibility

The semantics of local types is defined by a term rewriting system modulo an equational theory. The semantics can be used to define both a subtype relation over local types and the notion of multiparty compatibility.

The rewrite rules and equational theory are presented in Fig. 4. As standard for term rewriting, the equations can be applied at any point in a derivation, and the rules can be applied in any context, where a context $\mathcal{C}\{\ \}$ is any local type with one hole in which any local type can be plugged. Thus we have the following implicit rules:

$$\mathcal{C}\{\ T\ \} \longrightarrow \mathcal{C}\{\ U\ \} \text{ only if } T \longrightarrow U \quad \text{context closure}$$

$$T \longrightarrow U \text{ only if } T \equiv U \quad \text{congruence}$$

We name the term rewriting system in Fig. 4 multiplicative additive system virtual (MAV) since our system combines systems multiplicative additive linear logic with mix (MALL) [17] and basic system virtual (BV) [9], both of which are consistent proof calculi. The equational system ensures that ; is a monoid and **par** and **sync** are commutative monoids. We briefly explain the rewrite rules.

- The atomic interaction rules enable a negative atom and positive atom to annihilate each other, whenever the carried sort of the negated atom is a subsort of the carried sort of the positive atom. Assuming we have a subsorting system, that defines any preorder, we extend the system atoms as follows.

$$c(S0) \text{ to } P \leq c(S1) \text{ to } P \text{ only if } S0 \leq S1$$
$$c(S0) \text{ from } P \leq c(S1) \text{ from } P \text{ only if } S0 \leq S1$$

For example, the subsorting can be given by subtyping for XML Schema [2].
- The switch rule generalises the rule for the tensor product in linear logic. The rule focusses a parallel composition on where an interaction takes place.
- The seq rule arises in the theory of pomsets [8]. The rule strengthens causal dependencies to introduce a barrier across two parallel threads.
- The left choice and right choice rules represent an internal choice where the protocol has control over the branch to select. The external choice rule, represents when we cannot determine at compile time what branch will be selected; hence must analyse both possibilities. The tidy rule simply acknowledges when two branches in an external choice have successfully closed. The medial is essential for the co-existence of seq and external choice.

We extend the complementation operator over atoms to all local types using the following function that transforms a type into its *co-type* [10].

$$\sim(P \& Q) = \sim P \text{ or } \sim Q \qquad \qquad \sim(P \text{ or } Q) = \sim P \& \sim Q$$

$$\sim\text{par } T \text{ and } U = \text{sync } \sim T \text{ and } \sim U \qquad \sim\text{sync } T \text{ and } U = \text{par } \sim T \text{ and } \sim U$$

$$\sim(T\ ;\ U) = \sim T\ ;\ \sim U \qquad \qquad \sim\{\} = \{\} \qquad \qquad \sim\sim A = A$$

The above function transforms any local type into a local type in *negation normal form*, where complementation applies only to atoms, as permitted by the syntax in Fig. 3. We deliberately do not include complementation for arbitrary types in the syntax for local types, since the contravariant nature of complementation complicates the rewriting system without any gain in expressive power [9].

In the calculus of structures a *proof* is a special derivation that reduces to the unit type $\{\}$, representing a successfully completed session.

Definition 1. *If for any type* $T \longrightarrow \{\}$, *according to the term rewriting system in Fig. 4, then we write* $\vdash T$, *and say that* T *is provable.*

$$\textbf{par} \sim A \textbf{ and } B \longrightarrow \{\} \text{ only if } A \leq B \quad \text{atomic interaction}$$

$$\textbf{par} \{ \textbf{ sync } T \textbf{ and } U \} \textbf{ and } V \longrightarrow \textbf{sync } T \textbf{ and } \{ \textbf{ par } U \textbf{ and } V \} \quad \text{switch}$$

$$\textbf{par} \{ T \ ; \ U \} \textbf{ and } \{ V \ ; \ W \} \longrightarrow \{ \textbf{ par } T \textbf{ and } V \} \ ; \ \{ \textbf{ par } U \textbf{ and } W \} \quad \text{seq}$$

$$T \textbf{ or } U \longrightarrow T \quad \text{left choice} \qquad T \textbf{ or } U \longrightarrow U \quad \text{right choice} \qquad \{\} \& \{\} \longrightarrow \{\} \quad \text{tidy}$$

$$\textbf{par} \ T \textbf{ and } \{ U \& V \} \longrightarrow \{ \textbf{ par } T \textbf{ and } U \} \& \{ \textbf{ par } T \textbf{ and } V \} \quad \text{external choice}$$

$$\{ T \ ; \ U \} \& \{ V \ ; \ W \} \longrightarrow \{ T \& V \} \ ; \ \{ U \& W \} \quad \text{medial}$$

$$\textbf{par} \{ \textbf{ par } T \textbf{ and } U \} \textbf{ and } V \equiv \textbf{par } T \textbf{ and } \{ \textbf{ par } U \textbf{ and } V \}$$
$$\textbf{sync} \{ \textbf{ sync } T \textbf{ and } U \} \textbf{ and } V \equiv \textbf{sync } T \textbf{ and } \{ \textbf{ sync } U \textbf{ and } V \}$$
$$\textbf{sync } T \textbf{ and } \{\} \equiv T \qquad \textbf{par } T \textbf{ and } \{\} \equiv T$$
$$\{ T ; U \} \ ; \ V \equiv T ; \{ U \ ; \ V \} \qquad \{\} \ ; \ T \equiv T \qquad T \ ; \ \{\} \equiv T$$
$$\textbf{par } T \textbf{ and } U \equiv \textbf{par } U \textbf{ and } T \qquad \textbf{sync } T \textbf{ and } U \equiv \textbf{sync } U \textbf{ and } T$$

Fig. 4. Term rewriting system modulo an equational theory for local types.

The following result is a generalisation of a consistency result called *cut elimination* that appears commonly in proof theory.

Theorem 1. *Suppose that there is a proof using the extra rules:*

– *par $\sim T$ and $T \longrightarrow \{\}$ (interact)*
– *$\{\} \longrightarrow$ sync $\sim T$ and T (co-interact)*

Given such a proof, a new proof can be constructed that uses only the rules in Fig. 4. We say that the rules interact and co-interact are admissible.

The main results in this paper are corollaries of the above proof-theoretic result. The proof of Theorem 1 involves a technique known as *splitting* introduced in [9]. Choice operators, known as additives, are handled using techniques similar to Theorem 6 in [4], for which we require the following notion of a killing context.

Definition 2. *A killing context $T\{ \cdot, \cdot, \ldots, \cdot \}$ is an n-ary context such that*

$$T\{ \ \} ::= \{ \cdot \} \mid T\{ \ \} \& T\{ \ \}$$

where $\{ \cdot \}$ is a hole into which any local type can be plugged.

The splitting lemma below simulates sequent calculus style rules in a context where the root formula is a parallel composition. The proof of the splitting lemma is quite involved, so receive special attention in a companion paper [13].

Lemma 1 (Splitting). *The following statements hold.*

- *For any atom A, if $\vdash$ **par** $\sim A$ **and** T, then there exist atoms $B_1, B_2, \ldots, B_n$ such that $A \leq B_i$ for $1 \leq i \leq n$ and n-ary killing context $\mathcal{T}\{\ \}$ where $T \longrightarrow \mathcal{T}\{\ B_1, B_2, \ldots, B_n\ \}$.*
- *For any atom A, if $\vdash$ **par** A **and** T, then there exist atoms $B_1, B_2, \ldots, B_n$ such that $B_i \leq A$ for $1 \leq i \leq n$ and n-ary killing context $\mathcal{T}\{\ \}$ where $T \longrightarrow \mathcal{T}\{\ \sim B_1, \sim B_2, \ldots, \sim B_n\ \}$.*
- *If $\vdash$ **par** $\{T \& U\}$ **and** V, then $\vdash$ **par** T **and** V and $\vdash$ **par** U **and** V.*
- *If $\vdash$ **par** $\{T \text{ or } U\}$ **and** V, then there exist local types W_i such that either $\vdash$ **par** T **and** W_i or $\vdash$ **par** U **and** W_i, for $1 \leq i \leq n$, and n-ary killing context $\mathcal{T}\{\ \}$ where $V \longrightarrow \mathcal{T}\{\ W_1, W_2, \ldots, W_n\ \}$.*
- *If $\vdash$ **par** $\{$ **sync** S **and** T $\}$ **and** U, then there exist local types V_i and W_i such that $\vdash$ **par** S **and** V_i and $\vdash$ **par** T **and** W_i, for $1 \leq i \leq n$, and n-ary killing context $\mathcal{T}\{\ \}$ where $U \longrightarrow \mathcal{T}\{\ $**par** V_1 **and** $W_1, \ldots, $**par** V_n **and** $W_n\ \}$.*
- *If $\vdash$ **par** $\{S\ ;\ T\}$ **and** U, then there exist local types V_i and W_i such that $\vdash$ **par** S **and** V_i and $\vdash$ **par** T **and** W_i, for $1 \leq i \leq n$, and n-ary killing context $\mathcal{T}\{\ \}$ where $U \longrightarrow \mathcal{T}\{\ V_1\ ;\ W_1, V_2\ ;\ W_2, \ldots, V_n\ ;\ W_n\ \}$.*

The above splitting result is key to solving two further lemmas, the proof of which are provided in a companion paper [13]. Hence, in the interest of focusing on the relevance of MAV to sessions, we provide only statements of the lemmas.

Lemma 2 (Context Reduction). *If, for any type V, $\vdash$ **par** T **and** V yields $\vdash$ **par** U **and** V, then, for any context $\mathcal{C}\{\ \}$, $\vdash \mathcal{C}\{\ T\ \}$ yields $\vdash \mathcal{C}\{\ U\ \}$.*

The following result, shows that rules complimentary to those that appear in Fig. 4 can be eliminated. By a complementary rule, or *co-rule*, we mean a rule where the direction of rewriting is reversed and co-typing is applied to both local types in the rewrite rule. The proof follows from splitting and the context lemma.

Lemma 3 (Co-rule Elimination). *The following statements hold.*

- *If $\vdash \mathcal{C}\{$ **sync** A **and** $\sim B$ $\}$, where $A \leq B$, then $\vdash \mathcal{C}\{\ \}$.*
- *If $\vdash \mathcal{C}\{$ **sync** $\{\ T\ ;\ U\ \}$ **and** $\{\ V\ ;\ W\ \}\ \}$,*
  *then $\vdash \mathcal{C}\{\ \{$ **sync** T **and** $V\ \}\ ;\ \{$ **sync** U **and** $W\ \}\ \}$.*
- *If $\vdash \mathcal{C}\{\ T \& U\ \}$, then $\vdash \mathcal{C}\{\ T\ \}$.*
- *If $\vdash \mathcal{C}\{\ T \& U\ \}$, then $\vdash \mathcal{C}\{\ U\ \}$.*
- *If $\vdash \mathcal{C}\{$ **sync** T **and** $\{\ U \text{ or } V\ \}\ \}$,*
  *then $\vdash \mathcal{C}\{\ \{$ **sync** T **and** $U\ \}$ **or** $\{$ **sync** T **and** $V\ \}\ \}$.*
- *If $\vdash \mathcal{C}\{\ \{\} \text{ or } \{\}\ \}$, then $\vdash \mathcal{C}\{\ \}$.*
- *If $\vdash \mathcal{C}\{\ \{\ P\ ;\ Q\ \}$ **or** $\{\ R\ ;\ S\ \}\ \}$,*
  then $\vdash \mathcal{C}\{\ \{\ P \text{ or } R\ \}\ ;\ \{\ Q \text{ or } S\ \}\ \}$.

Theorem 1, follows from the above result, by induction on the size of the local type in any interaction or co-interaction rule. Thereby we have established the consistency of the system MAV. The following section, demonstrates why consistency of a calculus is more than a theoretical curiosity.

3.1   A Subtyping Relation for Sessions

We use the semantics of local types to define a subtype relation over local types.

Definition 3. *For local types T and U, if $\vdash$ **par** $\sim T$ **and** U, then $T \leq U$, pronounced T is a subtype of U.*

From Theorem 1 we immediately establish that subtyping is consistent in the following sense.

Corollary 1. *Subtyping is a precongruence: a reflexive, transitive relation that holds in any context.*

Consider the running 2PC example. The **Leader** local protocol in Fig. 2 is a subtype of the following local protocol **Leader′**.

> **par** *prepare* (*Timestamp*) **from** *Participant*
> **and** *L̲begin* (*Payload*) **from** *Client* ;
> **par** $\sim$*p̲_commit* (*Timestamp*) **to** *Participant*
> **and** $\sim$*c̲_commit* (*Timestamp*) **to** *Client*

The difference between the local types for **Leader** and **Leader′** is that **Leader′** waits for the *L̲begin* and *prepare* messages in parallel. Thus **Leader**; can potentially consume the *prepare* message before consuming the *L̲begin* message, which is not possible in **Leader**.

Subsorting. The use of subsorts allows us to recover a classic property of subtyping for channel types [20]: send types are contravariant and receive types are covariant. Immediately, from the atomic interaction rules we obtain, that if $S0 \leq S1$, then both $\sim c(S1)$ **to** $P \leq \sim c(S0)$ **to** P and $c(S0)$ **from** $P \leq c(S1)$ **from** P hold. Notice that the complementation operator prefixing the send event induces the expected contravariance. For example, in 2PC the sender may send a natural number timestamp, when an integer timestamp was expected, assuming that $nat \leq int$ is in the subsorting system. This agrees with related work [20] on subtyping with respect to I/O types for channels.

Subtyping for Choice. The subtype system derived from the extended calculus, reflects existing work on session subtyping involving choice [6]. Consider the extended two phase commit example, with local types **Leader″**, **Participant′**, and **Client′** in Fig. 5. Note that **par**, **sync** and semi-colon are assumed to have a higher precedence than & and **or**.

The example local types **Leader″** and **Client′** involve an external choice. The local type **Leader″** has a choice that allows an abort message to be received from the participant, at which point the client must be notified about the abort. The client has the choice of receiving the commit message or receiving the abort message.

Client' :   **Participant'** :

par $\sim$*p_begin*(*Payload*) **to** *Participant*   *p_begin*(*Payload*) **from** *Client* ;
and $\sim$*L_begin*(*Payload*) **to** *Leader* ;   { $\sim$*prepare*(*Timestamp*) **to** *Leader* ;
{ *commit*(*Timestamp*) **from** *Leader*   *p_commit*(*Timestamp*) **from** *Leader*
  or   &
  c_abort(*Error*) **from** *Leader* } $\sim$*p_abort*(*Error*) **to** *Leader* }

    Leader'' :   *L_begin*(*Payload*) **from** *Client*;
        { *prepare*(*Timestamp*) **from** *Participant* ;
        par $\sim$*p_commit*(*Timestamp*) **to** *Participant*
        and $\sim$*c_commit*(*Timestamp*) **to** *Client*
        or
        p_abort(*Error*) **from** *Participant* ;
        $\sim$*c_abort*(*Error*) **to** *Client* }

Fig. 5. Example of roles in a commit protocol with the choice to abort.

The local type **Leader''** is a super-type of the local type **Leader**, since **Leader''** can always (internally) choose the left branch of the choice in the protocol. Similarly, the local type **Client'** is a super-type of **Client**.

Now consider the local type **Participant'**. In contrast to **Leader''** and **Client'**, the local type **Participant'** is *not* a supertype of **Participant**. This contrast is due to the presence of external choice rather than internal choice. An external choice is used since we cannot determine at compile-time whether the participant will commit or abort; hence both branches must be analysed.

3.2   Multiparty Compatibility

The semantics of local types in Fig. 4 can also be used to determine whether a session can successfully close, without hanging sends or receives. The following definition is the essence of the idea of *multiparty compatibility* in [5].

Definition 4 (Multiparty Compatibility). *If* T_1, T_2, ... T_n *are local types such that **par** T_1 **and** T_2 ... **and** T_n is provable, then T_1, T_2, ... T_n are said to be multiparty compatible.*

The following example, due to Tiu [21], emphasises that we could not express multiparty compatibility using natural deduction.

Role P : $\sim$*begin*(*Data*) **to** *Q* ;   *Role Q* : {
    {   **par** *begin*(*Data*) **from** *P*
      par $\sim$*fun*(*Control*) **to** *Q*   **and** *fun*(*Control*) **from** *P*
      and *done*(*Data*) **from** *Q*   } ;
    } $\sim$*done*(*Data*) **to** *P*

Notice that the causal dependency forced by role Q between receiving a message on channel *fun* and sending a message on channel *done*, induces a dependency at role P; specifically the send on *fun* must happen before the receive on *done*. In the proof of multiparty compatibility, this dependency is imposed by applying a rule, within sequential composition structure, within a par structure. Application of rules in a context alternating between structures is known as *deep inference*. Natural deduction, traditionally used to express type systems, cannot express the scenario above.

The projection of any global type onto its local types for each participant and channel is multiparty compatible.

Lemma 4. *For any G with set of roles and channels I, the multiset of local types $(G \restriction_i)_{i \in I}$ is multiparty compatible.*

Proof. The proof is by induction on the structure of G. The only base case is $c(S)$ from P to Q, for which the following rewrites hold using *switch* and *atomic interaction*.

par $G \restriction_P$ and $G \restriction_Q$ and $G \restriction_c =$
par $\sim c(S)$ to Q and $c(S)$ from P and $\{$ sync $c(S)$ to Q and $\sim c(S)$ from P $\}$
$\longrightarrow$ sync $\{$ par $\sim c(S)$ to Q and $c(S)$ to Q $\}$ and
$\{$ par $\sim c(S)$ from P and $c(S)$ from P $\}$ $\longrightarrow \{\}$

Hence the local types $G \restriction_P, G \restriction_Q, G \restriction_c$ are multiparty compatible.

Consider the case of sequential composition. Assume that G_0 and G_1 are multiparty compatible and consider $G_0 ; G_1$. Hence for $i_1, i_2, \ldots \in I$. By repeated application of the seq rule and the induction hypotheses.

par $\{$ $(G_0 ; G_1) \restriction_{i_1}$ $\}$ and $\{$ $(G_0 ; G_1) \restriction_{i_2}$ $\}$ and $\ldots$
$=$ par $\{$ $G_0 \restriction_{i_1} ; G_1 \restriction_{i_1}$ $\}$ and $\{$ $G_0 \restriction_{i_2} ; G_1 \restriction_{i_2}$ $\}$ and $\ldots$
$\longrightarrow$ par $G_0 \restriction_{i_1}$ and $G_0 \restriction_{i_2}$ and $\ldots$; par $G_1 \restriction_{i_1}$ and $G_1 \restriction_{i_2}$ and $\ldots$
$\longrightarrow \{\}$

Hence $G_0 ; G_1$ is multiparty compatible.

Consider the case of choice. Assume that G_0 and G_1 are multiparty compatible and consider choice at P G_0 or G_1. Hence for $i_1, i_2, \ldots \in I \setminus \{P\}$. By repeated application of the external choice, left choice, right choice and the induction hypotheses.

par (choice at P G_0 or G_1) $\restriction_P$ and (choice at P G_0 or G_1) $\restriction_{i_1}$ and $\ldots$
$=$ par $\{$ $G_0 \restriction_P \& G_1 \restriction_P \}$ and $\{$ $G_0 \restriction_{i_1}$ or $G_1 \restriction_{i_1} \}$ and $\ldots$
$\longrightarrow$ par $G_0 \restriction_P$ and $\{$ $G_0 \restriction_{i_1}$ or $G_1 \restriction_{i_1}$ $\}$ and $\ldots$
$\&$ par $G_1 \restriction_P$ and $\{$ $G_0 \restriction_{i_1}$ or $G_1 \restriction_{i_1}$ $\}$ and $\ldots$
$\longrightarrow$ par $G_0 \restriction_P$ and $G_0 \restriction_{i_1}$ and $\ldots$ $\&$ par $G_1 \restriction_P$ and $G_1 \restriction_{i_1}$ and $\ldots$
$\longrightarrow \{\} \& \{\} \longrightarrow \{\}$

Hence choice at P G_0 or G_1 is multiparty compatible.

The inductive case for parallel composition is similar. Hence the result follows by induction on the structure of G. □

A consequence of the above lemma is that the family of all projections from the global type in Fig. 1 is multiparty compatible.

Subtyping allows local protocols to be weakened while retaining multiparty compatibility. The following lemma is an immediate consequence of Corollary 1.

Lemma 5. *If T_1, T_2, ..., T_n are multiparty compatible, and $T_i \leq U_i$, for $1 \leq i \leq n$, then U_1, U_2, ...U_n are multiparty compatible.*

We now introduce the notion of coherence, which defines families of local protocols and channels, that respect a global type.

Definition 5. *A multiset of local types $(T_i)_{i \in I}$, where I is a set of roles and channels, is coherent (with respect to G) if there exists a global type G such that for all $i \in I$, $G \lceil_i \leq T_i$, where $\leq$ is the subtyping relation.*

The protocol based on Tiu's counter example is *coherent* with respect to the following global type.

$$\begin{aligned} &begin\,(Data) \text{ from } P \text{ to } Q\,; \\ &fun\,(Function) \text{ from } P \text{ to } Q\,; \\ &done\,(Data) \text{ from } Q \text{ to } P \end{aligned}$$

Notice that, if type equality rather than subtyping is used in the definition of coherence, then Tiu's counter example is not coherent. Thus subtyping relaxes the corresponding definition in [12].

The proof of the following proposition follows from Lemmas 4 and 5.

Proposition 1. *Any coherent protocol is multiparty compatible.*

Proof. Assume that $(T_i)_{i \in I}$ is coherent. Hence there exists G such that for all $i \in I$, $G \lceil_i \leq T_i$. By Lemma 4, the multiset of of protocols $(G \lceil_i)_{i \in I}$ is multiparty compatible. Furthermore, by Lemma 5, since for all $i \in I$, $G \lceil_i \leq T_i$, $(T_i)_{i \in I}$ is also multiparty compatible.   □

The converse of Proposition 1 is more difficult, since given only the local protocols, we must construct, or *synthesise*, a global protocol given only the local types. In general synthesis of a global protocol is not possible [5], hence an open question is the following: under what conditions is a multiparty compatible family of local protocols is coherent.

The protocols **Client**, **Leader$'$**, **Participant** are coherent, since the definition of coherence permits subtyping. However they are also coherent with respect to the global protocol below.

$$\begin{aligned} &\text{par } \{\ p\_begin\,(Payload) \text{ from } Client \text{ to } Participant\,; \\ &\qquad\quad prepare\,(Timestamp) \text{ from } Participant \text{ to } Leader\ \} \\ &\text{and } l\_begin\,(Payload) \text{ from } Client \text{ to } Leader\,; \\ &\text{par } c\_commit\,(Timestamp) \text{ from } Leader \text{ to } Client \\ &\text{and } p\_commit\,(Timestamp) \text{ from } Leader \text{ to } Participant \end{aligned}$$

The global type above is more general than the global type in Fig. 1, with respect to the subtyping relation over global types defined below.

Definition 6. *For global types G_0 and G_1 with set of participants and channels I, if for all $i \in I$, $G_0 \lceil_i \leq G_1 \lceil_i$, then $G_0 \leq G_1$.*

Following [18], we say that the most general coherent global protocol, with respect to the above subtyping relation, with respect to the multiset of protocols, is the *principal global type* for that multiset of local protocols. Hence the above global type is the principal global type for **Client, Leader', Participant**.

For the local protocols **Client'**, **Leader"** and **Participant'** from Fig. 5, the principal global type is as follows.

> **par** *p_begin*(*Payload*) **from** *Client* **to** *Participant*
> **and** *l_begin*(*Payload*) **from** *Client* **to** *Leader* ;
> **choice at** *Participant*
>   { *prepare*(*Timestamp*) **from** *Participant* **to** *Leader* ;
>   **par** *c_commit*(*Timestamp*) **from** *Leader* **to** *Client*
>   **and** *p_commit*(*Timestamp*) **from** *Leader* **to** *Participant* }
>   **or** { *p_abort*(*Error*) **from** *Participant* **to** *Leader* ;
>   *c_abort*(*Error*) **from** *Leader* **to** *Client* }

Notice that, since subtyping for external choice and internal choice are dual to each other, there is no subtype relationship between the global type above and the global type in Fig. 1. Subtyping of global protocols should preserve coherence.

Proposition 2. *If $(T_i)_{i \in I}$ is coherent with respect to G_1 and $G_0 \leq G_1$, then $(T_i)_{i \in I}$ is coherent with respect to G_0.*

The proof follows immediately from the definitions.

Asynchronous Sessions. Assume that we use asynchronous communication channels, where a send message event happens before the corresponding receive message event, and furthermore the order messages are received are not related to the order in which messages are sent. The projection to asynchronous channels is the same as the projection for synchronous channels except the following case.

$$d(S) \text{ from } P \text{ to } Q\lceil_c = \begin{cases} \text{sync } c(S) \text{ to } Q \ ; \ {\sim}c(S) \text{ from } P & \text{if } c = d \\ \{\} & \text{otherwise} \end{cases}$$

We can establish that, for protocols that use synchronous channels and can successfully complete, the protocols can successfully complete using asynchronous channels in place of synchronous channels. This observation follows immediately from Lemma 4, Corollary 1, and the observation that sync T and $U \leq T \ ; \ U$.

Corollary 2. *If G is a global protocol, where I is the set of roles and channels appearing in G, then using asynchronous channels, $(G\lceil_i)_{i \in I}$ is multiparty compatible.*

However, the converse does not hold. There exist sessions that may successfully complete using asynchronous channels, that can never complete successfully using synchronous channels. The methodology in this work can also be adapted to evaluate the termination potential of protocols where channels are queues of length up to two, for which stronger guarantees on the order in which messages are receive on channels are guaranteed [12].

3.3 Complexity and a Path to Implementation

Deciding provability in the calculus MAV is a PSPACE-complete problem. This complexity bound can be established directly from existing results. In particular, since the calculus extends MALL which is PSPACE-hard [17], there is a trivial polynomial reduction from MALL to MAV, i.e. the direct embedding of propositions, such that a proposition is provable in MALL if and only if its embedding is provable in MAV. Furthermore, by the argument in [17], the length of each independent branch in a proof is polynomial.

Proposition 3. *The problem of deciding whether a local type in MAV is provable is PSPACE-complete.*

A consequence of the above complexity result is provability of local types in MAV can be reduced to QBF, the canonical PSPACE-complete problem, for which sufficiently efficient solvers exist. Thereby properties of sessions, such as multiparty compatibility, can be verified for protocols of a realistic size.

4 Related Work and Conclusion

Correspondences between session types and variants or extensions of linear logic have been studied in related work. The study of the "proofs as processes" interpretation of *intuitionistic linear logic* using the linear λ-calculus was initiated by Abramsky [1], and has been adapted explicitly to asynchronous sessions [7]. An alternative approach due to Caires and Pfenning [3] assigns propositions in intuitionistic linear logic to channel names, where the proposition represents the session performed on the named channel. Wadler [22] brings light to the linear λ-calculus and channel approaches, by proving that a variant of the linear λ-calculus can be translated faithfully into a process calculus and type system where propositions in (classical) linear logic are assigned to channel names. In both the intuitionistic [3] and classical [22] interpretations, intuitively, the tensor product is interpreted asymmetrically as follows: "$A \otimes B$ is the type of a channel that outputs an A *and then* behaves as B." Both approaches argue that the symmetry of the tensor product can be recovered using an isomorphism induced by a process that flips the order of actions.

We make a different choice. We interpret sequentiality using an explicit noncommutative operator. This relieves the commutative operators so that they can be used to model symmetric features such as parallel composition. For the calculus in this work, the results presented, notably the consistency of subtyping (Corollary 1) and the multiparty compatibility of coherent protocols (Proposition 1), follow directly from the proof theoretic result in Theorem 1. Thus, by adopting the calculus of structures to express the semantics of local types, we reduce several problems in session types to a generalised cut elimination result.

Acknowledgements. This work is supported by a grant of the Romanian National Authority for Scientific Research, project number PN-II-ID-PCE-2011-3-0919. The second author received support from MOE Tier 2 grant MOE2014-T2-2-076.

References

1. Abramsky, S.: Computational interpretations of linear logic. Theoret. Comput. Sci. **111**(1), 3–57 (1993)
2. Benzaken, V., Castagna, G., Frisch, A.: CDuce: an XML-centric general-purpose language. ACM SIGPLAN Not. **38**(9), 51–63 (2003)
3. Caires, L., Pfenning, F.: Session types as intuitionistic linear propositions. In: Gastin, P., Laroussinie, F. (eds.) CONCUR 2010. LNCS, vol. 6269, pp. 222–236. Springer, Heidelberg (2010)
4. Chaudhuri, K., Guenot, N., Straßburger, L.: The focused calculus of structures. In: EACSL, vol. 12, pp. 159–173 (2011)
5. Deniélou, P.-M., Yoshida, N.: Multiparty compatibility in communicating automata: characterisation and synthesis of global session types. In: Fomin, F.V., Freivalds, R., Kwiatkowska, M., Peleg, D. (eds.) ICALP 2013, Part II. LNCS, vol. 7966, pp. 174–186. Springer, Heidelberg (2013)
6. Gay, S., Hole, M.: Subtyping for session types in the pi calculus. Acta Informatica **42**(2–3), 191–225 (2005)
7. Gay, S.J., Vasconcelos, V.T.: Linear type theory for asynchronous session types. J. Funct. Program. **20**(1), 19 (2010)
8. Gischer, J.L.: The equational theory of pomsets. Theoret. Comput. Sci. **61**(2–3), 199–224 (1988)
9. Guglielmi, A.: A system of interaction and structure. ACM Trans. Comput. Logic **8**, 1–64 (2007)
10. Honda, K.: Types for dyadic interaction. In: Best, E. (ed.) CONCUR 1993. LNCS, vol. 715, pp. 509–523. Springer, Heidelberg (1993)
11. Honda, K., Mukhamedov, A., Brown, G., Chen, T.-C., Yoshida, N.: Scribbling interactions with a formal foundation. In: Natarajan, R., Ojo, A. (eds.) ICDCIT 2011. LNCS, vol. 6536, pp. 55–75. Springer, Heidelberg (2011)
12. Honda, K., Yoshida, N., Carbone, M.: Multiparty asynchronous session types. ACM SIGPLAN Not. **43**(1), 273–284 (2008)
13. Horne, R.: The consistency and complexity of multiplicative additive system virtual. Sci. Ann. Comput. Sci. **XXV**(2), 245–316 (2015). doi:10.7561/SACS.2015.2.245
14. Hu, R., Neykova, R., Yoshida, N., Demangeon, R., Honda, K.: Practical interruptible conversations. In: Legay, A., Bensalem, S. (eds.) RV 2013. LNCS, vol. 8174, pp. 130–148. Springer, Heidelberg (2013)
15. Hu, R., Yoshida, N., Honda, K.: Session-based distributed programming in java. In: Vitek, J. (ed.) ECOOP 2008. LNCS, vol. 5142, pp. 516–541. Springer, Heidelberg (2008)
16. Kahramanogullari, O.: Maude as a platform for designing and implementing deep inference systems. ENTCS **219**, 35–50 (2008)

17. Lincoln, P., et al.: Decision problems for propositional linear logic. Ann. Pure Appl. Logic **56**(1), 239–311 (1992)
18. Mostrous, D., Yoshida, N., Honda, K.: Global principal typing in partially commutative asynchronous sessions. In: Castagna, G. (ed.) ESOP 2009. LNCS, vol. 5502, pp. 316–332. Springer, Heidelberg (2009)
19. Ng, N., Yoshida, N., Honda, K.: Multiparty session C: safe parallel programming with message optimisation. In: Furia, C.A., Nanz, S. (eds.) TOOLS 2012. LNCS, vol. 7304, pp. 202–218. Springer, Heidelberg (2012)
20. Pierce, B., Sangiorgi, D.: Typing and subtyping for mobile processes. In: LICS 1993, pp. 376–385. IEEE (1993)
21. Tiu, A.: A system of interaction, structure II: the need for deep inference. Logical Methods Comput. Sci. **2**(2), 1–24 (2006)
22. Wadler, P.: Propositions as sessions. J. Funct. Prog. **24**(2–3), 384–418 (2014)

Using Refinement in Formal Development of OS Security Model

Petr N. Devyanin[1(✉)], Alexey V. Khoroshilov[2], Victor V. Kuliamin[2], Alexander K. Petrenko[2], and Ilya V. Shchepetkov[2]

[1] Educational and Methodical Community of Information Security, Moscow, Russia
peter_devyanin@hotmail.com
[2] Institute for System Programming, Russian Academy of Sciences, Moscow, Russia
{khoroshilov,kuliamin,petrenko,shchepetkov}@ispras.ru

Abstract. The paper presents work in progress on formal development of an operating system security model for the purpose of its deductive verification. We consider two approaches to formalize the security model. The first one is to build a monolithic model, another one is to build a hierarchical model using the refinement technique. The main criteria for comparison are costs of development, simplicity of maintenance and confidence in the quality of the formal model. The results are twofold. On the one hand, refinement helped us to deal with complexity of the formal model, to improve its readability and to simplify automatic proofs. However, deep understanding of the security model details and careful planning were absolutely necessary to build a reasonable hierarchical model. The monolithic approach allowed to quickly start formalization and helped to study the details of the security model, but the resulting formal model became hard to maintain and explore.

Keywords: Security model · Formal verification · Refinement · Event-B

1 Introduction

Traditionally computer security models are expressed by combining a natural language and mathematical notations. Proofs of their correctness and consistency are performed by hand. Such proofs are error prone and not completely reliable. Besides, the reliability of manual proofs decreases with increasing size and complexity of the models.

Formal methods are promising approaches for specification and verification of software systems [10]. Validation of the RBAC ANSI 2012 standard confirmed that they could be successfully used for proving the correctness of security models [8]. Although this standard is widely used in industry, numerous problems were identified and fixed with the help of formal method B [1].

The research was supported by the Ministry of Education and Science of the Russian Federation (unique project identifier RFMEFI60414X0051).

M. Mazzara and A. Voronkov (Eds.): PSI 2015, LNCS 9609, pp. 107–115, 2016.
DOI: 10.1007/978-3-319-41579-6_9

In this paper we present a work in progress on formal analysis of a mandatory entity-role security model of access and information flows control in Linux (the MROSL DP-model [7]), which provides:

- Mandatory integrity control (MIC).
- Mandatory access control (MAC).
- Role-based access control (RBAC).

The model was implemented in Astra Linux Special Edition[1] as a Linux Security Module by RPA RusBITech in 2014.

In the previous work [6] we chose formal method Event-B and the Rodin platform [2,3] for the MROSL DP-model formalization and verification in order to confirm that the model satisfies the main security requirements – ability to protect entities and subjects from violating their integrity and security levels through authorized accesses.

Like many other formal methods, Event-B allows to develop formal specifications using refinement — a well-known and a widely recommended technique for incremental development [4,9]. Numerous systems were formalized with it [5,11]. Refinement helps to deal with the complexity of systems by decomposing their specifications into separate components. However, it is not clear what disadvantages refinement has, or what additional benefits it offers.

The paper presents the results of comparison of two MROSL DP-model specifications that were developed using different approaches: without use of the refinement technique and with it.

Next section of the paper describe the MROSL DP-model in detail. Sections 3 and 4 give an overview of Event-B and the refinement technique. Section 5 describes formalization of the model. Section 6 provides the comparison of developed specifications. Section 7 summarizes the results of development and verification and outlines further work of the project.

2   Main Features of the MROSL DP-model

Concepts used in the model are entities, sessions, user accounts and roles. Entities represent data objects like files, directories, sockets, etc. Sessions are operating system processes and each of them has the corresponding user account on behalf of which it operates. Roles are containers of permissions allowing to perform certain operations. The main complexity of the model derives from the non-trivial connections between these concepts that in most cases are expressed as functions.

The MROSL DP-model contains three main security features: MIC, MAC and RBAC. Due to MIC each entity, session, user account and role has an integrity level, which can be high or low. High-integrity entities (roles, etc.) are protected from modification by low-integrity sessions. MAC provides a security label to each entity, session, user account and role. MAC prohibits read accesses

---

[1] http://www.astra-linux.com.

to an entity for sessions that do not have greater-or-equal security label (labels are partially ordered). Also it prohibits write accesses to an entity for sessions that do not have the same security label. RBAC strictly limits session rights to perform various operations by providing a set of roles (containers of rights) to each session.

The security model defines 44 operations. 34 of these operations can create or remove entities, sessions, user accounts or roles, change integrity and security labels, add or remove accesses. In addition, 10 operations are defined for more precise security analysis in terms of information flows. Each operation is defined by precondition and postcondition.

Postconditions must not violate any constraints defined in the model. Some of these constraints describe the environment of the security model (e.g. filesystem, processes, accesses), while others define security features mentioned above. Due to the large number of the constraints and their complex nature it is hard to verify the MROSL DP-model by hand without mistakes. Formalizing the model into a machine-readable form allows to prove its correctness in a machine checkable way.

3   Event-B and Rodin

Capability of combining automatic and interactive proofs along with the stories of its successful use for a number of complex projects convinced us to use a B dialect called Event-B. It has a simple notation and comes with a great tool support in the form of the Rodin Platform[2].

An Event-B model (or specification) consists of *contexts* and *machines*. Contexts contain the static parts of the specification: definitions of *constants* and their *axioms*. Machines contain the dynamic or behavioral parts of the specification: *variables*, *invariants* and *events*. Variables and constants can be sets, binary relations, functions, numbers or Boolean data. Values of variables form the current state of the specification and invariants constrain it.

Events represent the way the state may evolve. Each event consists of parameters, guards and actions, though any two of them are optional. Guards restrict values of parameters and states under which the event can occur, while actions change current state of the specification by modifying its variables. The correctness of each change of the specification state needs to be proven since invariants are supposed to hold whenever variable values change.

The Rodin platform supports both modelling and proving and integrates them in a seamless way. Both automatic and interactive proofs are supported. For each case that requires a proof — unambiguity of expressions, invariant preservation and refinement between models (if the refinement technique is used) — Rodin generates a corresponding proof obligation. Full proof of a model means that all generated proof obligations are discharged.

---

[2] http://www.event-b.org/.

4   Refinement

Refinement technique is well known and supported by many formal methods. Instead of making a monolithic specification that contains all details of the system, refinement offers to build a series of specifications, where each specification is a refinement of the previous one (or abstract one) and the last one is the most concrete one. It allows to build a specification gradually, adding new features step by step, and thus to deal with complexities that arise during formalization of large systems.

There are two major approaches of refinement: *posit-and-prove* and *rule-based* [5]. In the first approach each refinement step must be proved to be correct, while in the second approach refinement is performed automatically using transformation rules, from which it follows that this refinement is correct by construction.

Refinement can be used in two ways. The aim of *horizontal* refinement (often called *superposition* refinement) is to add complexity to the specification by introducing new properties and events extending old ones. The second way is to use refinement to add details to data structures, such as replacing an abstract variable by a concrete one (*vertical* or *data* refinement).

5   Development

Formalization of the MROSL DP-model is a tricky task because of the size of the model (200 pages) and its complex nature. We started from the development of a monolithic specification that represents the entire security model. Then we used this knowledge to develop a new specification with the refinement technique.

To develop the monolithic specification, we used an iterative approach adding small parts of the system step by step and proving their correctness. It allowed to quickly notice and to fix problems occurring due to misunderstanding of the description of the system, but sometimes it was necessary to repeat existing proofs since every change of the specification could violate them. With this approach we developed the formal specification of the MROSL DP-model and proved its correctness. It took more than a year of work. A number of inaccuracies in the initial description of the model was identified and fixed.

	Number	Lines of code
Finite sets	7	7
Constants	26	26
Axioms	39	83
State variables	48	48
Invariants	161	394
Events	43	1954

Fig. 1. The composition and the size of the monolithic specification.

The size of this specification is approximately 2 500 lines of code, which is quite small compared with the textual description. More details can be seen in Fig. 1.

On top of this experience we developed a refined specification. Despite the fact that we were perfectly familiar with the MROSL DP-model at that moment, several times we had to completely rewrite the specification due to inaccurate planning. As a result we managed to decompose the original model into 16 parts and to determine the order in which they should be implemented as a series of specifications. Our refinement was correct by construction, so no additional proof obligations were generated.

6   Comparison

During the analysis of the refined specification we noticed some differences from the monolithic one. The refined version is easier to understand, more human readable and structured. Moreover, refinement provides a natural way to add new details to the specification. It is easier to change the specification, and, unlike the monolithic specification, changes can affect fewer of discharged proofs. We kept possible changes in mind during refinement planning, and it helped to achieve our additional goal – to simplify maintenance.

Despite the aforementioned advantages of the refined specification, most design decisions (which data structures to use, how to express invariants better, etc.) are the same. The main comparison characteristics like the size of the specification and the difficulty of interactive proofs are also similar in our case. However, the development of the monolithic specification required much less effort — due to the absence of refinement planning, which is quite a difficult task, so our main goal (to prove correctness of the model) is achieved faster with it.

Better readability of the refined model can be exposed with two examples[3]. Figure 2 demonstrates a part of the **create_session** event from the monolithic specification. This event is an analogue of the corresponding operation from the MROSL DP-model. It models the creation of a new session. It has parameters, preconditions (guards, in terms of Event-B) and postconditions (actions). Guards and actions are lines with @grd and @act labels, parameters are defined in the **any** section.

Arrows in Fig. 2 group related guards and actions by parts of the model to which they belong. It is easy to notice a lack of structure here: a lot of closely related guards and actions are scattered throughout the text. For instance, @grd2 — @grd4, @grd7 — @grd9, @grd25, @act6, @act7 are represent profiles and executable files. Moreover, parts of one event can be associated not only with each other, but also with the existing invariants and parts of other events. There is no way to denote their connection in Event-B without use of refinement.

Actually the refined model is a series of specifications. Each of them describes a specific feature of the MROSL DP-model. Figure 3 represents one of the refinement steps — adding the specification modeling profiles and executable files.

---

[3] These examples are provided with permission of RPA RusBITech.

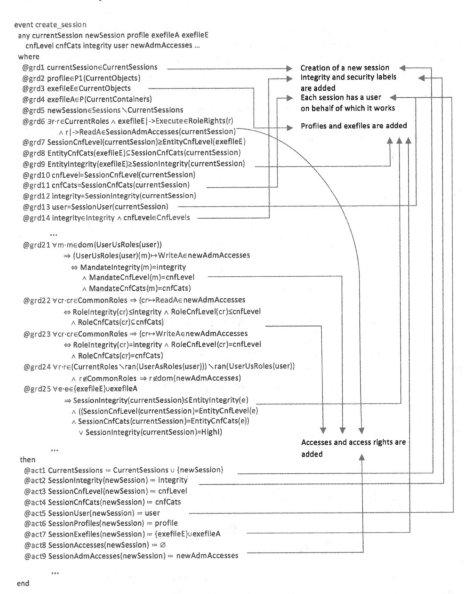

Fig. 2. A part of the `create_session` event from the monolithic specification.

We can see how a particular feature — profiles and exefiles — affects existing events (`create_user`, `set_user_labels` and `create_session`) and the requirements (invariants) it must satisfy. This specification is quite compact, it is easy to understand and maintain.

To achieve this it is vital to know possibilities of refinement, its restrictions, features of the chosen formal method, and of course the system itself. Each wrong

```
machine N11 refines N10 sees C3

...

invariants
   @UserProfiles_type UserProfiles∈CurrentUserAccounts→P1(CurrentEntities)
   @SessionProfiles_type SessionProfiles∈CurrentSessions→P(Entities)
   @SessionExefiles_type SessionExefiles∈CurrentSessions→P(Entities)
   @UserProfilesIntIsCorrect
      ∀u,p·u∈CurrentUserAccounts ∧ p∈UserProfiles(u) ⇒ UserIntegrity(u)=EntityIntegrity(p)
   @UserProfilesCnfIsCorrect
      ∀u,p·u∈CurrentUserAccounts ∧ p∈UserProfiles(u) ⇒ UserCnfLevel(u)=EntityCnfLevel(p)

   ...

events

...

event create_user extends create_user
 any profiles
 where
   @grd33 profiles∈P1(CurrentEntities)
   @grd34 ∀p·p∈profiles ⇒ EntityIntegrity(p)=integrity
   @grd35 ∀p·p∈profiles ⇒ EntityCnfLevel(p)=cnfLevel
 then
   @act16 UserProfiles(user) ≔ profiles
end

event set_user_labels extends set_user_labels
 any profiles
 where
   @grd58 profiles∈P1(CurrentEntities)
   @grd59 ∀p·p∈profiles ⇒ EntityIntegrity(p)=integrity
   @grd60 ∀p·p∈profiles ⇒ EntityCnfLevel(p)=cnfLevel
 then
   @act16 UserProfiles(user) ≔ profiles
end
 ...
event create_session extends create_session
 any exefileA exefileE profile
 where
   @grd12 profile∈P1(CurrentObjects)
   @grd13 exefileE∈CurrentObjects
   @grd14 exefileA∈P(CurrentContainers)
   @grd15 EntityCnfLevel(exefileE)⊆SessionCnfLevel(currentSession)
   @grd16 EntityCnfLevel(exefileE)⊆UserCnfLevel(user)
   @grd17 EntityIntLevel(exefileE)≥integrity
 then
   @act7 SessionProfiles(newSession) ≔ profile
   @act8 SessionExefiles(newSession) ≔ {exefileE}∪exefileA
end
end
```

Fig. 3. A part of the refined specification related to profiles and executable files.

decision can eventually lead to the need of total redesign of a specification. In some cases wrong refinement can even complicate formalization and analysis.

In our experience, automatic provers operate a little better on the refined specification. Some statistics can be found in Fig. 4. It could be explained by the fact that the Rodin platform was specifically designed to support the refinement technique.

Specifications	Monolithic	Refined
Automatically proved	70% of the model	75% of the model

Fig. 4. Statistics of operation of automatic provers.

The MROSL DP-model contains precise description of operations in form of preconditions and postconditions. It simplifies the development of both specifications, but also restricts the refinement possibilities. Thus, in our case (and for the class of similar systems) refinement offers only better readability and structure of specifications, in exchange for increased complexity of development.

7   Conclusions and Future Work

We completed formalization and verification of the MROSL DP-model using formal method Event-B in two ways — without use of the refinement technique and with it. The approach without refinement allowed us to develop a monolithic specification that contains the entire security model, while refinement was used to build an ordered series of specifications, where each specification is a refinement of the previous one (or abstract one) and the last one is the most concrete one.

We have found that refinement improves readability and simplifies automatic proofs. But to achieve this it is vital to know possibilities of refinement, its restrictions, features of the chosen formal method, and the system under verification (the MROSL DP-model, in our case). Careful planning is also needed. The development of the monolithic specification required much less effort, but the resulting specification is hard to maintain and explore.

On the next steps of the project we are going to use refinement for formalization and verification of a hierarchical MROSL DP-model, which is under development. It will contain a basic layer that can be extended to a security model of hypervisor, operating system, etc. We believe that there will be difficulties with refinement due to a nonlinear hierarchy of the model and multiple inheritance.

References

1. Abrial, J.-R.: The B-Book: Assigning Programs to Meanings. Cambridge University Press, Cambridge (1996)

2. Abrial, J.-R.: Modeling in Event-B: System and Software Engineering. Cambridge University Press, Cambridge (2010)
3. Abrial, J.-R., Butler, M., Hallerstede, S., Hoang, T.S., Mehta, F., Voisin, L.: Rodin: an open toolset for modelling and reasoning in Event-B. Int. J. Softw. Tools Technol. Transfer **12**(6), 447–466 (2010)
4. Abrial, J.-R., Hallerstede, S.: Refinement, decomposition, and instantiation of discrete models: application to Event-B. Fundamentae Informatica **77**(1,2), 1–28 (2007)
5. Damchoom, K.: An incremental refinement approach to a development of a flash-based file system in Event-B. Ph.D. thesis, University of Southampton, School of Electronics and Computer Science (2010)
6. Devyanin, P.N., Khoroshilov, A.V., Kuliamin, V.V., Petrenko, A.K., Shchepetkov, I.V.: Formal verification of OS security model with alloy and Event-B. In: Ait Ameur, Y., Schewe, K.-D. (eds.) ABZ 2014. LNCS, vol. 8477, pp. 309–313. Springer, Heidelberg (2014)
7. Devyanin, P.N.: Security models of computer systems: access control and information flows (in Russian). Hot line - Telecom (2013)
8. Huynh, N., Frappier, M., Mammar, A., Laleau, R., Desharnais, J.: Validating the RBAC ANSI 2012 standard using B. In: Ait Ameur, Y., Schewe, K.-D. (eds.) ABZ 2014. LNCS, vol. 8477, pp. 255–270. Springer, Heidelberg (2014)
9. Wirth, N.: Program development by stepwise refinement. CACM Commun. ACM **14**, 221–227 (1971)
10. Woodcock, J., Larsen, P.G., Bicarregui, J., Fitzgerald, J.: Formal methods: practice and experience. ACM Comput. Surv. **41**(4), 1–39 (2009)
11. Yeganefard, S., Butler, M., Rezazadeh, A.: Evaluation of a guideline by formal modelling of cruise control system in Event-B. In: NFM 2010, pp. 182–191 (2010)

Conflict Resolution in Multi-agent Systems with Typed Connections for Ontology Population

Natalia Garanina$^{(\boxtimes)}$, Elena Sidorova, and Stepan Anokhin

A.P. Ershov Institute of Informatics Systems,
Lavrent'ev av., 6, Novosibirsk 630090, Russia
{garanina,lena}@iis.nsk.su, saanokhin@gmail.com

Abstract. The paper presents a conflict resolution algorithm for multi-agent systems with agents connected by relations of different types and worth. The result of conflict resolution is a conflict-free set of agents. We apply this algorithm for the ambiguity resolution problem in ontology population based on multiagent natural language text analysis.

1 Introduction

The motivation of our work is studying the problem of ambiguity resolution in the framework of ontology population from natural language texts. In [4] we suggest text analysis algorithms producing a system of information agents. However, features of natural language cause the ontology population ambiguities, which those agents have to resolve.

The ambiguity problem in a natural language processing can be classified into the following types: syntactic, lexical, structural, semantic, pragmatic ambiguity etc. The widespread approach WSD (Word Sense Disambiguation) resolves ambiguity for isolated words using subject information [1,9]. However, for disambiguation in the framework of ontology population the problem has to be solved for ontology instances of classes and relations retrieved from a given text which could populate a given ontology. Also there may be necessary to consider word-complexes not isolated words only.

The allied approach to ontology-driven disambiguation which uses a context of a given input text is suggested in [8]. Sequential sentence-by-sentence ambiguity resolution is performed. For every sentence, a set of semantic interpretation is constructed. Each interpretation is represented by a graph with vertices as ontology entities and edges as ontology relations. Every next sentence may increase scores of some interpretation of the previous ones. Hence the preference of alternative meaning of words is based on ontology relations. This approach has low accuracy because such on-the-fly choice of alternative takes into account the nearest context mainly. Our approach uses the maximal context available from

---

The research has been supported by Russian Foundation for Basic Research (grant 13-01-00643, 15-07-04144, 13-07-00422).

M. Mazzara and A. Voronkov (Eds.): PSI 2015, LNCS 9609, pp. 116–129, 2016.
DOI: 10.1007/978-3-319-41579-6_10

an input text for choosing alternative. Connections between ontology objects (class and relation instances) correspond to informational dependance of the text. Since the approach does not require complete sentence parsing, this considerably simplify the text analysis for ontology population.

We generalize this particular problem of ambiguity resolution for ontology population to a problem of conflict resolution in multi-agent system with typed weighted connections. This abstraction is a basis for resolution of various types of text ambiguities. The presence and evolution of typed connections, affecting internal and external states of an agent, are the main matter of the proposed systems. Such simple models can be used for study and analysis of dynamical multi-agent systems, for instance, social communities and networks, models of cloud distributed computing, etc. In particular, it may be necessary to solve this class of problems of conflict resolution in groups of agents taking into account the number and quality of connections inside a group of agents. An example of such a problem could be the task of determining the election winners in any socially significant structure or club in which the presence and weight of the connections between certain members of the election are important as well as their own weight.

The works on multi-agent systems usually focus on the behavior of agents, methods of communication between agents, knowledge and beliefs of an agent about environment and other agents, etc. [3, 11]. Works concerning conflict resolution process usually consider the process in terms of the behavior of the agent depending on its internal state, reasoning and argumentation methods etc. [7]. The dynamics of the agents connections is not a subject of these researches. There are papers related to the dynamics of weighted connections, but those connections are not the typed and their changes does not affect the internals of the agent [6]. On the other hand there are works on the study of social networks in which the agents are connected by the typed connections, but their weight is irrelevant [2].

In this paper, we propose an algorithm for the conflict resolution in the multi-agent system with typed weighted connections. Protocols of the agents executing this algorithm are presented. It is shown that the algorithm of conflict resolution can be used to resolve ambiguities in the process of semantic analysis of a natural language text for ontology population of subject domains.

The rest of the paper is organized as follows. The next Sect. 2 gives base definitions and the problem statement. Section 3 describes agents of our systems, their action protocols, and the main conflict resolution algorithm. The following Sect. 4 shows that the extended base multi-agent text analysis algorithm for ontology population forms a multi-agent system with typed connections and the conflict resolution algorithm can be used for the context-depending ambiguity resolution. We conclude in the last Sect. 5 with a discussion of further research.

2   Problem Statement and Base Definitions

Let a set of conflict types be $CTypes = \{remove, delete, decrease\}$. We define *Multi-agent System with Typed Connections* (MASC) as a tuple $S = (A, C, I_C, w_C, w_A, T_A, T_C)$, where

- A is a finite set of agents;
- C is a finite set of connection;
- mapping $I_C : C \longrightarrow 2^{A \times A}$ is an interpretation function of (directed) connections between agents;
- mapping $w_A : A \longrightarrow \mathbb{N}$ is a worth function for agents;
- mapping $w_C : C \longrightarrow \mathbb{N}$ is a worth function for connections;
- mapping $T_A : A \longrightarrow CTypes \times 2^C$ matches agents with types and
  $\forall a \in A\ (\exists ct \in CTypes, Con \subseteq C\ :\ (Con \neq \emptyset \wedge T_A(a) = (ct, Con)) \Rightarrow (\forall c \in Con \exists a' \in A\ :\ (a, a') \in I_C(c) \vee (a', a) \in I_C(c))$, i.e. connections in an image of the function must be connections of the corresponding agent;
- mapping $T_C : C \times A \times A \longrightarrow CTypes$ matches connections with types and
  $\forall c \in C, a, a' \in A : T_C(c, a, a') \neq \emptyset \Leftrightarrow (a, a') \in I_C(c)$, i.e. this function is defined for an instances of connections;
  mapping $T_D : C \times A \longrightarrow \mathbb{N}$ matches connections of *decrease* type with natural numbers: $\forall c \in C, a, a' \in AT_C(c, a, a') = decrease \Rightarrow T_D(c, a) = d$.

For every agent $a \in A$ we define the following sets of agents and connections. The similar definitions are used in the graph theory, but we would like to reformulate them for the clarity. We omit symmetric definitions of ancestors $Anc*$ (for descendants $Des*$) and predecessors $Pred*$ (for successors $Succ*$) for the brevity:

- $C_a = \{c \in C | \exists a' \in A : (a, a') \in I_C(c) \bigvee (a', a) \in I_C(c)\}$ is connections of a;
- $Des_a^c = \{a' \in A \mid (a, a') \in I_C(c)\}$ is a set of descendants by c connection;
- $Des_a = \bigcup_{c \in C_a} Des_a^c$ is a set of descendants;
- $Succ_a^c = Des_a^c \cup \bigcup_{a' \in Des_a^c} Succ_{a'}^c$ is a set of successors by c connection;
- $Succ_a = Des_a \cup \bigcup_{a' \in Des_a} Succ_{a'} = \bigcup_{c \in C_a} Succ_a^c$ is a set of successors.

We deal with MASC in which $Succ_a^c \cap Pred_a^c = \emptyset$, i.e. every connection has no cycle. We consider conflicts of agents which resolution depends on degree of connectivity of an agent with other agents, on its own worth, and on its influence determined by its type. The degree of connectivity is determined by a weight of an agent which could be defined as follows. For every $a \in A$ mapping

- $wt_{Des}^a : C \longrightarrow \mathbb{N}$ is *the weight function of connection successors* defined by
  $wt_{Des}^a(c) = \sum_{a' \in Des_a^c} wt_{Des}^{a'}(c) + w_A(a)$;
- $wt_{Anc}^a : C \longrightarrow \mathbb{N}$ is *the weight function of connection predecessors* defined by
  $wt_{Anc}^a(c) = \sum_{a' \in Anc_a^c} wt_{Anc}^{a'}(c) + w_A(a)$;
- $wt : A \longrightarrow \mathbb{N}$ is *the weight function of agents* defined by
  $wt(a) = \sum_{c \in C_a} (wt_{Des}^a(c) + wt_{Anc}^a(c) - 2w_A(a)) + w_A(a)$.

The *weight of system* S is $wt(S) = \sum_{a \in A} wt(a)$.

Let *conflict set* $Conf \subseteq A \times A$ be a given set of conflict pairs of agents, and $Conf$ satisfies the following inheritance property: $\forall (a, b) \in Conf (\exists a', b' \in A, c \in C\ :\ (a, a') \in I_C(c) \wedge (b, b') \in I_C(c) \bigvee (a', a) \in I_C(c) \wedge (b', b) \in I_C(c)) \Rightarrow (a', b') \in Conf)$, i.e. descendants or ancestors by the same connection inherit the conflict. For every $(a, a') \in Conf$, agent a' is a *minor agent* if a wins over

a'. Determination of the winner depends on the weights of conflicting agents. Successors and predecessors of the minor agent could be involved in its conflict also. We say that *a conflict is resolved* if agent a, which is the minor agent (or is the agent involved by agent b via connection c), performs the following *conflict actions*:

1. if $T_A(a) = (remove, \emptyset)$ (or $T_C(c, b, a) = remove$), then a removes itself from A with all its connections and involves all its descendants and ancestors to perform conflict actions induced the corresponding connections;
2. if $T_A(a) = (delete, Del)$ (or $T_C(c, b, a) = delete$), then it deletes all connections in Del (or $Del = \{c\}$), and involves its descendants and ancestors connected by these connections to perform conflict actions induced the corresponding connections;
3. if $T_A(a) = (decrease, Dec)$ (or $T_C(c, b, a) = decrease$), then it decreases its own worth for all connections from $Dec = \{c \mid T_C(c, a, a') = decrease \vee T_C(c, a', a) = decrease\}$ (or $Dec = \{c\}$) by number $\sum_{c \in Dec} T_D(c, a)$, and involves its descendants and ancestors connected by these connections to perform conflict actions induced the corresponding connections.

A conflict pair of agents is deleted from $Conf$ after conflict resolution. Conflict actions can decrease the weight of all involved agents and their successors and predecessors. Hence, the set of minor agents is unstable in general. Moreover, the first conflict action reduces the conflict set and the set of agents in MASC. Hence the system is dynamic due to conflict resolution. Change of the system weight with the fixed weight function depends on a policy of conflict actions for every agent. *Problem of conflict resolution in MASC* is to get a conflict-free MASC of the maximal weight. We develop a multiagent algorithm that produces such system.

3   Conflict Resolution in MASC

For constructing the conflict-free multiagent system of the maximal weight by resolving a chain of conflicts we should know how much each conflict resolution step affects the system weight. Hence, for every agent in conflict, it is necessary to compute its *conflict weight* which is the difference between the system weight before and after the agent conflict resolution. Really the conflict weight of every conflict agent is the sum of induced "conflict weights" of all agents involved by it. Our algorithm for constructing the conflict-free set uses distributed computing of this function with polynomial complexity.

Action protocols for conflict resolution used by MASC agents form a multiagent system of conflict resolution MACR. The system MACR includes set of MASC agents and an agent-master. Note that a fully distributed version of our algorithm could be developed but it should be quite ineffective. The result of agent interactions by protocols described below is the conflict-free MASC. All agents execute their protocols in parallel until the master detects termination. The system is dynamic because MASC agents can be deleted from the system.

The agents are connected by synchronous duplex channels. The master agent is connected with all agents, MASC agents are connected with their ancestors and descendants. Messages are transmitted instantly via a reliable medium and stored in channels until being read.

Let $A = \{a_1, ..., a_n\}$ be a MASC agents set, and M be the master agent. Let Ai be an interface protocol of agent a_i, and M be the protocol of actions of the agent-master M. Then multi-agent conflict resolution algorithm MACR can be presented in pseudocode as follows:

MACR:: parallel {A1} ...{An} {M}

Our algorithm for constructing a conflict-free MASC of the maximal weight is a greedy algorithm. At every step it chooses for resolution a conflict which has the maximal effect to the system weight. This effect depends on conflict actions of involved agents. Hence the following algorithms should be implemented: calculating of agents' weights, calculating of agents' conflict weights, the main algorithm for constructing a conflict-free set of agents of the maximal weight. The weights' calculation should be performed by MASC agents, but constructing a conflict-free set should be conducted by the master agent.

We define an interface protocol Ai for system agents, which specifies agent's reactions for incoming messages. Messages for a system agent include actions act which agent should to perform and information for those actions body: $\text{msg} = \text{act} \times \text{body}$, where $\text{act} = \{\text{start}, \text{stop}, \text{ToAct}, \text{ToChange}\}$, where ToAct is to perform a conflict action protocol, ToChange is to change weight protocol, and their parameters body described below at the protocols' definitions. An agent stays in a wait mode until an input message causes the agent to react. Let function get(Set) gets an arbitrary element in nonempty set Set and removes it from the set.

Interface Protocol of Agent a.

```
Ai (a) ::
 set of msg Input; msg mess = (start, null);
1. while ( mess.act != stop )
2.    if ( Input != ∅ ) then {
3.       mess = get (Input);
4.       if(mess.act = ToAct) then a.Act(mess.body);
5.       if(mess.act = ToChange) then a.ChangeWeight(mess.body);}
```

(1) The Main Algorithm for Conflict Resolution

Let us give an informal description of protocol Master. Let $Conf_A = \{a \in A | \exists b \in A (a,b) \in Conf\}$ be a set of agents in a conflict. Until this set becomes empty master should repeat the following steps: (1) to compute agents' weights by launching agents to perform protocols WeightComp in parallel; (2) to compute agents' conflict weights by launching conflict agents to perform protocols Act in sequence; before every launching local data of every agent should be saved, and after they should be restored for correct computations of conflict weights; (3) to find the minor partner of the agent of maximal impact for the system weight, with the maximal difference in their conflict weights; (4) to resolve the conflict of these agents by launching the minor agent to perform protocol Act; (5) to remove the conflict of the agent and conflicts of deleted agents from the conflict set; (6) to remove from A agents which perform (induced) conflict action 1; (7) to recalculate the set of conflicts and the set of agents in conflicts. We consider the master can detect termination moments of other agents' parallel computations at every step. The protocol of conflict weights computing and weights changing belongs to the class of wave echo algorithms [10].

Let integer weight of agent a be $a.\mathtt{wt}$, its conflict weight be $a.\mathtt{cwt}$, boolean variable $a.\mathtt{Rmvd}$ is true if a is removed by its conflict action 1, and false otherwise. Let function $\mathtt{save\_data(a)}$ saves data of agent a (its current weight, worth, set of connections, sets of descendants and ancestors, and existence status), and function $\mathtt{restore\_data(a)}$ restore these data. Let function ($\mathtt{max\_wConf}(X)$) ($\mathtt{min\_wConf}(X)$) return the agent of the maximal (minimal) conflict weight in set of agents X. Let Del_A be set of agents removed from A due to particular conflict resolution.

Protocol of the Master Agent for Conflict Resolution.

```
Master ::
agent a, b;
1. while ( Conf_A ≠ ∅ ){
2.        forall a∈ A in_parallel WeightComp(a);
3.        forall a∈ Conf_A in_sequence {
4.                forall b∈ A save_data(b);
5.                a.Act(T_A(a).type, null, null, true);
6.                forall b∈ A restore_data(b); }
7.        a = max_wConf( Conf_A );
8.        b = min_wConf( PartConf_a );
9.        b.Act( T_A(b).type, null, null, false);
10.       Conf = Conf \ {(a,b)};
11.       A = A \ Del_A;
12.       recalculate( Conf );
13.       recalculate( Conf_A );}
14. forall a∈ A in_parallel send ( stop ) to a;
```

(2) Computing Agents' Weight

Let the set of connection of agent a be $C_a = \{c_1, \ldots, c_n\}$. Following the definitions of the weights the agent launches parallel calculations of the sum weight by every connection c_i for successors $\mathtt{Des}(c_i)$ and for predecessors $\mathtt{Anc}(c_i)$ (line 1) and stores calculated weights in arrays $\mathtt{w\_Des}$ and $\mathtt{w\_Anc}$ respectively. When these parallel calculations are finished, the agent computes its own weight (lines 2–4). The calculation processes have local channels $\mathtt{Input}$ for messages with integer weights of successors (predecessors). They send the weights increased by $w_A(a)$ to predecessors (successors) respectively. We omit the similar description of predecessors' processes $\mathtt{Anc}(c_i)$ for the brevity. All these agent's weights are accessible to the agent for changing in its other protocols.

Protocol of Agent a for Weight Compute.

```
WeightComp (a) ::
```

```
array [C_a] of int: w_Des, w_Anc;
int w_Des_own = 0, w_Anc_own = 0;
```
1. `parallel forall` $c_i \in C_a$ `{Des(`c_i`)} {Anc(`c_i`)}`
2. `w_Des_own =` $\sum_{c_i \in C_a}$`w_Des[`c_i`]` `;`
3. `w_Anc_own =` $\sum_{c_i \in C_a}$`w_Anc[`c_i`]` `;`
4. `a.wt = w_Des_own + w_Anc_own +` $w_A(a)$`;`

`   a.Des(`c_i`) ::`
```
     set of int Input;
     int NumD =
```
$|Des_a^{c_i}|$`;`
1. `w_Des[`c_i`] = 0;`
2. `while( NumD != 0 )`
3. `        if ( Input !=` $\emptyset$ `) then {`
4. `        w_Des[`c_i`] = w_Des[`c_i`] + get( Input ); NumD = NumD - 1;}`
5. `forall ( b`$\in Anc_a^{c_i}$ `) send w_Des[`c_i`]*`$w_C(c_i)$`+`$w_A(a)$ `to b.Des(`c_i`);`

(3) Computing Agents' Conflict Weight

An input for the next protocol Act is a message of the form mess = (ct, x, c, wc), where ct is conflict action type, x is an agent which induce this action, c is a connection with this agent, and wc is true if a conflict weight is computing. Let a *starting agent* have no inducing agent. This protocol a removed agent should not perform (line 1). In (lines 2–5) an agent depending on the type of its conflict action (1) determines its difference in the own weight in variable of temporal conflict weight wConf, (2) forms sets of connections with descendants and ancestors which weights are changing due to this action, and (3) specifies the amount of these changes in variable w (lines 4, 6, 7). Then the agent sends the corresponding messages to the partners (lines 6, 7). The agent launches a wave of weight changing of its successors and predecessors and waits when it finishes (line 8). The agent has local channel Input for messages with changed integer weights of its successors and predecessors. In line 9 it adds these weights to its temporal conflict weight. Note that at this moment the conflict weight characterizes a change in the agent's weight (line 10). Further the agent depending on its conflict type launches a wave of conflict actions of its involved partners (lines 13, 14). If the agent computes its conflict weight it waits when the wave finishes (line 16). Now the local channel Input stores messages with integer induced conflict weights of involved successors and predecessors. In line 16 the agent sums these weights with its temporal conflict weight. If the agent is not a starting agent then it sends its induced conflict weight to the agent which has involved it (line 18). If the agent is a starting agent then it stores its conflict weight (line 19). If the agent is involved in conflict resolution then it can change its local data (lines 20–21).

Protocol of Agent a for Conflict Actions.

```
Act( mess = (ct, x, c, wc) ) :: {
  int w, wConf;
  agent b; connection c;
  set of connections Con;
  set of agents Desa = ∅, Anca = ∅, Part = ∅;
```

```
    set of int Input;
1.  if( a.Rmvd ) then send(doneAct, 0) to x; return;
2.  if( ct = remove ) then act = delMe; Con = C_a;
                        wConf = a.wt; a.Rmvd = true;
3.  if( ct = delete ) then act = delMe;
                        if( x = null ) Con = Del; else Con = c;
                        wConf=∑_{e∈Del}(w_Des[e]+w_Anc[e])*w_C(e);
4.  if( ct = decrease ) then act = decMe; Con = C_a;
                        if( x = null ) w = ∑_{e∈Dec} T_D(e,a);
                        else w = T_D(c,a);
                        wConf = w; w_A(a) = w_A(a) - w;
5.  forall c∈Con {
6.     forall b∈ Des_a^c \ {x};
                if( ct != decrease ) w = w_Anc[c]+w_A(a);
                send (ToChange, act, a, c, w, Anc) to b;
                Desa = Desa∪{b};
7.     forall b∈ Anc_a^c \ {x};
                if( ct != decrease ) w = w_Des[c]+w_A(a);
                send (ToChange, act, a, c, w, Des) to b;
                Anca = Anca∪{b}; }
8.  wait (doneWt) fromall b∈Desa∪Anca;
9.  while ( Input != ∅ ) wConf = wConf + get( Input );
10. a.wt = a.wt - wConf;
11. if ( ct = decrease ) then
                if ( x = null ) Con = Dec; else Con = c;
12. forall c∈Con {
13.        forall b∈ Des_a^c \ {x};
                send (ToAct, T_C(c,a,b), a, c, wc) to b;
                Part = Part∪{b};
14.        forall b∈ Anc_a^c \ {x};
                send (ToAct, T_C(c,b,a), a, c, wc) to b;
                Part = Part∪{b}; }
15. if ( wc ) then
16.        wait (doneAct) fromall b∈Part;
17.        while ( Input != ∅ ) wConf = wConf + get( Input );
18.        if ( x != null ) then send (doneAct, wConf) to x;
19.        else a.cwt = wConf;
20. else if ( ct = remove ) then Del_A = Del_A ∪ {a};
21.        if ( ct = delete ) then Des_a = Des_a\Desa;
                        Anc_a =Anc_a\Anca;   }
```

The next protocol input is a message of the form mess = (act, x, c, w, Rel), where act specifies should the agent a remove (act = delMe) agent x from its ancestors (Rel = Anc) or descendants (Rel = Des) by connection c (lines 1–6). In any case, the agent decreases its corresponding weights by w. Decreasing of the weights affects weights of its successors and predecessors. The agent initiates changing of the weights in line 7 and waits when it finishes (line 8). The local channel `Input` accumulates changing of these weights. The agent sums the differences with its weight difference `w_df` and sends the result to agent x which has induced its weight change (lines 9–11). Its own weight should be decreased by `w_df` also (line 12).

Protocol of Agent a for its Weight Changing.

```
ChangeWeight( mess = (act, x, c, w, Rel) ) :: {
    int w_df;
    agent b;
    set of agents Parts;
    set of int Input;
```
1.   `if( Rel = Anc ) then w_Anc[c] = w_Anc[c] - w;`
2.   `if( act = delMe ) then` $Anc_a^c = Anc_a^c \setminus \{x\}$`;`
3.   `Parts =` Des_a^c`;`
4.   `else w_Des[c] = w_Des[c] - w;`
5.   `if( act = delMe ) then` $Des_a^c = Des_a^c \setminus \{x\}$`;`
6.   `Parts =` Anc_a^c`;`
7.   `forall b∈Parts send (ToChange, decMe, a, c, w, Rel);`
8.   `wait (doneWt) fromall b∈Parts;`
9.   `w_df = w*`$w_C(c)$`;`
10. `while( Input != ∅ ) w_df = w_df + get( Input );`
11. `send (doneWt, w_df) to x;`
12. a`.wt =` a`.wt - w_df; }`

Outline of the main conflict-resolution algorithm performed by the agent-master. Weights of agents are computed in parallel, then conflict weights of conflict agents are computed in sequence. The conflict weights correspond to degree of the agents' influence to post-conflict weight of the system. During computation of conflict weights, changes of the weight and connections of a conflict agent are simulated. The difference between the whole system weights before and after the simulation is calculated. Then the most influential agent is chosen and its least influential conflict partner (the minor agent) performs its conflict action resolving the conflict. If after the resolution there are conflict agent in the system then the above steps repeat again. Correctness of the main algorithm follows from correctness of weights computing and the proper choice of a conflict for resolution due to inheritance property of a conflict set. Really, at every resolution step the agent with the maximal impact to the system weight has to remain in the system.

Outline of the weight computing algorithm performed by every system agent. Parallel computation starts with agents without descendants/ancestors. Connection's ancestors/descendants of every agent accumulate the values from the connection's descendants/ancestors. They sum these values with their worth and send this sum to the connection's ancestors/descendants. The own weight of an agent is the sum of its worth and weight values of all connections. Correctness of the algorithm is based on acyclicity of every connection and could be proved by induction on a structure of the connection graph.

Outline of the conflict weight computing algorithm performed by the conflict agents. The computation is started by a conflict agent. It can remove itself from the system with all its connections, or delete some of its connections, or decrease its worth for some of its connections. In every case, its weight and the weights of partners linked with the agent by these connections are decreased. Hence the agent launches computations of these weight changes. It waits for the end of all computations to guarantee their correctness. Before the computations start, the agent fixes the system weights difference caused by itself directly without taking into account the weight differences caused by involved agents. To calculate the latter differences, the agent launches computations of induced conflict weights of the involved agents in recursive and parallel mode. Due to additivity of conflict weights and acyclicity of connections the conflict weight computation is correct. This fact could be proved by induction on a structure of the connection graph.

A time complexity of recursive parallel algorithms for weights, changes of weights, and conflict weights computations depends on number of connections and is equal to $O(n^2)$, where n is the number of the system agents. The most complicated computation of the main algorithm is the sequential computation of the conflict weights. It takes $O(n^3)$ time. Hence, the general time complexity of the multi-agent algorithm for construction of the conflict-free set of agents is equal to $O(n^3)$.

4   Ambiguity Resolution

The proposed algorithm is applicable for conflict resolution to resolve ambiguities (homonymy) in the framework of ontology population from natural language texts. Paper [4] presents the basic algorithm of semantic analysis of a natural language text for a given domain ontology. In this multi-agent algorithm, agents of two main kinds interact: information agents correspond to meaningful units of the information being retrieved, and rule agents implement population rules of a given ontology and a semantic-syntactic model of a language. The result of the algorithm is a multi-agent system composed of information (class and relation) agents and lexical objects related to instances of classes and relations of the ontology. However, due to the features of natural language, several information agents may correspond to the same fragments of the text. This fact generates semantic ambiguity: the ontology can be populate by the only one of them. In the paper [5] we proposed to evaluate the cardinality of agents' contexts, i.e. how much an agent is related with the other agents of the resulting system via the information contained in it, and to choose the agents the most integrated in the text. The resulting system can be regarded as multi-agent information system with typed connections and the conflict resolution algorithm, removing the less integrated agents from the system, can be used for resolving ambiguity. This multi-agent system is a system of information dependencies. In these systems agents can use information from predecessors and can pass the (processed) information to successors. Naturally, there are no cycles because of information transfer. The weight functions for agents and winners in conflicts should correspond to information worth of agents and their connectivity with other agents. Note, that in information systems only descenders can be involved in a conflict.

Let A^O be a finite set of information agents and Atr be a set of attributes of information agents. For $a_1, a_2 \in A^O$ we say that

- $a_1 \xrightarrow{\alpha^{tut}} a_2$ if there is a rule which updates a_2 using attribute α from a_1;
- $a_1 \xrightarrow{\alpha^{par}} a_2$ if there is a rule which generates a_2 using attribute α from a_1;
- $a_1 \xrightarrow{a_1^{par}} a_2$ if a_2 is a relation agent and there is a rule which generates a_2 using class agent a_1 or an object agent from relation agent a_1.

We define the system as a tuple $S^O = (A^O, C^O, I_C^O, w_C^O, w_A^O, T_A^O, T_C^O)$, where

- A^O is a finite set of information agents;
- $C^O = \{\alpha \in Atr \mid \exists a, b \in A^O : a \xrightarrow{\alpha} b\} \cup \{a \in A^O \mid \exists b \in A^O : a \xrightarrow{a} b\}$
- mapping $I_C^O : C \longrightarrow 2^{A \times A}$ connects two agents $a, b \in A^O$: $I_C^O(c) = (a, b)$ iff $a \xrightarrow{c} b$;
- mapping $w_A^O : A \longrightarrow 1$ is a worth function for agents;
- mapping $w_C^O : C \longrightarrow 1$ is a worth function for connections;
- mapping $T_A^O : A \longrightarrow \{remove\} \times \emptyset$ permits only removal of conflict agents;
- mapping $T_C^O : C \times A \times A \longrightarrow \{remove, delete\}$ defines types of connections: $T_C^O(c, a, b) = remove$ iff $a \xrightarrow{c^{par}} b$ and $T_C^O(c, a, b) = delete$ iff $a \xrightarrow{c^{tut}} b$.

For performing the suggested conflict resolution algorithm the base protocols for information and rule agents should be expanded by features to store information about generating and updating agents. For this purpose, on generating (updating) agent a by attribute α or object agent b, a rule agent sends

1. the name of generated (updated) agent a with information about typed connection c^{par} (c^{tut}) to owners of the attribute or object, and
2. a list of names of the attribute or object owners with information about typed connection c^{par} (c^{tut}) to agent a.

The agents store these data in descendant and ancestor lists respectively.

Set of conflicts $Conf^O$ corresponds to ambiguities in a text and can be calculated using information about text positions of information agents. It satisfies inheritance property due to transferring information about values of attributes or objects, which correspond to appointed text position. Now we can apply the above algorithm of conflict resolution to multi-agent system S^O generated by the enriched basic algorithm and then use the ambiguity-free set of information agents for ontology population.

Consider now the performance of the conflict resolution algorithm in a particular case of syntactic ambiguity in the following sentence:

On October 22, 2013, an official ceremony was held in the Nenets Autonomous District to mark the start of pilot oil production *at the A. Titov field.*

We consider *Energetics* as an ontology subject domain. Thesaurus of this subject area among others should contain single-word terms *pilot, oil* and *production* together with multi-word terms *pilot oil* and *oil production*. Thus the ambiguity in the example above is the following:

[[pilot [oil production]] ⟷ [[pilot oil] production]]

During the multiagent algorithm initialization for the above sentence the following lexical objects L1–L5 is created with semantic attributes from the thesaurus (see Fig. 1). As a result of main stage of multiagent algorithm by the means of rule-agents implementing search of information concerning activities related to the oil production, an informational agents I1–I4 and R1–R3 corresponding to the ontological classes and relations is created.

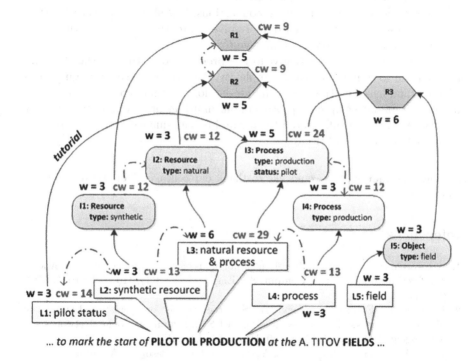

... to mark the start of **PILOT OIL PRODUCTION** at the A. TITOV **FIELDS** ...

Fig. 1. An example of conflicting agents.

Thus the main stage of the analysis in our example results in the following list of conflicts: (L1,L2), (L2,L3), (L3,L4), (I1,I2), (I3,I4), (R1,R2). Calculated weights of agents are also depicted at Fig. 1. The conflict resolution algorithm deletes agents L2, I1, and R1 at the first iteration, and L4 and I4 at the second one. The result of the algorithm is the set of information agents I2, I3, I5, R2, and R3. Thereby all remaining conflicts are resolved automatically.

5   Conclusion

This paper proposes to consider a special kind of multi-agent systems with typed connections. For the operation of such systems, the weight and type of relations between the agents is of particular importance. In particular, conflict resolution for agents is based on the comparison of agents' weights depending on the quantity and quality of connections within the system. We study the conflict resolution process in information systems, in which connections of agents are determined by the transfer of information. The suggested algorithm of conflict resolution is based on the calculation of agents' weights and their impact on the state of the system in the process of conflict resolution. An extended multi-agent system of the semantic analysis of natural language text for ontology population is an information system with typed connections. It is shown that the algorithm of conflict resolution can be used to resolve contextual ambiguity that often arises in the analysis of natural language texts.

In the near future we plan to give formal proofs of correctness of the algorithm proposed and to estimate its time complexity. We propose use an ambiguity resolution method based on this algorithm for ontology instances relied on unreliable information. In a development process of our multi-agent system of text analysis we intend to carry out integrated testing and to rate quality of these algorithms in terms of accuracy and recall.

Acknowledgements. We would like to thank our colleague Igor Anureev for help and discussions.

References

1. Alfawareh, H.M., Jusoh, S.: Resolving ambiguous entity through context knowledge and fuzzy approach. Int. J. Comput. Sci. Eng. (IJCSE) **3**(1), 410–422 (2011). ISSN: 0975-3397
2. Bergenti, F., Franchi, E., Poggi, A.: Selected models for agent-based simulation of social networks. In: Proceedings of 3rd Symposium on Social Networks and Multiagent Systems (SNAMAS 2011), pp. 27–32 (2011)
3. Fagin, R., Halpern, J.Y., Moses, Y., Vardi, M.Y.: Reasoning About Knowledge. MIT Press, Cambridge (1995)
4. Garanina, N., Sidorova, E., Bodin, E.: A multi-agent text analysis based on ontology of subject domain. In: Voronkov, A., Virbitskaite, I. (eds.) PSI 2014. LNCS, vol. 8974, pp. 102–110. Springer, Heidelberg (2015)
5. Garanina, N.O., Sidorova, E.A.: Ontology population as algebraic information system processing based on multi-agent natural language text analysis algorithms. Program. Comput. Softw. **41**(3), 140–148 (2015)
6. De Gennaro, M.C., Jadbabaie, A.: Decentralized control of connectivity for multi-agent systems. In: Proceedings of 45th IEEE Conference on Decision and Control, pp. 3628–3633 (2006)
7. Huhns, M.N., Stephens, L.M.: Multiagent systems and societies of agents. In: Multiagent Systems, pp. 79–120. MIT Press (1999)

8. Kim, D.S., Barker, K., Porter, B.W.: Improving the quality of text understanding by delaying ambiguity resolution. In: Proceedings of the 23rd International Conference on Computational Linguistics (Coling 2010), Beijing, pp. 581–589, August 2010

9. Navigli, R.: Word sense disambiguation: a survey. ACM Comput. Surv. **41**(2), 169 (2009)

10. Tel, G.: Introduction to Distributed Algorithms. Cambridge University Press, Cambridge (2000)

11. Wooldridge, M.: An Introduction to Multiagent Systems. Willey & Sons Ltd., New York (2002)

Maximally-Polyvariant Partial Evaluation in Polynomial Time

Robert Glück

DIKU, Department of Computer Science,
University of Copenhagen, Copenhagen, Denmark

Abstract. Maximally-polyvariant partial evaluation is a strategy for program specialization that propagates static values as accurate as possible. The online partial evaluator presented here achieves this precision in time polynomial in the number of partial-evaluation configurations. This is a significant improvement because a conventional partial evaluator can take exponential time, and no fast algorithm was known for maximally-polyvariant specialization. For an important class of quasi-deterministic specialization problems, our algorithm performs in linear time, even for linear-time specialization of a naive string matcher into a linear-time matcher, which was Futamura's long-standing open challenge. Our results are presented using a recursive flowchart language.

1 Introduction

Partial evaluation, also known as mixed computation, is a well-known technique for program specialization based on aggressive constant propagation and extensive call unfolding [11,24]. *Maximally-polyvariant* partial evaluation (polymax PE) is a recent strategy that has no intentional loss of information and is as accurate as possible in propagating static values [8]. It overcomes an inherited limit [26] present in almost all partial evaluators of recursive languages, the *monovariant* specialization of procedure exits. The increased accuracy allows a maximally-polyvariant partial evaluator to achieve, among others, the Bulyonkov effect [7], that is, constant folding while specializing an interpreter.

However, accuracy has its price: specialization time. A straightforward realization of such a partial evaluator can take exponential time for specializing programs. The online partial evaluator presented in this paper achieves the same precision in time polynomial in the number of partial-evaluation configurations. For an important class of quasi-deterministic specialization problems our algorithm performs in linear time, which includes Futamura's long-standing open challenge [14]: the *linear-time specialization* of a naive string matcher into a *linear-time matcher*. Previously it was conjectured that a binding-time-improved naive matcher would expose enough static computations to the caching of a hypothetical memoizing partial evaluator [1]. However, no such partial evaluation method existed and the binding-time improvements were not trivial. Our solution to Futamura's challenge involves applying a new algorithm to a naive

© Springer International Publishing Switzerland 2016
M. Mazzara and A. Voronkov (Eds.): PSI 2015, LNCS 9609, pp. 130–148, 2016.
DOI: 10.1007/978-3-319-41579-6_11

string matcher that is similar to a deterministic pushdown matcher [3]. The naive matcher is thereby specialized into an efficient linear-time matcher in linear time. This is remarkable because *both* parts of Futamura's challenge are solved. Previously, it was unknown that the *KMP test* [28] could be passed by an accurate partial evaluator without sophisticated binding-time improvements. Known solutions to the KMP test include Futamura's generalized partial computation utilizing a theorem prover [14], Turchin's supercompilation with unification-based driving [18], and various binding-time-improved matchers [1,9]. Our approach provides fresh insights into fast partial evaluation and accurate program staging.

We present our results using a recursive flowchart language, as it is commonly used for studying the principles of partial evaluation (*e.g.*, [6,15,19,21,23]), which should make our results readily comparable and comprehensible.

To summarize, the main contributions of this investigation are

- a method for maximally-polyvariant partial evaluation in polynomial time that speeds up to linear time for quasi-deterministic specialization problems,
- a solution to Futamura's challenge, a classic problem of partial evaluation.

As a result, a class of specialization problems can now be solved faster than before with high precision, which may enable faster Ershov's generating extensions [11], *e.g.*, for a class similar to Bulyonkov's analyzer programs [6]. This is significant because *super-linear program staging* by partial evaluation becomes possible: the time to run the partial evaluator *and* its residual program is linear in the input, while the original program is not, as for the naive matcher.

In Sect. 2, we define the recursive flowchart language. Section 3 lays out maximally-polyvariant partial evaluation, and presents our main technical result, the polynomial-time graph-based algorithm. In Sect. 4, we present the linear-time specialization of a naive string matcher. Section 5 discusses related work, and Sect. 6 concludes the paper.

We assume the reader is familiar with the basic notions of partial evaluation (a good source is [21] or [24, Part II]).

2   A Recursive Flowchart Language

The basic aspects of computation in a flowchart language are store transformations by assignments and control transfers by jumps. Our recursive flowchart language has been slightly modified from that in [8] but has the same format.[1]

Syntax. Figure 1 defines the abstract syntax of the language. A program is a sequence of labeled *basic blocks* containing either an assignment and a jump, a call, or a return statement. An *assignment* $x := o(x^*)$ contains the application of an n-ary operator o to arguments x^*. For simplicity, only variables are allowed as arguments. Nested expressions can be built using several assignments. Constants are represented by nullary operators.

---

[1] Multiple return variables; tests are evaluated in the assignment-updated store.

Grammar

$$q ::= b^+$$
$$b ::= l : a\ j$$
$$\mid\ l : \texttt{call}\ l\ l$$
$$\mid\ l : \texttt{return}\ x^*\ l$$
$$a ::= x\ :=\ o(x^*)$$
$$j ::= \texttt{case}\ t(x^*)\ l^+$$

Syntax Domains

$q \in$ Programs	$j \in$ Jumps	$o \in$ Operators
$b \in$ Basic-Blocks	$l \in$ Labels	$t \in$ Tests
$a \in$ Assignments	$x \in$ Variables	

Fig. 1. Syntax of the recursive flowchart language

A *jump* $\texttt{case}\ t(x^*)\ l^+$ contains the application of an n-ary test t to arguments x^* and labels l^+. Control will be transferred to one of the labels in l^+.

A *call statement* $\texttt{call}\ l'\ l''$ transfers control to a procedure whose entry block is labeled l' and copies the whole store. When the procedure returns, control is transferred to label l'' (possibly offset by the label in the return statement; see below) and the values of the specified variables are copied back into the original store. We do *not* demand a distinguished entry point of a procedure; one may call to any basic block in a program, from where execution will then proceed until a return statement is met.

A *return statement* $\texttt{return}\ x^*\ l$ returns the values of variables x^* to the call. It also includes an offset label l which is "added" to the return label given in the call. The offset makes it easy to return to different basic blocks. The special label nil $\in$ Labels is used as the empty label. We assume that the concatenated target labels all exist in the program. A conventional return corresponds to $\texttt{return}\ x$ nil.

A program q is represented by a *block map* Γ that maps label l into the basic block labeled l in q. We assume that every program q considered is well-formed.

Programs are written in a concrete syntax using syntactic sugar. For example, we write $\texttt{goto}\ l$ instead of $\texttt{case}\ t_{\texttt{true}}()\ l$, and several assignments in a basic block. The string matcher is such a program (Fig. 7).

Semantics. Evaluation of a program proceeds sequentially from one block to another. A *computation state* is a pair (l, σ) that contains label l of the current basic block and the values of the program's variables in store σ. A *store* $\sigma \in$ Stores is a partial function from Variables to Values. We denote by *variable update* $\sigma[x \mapsto v]$ the store like σ except that x maps to v, by *store update* $\sigma \cdot \sigma'$ the store like σ except that all variables in σ' map to their value in σ', and by *selection* $\sigma_{x_1,\ldots,x_n}$ the store that maps $x_1,\ldots,x_n$ to their value in σ. A *stack of states* $r \in$ Stacks represents the current state of execution of a program.

The rules in Fig. 2 define a transition relation $\rightarrow_{int}$ between stacks of states. A judgment $\Vdash_\Gamma r \rightarrow_{int} r'$ represents a transition from stack r to stack r' in

Assignment

$$\frac{\forall i \, . \, \sigma(x_i) = v_i \quad [\![o]\!](v_1, \ldots, v_n) = v}{\sigma \vdash x := o(x_1, \ldots, x_n) \Rightarrow \sigma[x \mapsto v]} \quad \text{(E1)}$$

Jump

$$\frac{\forall i \, . \, \sigma(x_i) = v_i \quad [\![t]\!](v_1, \ldots, v_n, l_1, \ldots, l_m) = l}{\sigma \vdash \mathbf{case} \ t(x_1, \ldots, x_n) \ l_1, \ldots, l_m \Rightarrow l} \quad \text{(E2)}$$

Basic Block

$$\frac{\Gamma(l) = a \ j \quad \sigma \vdash a \Rightarrow \sigma' \quad \sigma' \vdash j \Rightarrow l'}{\Vdash_\Gamma (l, \sigma) \colon r \rightarrow_{int} (l', \sigma') \colon r} \quad \text{(E3)}$$

$$\frac{\Gamma(l) = \mathbf{call} \ l' \ l''}{\Vdash_\Gamma (l, \sigma) \colon r \rightarrow_{int} (l', \sigma) \colon (l'', \sigma) \colon r} \quad \text{(E4)}$$

$$\frac{\Gamma(l) = \mathbf{return} \ x_1, \ldots, x_n \ l''}{\Vdash_\Gamma (l, \sigma) \colon (l', \sigma') \colon r \rightarrow_{int} (l', \sigma') \cdot (l'', \sigma_{x_1, \ldots, x_n}) \colon r} \quad \text{(E5)}$$

Semantic Values

$$
\begin{aligned}
r &\in \text{Stacks} &&= (\text{Labels} \times \text{Stores})^* \\
l &\in \text{Labels} &&= \text{Block-Labels} \cup \{\, \text{nil} \,\} \\
\sigma &\in \text{Stores} &&= \text{Variables} \rightharpoonup \text{Values} \\
\Gamma &\in \text{Block-Maps} &&= \text{Block-Labels} \rightharpoonup \text{Basic-Blocks}
\end{aligned}
$$

Fig. 2. Operational semantics of the recursive flowchart language

program Γ. The rules are defined with respect to the semantics of Operators and Tests. Each test name is mapped to a function from value/label tuples to labels e.g.: $[\![t]\!](v_1, \ldots, v_n, l_1, \ldots, l_m) = l$. We assume that the test always returns one of its input labels, $l \in \{l_1, \ldots, l_m\}$, and that the outcome of the test does not depend on those labels, only on $v_1, \ldots, v_n$.

At a call, the current store is paired with the return label then pushed on the call stack, and control is shifted to the called label. On return, the state is popped off the stack and evaluation continues at state $(l', \sigma') \cdot (l'', \sigma'') = (l' \cdot l'', \sigma' \cdot \sigma'')$, where l'' is the offset label and $\sigma'' = \sigma_{x_1, \ldots, x_n}$ is the returned store. We regard labels as strings, and use an auxiliary function, $\cdot$, to concatenate labels (*e.g.*, cont·ab = contab). The empty label, nil, is syntactic sugar for the empty string (*e.g.*, nil·ab = ab). A call statement can specify an empty label, call l nil, as long as the offset label in the return exists in the program. The rules of the operational semantics are straightforward and should not need particular explanation.

3   Maximally-Polyvariant Partial Evaluation

A partial evaluator tries to precompute as much as possible, given part of a program's input. The essential difference between interpretation and partial evaluation is that a partial evaluator operates over a *partial store* in which values of the variables are not all known. Abstractly, three steps are performed [21,23]:

1. Collection of all reachable configurations.
2. Block specialization and code generation.
3. Post-processing of the residual program.

Starting from an initial configuration containing a partial store, the first step of partial evaluation determines the set of all reachable configurations. The second step produces specialized blocks for the residual program using the reachable configurations. The third step, post-processing, performs conventional local optimizations and eliminates redundant code (*e.g.*, jumps caused by blocks chained by one-way jumps). The two last steps can be performed in time linear in the number of reachable configurations and will not be considered further (*cf.* [21]). We will focus on the key problem of a fast collection.

To distinguish known (*static*) and unknown (*dynamic*) values, we use a special value $D \notin$ Values. A *partial store* is a store σ that maps variables to Values$_D$ = Values $\cup \{ D \}$ such that

- If a variable x has a static value v, then $\sigma(x) = v$.
- If a variable x has a dynamic value, then $\sigma(x) = D$.

A variable x is either static or dynamic: there are no partially static values. A *configuration* (l, σ) consists of a label l and a partial store σ, and represents a set containing all states in which the static variables are fixed to their static values in the configuration. Below we refer to partial stores simply as stores.

Block traversal. We give the rules for handling the three types of basic blocks, and then use the rules to define an (inefficient) stack- and an (efficient) graph-based collection. The four rules B1–B4 for assignments and jumps in Fig. 3 are simple. The evaluation of operators (tests) now depends on the partial store σ. If all arguments of an operator (test) are static, it is evaluated. Otherwise, in the case of an assignment, the value of x becomes dynamic. In the case of a test, all labels in the jump are returned (*i.e.*, all labels to which control might be passed). Dynamic tests lead to branching traces in partial evaluation (all possible control flows have to be considered when collecting the reachable configurations).

The traversal of a basic block is formalized as a judgment $\vdash_\Gamma c \Rightarrow P$ that relates a configuration c to a *set of steps* P, which determines how to proceed with the collection. The next step can be *forward* ($\uparrow$) to a new configuration or *return* ($\downarrow$) with a configuration. The rules B5–B7 at the bottom of Fig. 3 define P. An assignment block yields a set of several forward steps if the test is dynamic, $P = \{\uparrow(c, c_1), \ldots, \uparrow(c, c_m)\}$, a singleton otherwise. A call block yields a forward step containing caller c, callee c', and continuation c'', $P = \{ \uparrow((c, c''), c') \}$. A return block yields a step that returns c', called a *terminator of* c, $P = \{ \downarrow(c, c') \}$.

In general, a *step* $p \in P$ has the form

$$p \ ::= \ \uparrow(k, c) \ | \ \downarrow(k, c)$$
$$k \ ::= \ c \ | \ (c, c) \ | \ ()$$

where $\uparrow(k, c)$ is a step forward from a predecessor k to a configuration c, and $\downarrow(k, c)$ returns a terminator c to k. A *predecessor* k can be a single configuration,

---

Assignment

$$\frac{\forall i \,.\, \sigma(x_i) = v_i \quad [\![o]\!](v_1, \ldots, v_n) = v}{\sigma \vdash_{pe} x := o(x_1, \ldots, x_n) \Rightarrow \sigma[x \mapsto v]} \tag{B1}$$

$$\frac{\exists i \,.\, \sigma(x_i) = D}{\sigma \vdash_{pe} x := o(x_1, \ldots, x_n) \Rightarrow \sigma[x \mapsto D]} \tag{B2}$$

Jump

$$\frac{\forall i \,.\, \sigma(x_i) = v_i \quad [\![t]\!](v_1, \ldots, v_n, l_1, \ldots, l_m) = l}{\sigma \vdash_{pe} \mathbf{case}\ t(x_1, \ldots, x_n)\ l_1, \ldots, l_m \Rightarrow \{l\}} \tag{B3}$$

$$\frac{\exists i \,.\, \sigma(x_i) = D}{\sigma \vdash_{pe} \mathbf{case}\ t(x_1, \ldots, x_n)\ l_1, \ldots, l_m \Rightarrow \{l_1, \ldots, l_m\}} \tag{B4}$$

Basic Block

$$\frac{\Gamma(l) = a\ j \quad \sigma \vdash_{pe} a \Rightarrow \sigma' \quad \sigma' \vdash_{pe} j \Rightarrow L}{\vdash_\Gamma (l, \sigma) \Rightarrow \{\uparrow((l, \sigma), (l', \sigma')) \mid l' \in L\}} \tag{B5}$$

$$\frac{\Gamma(l) = \mathtt{call}\ l'\ l''}{\vdash_\Gamma (l, \sigma) \Rightarrow \{\uparrow(((l, \sigma), (l'', \sigma)), (l', \sigma))\}} \tag{B6}$$

$$\frac{\Gamma(l) = \mathtt{return}\ x_1, \ldots, x_n\ l''}{\vdash_\Gamma (l, \sigma) \Rightarrow \{\downarrow((l, \sigma), (l'', \sigma_{x_1, \ldots, x_n}))\}} \tag{B7}$$

Fig. 3. Traversing a basic block with a configuration (l, σ)

a pair of configurations, or empty. When empty, it is denoted by $()$, as in the case of an initial configuration which has no predecessor.

3.1 Stack-Based Collection of Reachable Configurations

Intuitively, to collect all reachable configurations, all possible computation traces through a program have to be followed, starting from an initial configuration. Rather than relating stacks of call states (like $\rightarrow_{int}$), the stack-based collection relates stacks of predecessors. Every configuration passed during a forward step is placed on the stack. Understanding the stack-based collection will be useful when we introduce an efficient graph-based collection.

Let $c_0 = (l_0, \sigma_0)$ be the *initial configuration* where l_0 is the initial label of a program Γ and σ_0 is the store holding the values of the static variables given as input to the partial evaluator (all other variables are dynamic). A configuration c is considered *reachable from* c_0 if it is the target of a forward step $\uparrow(k, c)$. The *set of reachable configurations* is the set of configurations in the closure:

$$Poly_{stack} = \{\, c \mid\, \vdash_\Gamma \langle \uparrow((), c_0), \epsilon \rangle \rightarrow^*_{stack} \langle \uparrow(k, c), r \rangle \,\}.$$

The collection starts with the initial step $\uparrow((), c_0)$ and the empty stack ϵ. Figure 4 defines the three collection rules S1–S3 of relation $\rightarrow_{stack}$. The rules are similar

$Step$

$$\frac{\vdash_\Gamma c \Rightarrow P \quad p \in P}{\Vdash_\Gamma \langle \uparrow(k,c),r \rangle \rightarrow_{stack} \langle p,k:r \rangle} \tag{S1}$$

$$\frac{}{\Vdash_\Gamma \langle \downarrow(c,t),k:r \rangle \rightarrow_{stack} \langle \downarrow(k,t),r \rangle} \tag{S2}$$

$$\frac{}{\Vdash_\Gamma \langle \downarrow((c,c'),t),r \rangle \rightarrow_{stack} \langle \uparrow(c,c'\cdot t),r \rangle} \tag{S3}$$

$Semantic\ Values$

$$
\begin{aligned}
r &\in \text{Stacks} &&= \text{Preds}^* \\
p &\in \text{Steps} &&= \uparrow(\text{Preds} \times \text{Configs}) \cup \downarrow(\text{Preds} \times \text{Configs}) \\
k &\in \text{Preds} &&= \text{Configs} \cup (\text{Configs} \times \text{Configs}) \cup \{\,()\,\} \\
c &\in \text{Configs} &&= \text{Labels} \times \text{Pe-Stores} \\
\sigma &\in \text{Pe-Stores} &&= \text{Variables} \rightarrow (\text{Values} \cup \{\,D\,\})
\end{aligned}
$$

Fig. 4. Stack-based collection of reachable configurations

to the original semantics in Fig. 3 except that the transition sequence may branch and that every predecessor is pushed on the stack.

The first rule S1 for a $\uparrow$-step selects a step $p \in P$ among those determined by the block traversal, and pushes the predecessor k of c on the stack r. The last two rules S2 and S3 for $\downarrow$-steps propagate a terminator t down the stack until the most recent call is on top (a configuration pair). Rule S3 mimics the return-block rule E5 of the original semantics, and yields a $\uparrow$-step to the following configuration obtained by updating the continuation configuration with terminator t.

A partial evaluator can produce a residual program if the set of reachable configurations is finite. This is the case when the static values in the stores of the reachable configurations vary only finitely. Because this is not always the case, the partial evaluator defined by the rules in this paper may not terminate for every initial configuration c_0 of a program Γ, which for non-trivial specialization is considered acceptable in most of the literature on partial evaluation.

Maximally polyvariant. A distinguishing feature of the collection is that all basic blocks are handled in a polyvariant manner. There is no intentional loss of static values due to generalization of configurations. A call can have *multiple terminators* due to branching transitions, which leads to multiple configurations that need to be explored after a call. This polyvariant handling of terminators avoids the *monovariant return approximation* of conventional partial evaluators [24], in which the result of a call is dynamic if one of its arguments is dynamic. The partial evaluator defined by the rules in Figs. 3 and 4 is *maximally polyvariant* [8]. Among others, it achieves the Bulyonkov effect [7], that is, constant folding while specializing an interpreter. However, accuracy has its price. Multiple terminators are the "complexity generator" of maximally polyvariant partial evaluation because multiple continuations need to be explored after a call, and this degree of branching is not bound by a program-dependent constant, but depends on the static values in the initial configuration c_0. In a conventional partial evaluator, a recursive call has at most one terminator regardless of the initial configuration.

3.2 Graph-Based Collection of Reachable Configurations

A naive implementation of the stack-based rules in Fig. 4 may take *exponential time* to collect all reachable configurations. The same transition sequence may be repeated many times, and there is no way in which one could reuse steps done previously. It may be *nonterminating* even if the set of reachable configurations is finite because the stack may grow forever without reaching new configurations. Both problems can be avoided by taking advantage of the following observation about sharing transitions sequences and terminators [16].

Observation 1 (terminator sharing). *For any program Γ, the following implication holds for all configurations c, t, predecessors k, and stacks r:*

$$\Vdash_\Gamma \langle \uparrow((), c), \epsilon \rangle \to^*_{stack} \langle \downarrow((), t), \epsilon \rangle \implies \Vdash_\Gamma \langle \uparrow(k, c), r \rangle \to^*_{stack} \langle \downarrow(k, t), r \rangle .$$

That is, if a step to a configuration c in an empty context (empty predecessor, empty stack) yields a terminator t, so will a step to c in any context (k, r). We will use this observation in two ways to avoid redundant transitions.

1. Once t is known as a terminator of c, it can be reused. To illustrate this, suppose we reach c in two different contexts, $\langle \uparrow(k_1, c), r_1 \rangle$ and $\langle \uparrow(k_2, c), r_2 \rangle$. Then we can make a shortcut using t without repeating the intermediate transitions:

$$\vdash_\Gamma \langle \uparrow(k_1, c), r_1 \rangle \to_{shortcut} \langle \downarrow(k_1, t), r_1 \rangle ,$$
$$\vdash_\Gamma \langle \uparrow(k_2, c), r_2 \rangle \to_{shortcut} \langle \downarrow(k_2, t), r_2 \rangle .$$

2. If the same terminator is returned into the same context, the subsequent transitions are identical. To illustrate this, suppose two configurations c_1 and c_2 that return the same terminator t are reached in the same context, $\langle \uparrow(k, c_1), r \rangle$ and $\langle \uparrow(k, c_2), r \rangle$. Then the transitions following $\langle \downarrow(k, t), r \rangle$ need not be repeated:

$$\Vdash_\Gamma \langle \uparrow(k, c_1), r \rangle \to^*_{stack} \langle \downarrow(k, t), r \rangle ,$$
$$\Vdash_\Gamma \langle \uparrow(k, c_2), r \rangle \to^*_{stack} \langle \downarrow(k, t), r \rangle .$$

The central idea of the graph-based rules is to take advantage of these properties. Instead of following each single path, as with the stack-based rules, we will search *concurrently* along all paths for reachable configurations. A forward step ($\uparrow$) then traverses a forward edge in a directed graph, which may be cyclic, and a return step ($\downarrow$) propagates a terminator backward along an edge. We define the rules such that the collection (i) traverses an edge just once, and (ii) returns the same terminator along an edge just once. For this we memoize the predecessors (in a relation K) and the terminators (in a relation T) of each configuration. Relation K is the reverse graph that points from configurations to their predecessors.

   We write $K(c) = \{ k \mid (c, k) \in K \}$ to denote the predecessors of c in K, and $T(c) = \{ t \mid (c, t) \in T \}$ to denote the terminators of c in T. Then $k \in K(c)$

Step		
	$$\dfrac{K(c) = \emptyset \quad \vdash_\Gamma c \Rightarrow P}{\Vdash_\Gamma \langle \uparrow(k,c), K, T\rangle \rightarrow_{pe} \langle P, K \cup (c,k), T\rangle}$$	(R1)

$$\frac{K(c) \neq \emptyset \quad k \notin K(c)}{\Vdash_\Gamma \langle \uparrow(k,c), K, T\rangle \rightarrow_{pe} \langle \{\, \downarrow(k,t) \mid t \in T(c)\,\}, K \cup (c,k), T\rangle} \tag{R2}$$

$$\frac{t \notin T(c)}{\Vdash_\Gamma \langle \downarrow(c,t), K, T\rangle \rightarrow_{pe} \langle \{\, \downarrow(k,t) \mid k \in K(c)\,\}, K, T \cup (c,t)\rangle} \tag{R3}$$

$$\frac{}{\Vdash_\Gamma \langle \downarrow((c,c'),t), K, T\rangle \rightarrow_{pe} \langle \{\, \uparrow(c,c'{\cdot}t)\,\}, K, T\rangle} \tag{R4}$$

Control

$$\frac{\Vdash_\Gamma \langle p, K, T\rangle \rightarrow_{pe} \langle P', K', T'\rangle}{\Vdash_\Gamma \langle p \uplus P, K, T\rangle \rightarrow_{pe} \langle P \cup P', K', T'\rangle} \tag{C1}$$

$$\frac{\Vdash_\Gamma \langle p, K, T\rangle \nrightarrow_{pe}}{\Vdash_\Gamma \langle p \uplus P, K, T\rangle \rightarrow_{pe} \langle P, K, T\rangle} \tag{C2}$$

Semantic Values (See Fig 4.)

Fig. 5. Graph-based collection of reachable configurations

means that k is a predecessor of c, and $t \in T(c)$ that t is a terminator of c. We often omit the parenthesis around singletons, *e.g.*, $T \cup (c,t)$ is $T \cup \{\,(c,t)\,\}$.

The set of reachable configurations is the set of configurations in the closure:

$$Poly_{graph} = \{\, c \mid \Vdash_\Gamma \langle \{\uparrow((), c_0)\,\}, \emptyset, \emptyset\rangle \rightarrow_{pe}^* \langle \uparrow(k,c) \cup P, K, T\rangle \,\}.$$

The collection starts with a pending set P that contains the initial step $\uparrow((), c_0)$, and empty sets K, T. Figure 5 defines the six collection rules of relation $\rightarrow_{pe}$. Set P is maintained by two control rules (C1, C2). C1 adds steps P' to P if one of the four rules (R1–R4) applies to a step p in the pending set. If none of the four rules applies, p is removed by C2 ($\uplus$ is the union of disjoint sets). The control rules can be applied in any order and until the pending set is empty.

The application of rules R1–R4 maintains two invariants for all c:

$$K(c) \neq \emptyset \implies c \text{ "was traversed"},$$
$$k \in K(c) \,\wedge\, t \in T(c) \implies \downarrow(k,t) \text{ "was generated"}.$$

R1 $\uparrow(k,c)$: A basic block is traversed with configuration c, $\vdash_\Gamma c \Rightarrow P$, if this was not done before, $K(c) = \emptyset$. The first predecessor k of c is recorded by adding k to $K(c)$. Each application of R1, as well as of R2 and R3, disables a condition that enabled it (here, $K(c) \neq \emptyset$ afterwards).

R2 $\uparrow(k,c)$: If c is reached from a new predecessor, $k \notin K(c)$, and c was already traversed, $K(c) \neq \emptyset$, all known terminators $t \in T(c)$ are returned to k, and the invariant is maintained by adding k to $K(c)$. Note that even if no terminator has yet been found for c, k is recorded as a predecessor of c.

R3 $\downarrow(c,t)$: A terminator t passed back to c is only propagated to the predecessors of c, $K(c)$, if t is a new terminator of c, that is $t \notin T(c)$. The invariant is maintained by adding t to $T(c)$; otherwise, $\downarrow(k,t)$ was already added to P.

R4 $\downarrow((c,c'),t)$: Essentially the same as the corresponding rule S3 in Fig. 4.

We state without proof: For all Γ and all initial c_0, $Poly_{stack} = Poly_{graph}$.

Termination. If the set of reachable configurations is finite for a given program Γ and initial c_0, the transition sequence terminates with an empty pending set:

$$\Vdash_\Gamma \langle \{ \uparrow((),c_0) \}, \emptyset, \emptyset \rangle \rightarrow^*_{pe} \langle \emptyset, K, T \rangle$$

If the set of reachable configurations is finite, so is the set of possible steps. Rule C1 adds new steps to P as long as a R1–R4 rule applies to some p in P, but this can only be the case a finite number of times. Each application of R1–R3 disables a condition that enabled it (*e.g.*, if $t \notin T(c)$ before applying R3, then $t \in T(c)$ afterwards). Thus, only a finite number of steps can be added by R1–R3, including $\downarrow$-steps. This limits how often R4 can turn a $\downarrow$- into a $\uparrow$-step. Hence, rule C2 eventually removes all steps from P, and no more rules apply.

Polynomial-Time Complexity. We will now show that the time to collect all reachable configurations is (i) *cubic* in the number of reachable configurations, and (ii) *polynomial* in the static variety of the program variables. We begin by assuming a suitable data structure for sets such that the union of two sets with cardinalities u and v takes at most time $O(u+v)$, and the creation of a set from n elements takes at most time $O(n)$. Set operations that take constant time are testing the membership of an element, and picking and removing an element from a set. We assume a random-access machine with a uniform cost model.

Let n be the number of reachable configurations for a given program Γ and initial c_0. Then sets K and T contain at most $O(n^2)$ elements, and there are at most $O(n^2)$ steps of the form $\uparrow(k,c)$ and $\downarrow(k,t)$. (There are at most $O(n)$ predecessors $k = (c_1, c_2)$ because the stores in c_1, c_2 are by construction in B6 always identical.) Any subset $K(c)$ and $T(c)$ has at most $O(n)$ elements.

Assuming that the evaluation of primitive operators o and tests t takes constant time, the traversal of a basic block, $\vdash_\Gamma c \Rightarrow P$, takes constant time (Fig. 3).

The time to perform the collection depends on how many steps are added to P by C1 (Fig. 5). Steps can only be added by C1 if a R1–R4 rule applies to some p. R1 can only be applied once to each of the n configurations, and each application yields $O(1)$ steps. R2 and R3 can only be applied once to each of the $O(n^2)$ possible steps, and each application yields at most $O(n)$ steps. Thus, R1–R3 can add up to $O(n^3)$ steps. R4 cannot be applied more often than the $\downarrow$-steps added by R1–R3. Together, C1 and C2 apply at most $O(n^3)$ times. Thus, the collection time is *cubic $O(n^3)$ in the number of reachable configurations*.

The number of reachable configurations, n, depends on the number of stores, which depends on the number of static values to which each variable in a given program can be bound during the collection (there is only one dynamic value D).

Assuming that each of the j program variables is bound at most to m static values, there are at most $O(m^j)$ different stores, where j is a program-dependent constant. Thus, there are at most $O(m^j)$ reachable configurations. The collection takes time $O(n^3)$, and thus is *polynomial $O(m^j)$ in the static variety m*, a function of the initial configuration c_0. (This coincides with the time to simulate 2N-PDAs with j heads on a read-only input tape of length m [2].)

Linear-time case. The time to collect the reachable configurations is dominated by the number of steps added to P. If we identify conditions under which only a linear number of steps is added, the collection takes linear time. Among R1–R4 in Fig. 5, R2 and R3 are the "complexity generators" as each application can produce $O(n)$ steps depending on the size of sets $T(c)$ and $K(c)$, respectively.

Table 1. Linear-time case: configuration types and their predecessors and terminators

c	$|C(c)|$	$|K(c)|$	$|T(c)|$
x	$O(1)$	$O(1)$	$O(n)$
y	$O(1)$	$O(n)$	$O(1)$
z	$O(n)$	$O(1)$	$O(1)$
Σ	$O(n)$	$O(n)$	$O(n)$

Consider a set of reachable configurations, C, that consists of three disjoint sets X, Y, Z such that $C = X \uplus Y \uplus Z$. We assume every $x \in X, y \in Y, z \in Z$ has the number of predecessors, $|K(\cdot)|$, and terminators, $|T(\cdot)|$, given by Table 1, and there are $O(1)$ configurations in X and Y, and $O(n)$ in Z. Then the size of sets K and T is $O(n)$. It is easy to verify that there are at most $O(n)$ applications of R1–R4 producing in total at most $O(n)$ steps. Thus, the collection time is $O(n)$. (This coincides with the time to simulate 2D-PDAs, which is linear in the length of the read-only input tape [10].) The specialization of a naive matcher below can be carried out in linear time because it is an instance of this special case.

Block Specialization. Block specialization can be done in *time* linear in the number of reachable configurations and generates residual programs of *size* linear in the number of reachable configurations (at most one block per configuration) [8,19]. Importantly, all static calls are replaced by unconditional jumps. The return configuration of a static call c is the terminator t in singleton $T(c)$. Replacing static calls by their static result is standard in partial evaluation [24]. It ensures that static calls are not evaluated again by the residual program.

4   Linear-Time Specialization of a Naive String Matcher

The specialization of a naive string matcher into an efficient linear-time matcher is a classic problem of partial evaluation first considered in 1987 [14]. Given an inefficient quadratic-time matcher that searches for the first occurrence of a pattern p in a string s, the task of a partial evaluator is to specialize the matcher with respect to p into a residual matcher that searches for p in a string in linear time. Let m be the length of a pattern p and let n be the length of a string s, then two types of problems arise [12]:

1. Can we obtain for any p an $O(n)$-time residual matcher of size $O(m)$ by partial evaluation of the naive matcher?
2. Can we obtain from the naive matcher and the partial evaluator an $O(m)$-time program generator that produces matchers of Type 1 for any p?

The Type 1 problem was solved in different ways by several partial evaluators, including generalized partial computation by employing a theorem prover [13], perfect supercompilation based on unification-based driving [18], and offline partial evaluation after binding-time improvement of a naive matcher [9]. The solutions were thoroughly investigated in several publications (see [1] for references).

The Type 2 problem remained unsolved until this study, though it had been pointed out [1] that manual binding-time improvement of a naive matcher could expose static functions to the caching of a hypothetical memoizing partial evaluator. However, no such method for partial evaluation existed.

We are going to show that the graph-based partial evaluation method that we introduced in Sect. 3 solves *both* types of problems. Our method relies solely on maximally-polyvariant constant propagation, and not the addition of a theorem prover, perfect driving, or sophisticated binding-time improvements.

A new approach. We approach Futamura's challenge from a new angle. It was noted [3, p. 336], [25, p. 338] that a naive matcher programmed as a *2-way deterministic pushdown automaton* (2D-PDA) can be simulated in *linear time* $O(m + n)$ given p *and* s using Cook's construction [10]. This is noteworthy because the same matcher run as a standard PDA takes *quadratic time* $O(m \cdot n)$.

We are going to use such a matcher as the source program for our partial evaluator. We assume that the reader is familiar with the basics of PDA, and recalls that they consist of a stack, a read-only tape, and a finite-state control. The sets of stack symbols, tape symbols, and states are fixed for a given PDA.

To understand how to write such a matcher in our flowchart language (Sect. 2), we are first going to look into the workings of a naive pushdown matcher taken from the literature [3, p. 338]. It is not a common practice to imitate a pushdown automaton in a recursive language, but this approach will lead us to our goal of improving the asymptotics of both problem types from quadratic to linear.

Naive pushdown matcher. Figure 6 shows the naive matcher written in a pushdown programming language [5] with instructions that push and pop the stack (push, pop), move the tape head (left, right), test the symbol on the stack top and under the tape head (iftop=, iftape=), test the emptiness of the stack and the end of the tape (bottom?, rightend?), and halt (accept, reject). The input on the read-only tape has the form $s_n \ldots s_1 \$ p_1 \ldots p_m$ where $s^R = s_n \ldots s_1$ is the

```
(copy     ((iftape= A) (push A) right (goto copy))          ; copy A to stack
          ((iftape= B) (push B) right (goto copy))          ; copy B to stack
          ((iftape= $) right          (goto compare)))      ; start match

(compare (rightend?   accept)                               ; p did match
         (bottom?     reject)                               ; p didn't match
         ((iftape= A) (iftop= A) pop right (goto compare))  ; both are A
         ((iftape= B) (iftop= B) pop right (goto compare))  ; both are B
         (left        (goto restore)))                      ; p isn't prefix

(restore ((iftape= A) (push A) left (goto restore))         ; restore A
         ((iftape= B) (push B) left (goto restore))         ; restore B
         ((iftape= $) pop right      (goto compare)))       ; restart match
```

Fig. 6. A naive string matcher in a 2D-PDA language (adapted from [5])

```
((p s) (match)                                    ; match(p,s)
  (match    ((t := '()) (q := '())) (goto copy))  ; initialize

  (copy     (if (pair? s) spush compare))         ; start match
  (spush    (call sarg ()))                       ; copy character
  (sarg     ((t := (hd s)) (s := (tl s))) (goto copy)) ; to stack

  (compare (if (null? p) accept cempty?))         ; p did match
  (cempty? (if (null? t) reject cequal?))         ; p didn't match
  (cequal? (if (= (hd p) t) cnext restore))       ; both are equal
  (cnext    ((q := (cons (hd p) q)) (p := (tl p))) ; move right on p
            (return (p q) compare))               ; continue match

  (restore (if (pair? q) rpush rpop))             ; restore
  (rpush    (call rarg ()))                        ; push by call
  (rarg     ((t := (hd q)) (p := (cons t p)))      ; restore character
            (q := (tl q)) (goto restore))          ; move left on p
  (rpop     (return (p q) compare))                ; restart match

  (accept   ((p := 'accept)) (goto spop))          ; return accept
  (reject   ((p := 'reject)) (goto spop))          ; return reject
  (spop     (return (p) spop)))                    ; pop to halt
```

Fig. 7. A naive string matcher in recursive flowchart (with syntactic sugar)

reversed string, $p = p_1 \ldots p_m$ the pattern, and $ a separator that differs from the characters in s and p ($m, n \geq 0$). Initially, the head is positioned at the left-most character on the tape and the stack is empty. The matcher in the figure is defined over the tape alphabet $\{ A, B, \$ \}$, and is easily extended to larger alphabets.

The matcher works in two phases. First, the string $s_n \ldots s_1$ is copied from the tape to the stack by reading the characters from the left to the right, and pushing them onto the stack until the separator $ is read (block `copy`), which means that s_n is on the bottom of the stack and s_1 on its top (thus, it is convenient, but not necessary, to have the string in reversed order). After loading the string onto the stack, this part of the tape is never read again.

Second, the pattern $p_1 \ldots p_m$ is compared with the string on the stack (block `compare`). The tape head (initially p_1) and the stack top (initially s_1) are compared. As long as the comparison is successful ($p_i = s_j$), the tape head moves right (p_{i+1}) and the stack is popped (s_{j+1}). The comparison continues until the match is complete (`accept`), the stack is empty (`reject`), or a mismatch occurs ($p_i \neq s_j$). In case of a mismatch, the successfully matched prefix $p_1 \ldots p_{i-1}$ is used to restore the stack (block `restore`), and matching starts again after popping the top of the restored stack, which is the next prefix of s. The repeated restoring and rematching makes this a quadratic-time matcher.

Naive flowchart matcher. We are going to simulate the working of this pushdown matcher in flowchart. Recursive flowchart does not provide a pushdown stack, but allows imitation of its behavior by calling and returning on the call stack. This leads to an unusual recursive matcher. Instead of an input tape, the program has two input variables, p and s, which hold pattern and string as character lists.

The matcher moves one-way on the string and two-way on the pattern. To allow two-way operation, position i on a pattern p is represented by two variables: p $= (p_i \ldots p_n)$, q $= (p_{i-1} \ldots p_1)$. A right move yields p $= (p_{i+1} \ldots p_n)$, q $= (p_i \ldots p_1)$; analogously for a left move. Initially, p $= (p_1 \ldots p_n)$, q $= ()$. List operators select the head and tail of a list (`hd`, `tl`), add an element to the front of a list (`cons`), and test for a pair and an empty list (`pair?`, `null?`).

The flowchart matcher in Fig. 7, written in concrete syntax, proceeds in two phases just as the pushdown matcher. The two input variables (p, s) and the initial block (`match`) are specified in the program header. After recursively building the call stack, where each call assigns the current head of s to a local variable t ('top'), matching starts by comparing the head of p against t. If equal, matching continues by returning the tail of p; otherwise, the call stack is recursively rebuilt from the pattern. After the first phase, during which p and q are unchanged, s is no longer live in the second phase. There are two recursive calls in the matcher (underlined). The variables live at a call to `sarg`, and thus its implicit arguments, are p, q, s; those live at a call to `rarg` are p, q. Variable t is local to each recursive invocation because it is not live at the called blocks.

During partial evaluation, the equality test in block `cequal?` will be static or dynamic depending on whether t is assigned a character of the static pattern by `rarg` or the dynamic string by `sarg`. Analysis of what a call to `rarg` returns reveals that it locates the longest prefix of p that is a proper suffix of the successfully matched $p_1 \ldots p_{i-1}$ (*cf.* [1]). This is a static quadratic-time subproblem that our partial evaluator simulates in linear time by memoizing terminators.

We use a programming technique in which only the offset label in a return statement determines the target block. This makes the program more compact,

```
((s) (0_match_0)                                              ; match_AAB(s)
  (0_match_0    (if (pair? s) 0_spush_1 0_compare_2))
  (0_spush_1    (call 2_sarg_2 0_))
  (2_copy_2     (if (pair? s) 2_spush_2 2_compare_2))         ; copy character
  (2_spush_2    (call 2_sarg_2 2_))                           ; to stack
  (2_sarg_2     ((t := (hd s)) (s := (tl s))) (goto 2_copy_2))

  (2_compare_2  (if (null? t) 2_spop_3 2_cequal?_2))          ; p didn't match
  (2_cequal?_2  (if (= 'A t) 2_cnext_2 2_restore_2))          ; t equal A
  (2_cnext_2    (return () compare_4))                        ; continue match
  (2_restore_2  (return () compare_2))                        ; restart match

  (2_compare_4  (if (null? t) 2_spop_3 2_cequal?_4))          ; p didn't match
  (2_cequal?_4  (if (= 'A t) 2_cnext_4 2_compare_2))          ; t equal A
  (2_cnext_4    (return () compare_5))                        ; continue match

  (2_compare_5  (if (null? t) 2_spop_3 2_cequal?_5))          ; p didn't match
  (2_cequal?_5  (if (= 'B t) 2_spop_7 2_compare_4))           ; t equal B

  (2_spop_3     (return () spop_3))                           ; pop to reject
  (2_spop_7     (return () spop_7))                           ; pop to accept

  (0_compare_2  ((p := 'reject)) (goto 0_spop_f))             ; return reject
  (0_compare_4  ((p := 'reject)) (goto 0_spop_f))             ; return reject
  (0_compare_5  ((p := 'reject)) (goto 0_spop_f))             ; return reject
  (0_spop_3     ((p := 'reject)) (goto 0_spop_f))             ; return reject
  (0_spop_7     ((p := 'accept)) (goto 0_spop_14))            ; return accept
  (0_spop_f     (return (p) spop_d))                          ; halt
  (0_spop_14    (return (p) spop_12)))                        ; halt
```

Fig. 8. A linear-time residual matcher for pattern p = (A A B) after post-processing

but is otherwise not essential. Recall that upon a return, two labels are appended, l' on the call stack and l'' in the return statement, and control returns to block $l' \cdot l''$ (*cf.* E5, Fig. 2). Thus, when the label on the call stack is empty, $l' = $ nil, control returns to block $l'' = $ nil $\cdot l''$. For example, (return (p q) compare) returns to block compare provided the corresponding call was (call rarg ()), where () represents the empty label nil.[2] A return can update the values of several variables in the target block (here, p, q are updated in block compare).

Fast residual matcher. To illustrate the residual matchers, we specialize the naive matcher in Fig. 7 with respect to p = (A A B) using the maximally-polyvariant partial evaluator. After postprocessing including transition compression, inlining constants, and adding syntactic sugar, this yields the residual matcher in Fig. 8.

Again, the residual matcher consists of two phases. As before, the first phase recursively builds the call stack in time and size proportional to the length of s

---

[2] A return block that returns to itself halts a program: (spop (return (p) spop)).

(blocks 2_copy_2 to 2_sarg_2). Unlike the naive matcher in Fig. 7, the second phase performs the matching *without* restoring any part of the string (blocks 2_compare_2 to 2_cequal?_5). Control is dispatched depending on the outcome of the tests, and only jumps or returns to the next test; there are no restore calls. The pattern is hard-coded. The residual matcher takes time linear in the length of s and its size is linear in the length of p. It satisfies the conditions of a Type 1 matcher (this is the case for all residual matchers; see below). The residual variants of block spop are artifacts of specializing the outermost call sarg with respect to static $t = ()$, and inlining constants by post-processing.

The residual matcher is a linear-time *Morris-Pratt matcher* [1,3]. A Morris-Pratt matcher performs some redundant tests because negative information obtained during the last mismatch is not exploited in the next match. For example, in our residual matcher, when the two tests (null? t) and (= 'A t) fail at blocks 2_compare_4 and 2_cequal?_4, they are repeated at blocks 2_compare_2 and 2_cequal?_2 before restarting the match. Only a program-dependent number of redundant tests is performed, so the linear-time performance of a Morris-Pratt matcher is not affected. Negative information about tests is not exploited by the partial evaluator as done by perfect driving in supercompilation [17,18].

Linear-time specialization. From the analysis in the previous section we know that the graph-based collection takes time linear in the number of configurations under the conditions in Table 1. To show that is the case when specializing the naive matcher in Fig. 7 with respect to a static pattern, we check all configurations that can occur. We use the fact that the matcher runs in two phases.

During the first phase, the static variables (p, q) representing the pattern are unchanged; all operations on the dynamic variable s are suspended. Thus, in the first phase, the number of configurations and their predecessors is $O(1)$. According to Table 1, the number of terminators is of no concern for configurations of type x (in fact, it is $O(m)$ because all pattern positions may be returned).

In the second phase, the static variables (p, q) may represent every position in the static pattern, which means the number of possible configurations is $O(m)$. Because the only variables live at a call to block rarg are static (p, q), all restore calls are precomputed, and never occur in the residual matcher. A static call is deterministic and, if it terminates, has exactly one terminator. Thus, the second phase has $O(m)$ configurations, and for each configuration the number of terminators and predecessors is $O(1)$ (configurations of type z).

The conditions in Table 1 are satisfied and the collection takes time $O(m)$. The number of configurations in both phases is $O(m)$, and so is the size of the residual matcher obtained by block specialization. A trivial specialization of the partial evaluator yields an $O(m)$-time generating extension, which is sufficient to satisfy the Type 2 requirement and solve Futamura's challenge.

5   Related Work

Parsing algorithms make use of sharing to achieve polynomial-time performance. Generalized LR parsing in particular uses a related graph-structured representation of parsing stacks [20]. Most algorithms rely on the 1-way nature of parsing, and often treat left recursion as a special case, *e.g.* by grammar transformation, while our partial evaluation method assumes no directionality when exploring the configuration space. Our method examines only those configurations that are reachable from the initial configuration, while the classic simulation methods for 2-way pushdown automata also examine unreachable pushdown configurations bottom-up [2,10]; exceptions are the 2D-PDA simulations [22,27]. Methods for model checking of recursive procedures [4] also make use of pushdown systems. Related work on partial evaluation was discussed throughout the paper.

6   Conclusion

We presented an efficient method for maximally-polyvariant partial evaluation of recursive flowchart languages that makes use of computation sharing by memoization and a graph-structured stack representation. We exploited analogies with pushdown automata for the linear-time specialization of a naive string matcher.

A main result of this investigation is that super-linear program staging by partial evaluation is possible. Three keys to the solution are:

1. high accuracy by maximally-polyvariant partial evaluation (allows recursive procedures with multiple terminators),
2. fast partial evaluation by a polynomial-time reachability algorithm (solves a class of quasi-deterministic reachability problems in linear time), and a
3. source program structure analogous to pushdown systems (exposes recursive subproblems to memoization).

A direction for future work is to investigate how more deeply specialized generating extensions can be obtained from the mechanisms above, and practical issues related to super-linear staging and the generation of fast program generators.

Acknowledgments. The author would like to thank Andrei Klimov and the anonymous reviewers for their comments, and Chung-chieh Shan for discussions of parsing. It is a great pleasure to thank Akihiko Takano for providing the author with excellent working conditions at the National Institute of Informatics, Tokyo, and Masami Hagiya and Zhenjiang Hu for their invaluable support.

References

1. Ager, M.S., Danvy, O., Rohde, H.K.: Fast partial evaluation of pattern matching in strings. ACM TOPLAS **28**(4), 696–714 (2006)
2. Aho, A.V., Hopcroft, J.E., Ullman, J.D.: Time and tape complexity of pushdown automaton languages. Inf. Control **13**(3), 186–206 (1968)
3. Aho, A.V., Hopcroft, J.E., Ullman, J.D.: The Design and Analysis of Computer Algorithms. Addison-Wesley, Reading (1974)
4. Alur, R., Bouajjani, A., Esparza, J.: Model checking procedural programs. In: Clarke, E.M., Henzinger, T.A., Veith, H. (eds.) Handbook of Model Checking. Springer, Heidelberg (2016)

5. Amtoft-Hansen, T., Nikolajsen, T., Träff, J.L., Jones, N.D.: Experiments with implementations of two theoretical constructions. In: Meyer, A.R., Taitslin, M.A. (eds.) Logic at Botik 1989. LNCS, vol. 363, pp. 119–133. Springer, Heidelberg (1989)

6. Bulyonkov, M.A.: Polyvariant mixed computation for analyzer programs. Acta Informatica **21**(5), 473–484 (1984)

7. Bulyonkov, M.A.: Extracting polyvariant binding time analysis from polyvariant specializer. In: Partial Evaluation and Program Manipulation, pp. 59–65. ACM (1993)

8. Christensen, N.H., Glück, R.: Offline partial evaluation can be as accurate as online partial evaluation. ACM TOPLAS **26**(1), 191–220 (2004)

9. Consel, C., Danvy, O.: Partial evaluation of pattern matching in strings. Inf. Process. Lett. **30**(2), 79–86 (1989)

10. Cook, S.A.: Linear time simulation of deterministic two-way pushdown automata. In: Freiman, C.V., Griffith, J.E., Rosenfeld, J.L. (eds.) Information Processing 71, pp. 75–80. North-Holland, Amsterdam (1972)

11. Ershov, A.P.: On the partial computation principle. Inf. Process. Lett. **6**(2), 38–41 (1977)

12. Futamura, Y., Konishi, Z., Glück, R.: Automatic generation of efficient string matching algorithms by generalized partial computation. In: Asian Symposium on Partial Evaluation and Program Manipulation, pp. 1–8. ACM (2002)

13. Futamura, Y., Konishi, Z., Glück, R.: Program transformation system based on generalized partial computation. New Gener. Comput. **20**(1), 75–99 (2002)

14. Futamura, Y., Nogi, K.: Generalized partial computation. In: Bjørner, D., Ershov, A.P., Jones, N.D. (eds.) Partial Evaluation and Mixed Computation, North-Holland, pp. 133–151 (1988)

15. Glück, R.: A self-applicable online partial evaluator for recursive flowchart languages. Softw. Pract. Experience **42**(6), 649–673 (2012)

16. Glück, R.: A practical simulation result for two-way pushdown automata. In: Han, Y.-S., Salomaa, K. (eds.) Implementation and Application of Automata. LNCS, vol. 9705. Springer, Heidelberg (2016)

17. Glück, R., Jørgensen, J.: Generating transformers for deforestation and supercompilation. In: LeCharlier, B. (ed.) SAS 1994. LNCS, vol. 864, pp. 432–448. Springer, Heidelberg (1994)

18. Glück, R., Klimov, A.V.: Occam's razor in metacomputation: the notion of a perfect process tree. In: Cousot, P., Falaschi, M., Filé, G., Rauzy, A. (eds.) WSA 1993. LNCS, vol. 724, pp. 112–123. Springer, Heidelberg (1993)

19. Gomard, C.K., Jones, N.D.: Compiler generation by partial evaluation: a case study. Structured Program. **12**(3), 123–144 (1991)

20. Grune, D., Jacobs, C.J.H.: Parsing Techniques: A Practical Guide. Monographs in Computer Science, 2nd edn. Springer, New York (2008)

21. Hatcliff, J.: An introduction to online and offline partial evaluation using a simple flowchart language. In: Hatcliff, J., Mogensen, T.Æ., Thiemann, P. (eds.) Partial Evaluation 1998. LNCS, vol. 1706, pp. 20–82. Springer, Heidelberg (1999)

22. Jones, N.D.: A note on linear time simulation of deterministic two-way pushdown automata. Inf. Process. Lett. **6**(4), 110–112 (1977)

23. Jones, N.D.: Automatic program specialization: a re-examination from basic principles. In: Bjørner, D., Ershov, A.P., Jones, N.D. (eds.) Partial Evaluation and Mixed Computation, North-Holland, pp. 225–282 (1988)

24. Jones, N.D., Gomard, C.K., Sestoft, P.: Partial Evaluation and Automatic Program Generation. Prentice-Hall, Englewood Cliffs (1993)

25. Knuth, D.E., Morris, J.H., Pratt, V.R.: Fast pattern matching in strings. SIAM J. Comput. **6**(2), 323–350 (1977)
26. Mogensen, T.Æ.: Evolution of partial evaluators: removing inherited limits. In: Danvy, O., Glück, R., Thiemann, P. (eds.) Partial Evaluation. LNCS, vol. 1110, pp. 303–321. Springer, Heidelberg (1996)
27. Rytter, W.: A simulation result for two-way pushdown automata. Inf. Process. Lett. **16**(4), 199–202 (1983)
28. Sørensen, M.H., Glück, R., Jones, N.D.: A positive supercompiler. J. Funct. Program. **6**(6), 811–838 (1996)

Dynamics Security Policies and Process Opacity for Timed Process Algebras

Damas P. Gruska[✉]

Institute of Informatics, Comenius University,
Mlynska dolina, 84248 Bratislava, Slovakia
gruska@fmph.uniba.sk

Abstract. Process opacity for dynamic security policies is formalized and studied. The dynamic security policies influence what an intruder can observe as well as which part of system's behaviour is classified at a given moment. The resulting security properties are undecidable but under some realistic restrictions we obtain decidable ones.

Keywords: Dynamic security policy · Process opacity · Process algebras · Information flow

1 Introduction

Information flow based security properties (see [GM82]) assume an absence of any information flow between private and public systems activities. This means, that systems are considered to be secure if from observations of their public activities no information about private activities can be deduced. This approach has found many reformulations and among them opacity (see [BKR04, BKMR06]) could be considered as the most general one and many other security properties could be viewed as its special cases (see, for example, [Gru07]). In [Gru15] opacity is modified (the result is called process opacity) in such a way that instead of process's traces we focus on properties of reachable states. Hence we assume an intruder who is not primarily interested whether some sequence of actions performed by a given process has some given property but we consider an intruder who wants to discover whether this process reaches a state which satisfied some given (classified) predicate. It turns out that in this way we could capture some new security flaws. Both opacity and process opacity are based on fixed (static) security policy which is not changed during system computation. This approach seems to be rather restrictive for applications where their security policies (classification, declassification etc.) change dynamically. Hence, there is a growing research and a number of papers devoted to dynamic security properties tailored for various formalizations and computational paradigms. For instance, in the case of imperative programs, security policy requires that values of classified

Work supported by the grant VEGA 1/1333/12.

M. Mazzara and A. Voronkov (Eds.): PSI 2015, LNCS 9609, pp. 149–157, 2016.
DOI: 10.1007/978-3-319-41579-6_12

variables could not be obtained by observing public ones, what can be formalizes by an equivalence relation on values of program's variables. In the case of dynamic security policies, this relation can change during a computation (see, for example, [DHS15]). In general, a dynamic security policy permits different information flows at different points during program/system's execution.

The aim of this paper is to formalize process opacity for dynamic security policies. Here the dynamic security policies define what an intruder can observe as well as which part of system's behaviour is classified at a given moment. Since our plan is to elaborate techniques for description of timing attacks and to verify systems security against them, we have decided to work with a timed process algebra which can be used for description of timing behavior of systems. We do not consider value-passing algebra since we focus on actions and not on communicated values. Considering also values and possible security types of variables would bring new challenges and we leave it for future work together with some other proposals which are mentioned in the next sections.

The paper is organized as follows. In Sect. 2 we describe the timed process algebra TPA which will be used as a basic formalism. In Sect. 3 we present some notion on information flow security and in the next section dynamic security policies for process opacity are defined and studied. Section 5 contains discussion and plans for future work.

2   Timed Process Algebra

In this section we define Timed Process Algebra, TPA for short. TPA is based on Milner's CCS but the special time action t which expresses elapsing of (discrete) time is added. The presented language is a slight simplification of Timed Security Process Algebra introduced in [FGM00]. We omit an explicit idling operator ι used in tSPA and instead of this we allow implicit idling of processes. Hence processes can perform either "enforced idling" by performing t actions which are explicitly expressed in their descriptions or "voluntary idling" (i.e. for example, the process $a.Nil$ can perform t action since it is not contained the process specification). But in both cases internal communications have priority to action t in the parallel composition. Moreover we do not divide actions into private and public ones as it is in tSPA. TPA differs also from the tCryptoSPA (see [GM04]). TPA does not use value passing and strictly preserves *time determinancy* in case of choice operator $+$ what is not the case of tCryptoSPA.

To define the language TPA, we first assume a set of atomic action symbols A not containing symbols τ and t, and such that for every $a \in A$ there exists $\bar{a} \in A$ and $\bar{\bar{a}} = a$. We define $Act = A \cup \{\tau\}, At = A \cup \{t\}, Actt = Act \cup \{t\}$. We assume that $a, b, \ldots$ range over A, $u, v, \ldots$ range over Act, and $x, y \ldots$ range over $Actt$. Assume the signature $\Sigma = \bigcup_{n \in \{0,1,2\}} \Sigma_n$, where

$$\Sigma_0 = \{Nil\}$$
$$\Sigma_1 = \{x. \mid x \in A \cup \{t\}\} \cup \{[S] \mid S \text{ is a relabeling function}\}$$
$$\cup \{\backslash M \mid M \subseteq A\}$$
$$\Sigma_2 = \{\mid, +\}$$

with the agreement to write unary action operators in prefix form, the unary operators $[S], \backslash M$ in postfix form, and the rest of operators in infix form. Relabeling functions, $S : Actt \rightarrow Actt$ are such that $\overline{S(a)} = S(\bar{a})$ for $a \in A, S(\tau) = \tau$ and $S(t) = t$.

The set of TPA terms over the signature Σ is defined by the following BNF notation:

$$P :: = X \mid op(P_1, P_2, \ldots P_n) \mid \mu X P$$

where $X \in Var$, Var is a set of process variables, $P, P_1, \ldots P_n$ are TPA terms, $\mu X-$ is the binding construct, $op \in \Sigma$.

The set of CCS terms consists of TPA terms without t action. We will use an usual definition of opened and closed terms where μX is the only binding operator. Closed terms which are t-guarded (each occurrence of X is within some subterm $t.A$ i.e. between any two t actions only finitely many non timed actions can be performed) are called TPA processes.

We give a structural operational semantics of terms by means of labeled transition systems. The set of terms represents a set of states, labels are actions from $Actt$. The transition relation $\rightarrow$ is a subset of $TPA \times Actt \times TPA$. We write $P \xrightarrow{x} P'$ instead of $(P, x, P') \in \rightarrow$ and $P \not\xrightarrow{x}$ if there is no P' such that $P \xrightarrow{x} P'$. The meaning of the expression $P \xrightarrow{x} P'$ is that the term P can evolve to P' by performing action x, by $P \xrightarrow{x}$ we will denote that there exists a term P' such that $P \xrightarrow{x} P'$. We define the transition relation as the least relation satisfying the inference rules for CCS plus the following inference rules:

$$\frac{}{Nil \xrightarrow{t} Nil} \quad A1 \qquad \frac{}{u.P \xrightarrow{t} u.P} \quad A2$$

$$\frac{P \xrightarrow{t} P', Q \xrightarrow{t} Q', P \mid Q \not\xrightarrow{\tau}}{P \mid Q \xrightarrow{t} P' \mid Q'} \quad Pa \qquad \frac{P \xrightarrow{t} P', Q \xrightarrow{t} Q'}{P + Q \xrightarrow{t} P' + Q'} \quad S$$

Here we mention the rules that are new with respect to CCS. Axioms $A1, A2$ allow arbitrary idling. Concurrent processes can idle only if there is no possibility of an internal communication (Pa). A run of time is deterministic (S) i.e. performing of t action does not lead to the choice between summands of $+$. In the definition of the labeled transition system we have used negative premises (see Pa). In general this may lead to problems, for example with consistency of the defined system. We avoid these dangers by making derivations of τ independent of derivations of t. For an explanation and details see [Gro90].

For $s = x_1.x_2.\ldots.x_n, x_i \in Actt$ we write $P \xrightarrow{s}$ instead of $P \xrightarrow{x_1}\xrightarrow{x_2} \ldots \xrightarrow{x_n}$ and we say that s is a trace of P. The set of all traces of P will be denoted by $Tr(P)$. By ϵ we will denote the empty sequence of actions, by $Succ(P)$ we will denote the set of all successors of P i.e. $Succ(P) = \{P' \mid P \xrightarrow{s} P', s \in Actt^*\}$. If set $Succ(P)$ is finite we say that P is finite state process. We define modified transitions $\xRightarrow{}_M$ which "hide" actions from M. Formally, we will write $P\xRightarrow{x}_M P'$ for $M \subseteq Actt$ iff $P \xrightarrow{s_1} \xrightarrow{x} \xrightarrow{s_2} P'$ for $s_1, s_2 \in M^*$ and $P\xRightarrow{s}_M$ instead of $P\xRightarrow{x_1}_M\xRightarrow{x_2}_M \ldots \xRightarrow{x_n}_M$. We will write $P\xRightarrow{x}_M$ if there exists P' such that $P\xRightarrow{x}_M P'$. We will write $P\xRightarrow{\hat{x}}_M P'$

instead of $P \overset{\xi}{\Rightarrow}_M P'$ if $x \in M$. Note that $\overset{x}{\Rightarrow}_M$ is defined for arbitrary action but in definitions of security properties we will use it for actions (or sequence of actions) not belonging to M. We can the extend the definition of $\Rightarrow_M$ for sequences of actions similarly to $\overset{s}{\rightarrow}$. By $Sort(P)$ we will denote the set of actions from A which can be performed by P. The set of weak timed traces of process P is defined as $Tr_w(P) = \{s \in (A \cup \{t\})^* | \exists P'.P \overset{s}{\Rightarrow}_{\{\tau\}} P'\}$. Two process P and Q are weakly timed trace equivalent $(P \simeq_w Q)$ iff $Tr_w(P) = Tr_w(Q)$. We conclude this section with definitions M-bisimulation and weak timed trace equivalence.

Definition 1. Let $(TPA, Actt, \rightarrow)$ be a labelled transition system (LTS). A relation $\Re \subseteq TPA \times TPA$ is called a M-bisimulation if it is symmetric and it satisfies the following condition: if $(P, Q) \in \Re$ and $P \overset{x}{\rightarrow} P', x \in Actt$ then there exists a process Q' such that $Q \overset{\hat{x}}{\Rightarrow}_M Q'$ and $(P', Q') \in \Re$. Two processes P, Q are M-bisimilar, abbreviated $P \approx_M Q$, if there exists a M-bisimulation relating P and Q.

3 Information Flow

In this section we will present motivations for new security concepts which will be introduced in the next section. First we define an absence-of-information-flow property - Strong Nondeterministic Non-Interference (SNNI, for short, see [FGM00]). Suppose that all actions are divided into two groups, namely public (low level) actions L and private (high level) actions H. It is assumed that $L \cup H = A$. Process P has SNNI property (we will write $P \in SNNI$) if $P \backslash H$ behaves like P for which all high level actions are hidden (by action τ) for an observer. To express this hiding we introduce hiding operator $P/M, M \subseteq A$, for which it holds if $P \overset{a}{\rightarrow} P'$ then $P/M \overset{a}{\rightarrow} P'/M$ whenever $a \notin M \cup \bar{M}$ and $P/M \overset{\tau}{\rightarrow} P'/M$ whenever $a \in M \cup \bar{M}$. Formally, we say that P has SNNI property, and we write $P \in SNNI$ iff $P \backslash H \simeq_w P/H$. SNNI property assumes an intruder who tries to learn whether a private action was performed by a given process while (s)he can observe only public ones. If this cannot be done then the process has SNNI property. A generalization of this concept is given by opacity (this concept was exploited in [BKR04, BKMR06, Gru07] in a framework of Petri Nets, transition systems and process algebras, respectively. Actions are not divided into public and private ones at the system description level but a more general concept of observations and predicates is exploited. A predicate is opaque if for any trace of a system for which it holds, there exists another trace for which it does not hold and the both traces are indistinguishable for an observer (which is expressed by an observation function). This means that the observer (intruder) cannot say whether a trace for which the predicate holds has been performed or not.

Let us assume that an intruder tries to discover whether a given process can reach a state with some given property expressed by a (total) predicate. This might be process deadlock, capability to execute only traces s with time length less then n, capability to perform at the same time actions form a given set, incapacity to idle (to perform t action) etc. We do not put any restriction on such predicates but we only assume that they are consistent with some suitable behaviorial equivalence. The formal definition follows.

Definition 2. *We say that the predicate ϕ over processes is consistent with respect to relation $\cong$ if whenever $P \cong P'$ then $\phi(P) \Leftrightarrow \phi(P')$.*

As consistency relation $\cong$ we could take bisimulation ($\approx_\emptyset$), weak bisimulation ($\approx_{\{\tau\}}$) or any other suitable equivalence. A special class of such predicates are such ones (denoted as $\phi_{\cong}^Q$) which are defined by a given process Q and equivalence relation $\cong$ i.e. $\phi_{\cong}^Q(P)$ holds iff $P \cong Q$.

We suppose that the intruder can observe only some activities performed by the process. Hence we suppose that there is a set of public actions which can be observed and a set of hidden (not necessarily private) actions. To model observations we exploit the relation $\stackrel{s}{\Rightarrow}_M$. The formal definition of process opacity (see [Gru15]) is the following.

Definition 3 (Process Opacity). *Given process P, a predicate ϕ over processes is process opaque w.r.t. the set M if whenever $P \stackrel{s}{\Rightarrow}_M P'$ for $s \in (Actt \setminus M)^*$ and $\phi(P')$ holds then there exists P'' such that $P \stackrel{s}{\Rightarrow}_M P''$ and $\neg\phi(P'')$ holds. The set of processes for which the predicate ϕ is process opaque w.r.t. to the M will be denoted by POp_M^ϕ.*

Note that if $P \cong P'$ then $P \in POp_M^\phi \Leftrightarrow P' \in POp_M^\phi$ whenever ϕ is consistent with respect to $\cong$ and $\cong$ is such that it a subset of the trace equivalence (defined as $\simeq_w$ but insted of $\stackrel{s}{\Rightarrow}_{\{\tau\}}$ we use $\stackrel{s}{\Rightarrow}_\emptyset$).

4   Dynamic Security Policies

In this section we will generalize process opacity. First we define its persistent variant. It requires that not only process itself is process opaque but also all its successors are process opaque. The formal definition is the following.

Definition 4 (Persistent Process Opacity) *Given process P, a predicate ϕ over processes is persistently process opaque w.r.t. the set M if $P \in POp_M^\phi$ and whenever $P \stackrel{s}{\Rightarrow}_M P'$ for $s \in (Actt \setminus M)^*$ then $P' \in POp_M^\phi$. The set of processes for which the predicate ϕ is persistently process opaque w.r.t. to the M will be denoted by $PPOp_M^\phi$.*

Persistent process opacity is, in general, the stronger property then process opacity as it is stated by the following proposition.

Proposition 1. $PPOp_M^\phi \subseteq POp_M^\phi$ *and there exists M and ϕ such that the inclusion is proper.*

Proof. Sketch. The inclusion part follows directly form Definitions 3 and 4. Now let as assume that ϕ holds iff process cannot perform action h. Let $P = a.h.(a.h.Nil + a.Nil) + a.aNil$ then $P \in POp_{\{h\}}^\phi$ but $P \notin PPOp_{\{h\}}^\phi$.

Process opacity and persistent process opacity represent static security properties since neither predicates nor sets M can change during system's execution. To define dynamic security policy first we introduce a *security policy* as a pair (M, ϕ) with the first component being a set of actions non-visible for an intruder and the second component is a predicate over processes. We assume some fixed set L of actions which always visible to possible intruders. Some or all actions from $Actt \backslash L$ could become temporally visible. Actions from M, $M \subseteq Actt \backslash L$ are supposed to be invisible. Given security policy (M, ϕ) we define which processes satisfy this policy by means of process opacity.

Definition 5. *We say that process P satisfy security policy (M, ϕ) if $P \in POp_M^\phi$.*

Now we can define partial ordering on security policies. This ordering takes into account both the set of invisible actions as well as the strength of predicates.

Definition 6. *Given two security policies (M_1, ϕ_1) and (M_2, ϕ_2). We say that policy (M_1, ϕ_1) is stronger then (M_2, ϕ_2) (denoted by $\preceq$) iff $\phi_2 \Rightarrow \phi_1$ and $M_1 \subseteq M_2$. Let T be a set of policies. We will write $(M, \phi) \preceq T$ iff $(M, \phi) \preceq (M', \phi')$ for every $(M, \phi') \in T$.*

The ordering on security policies define security level for processes as it is stated by the following proposition.

Proposition 2. *Given two security policies (M_1, ϕ_1) and (M_2, ϕ_2) such that $(M_1, \phi_1) \preceq (M_2, \phi_2)$. Then $POp_{M_1}^{\phi_1} \subseteq POp_{M_2}^{\phi_2}$.*

Proof. Let $(M_1, \phi_1) \preceq (M_2, \phi_2)$. In [Gru15] we have proved that $POp_{M_1}^\phi \subseteq POp_{M_2}^\phi$ for $M_1 \subseteq M_2$ and $POp_M^{\phi_1} \subseteq POp_M^{\phi_2}$ if ϕ_2 implies ϕ_1. We complete the proof by applying these properties first for sets M_i and then for predicates ϕ_i.

Now we define dynamic security policy as a mapping which maps every visibly executed sequence s to a security policy. Then process satisfies dynamic policy if all its corresponding successors satisfy corresponding security policies. Formal definitions follow.

Definition 7. *Dynamic policy is a mapping D which maps every sequence $s, s \in L^*$ to a security policy.*

Definition 8. *We say that process P satisfies dynamic policy D (denoted by $P \in dsp(D)$) if for every $s \in L^*$ such that $P \overset{s}{\Rightarrow}_{Actt \backslash L} P'$ it holds $P' \in POp_M^\phi$ where $D(s) = (M, \phi)$.*

An alternative way how to define dynamic security policy could be by mappings which assign security policy to "present" security policy (and/or process P) and an execution path, i.e. mappings which assign $((M_1, \phi_1) \times s) \mapsto (M_2, \phi_2)$ $(P \times (M_1, \phi_1) \times s) \mapsto (M_2, \phi_2)$, $(P \times s) \mapsto (M_2, \phi_2))$, respectively (as regards the third possibility, see [DHS15]). Elaborating these approaches we leave for further work.

A special case of dynamic security policy is such one, which does not change security policy during execution. This case corresponds to persistent process opacity i.e. $P \in dsp(D)$ iff $P \in PPOp_M^\phi$ for D such that $D(s) = (M, \phi)$ for every $s, s \in L^*$. Moreover, also in the case of truly dynamic security policy D (which does not map every sequence to one given security policy), we can find appropriate "the strongest" persistent process opacity which guaranties $dsp(D)$ property as it is stated by the following proposition.

Proposition 3. *Given dynamic security policy D. Let $(M, \phi) \preceq I(D)$ where $I(D)$ is the image of D and $P \in PPOp_M^\phi$. Then $P \in dsp(D)$.*

Proof. Sketch. The proof follows from Proposition 2 and Definition 4.

Unfortunately, process security with respect to dynamic security policy is undecidable.

Proposition 4. *Process security with respect to dynamic security policy D (i.e. the question whether $P \in dsp(D)$) is undecidable in general.*

Proof. Sketch. The proof follows from Propositions 1, 3 and from undecidability of process opacity (see [Gru15]).

To obtain decidability of process opacity for dynamic security policies we put some restrictions on security policies as well as on mappings which assign them. First we model predicates by special processes called tests. For now we assume that action τ is not visible for an intruder, i.e. $\tau \in M$ for every security policy from $I(D)$. The tests communicate with processes and produce $\sqrt{}$ action if corresponding predicates hold for the processes. Then we model also dynamic security policy by a process which associate predicates with sequences of visible actions. In the subsequent proposition we show how to exploit this idea to express process opacity by means of appropriate M-bisimulation.

Definition 9. *We say that process T_ϕ is a test representing predicate ϕ if $\phi(P)$ holds iff $(P|T_\phi) \setminus At \approx_t \sqrt{_\phi}.Nil$ where $\sqrt{_\phi}$ is a new action indicating a passing of the test. If T_ϕ is the finite state process we say that ϕ is finitely definable predicate.*

Definition 10. *Suppose than dynamic security policy does not change a set of invisible actions, i.e. there exists M such $D(s) = (M, \phi_s)$ for every s. We say that process T_D defines dynamic security policy D iff $(T_D|s.Nil)[f]\setminus Sort(s.Nil) \approx T_{\phi_s}[f]$ for every $s \in L^*$ and appropriate choice of f. If T_D is the finite state process we say that dynamic security policy D is finitely definable.*

Note, that the renaming function f in the previous definition is needed to ensure that the whole sequence s is consumed by T_D to emulate T_{ϕ_s}. To formulate the proposition which reduces verification of security with respect to a given dynamic security policy to checking a variant of weak bisimulation, we need an auxiliary definition of contexts process (see, for example, [Gru10]).

Definition 11. *By context process we denote process which contains place holder(s) $\mathcal{H}$ i.e. in TPA term definition we allow also $\mathcal{H}$ alongside with process variable X. Let O be the context process. By $O[P]$ we denote process obtained from O by replacing all placeholders by P.*

Proposition 5. *Let dynamic security policy D is finitely definable and for every s, predicates ϕ, $\neg\phi$ are the finitely definable as well, where $D(s) = (M, \phi)$. Then there exists context process O such that $P \in dsp(M)$ iff $O[P] \approx_{M \cup \{t\}} F^n$ where $F = \sqrt{\phi} \cdot \sqrt{\neg\phi} . Nil + \sqrt{\neg\phi} \cdot \sqrt{\phi} . Nil + \sqrt{\neg\phi} . Nil$ and F^n denotes n parallel runs of F, where $n = |I(D)|$ i.e. n is equal to the size of the image of D.*

Proof. The main idea. To construct process context O we exploit process T_D and T_ϕ, $T_{\neg\phi}$. Process context duplicates necessary number copies of sequences of actions to corresponding copies of T_D processes as well as to T_ϕ and $T_{\neg\phi}$ processes. The auxiliary process B ("inside" O) produces visible actions for each copy of P or produces k actions which start validations of ϕ and $\neg\phi$, respectively, by corresponding tests. Then if process passes the test for validity of ϕ it has to pass also the test for validity of $\neg\phi$ (ordering is not important) or can pass only the test of validity of $\neg\phi$ or none. Note that time behaviour is checked by tests. This is the reason why we can use $\approx_{M \cup \{t\}}$ instead of $\approx_M$.

Now, thanks to the above introduced constructions, we can obtain a variant of decidable dynamic security policies. Actually, a limitation to finite states tests and policies are practically insignificant since the most of (if not all) practically important properties can be described by them.

Proposition 6. *Let dynamic security policy D is finitely definable and for every s, predicates ϕ, $\neg\phi$ are finitely definable as well, where $D(s) = (M, \phi)$. Process security with respect to dynamic security policy D is decidable in time $O((n.m.k.|A|)^3)$ for finite state processes, where n, m and k are numbers of states of P and the maximum of numbers of states of tests corresponding to ϕ and $\neg\phi$ and number of states of the process T_D corresponding to dynamic security policy D.*

Proof. According to Proposition 5 it is enough to prove that $\approx_{M \cup \{t\}}$ can be decided in time $O((n.m.k.|A|)^3)$. This can be done by the slight modification of the proof of complexity results for weak bisimulation (see [KS83]).

In the previous definitions and proposition we have assumed finite dynamic security policies, i.e. such ones for which image of D is finite. On the other side, we may restrict capabilities of an intruder and/or of dynamic security policy in such a way that we are interested only in executions s which contain less then some given number of t actions, i.e. to the case when the intruder has no more time to perform an attack than m time units. The proposed formalism can be easily extended to model such situations. We can also define dynamic security policies which do not depend on elapsing of time i.e. $D(s) = D(s')$ whenever $s|_A = s'|_A$, where $s|_A$ denote the sequence obtained from s by removing elements not contained in A. Similarly, we can define dynamic security policies which depend only on elapsing of time by requiring $D(s) = D(s')$ whenever $s|_{\{t\}} = s'|_{\{t\}}$.

5 Discussion and Further Work

We have presented the new security concept - dynamic security policies for process opacity and we have formalized it in the timed process algebra setting. We have shown that static persistent process opacity, which is strictly stronger then process opacity, is a special case of dynamic variant of process opacity. Moreover, by careful choice of processes expressing predicates as well as security policies we can obtain properties which can be effectively checked. We can model security with respect to limited time length of an attack, with a limited number of attempts to perform an attack and so on. We also plan to study dynamic security policies which assume intruders which are not only observers but can actively interact with the systems to be attacked.

References

[BKR04]   Bryans, J., Koutny, M., Ryan, P.: Modelling non-deducibility using Petri Nets. In: Proceedings of the 2nd International Workshop on Security Issues with Petri Nets and other Computational Models (2004)

[BKMR06] Bryans, J.W., Koutny, M., Mazaré, L., Ryan, P.Y.A.: Opacity generalised to transition systems. In: Dimitrakos, T., Martinelli, F., Ryan, P.Y.A., Schneider, S. (eds.) FAST 2005. LNCS, vol. 3866, pp. 81–95. Springer, Berlin (2006)

[DHS15]   van Delft, B., Hunt, S., Sands, D.: Very static enforcement of dynamic policies. In: Focardi, R., Myers, A. (eds.) POST 2015. LNCS, vol. 9036, pp. 32–52. Springer, Heidelberg (2015)

[FGM00]   Focardi, R., Gorrieri, R., Martinelli, F.: Information flow analysis in a discrete-time process algebra. In: Proceedings of 13th Computer Security Foundation Workshop. IEEE Computer Society Press (2000)

[GM04]   Gorrieri, R., Martinelli, F.: A simple framework for real-time cryptographic protocol analysis with compositional proof rules. Sci. Comput. Program. 50(1–3), 23–49 (2004)

[GM82]   Goguen, J.A., Meseguer, J.: Security policies and security models. In: Proceedings of IEEE Symposium on Security and Privacy (1982)

[Gro90]   Groote, J.F.: Transition systems specification with negative premises. In: Baeten, J.C.M., Klop, J.W. (eds.) CONCUR 1990. LNCS, vol. 458, pp. 332–341. Springer, Heidelberg (1990)

[Gru15]   Gruska, D.P.: Process opacity for timed process algebra. In: Voronkov, A., Virbitskaite, I. (eds.) PSI 2014. LNCS, vol. 8974, pp. 151–160. Springer, Heidelberg (2015)

[Gru10]   Gruska, D.P.: Process algebra contexts and security properties. Fundamenta Informaticae 102(1), 63–76 (2010)

[Gru07]   Gruska, D.P.: Observation based system security. Fundamenta Informaticae 79(3–4), 335–346 (2007)

[KS83]   Kanellakis, P.C., Smolka, S.A.: CCS expressions, finite state processes, and three problems of equivalence. In: Proceedings of The second annual ACM Symposium on Principles of Distributed Computing. ACM (1983)

Estimating Development Effort for Software Architectural Tactics

Mohamad Kassab[1,2(✉)] and Giuseppe Destefanis[3]

[1] Innopolis University, Kazan, Russia
[2] Engineering Division, The Pennsylvania State University, Malvern, PA, USA
muk36@psu.edu
[3] CRIM, Computer Research Institute of Montreal, Montreal, Canada
giuseppe.destefanis@crim.ca

Abstract. The increased awareness of the quality requirements as a key to software project and product success makes explicit the need to include them in any software project effort estimation activity. However, the existing approaches to defining size-based effort relationships still pay insufficient attention to this need. Furthermore, existing functional size measurement methods still remain unpopular in industry. In this paper, we propose the usage of the Analytic Hierarchy Process (AHP) technique in the effort estimation for architectural tactics derived to satisfy the quality requirements. The paper demonstrates the applicability of the approach through a case study.

Keywords: Quality requirements · Tactics · AHP · Requirements engineering · Effort estimation · Functional size

1 Introduction

The increasing software complexity and competition that exist in the software industry have highlighted the need to consider quality requirements as an integral part of software modeling and development. Quality requirements are characteristics that the system must possess in addition to the functionality. They play a critical role in driving architectural structure more than functionality during the software development; and they serve as an essential and distinguishing attributes of the final product.

Empirical reports consistently indicate that improperly dealing with quality requirements leads to project failures, or at least to considerable delays, and, consequently, to significant increases in the final cost [1].

While estimating development effort is a major activity in managing the scope of the requirements, this activity has been neglected for quality attributes in practice. From April 2013 through July 2013, we conducted a survey study on the requirements engineering (RE) current state of practice [2]. The survey drew 247 professional participants from 23 countries and from wide range of industries. Respondents were asked to base their responses on one project that they were either currently involved with or had taken part in during the past five years. Only 36 % of the survey participants reported on taking into account the quality requirements during the size/

© Springer International Publishing Switzerland 2016
M. Mazzara and A. Voronkov (Eds.): PSI 2015, LNCS 9609, pp. 158–169, 2016.
DOI: 10.1007/978-3-319-41579-6_13

effort estimation. For those who conducted estimation for the size/effort, "Expert Judgments" was the most popular technique.

While experiences show that quality requirements may represent more than 50 % of the total effort to produce a software product [3]; software developers are constantly under pressure to deliver on time and on budget. As a result, many projects focus on delivering functionalities at the expense of meeting quality requirements such as reliability, security, maintainability, portability, accuracy, among others. As software complexity grows and clients' demands on software quality requirements increase, these qualities can no longer be considered of secondary importance.

The need to deal comprehensively with the effect of quality attributes on the effort of building the software project generates the need to measure their functional size, as effort is a function of size [4]. Nevertheless, using the functional size measurement (FSMs) methods still remain unpopular in industry. In the RE state of practice survey that we conducted, out of the 60 % of those who reported on performing estimation for the size of requirements or the effort of building them, less than 7 % reported on the usage of any FSM method [2]. In addition, many quality requirements cannot have their functional size directly measured. This is mainly because many of these requirements cannot be operationalized in terms of functionalities but in other forms of architectural decisions.

The goal of this research is to investigate requirements-based tuned early estimation of the software effort. In particular, we propose the usage of the Analytic Hierarchy Process (AHP) technique in the effort estimation for quality requirements. These requirements are subjective and usually captured in qualitative format at the early stages of RE. Since AHP integrates qualitative approach with quantitative one, and subjective approach with objective one, it is appropriate for estimating the quality requirements at the beginning of development.

In the rest of this paper, Sect. 2 reviews related work, Sect. 3 introduces the background of quality-tactics relation and the AHP technique. In Sect. 4 we present our approach of incorporating the AHP for the quality effort estimation; and we demonstrate it through a case study. Finally we summarize and conclude the paper in the Sect. 5.

2   Related Work

Over the years, different estimation techniques have been developed in industry and academia, primarily with the objective of improving the accuracy of schedule, effort and cost estimation. These estimation techniques can primarily be subdivided into two major categories: formal methods and expert-judgment based methods. Overall, quality requirements received little attention compared to functionalities from these effort estimation techniques.

The existing function-point-based FSM techniques have so far addressed the topic of quality requirements only with respect to the task of adjusting the (unadjusted) FP counts to the project context or the environment in which the system is supposed to work. For example, the International Function Point Users Group (IFPUG) [5] has been approaching the inclusion of quality requirements in the final FP count by using qualitative judgments about the system's environment. The current version of the IFPUG Function Point Analysis (FPA) manual [6] speaks of a set of General System

Characteristics and Value Adjustment Factors all meant to address though in different ways – the quality requirements that a project may include.

Currently, there are five FSM models which are proposed by the COSMIC consortium and IFPUG member associations (namely, NESMA [7], FISMA [8], UKSMA [9], COSMIC [10], and IFPUG [6]) and which are recognized as ISO standards. In our earlier work [11], we compared and contrasted the ways in which quality requirements are treated in these FSM standards. For each standard, we looked at what quality requirements artifact is used as input to the FSM process, how this artifact is evaluated, and which FSM counting component reflects the NFRs. We found that all five FSM standards provide, at best, checklists which estimators can use to perform qualitative assessments of certain factors of the system's environment. However, these assessments reflect the subjective view of the professionals who run the FSM process. The FSM standards say nothing about what should be put in place to enable estimators to ensure the reproducibility of their assessment results regarding the NFRs in a project. For example, the Mark II FPA manual [9] refers to recent statistical analysis results and suggests that neither the Value Adjustment Factors from the IFPUG method [6] nor the Technical Complexity Adjustment (TCA) factors from the Mark II FPA method [9] represent well the influence on size of the various characteristics these two methods try to take into account. Indeed, the Mark II FPA manual says that the TCA factors are included only because of continuity with previous versions, and recommends that these factors be ignored altogether (p. 63 in [12]) when sizing applications within a single technical environment (where the TCA is likely to be constant).

Recently, "Software Non-functional Assessment Process" (SNAP) [13] was introduced as a measurement of non-functional software size. SNAP point sizing is a complement to a function point sizing, which measures functional software size. Nevertheless, as we pointed earlier, the usage of any FSM for estimation remains unpopular in the industry.

3   Background

3.1   Quality Requirements and Tactics

Quality is "the totality of characteristics of an entity that bear on its ability to satisfy stated and implied needs" [14]. Software Quality is an essential and distinguishing attribute of the final product. Tactics on the other hand are measures taken to implement the quality attributes [15]. For example, introducing concurrency for a better resource management is a tactic to improve system's Performance. Similarly, Authentication and Authorization are popular tactics to resist unwanted attacks on the system and improve the overall Security. In [15], the authors list the common tactics for the qualities: Availability, Modifiability, Performance, Security, Testability and Usability.

Tactics are considered as the building blocks from which software architectures are composed [15]; and the meeting point between requirements and architecture. Because qualities are being satisfied by implementing their corresponding set of tactics; the effort of building the quality requirements is in fact the effort of implementing their derived tactics. In this paper, our aim is to estimate the effort of building tactics that aim at satisfying the qualities.

3.2   The AHP Technique

The AHP [16, 17] is a technique for modeling complex and multi-criteria problems and solving them using a pairwise comparison process. Based on mathematics and psychology, it was developed by Thomas L. Saaty in the 1970s and has been extensively studied and refined since then. AHP was refined through its application to a wide variety of decision areas, including transport planning, product portfolio selection, benchmarking and resource allocation and energy rationing.

Simply described, AHP breaks down a complex and unstructured problems into a hierarchy of factors. A super-factor may include sub-factors. By pairwise comparison of the factors in the lowest level, we can obtain a prior order of factors under a certain decision criterion. The prior order of super-factors can be deduced from the prior order of sub-factors according to the hierarchy relations.

The AHP process starts by a detailed definition of the problem; goals, all relevant factors and alternative actions are identified. The identified elements are then structured into a hierarchy of levels where goals are put at the highest level and alternative actions are put at the lowest level. Usually, an AHP hierarchy has at least three levels: the goal level, the criteria level, and the alternatives level. This hierarchy highlights relevant factors of the problem and their relationships to each other and to the system as a whole.

Once the hierarchy is built, involved stakeholders (i.e., decision makers) judge and specify importance of the elements of the hierarchy. To establish the importance of elements of the problem, a pairwise comparison process is used. This process starts at the top of the hierarchy by selecting an element (e.g., a goal) and then the elements of the level immediately below are compared in pairs against the selected element. A pairwise matrix is built for each element of the problem; this matrix reflects the relative importance of elements of a given level with respect to a property of the next higher level. Saaty proposed the scale [1...9] to rate the relative importance of one criterion over another (See Table 1). Based on experience, a scale of 9 units is reasonable for humans to discriminate between preferences for two items [16, 17].

Table 1.   Pairwise comparison scale for AHP [16].

Intensity of judgment	Numerical rating
Extreme importance	9
Very strong importance	7
Strong importance	5
Moderate importance	3
Equal importance	1
For compromise between the above values	2, 4, 6, and 8

One important advantage of using AHP technique is that it can measure the degree to which manager's judgments are consistent. In the real world, some inconsistency is acceptable, and even natural. For example, in a sporting contest, if team A usually beats team B, and if team B usually beats team C, this does not imply that team A usually beats team C. The slight inconsistency may result because of the way the teams match up overall. The point is to make sure that inconsistency remains within some reasonable limits. If it exceeds a specific limit, some revision of judgments may be required. AHP technique provides a method to compute the consistency of the pairwise comparisons [16, 17].

4   Incorporating the AHP into Tactics Effort Estimation

4.1   AHP Hierarchy for Effort Estimation

The first step in the AHP process is to construct the hierarchy model. One challenge was to identify the elements of the criteria levels of the effort estimation AHP hierarchy.

We conducted a workshop that drew 24 professionals. During the workshop, professionals participated in a questionnaire and brainstorming session aiming at identifying the set of criteria that contributes to the effort of implementing the tactics. The participants reflected a diverse range of positions; describing themselves as programmers/developers, software/system engineers, or testers 46 % of the time. Architects, project/product managers, analysts, and consultants comprised the remaining 54 % of respondents; positions typically involved in the higher-level aspects of computerized system's technical design. Given this population, responses to the questionnaire are more likely to reflect the opinions and biases of any given project's development team rather than those of other groups represented in a software development effort.

The outcome of the workshop was the generation of Fig. 1 which presents the proposed AHP hierarchy model for the tactics effort estimation.

In the hierarchy, the effort as the object of decision-making appeared at the top level. The alternatives level, namely the bottom level, was composed of the tactics. In the middle, there were two criteria levels. One level had three criteria (level 2), i.e., Complexity, Inadvance in Technique, and Restriction from Developers. There was a convention that the weight of a super-criterion would increase with the increase of the sub-criterion's weights. Thus, we used "inadvance" as a criterion, but not "advance".

In the second criteria level (level 3), there were eight criteria, where functional size, Impact on architecture, association and interactivity are the sub-criteria of complexity, and so on. The contribution of sub-criteria of "Inadvance in Technique" and "Development Restrictions" towards the effort is trivial. The sub-criteria of "Complexity" are briefly explained below:

Functional size: Functional Size Methods have shifted the focus from measuring the technical characteristics of the software towards measuring the functionality of the software that is required by the intended users of the software. If the tactic corresponds to a functionality; then it will have a functional size that can be estimated and compared; otherwise if the tactic corresponds to other types of architectural decisions; then it will have no functional size. The effort is a function of size [4] where the increase in functional size increases the effort.

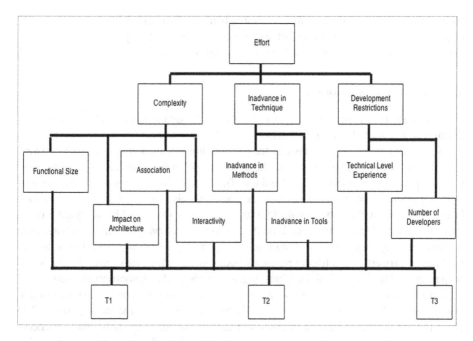

Fig. 1. AHP hierarchy model for the tactics effort estimation

Impact on Architecture: In [18], the authors identified six types of changes that an architectural structure or behavior might undergo when a tactic is implemented within the structure and they define a scale to rate these changes. For example, a tactic can have a minimum impact on the architecture when there are no major changes to be implemented to the current structure (e.g. minimal changes to be implemented within existing components); while it may have high impact on the architecture if the current structure require major changes (e.g. requiring the addition of 3 or more new components that will break the current structure). The higher the impact on the architecture is; the higher contribution to the effort. This criterion suggests also to take into account the order in which the tactics to be implemented. That is, if tactic B implemented after tactic A, then its implementation may require modification to the existing structure of A - a different effort from incorporating tactic B from scratch.

Association: This criterion suggests considering the range of items a tactic is associated to (e.g. functions, resources, processes, or the whole product). The wider this range is, the higher the effort will be.

Interactivity: Typically, systems have multiple important quality attributes, and decisions made to satisfy a particular quality may help or hinder the achievement of another quality attribute. The best-known cases of conflicts occur when the choice of a tactic to implement certain quality attribute contributes negatively towards the achievement of another quality. For example, decisions to maximize the system reusability and maintainability through the usage of "abstracting common services" tactic may come at the cost of the "response time". If a tactic contributes negatively to satisfy other qualities; then it contributes towards the increase in the effort and if it contributes positively towards the satisfaction of other qualities; then it contributes towards the decrease in the total effort.

4.2 Case Study Description

We demonstrate the incorporation of the AHP into quality/tactics effort estimation through an automated building system case study.

A company manufactures devices for the building automation domain and software applications that manage a network of these devices. With the hardware being commoditized, its profit margins have been shrinking. The internal development costs for the software applications that manage different devices have also been rising. To sustain their business long term, the company decides to create a new integrated building automation system. The intended system would broadly perform the following functions: manage field devices currently used for controlling building functions; define rules based on values of field device properties that trigger reactions; issue commands to set values of field device properties; and for life critical situations, trigger alarms notifying appropriate users.

Taking this approach would allow the company to reduce internal development costs – several existing applications will be replaced with the new system. The company could also achieve market expansion by entering new and emerging geographic markets and opening new sales channel in the form of Value Added Resellers (VARs).

In order to support a multitude of hardware devices and consider different languages and cultures, the system must be modifiable (a modifiability requirement). In order to support different regulations in different geographic markets, the system must respond to life threatening events in a timely manner (a performance requirement).

To apply the modifiability tactics, we aim to limit the impact of change and minimize the number of dependencies on the part of the system responsible for integrating new hardware devices. There are three design concerns related with modifiability: (1) Localize changes: this relates to adding a new field device; (2) Prevention of ripple effects: this relates to minimizing the number of modules affected as a result of adding a new field device; and (3) Defer binding time: this relates to the time when a new field device is deployed and the ability of non-programmers to manage such deployment.

We address these concerns by creating adaptors for field devices, an "anticipation of expected changes" tactic. We use two additional architectural tactics to minimize propagation of change. First we specify a standard interface to be exposed by all adaptors ("maintain existing interfaces"). Second, we use the adaptor as an "intermediary" responsible for semantic translation into a standard format, of all the data received from different field devices.

As of the performance quality attribute of the building automation system, there are two design concerns: (1) Resource Demand: the arrival of change of property value events from the various field devices and the evaluation of automation rules in response to these events are source of resource demand; and (2) Resource Management: the demand on resources may have to managed in order to reduce the latency of event and alarm propagation.

To address these concerns, we move the responsibility of rule evaluation and execution, and alarm generation, respectively to a newly added separate Logic & Reaction (L&R) component and an Alarm component. These components running outside the automation server can now be easily moved to dedicated execution nodes if necessary. In doing so, we are making use of the "increase available resources" tactic to address the resource management concern and the "reduce computational overhead" tactic to address the resource demand concern. We use an additional tactic to address the resource management concern. This tactic relies on introducing "concurrency" to reduce delays in processing time. Concurrency is used inside the L&R and Alarm components to perform simultaneous rule evaluations.

So to satisfy modifiability and performance qualities in the building automated systems; we introduced the five tactics: (1) an anticipation of expected changes; (2) maintain existing interfaces; (3) usage of an intermediary; (4) increase available resources; and (5) introducing concurrency.

4.3   AHP in Action

Construction of the hierarchy model is the first step in the problem solving process of the AHP technique. In the hierarchy, each of the eight criteria from level 3 is related to all tactics. In the automated building system case study, this means that each of the criteria: functional size, impact on architecture, association, interactivity, inadvance in methods, inadvance in tools, technical level experience, and number of developers is related to all tactics: an anticipation of expected changes; maintain existing interfaces; usage of an intermediary; increase available resources; and introducing concurrency.

Each of these relations between a level 3 criteria and tactics will be assessed via the pairwise comparison. The comparisons for this effort estimation problem applied on the building automation system case study are shown below (this is an actual execution of our approach by one of the architects participated in the workshop described earlier):

1. We start by the pairwise comparisons of evaluation criteria (level-2 elements in the decision hierarchy) – Table 2. This comparison represents the prioritization of the criteria in that level in respect to their impact on the effort. The weights values are calculated by; first calculating the geometric mean for each row; then dividing the geometric mean of each row by the total summation of geometric mean values from all rows. The geometric mean of n numbers, say, X1, X2,... Xn is given by: (X1 * X2 * ...* Xn)1/n.

Table 2. Pairwise comparisons matric for level-2 criteria in the automated home system.

	Complexity	Inadvace in technique	Development restrictions	Geometric Mean	Weight
Complexity	1	3	5	2.47	0.6
Inadvace in technique	0.33	1	0.2	0.4	0.1
Development restrictions	0.2	5	1	1	0.3

2. Similarly, we complete the pairwise comparisons of sub-criteria from the third levels with respect to level-2 criteria of the decision hierarchy (See Tables 3, 4 and 5).

Table 3. Pairwise comparisons matric for "Complexity" criterion

	Functional Size	Impact on architecture	Association	Interactivity	Weight
Functional size	1	5	5	5	0.6
Impact on architecture	0.2	1	3	3	0.2
Association	0.2	0.33	1	1	0.1
Interactivity	0.2	0.33	1	1	0.1

Table 4. Pairwise comparisons matric for "Inadvance in Technique" criterion

	Inadvance in methods	Inadvance in tools	Weight
Inadvance in methods	1	1	0.5
Inadvance in tools	1	1	0.5

Table 5. Pairwise comparisons matric for "Development Restrictions" criterion

	Technical experience level	Number of developers	Weight
Technical experience level	1	3	0.75
Number of developers	0.33	1	0.25

3. We then complete the pairwise comparisons of the tactics (elements of the lowest level in the hierarchy with respect to every crtiterion from level 3). Table 6 shows the pairwise comparison of the tactics with respect to "functional size" criterion. We will not show the pairwise computations with respect to other criteria in this paper due to the space constraints.

Table 6. Pairwise comparisons of tactics with respect to "functional size" criterion: (**T1**: Anticipation Expected Changes; **T2**: Maintain Existing Interfaces; **T3**: Usage of an Intermediary; **T4**: Increase Available Resources; **T5**: Introducing Concurrency)

	T1	T2	T3	T4	T5	Weight
T1	1	5	3	1	3	0.34
T2	0.2	1	0.33	0.2	0.33	0.05
T3	0.33	3	1	0.33	1	0.13
T4	1	5	3	1	3	0.34
T5	0.33	3	1	0.33	1	0.13

4. Once the normalized are computed for all levels of the hierarchy, they are combined by moving through the hierarchy starting at the lowest level. Figure 2 illustrates this procedure. For example, after one level of composition the average weights of the tactics (anticipation of expected changes, maintain existing interfaces, usage of an intermediary, increase available resources, introducing concurrency) with respect to "Development restrictions" are: (0.323, 0.165, 0.12, 0.325, 0.068) = 0.75 * (0.34, 0.13, 0.13, 0.34, 0.06) + 0.25 * (0.27, 0.27, 0.09, 0.28, 0.09).

Following this procedure, the overall weights for the tactics: (anticipation of expected changes, maintain existing interfaces, usage of an intermediary, increase available resources, introducing concurrency) are calculated to be (0.33, 0.11, 0.12, 0.34, 0.1).

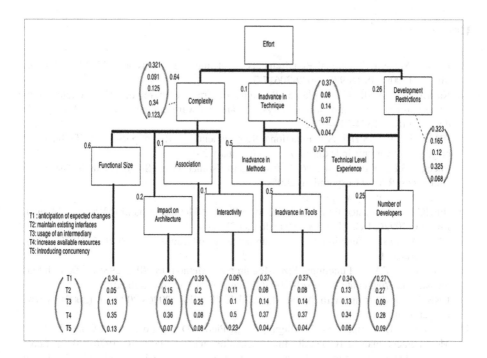

Fig. 2. Hierarchy composition of weights for the Home Automated system case study

5. Finally, if we know the effort of anyone among the five tactics from a historical project, then the effort of the others can be calculated. For example, if had known the effort of "introducing concurrency" from a previous project to be 3 person days; then the effort of "anticipation of expected changes" would be: (0.33/0.1) * 3 = 11 person days.

5 Conclusion

The quality effort estimation methodology presented in this paper aims at improving the predictive quality of the software industry's effort estimation models. The paper demonstrates the feasibility of the proposed approach on a case study.

The research we presented is multidisciplinary in nature, which opened multiple avenues of future work that we could effectively pursue. In our immediate next steps; we plan to validate our work further in real industrial settings. In addition, we plan on extending the effort estimation model to consider the cost estimation for the project.

We acknowledge that our solution proposal may sound complex for implementation by practitioners when large number of tactics are selected. Thus, we are also looking to automate the process of collecting the pairwise judgments and the final weights' calculations through implementing an automating tool for the process.

References

1. Kassab, M.: Non-functional Requirements: Modeling and Assessment. VDM Verlag Dr. Mueller (2009). ISBN 978-3-639-20617-3
2. Kassab, M., Neill, C., Laplante, P.: State of practice in requirements engineering: contemporary data, innovations in systems and software engineering. NASA J. (2014) doi:10.1007/s11334-014-0232-4
3. IBM website: SAS Hub Non Functional Requirements (NFRs). http://www.haifa.ibm.com/projects/software/nfr/index.html. Accessed January 2015
4. Pfleeger, S.L., Wu, F., Lewis, R.: Software Cost Estimation and Sizing Methods: Issues and Guidelines. RAND Corporation (2005)
5. FP Users Group. www.ifpug.org
6. IFPUG 4.1 Unadjusted Functional Size Measurement Method - Counting Practices Manual, ISO/IEC 20926, 1 October 2003, 1st edn (2003). www.ifpug.org
7. NESMA: NESMA functional size measurement method compliant to ISO/IEC 24570 (2006). www.nesma.nl
8. FISMA: FiSMA 1.1 Functional Size Measurement Method, ISO/IEC 29881 (2008). http://www.fisma.fi/wp-content/uploads/2008/07/fisma_fsmm_11_for_web.pdf
9. UKSMA: estimating with Mark II, v.1.3.1, ISO/IEC 20968:2002(E) (2002). www.uksma.co.uk
10. Abran, A., Desharnais, J.-M., Oligny, S., St-Pierre, D., Symons, C.: COSMIC FFP – Measurement manual (COSMIC implementation guide to ISO/IEC 19761:2003), École detechnologie supérieure – Université du Québec, Montréal, Canada (2003). http://www.gelog.etsmtl.ca/cosmic-ffp/manual.jsp
11. Kassab, M., Daneva, M., Ormandjieva, O.: A meta-model for the assessment of non-functional requirement size. In: Proceedings of the 34th Euromicro Conference Software Engineering and Advanced Applications – SEAA 2008, pp. 411–418 (2008)
12. ISO 14143-1: Functional size measurement – Definitions of concepts, International Organization for Standardization – ISO, Geneva (1988)
13. SNAP. http://www.ifpug.org/ISMA6/ITPC%20SNAP-SW%20Non-Functional%20Assessment%20Process-Sept13.pdf. Accessed May 2014
14. Glinz, M.: On non-functional requirements. In: 15th IEEE International Requirements Engineering Conference (RE 2007), Delhi, India, pp. 21–26 (2007)

15. Bass, L., Clements, P., Bass, L., Kazman, R.: Software Architecture in Practice, 3rd edn. Addison-Wesley, Reading (2013)
16. Saaty, T.L.: The Analytic Hierarchy Process. McGraw-Hill, New York (1980)
17. Saaty, T.L.: Decision Making for Leaders, Belmont. LifeTime Leaning Publications, California (1985)
18. Harrison, N.B., Avgeriou, P.: How do architecture patterns and tactics interact? A model and annotation. J. Syst. Softw. **83**(10), 1735–1758 (2010)

Clone Detection in Reuse of Software Technical Documentation

Dmitrij Koznov[1]([✉]), Dmitry Luciv[1], Hamid Abdul Basit[2], Ouh Eng Lieh[3], and Mikhail Smirnov[1]

[1] Saint Petersburg State University, Saint Petersburg, Russia
d.koznov@spbu.ru, dluciv@math.spbu.ru, smnsmn1979@gmail.com
[2] Lahore University of Management Sciences, Lahore, Pakistan
hamidb@lums.edu.pk
[3] National University of Singapore, Singapore, Singapore
issoel@nus.edu.sg

Abstract. As software documentation is becoming more and more complicated, efficiency of maintenance process could be increased through documentation reuse. In this paper, we apply software clone detection technique to automate searching of repeated fragments in software technical documentation to be reused. Our approach supports adaptive reuse, which means extracting "near duplicate" text fragments (repetitions with variations) and producing customizable reusable elements. We present a process and a tool, which can work with both DocBook documentation (widely used XML markup language) and DRL (DocBook extension with adaptive reuse features), as well as with plain text. Our tool is based on Clone Miner software clone detection tool, and integrated to DocLine environment (adaptive reuse documentation framework), providing visualization and navigation facilities on the clone groups found, and also supporting refactoring to extract clones into reusable elements.

Keywords: Software technical documentation · Documentation reuse · Software clone detection · Adaptive reuse · Refactoring · DocBook · DocLine · DRL

1 Introduction

Software documentation is a significant component of modern software. It is supposed to help software engineers to comprehend a given software system and accomplish development and modification tasks more efficiently [1]. There are two types of software documentation: technical documentation (requirement specifications, design documents, etc.), and user documentation (e.g., user guides). Sometimes API documentation is considered, that is a special case of technical documentation and describes application programming interfaces of reusable code libraries [2]. In this paper, we consider technical software documentation only.

© Springer International Publishing Switzerland 2016
M. Mazzara and A. Voronkov (Eds.): PSI 2015, LNCS 9609, pp. 170–185, 2016.
DOI: 10.1007/978-3-319-41579-6_14

It should be noted, that technical documentation may have considerable size and complex structure, and like the software itself, is constantly changed during development process. The quality of technical documentation is a well-known problem that has not been resolved in the last decades [3]. One of the reasons that leads to essential decrease of documentation quality during maintenance process is that documents may contain numerous repetitions. If there is no traceability between duplicate text fragments, we need to modify each fragment manually while making changes. But in practice it is hard to keep the documentation updated because of huge volumes and lack of time. That leads to accumulation of mistakes and contradictions in documentation.

The situation is even more complicated because very often duplicate information is "near duplicate", e.g., in one document the same software features may be described many times with different level of details. Also, there are sets of similar objects, which are described on the documentation: functions, interruptions, signals, etc. If objects belong to the same set then their descriptions have a lot of commonalities, but at the same time they differ from each other. This leads to repetitions with variations, and makes it difficult to apply usual text search techniques to find such repetitions. Moreover, it is necessary not only to search duplicate text fragments, but to manage them consistently.

Systematic reuse techniques attempt to simplify the software maintenance process. Different techniques of software reuse have been proposed [4,5]. One of these techniques is XVCL [6], which is based on adaptive reuse introduced by Paul Bassett [7]. These ideas were applied for software documentation reuse in DocLine framework [8]. In this context, refactoring of XML documentation technique was also explored [9] to simplify the maintenance process of existing documentation extracting reusable text fragments. But the challenge of automatically searching for reusable document fragments still remained open.

This paper closes the gap using software clone detection technique [10,11]. Our approach is designed for operating with XML documentation in DocBook [12] and DRL [8] markup languages, as well as with plain Text (i.e. ASCII/UNICODE format). DocBook is a wide-spread XML language for software documentation development in Linux/Unix community, while DRL is an extension of DocBook for implementation of adaptive reuse approach. We used Clone Miner [13] as a clone detection tool, filtering and correcting its outputs. Based on clones found by the tool, the approach supports refactoring of documentation, i.e. producing customizable reusable elements and inserting them into the text. We consider not only exact duplicates, but also "near duplicate" text fragments, applying adaptive reuse technique [6,7]. We implemented the approach as a tool that incorporates visualization and navigation facilities on the detected clone groups and provides seamless invocation of DocLine refactoring operations. The paper includes the results of the evaluation the proposed approach whereby we applied our tool for DocBook documentation of several open source projects, and, in particular, for Linux Kernel Documentation (LKD) [14].

2   Related Works

Technical documentation development currently widely employs XML markup languages. The widely used standards are DocBook [12] and DITA [15], both supporting modular approach and enabling development of reusable documentation components. In [8] adaptive software reuse technique of Bassett-Jarzabek [6,7], has been applied to documentation. But all of these approaches imply that documentation is developed as reusable modules from the very beginning, and they do not offer approaches and tools for searching and extracting repetitions. Meanwhile, documentation maintenance often requires eliminating inconsistencies, because previous corrections were local and made by different persons, in different manners. Searching "near duplicate" text fragments and extracting reusable text elements could simplify the maintenance process. Moreover, this may also lead to correction of descriptions of similar code objects (signals, functions of API, handlers, etc.) for better unification to facilitate future changes. The adaptive reuse technique of XVCL is helpful in this regard. In [9] refactoring of documentation was suggested to extract adaptive reusable elements. But no tools to search repeatable fragments were available.

A systematic review of the software documentation domain is presented in [16]. Below, we overview some of the studies, which provide automatic analysis and transformation of documentation.

Zhong et al. [17] suggested an approach to infer resource specifications from API documentation. The approach overcomes the problem that developers tend to ignore information in API documentation. But if some part of the code is automatically generated on technical documentation, the problem is solved. The paper proposes to generate resource specification on documentation.

An approach to detect documentation errors comparing code samples and corresponding document fragments is proposed in [18]. The approach is based on comparing code objects that are mentioned in the text (data types, procedures, variables, etc.) with the ones in the samples.

Garousi et al. [1] suggests to analyze the usage and quality of software projects' documentation during development and maintenance phases, based on projects' data and experts' opinion from a survey-based questionnaire.

Metrics to measure documentation quality are proposed in [19,20]. The authors also adapt the VizzAnalyzer clone detection tool [21] to provide a measurement of a documents uniqueness. However, further use of found clones is only briefly discussed and their automatic transformation for future reuse is not done.

To summarize, little attention is given to search repetitions in software technical documentation to extract reusable elements. The issue is only touched upon in [19,20], but no approach applies the idea of adaptive reuse to software technical documentation.

3   Background

3.1   DocBook

DocBook [12] is a collection of standards and tools for technical writing, particularly used for large and highly structured content. The key difference between DocBook and other structured formats (e.g., LaTeX) is that the style (bold, font size, italics etc.) is separated from the structured content. This allows one source document to have many presentations, such as HTML, PDF, etc. Unlike other document markup tools, DocBook is not WYSIWYG technology (What You See Is What You Get). It provides more flexibility, and allows to create more reliable documents, but demands for technical writers to be more experienced than Microsoft Word users (discussion about usage of markup languages by technical writers can be found in [22]). DocBook may be easily extended, and it is possible to use these extensions in practice: you only need to perform preprocessing specifications to eliminate extended constructs into plain DocBook, and after that you may use the standard DocBook utilities to get target document presentations (e.g., PDF).

3.2   DocLine

DocLine [8] is created for the development and maintenance of complicated software documentation basing on adaptive reuse [6,7] to operate with duplicate documentation fragments. Adaptive reuse means that reusable text fragments can be configured for each context where they are inserted.

DocLine provides a new XML markup language DRL, a model of documentation development process, and a toolset integrated into Eclipse IDE. DRL (Documentation Reuse Language) extends DocBook [12] providing two mechanisms of adaptive reuse: customizable information elements and multi-view item catalogs.

Customizable Information Elements. This can be understood with the help of a simple example. Let us consider a news aggregator that provides news feed from different sources. A description of the module to refresh news from RSS and Atom feeds can be the following:

```
When module instance receives refresh_news call, it  updates its
data from RSS and Atom feeds it is configured to listen to and
pushes new articles to the main storage.                          (1)
```

Meanwhile, the news aggregator can also use Twitter as a news feed, and the description of corresponding module can be as follows:

```
When module instance receives refresh_news call, it updates its
data from Twitter feeds it is subscribed to and pushes new
articles to the main storage.                                     (2)
```

To provide reuse of duplicate text in (1) and (2) using an adaptive reuse technique, the corresponding information element must be specified in DRL:

```
<infelement id="refresh_news">
When module instance receives refresh_news call, it updates its
data from <nest id="SourceType"></nest> and pushes new articles
to the main storage.</infelement>                          (3)
```

In this example, we define an information element (`<infelement/>` tag) and an extension point inside it (`<nest/>` tag). When this information element is included in a particular context, the extension point can be removed, replaced or appended with custom content without having to modify the information element itself. The following customization transforms(3) into (2):

```
<infelemref infelemid="refresh_news">
<replace-nest nestid="SourceType">Twitter feeds it is subscribed
to </replace-nest> </infelemref>                          (4)
```

The example (4) shows a reference to the information element defined in (3) (`<infelemref/>`) and the replacement of the extension point defined in this information element by new content (`<replace-nest/>`).

Multi-view Item Catalogs. In the documentation of most Software products one can find descriptions of typical items of the same kind. To organize adaptive reuse for that case a multi-view item catalog is introduced in DRL. The catalog contains a collection of items represented by a set of attributes. When a technical writer includes a catalog item into a particular context, s/he must indicate the corresponding representation template and the item identifier. Then, the content of the template will be inserted into the target context and all the references to the attributes will be replaced by corresponding attribute values. A particular case of the catalog is a dictionary, which contains a set of terms without presentation templates. Dictionaries are useful for creating glossary to unify naming policy in documentation. More details about multi-view item catalogs can be found in [8,9].

3.3   Refactoring Documentation

Refactoring is the process of changing a software system in such a way that it does not change the external behavior of the code, yet improves its internal structure [24]. In [9], refactoring was adapted to XML documentation maintenance. In this case, refactoring means the change of internal document specification (XML markup constructs), and preservation of output document presentation (e.g., pdf file). Based on this idea, a number of refactoring operations were designed for DocLine [9].The operations can be divided into the following groups:

1. Operations for extracting common assets, and, in particular, for transition to DRL from plain text or DocBook.

2. Operations to facilitate core assets tuning (extending their configurability).
3. Operations to facilitate the use of small-grained reuse constructions — dictionaries and multi-view item catalogs.
4. Operations for renaming various structural elements of documentation.

3.4   Software Clone Detection and Clone Miner

Very often software is reused by means of copy/paste. It produces duplicate code (software clones), and that may lead to serious maintenance problems. Clone detection methods and tools are aimed to find different kinds of duplicate code to perform refactoring based on reuse techniques. Systematic review of clone detection methods and tools can be found in [11], while interesting discussion about code cloning and clone detection is presented in [10].

This area is quite mature; there are a number of ready-to-use tools. We selected Clone Miner tool [13] as it is a simple command line tool that could easily integrate into the DocLine framework. Clone Miner is a token-based code clone detector. It converts the input source code into a string of lexical tokens and then applies suffix array based string matching algorithms to find the repeated parts of this string as clone groups.

The tool allows varying the minimal length of clones to be searched, measuring it in terms of the number of tokens. A token in the context of text documents is one single word separated from other words by some separator: '.', '(', ')', etc. For example, the following text fragment consists of 2 tokens: "FM registers".

Clone Miner was extended for this project to support plain text and Unicode inputs, which made it possible to apply the tool to Russian language documents as well.

4   The Process of Clone Detection and Refactoring

4.1   Overview

The general scheme of the process is shown in Fig. 1. The input of the process is a DRL file, which the user prepares for clone detection. After that s/he starts document clone detection by launching Clone Miner which generates the output results. Once the user gets the list of clone groups, s/he can execute the automated refactoring for any clone group. In refactoring, all occurrences of clone selected are replaced by references to reusable element definition.

4.2   Preparation for Clone Detection

DocLine operations are executed for DRL constructs, in particular, the searching of clones is applied to information elements. If the user wants to apply document clone detection for plain text or DocBook documents, s/he has to first perform refactoring operation "Transition to DRL". As a result, a new information element appears that includes the whole original text. Clone detection is then performed on this information element.

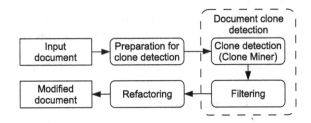

Fig. 1. Process overview

4.3   Clone Detection

We start Clone Miner in the "search in flat text" mode since actually we need flat text search: the repetitions in question might be found inside XML structures. Therefore, the found clones might violate XML markup. (5) shows a text fragment with a found clone *emphasized*. It includes the start tag but not the end tag. The clones become correct in terms of XML as a result of refactoring operations, and so does their context in the document.

```
<section id="file-tree-isa-directory">
<title>Reviving incoming calls </title>
<para>
Once you receive an incoming call, the phone gets CallerID
information and reads it out. But if...</para>
</section>                                                    (5)
```

4.4   Filtering

We use clones detected in refactoring, since it is the technical writer who is responsible for choosing the candidates for refactoring based on their semantic meaningfulness. Meanwhile the number of clone groups detected is so large that they need to be filtered. Our algorithm filters Clone Miner output by the following steps:

1. A clone group is rejected if clone length in the group is less than 5 symbols (e.g. "is a" contains 3 symbols): as a rule, such clones have no semantics, but usually a lot of such groups are found. Some terms can be lost, especially abbreviations, but this is the way to reduce considerably the number of insignificant clone groups. It should be reminded that we measure the clone length in number of tokens in the paper (it means the number of symbol sequences separated by the comma, space, etc.), but in this case we do it in terms of symbols, because the length is too small.
2. We eliminate the groups containing clones consisting only of XML constructs and do not contain output text: we have no task to organize XML markup constructs reuse.

3. We remove the clone groups consisting of phrases "that is", "there is a", etc.: these clones have no software semantics (this issue is discussed in Sect. 6). To avoid such clones we have elaborated the dictionary of such expressions based on our own experiments, and we check every clone group if its clones belong to the dictionary. In the future more sophisticated analysis techniques can be used, considering natural-language patterns embedded [23] into strictly defined DRL markup.

4.5 Refactoring

After previous steps, we have a set of clone groups. But our aim is to use clones to extract reusable elements. It can be done using the refactoring process described below. The process uses refactoring operations which have been suggested in [9], but some additional activities have to be performed. The schema of the refactoring process is presented in Fig. 2.

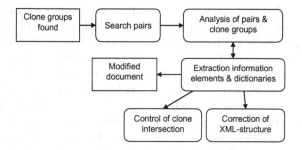

Fig. 2. Refactoring process

Searching Close Pairs. We have the list of clone groups found by Clone Miner in ($SetG$). To provide adaptive reuse, we search clone groups from $SetG$ where clones are located close to each other. For example, the following phrase can be found in the text 5 times with different variations (various port numbers): "inet daemon can listen on ... port and then transfer the connection to appropriate handler". In this situation we have 2 clone groups with 5 clones in every group: one group include clones "inet daemon can listen on", while the other includes "port and then transfer the connection to appropriate handler". We want to combine these clone groups in a single information element with one extension point to capture different port numbers.

To find out such kinds of clone groups we propose an algorithm. The algorithm works only with two clone groups, because our observations show that this is the most popular case (we plan to extend the algorithm in the future for n clone groups). We define the distance between two clones as the number of symbols between them (we do not consider a case of intersected text fragments). We define the distance between two clone groups G_1 and G_2 under the following constraints:

1. They have the same number of clones: $\#G_1 = \#G_2$.
2. We introduce an ordering for clones in a group based on their appearance in the document, and assign a number to each clone. As a result we have a set of clone pairs, where the first member belongs to one group, the second belongs to another, and for all pairs the first members belong to the same group, and the second members belong to the second one. Clones in the same pair are not intersecting, i.e. they are not overlapping in the text:
$\forall k \in (1..\#G_1)\ g_1^k \cap g_2^k = \emptyset$,
where g_1^k and g_2^k are members of G_1 and G_2 groups respectively.
3. For every pair of clones (one clone belongs to first group, another belongs to the second group, and both clones have the same number) clone from one group occurs before clone from the other group in the document:
$(\forall k \in (1..\#G_1)Before(g_1^k, g_2^k)) \bigvee (\forall k \in (1..\#G_1)Before(g_2^k, g_1^k))$,
where g_1^k and g_2^k are members of G_1 and G_2 groups respectively.

The distance between G_1 and G_2 is $dist(G_1, G_2) = \max(dist(g_1^k, g_2^k))$, where $dist(g_1^k, g_2^k)$ is a distance between clones (text fragments) g_1^k and g_2^k. We use this simple formula, because we have just one special requirement for distance between clone groups: if we choose a clone group it should be possible to compare a distances from this group to others to select the closest one. But we would not like to consider unreal distances, that is, variation of distances between clone pairs for selected groups should not be too big. For example, if the distance between the first clone pair is 1 symbol, and the distance between the second pair is 10 000 symbols then there is no chance, that these pairs are semantically connected, and it would not be sensible to create information element with extension point. Following our experiments, we have defined the maximum of distance variance between clones from two group as constant 2000: $Var(\{dist(g_1^k, g_2^k)|k \in (1..\#G_1), g_1^k \in G_1, g_2^k \in G_2\}) \leq 2000$. If the variance is greater, we do not consider this pair.

The algorithm of searching close pairs considers all clone groups from $SetG$ and for every group finds the closest one. If it is successful, a new pair is added to the set $PairG$. If it is not successful for selected clone group (e.g. there is no other clone group with the same number of clones) the resulting list have no pair with this clone group.

Analysis of Pairs & Clone Groups. In this step we combine the clone group pairs and the initial list of clone groups in a list L to present the information to the user for making decision: what text fragments should be extracted as information elements/dictionaries (elements of L we will call *candidates for refactoring* or shortly – *candidates*). The problem is that reusable text elements have to have some semantic, e.g. to be a typical description of a function or interruption. If reuse relies only on syntax and have no semantics, it looks useless. But it is hard to do such analysis automatically, that is why we provide browsing facilities to help the user to make the right decision.

L includes clone group pairs and single groups, which are not included in any pair: $L = PairG \bigcup \{G \mid G \in SetG \; \& \; \nexists P \in PairG : G = left(P) \vee G = right(P)\}$.

We order L by the length of elements measuring length in a symbols in descending order. The length of clone is the number of the symbols in a clone. The length of clone group is sum of lengths of all clones from a group: $\forall G \in L$ $length(G) = \#G \cdot length(g)$, where $g \in G$, and $\#G$ is a number of clones in G. It should be reminded that all clones from a group are duplicate text fragments, that is why all of them have equal length. The length of the clone group pair is the sum of the lengths of clone groups included in the pair: $length(Pair(G_1, G_2)) = length(G_1) + length(G_2)$. We can see elements at the top of the L, which contain most "amount" of text, and these elements are most preferable for reuse. The user should select manually a group or a pair to perform refactoring operations.

Extraction Information Elements & Dictionaries. For each clone group or clone group pair selected before the user can apply the following refactoring operations (see Sect. 3.3, group 1): *extracting information element, extracting information element with variations, or extracting to dictionary*.

Before executing these operations, we check if the selected clone group intersects with other clone groups, which have already been used to extract information elements/dictionaries. Clone Miner allows intersection of clone groups, as it has no information what will happen to the detected clones further. But in our case, such intersection leads to mistakes in refactoring operations.

If this checking was successful we perform transformation of selected text fragments to be reused and the remaining context into correct XML. As mentioned earlier, Clone Miner outputs XML-incorrect results, but DocLine can operate only with the correct DocBook/DRL fragments. Generally speaking, our algorithm opens/closes all the necessary tags, both in the clone and in the context from which it is extracted. However, these open/close actions should be "clever". For example, if we close and reopen the tag <para> (it marks a new paragraph), then we would have two paragraphs instead of one in the resulting text (i.e. text on pure DocBook that is produced after the elimination of DRL constructions and, in particular, after the substitution of reusable information elements). This is the direction of the future work.

Once the refactoring operation for selected candidates is successfully completed, it is removed from L, and document coordinates of the another elements of L are recalculated. After that the user goes back to the "Analysis of pairs & clone groups" step.

5   The Tool

To support the process presented above we implemented a Documentation Refactoring Toolkit [25], and integrated it into DocLine/Eclipse. The tool is implemented in Python and can be invoked as a standalone application (i.e. outside of Eclipse and DocLine). The tool provides navigation over detected candidates, and text browsing facility to observe clones in the source text. It is possible to perform extracting all clones from selected groups into reusable elements, i.e. perform refactoring.

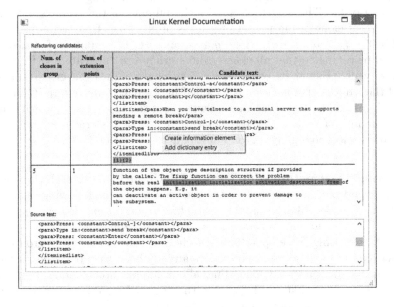

Fig. 3. Documentation refactoring toolkit

The main window is shown on the Fig. 3. The tool is launched for a document, while the title of the document is displayed as the title of the window. The lines of table in the section «Refactoring candidates» correspond to clone groups or pairs found for that document. In the pop up menu for a candidate the user can select a refactoring type – to create either an information element or a dictionary element. If the candidate is a pair, then variations are highlighted as yellow/green pieces of text in the «Candidate text» column.

The «Source text» section shows clones in the source document. If a selected candidate is a clone group then the user needs to select the number of the clone element in the group (see color numbers at the end of the first cell in the «Candidate text» column, Fig. 3). If a candidate is a pair (see the second cell in the «Candidate text» column), then the user needs to select a certain pair by clicking on the corresponding variation. In either case the «Source text» window will display the clone pair of clones in the source document.

6   Evaluation

We did our experiments using hand-made tests and third party DocBook documentation of open source industrial projects. The list of projects and corresponding documentation is presented in Table 1.

Table 1. Documentation used in experiments

Project	Documentation	Acronym	Size
Linux Kernel is an open operating system kernel, which is basis for Linux operating system	«Linux Kernel Documentation» is designed for programmers who use Linux Kernel [14]	LKD	892 KB
Zend Framework is an open source framework for developing web applications and services using PHP	«Zend PHP Framework documentation» is a programming guide [26]	Zend	2924 KB
Subversion is a versioning and revision control system	«Version Control with Subversion For Subversion 1.7» is a tool description for users and system administrators [27]	SVN	1810 KB
DocBook is a framework for single source documentation development	«DocBook 4 Definitive Guide» is the complete official documentation on DocBook markup language 4.0 [28]	DocBook	686 KB

Following GQM approach [29] we selected a set of questions to characterize the way of the assessment in our experiments:

- question 1: quality of documentation clone detection
- question 2: effectiveness of filtering clones
- question 3: evaluation of refactoring facilities

Addressing **question 1** we did experiments with Clone Miner and DocLine clone search facilities. The first experiment was carried out on hand-made tests for which we know exactly the number and the locations of clones. We found that Clone Miner made some mistakes, e.g., it sometimes skipped the last token in clones. We fixed these errors. After that our tool found correctly all the clones in hand-made tests.

To assess **question 2** we used third party documentation listed in Table 1. We used metrics, which are filtering types described in Sect. 4.4. The results are presented in Table 2. It should be noted, that filtering decreases the number of candidates by 13.2 % on average.

Numbers of refactoring candidates after filtration are presented in Table 3 for two cases: with the minimal lengths of clones of 1 and 5 (divided by slash in table). In the latter case the numbers of candidates are fewer and the situation looks more operable. However smaller clones, which were excluded in this case, can be used as dictionary elements or in other important situations. Therefore, we recommend that technical writer should work with candidates with the minimal length of clone equal to 1. To simplify operations with a large number of candidates our tool supports ordering by length.

Table 2. Filtering results

Metrics	LKD	Zend	SVN	DocBook	Average
Rejecting clones under 5 symbols in length, %	7.3	4.8	4.4	7.2	5.9
Rejecting pure XML markup clone groups, %	3.3	5.8	2.4	6.0	4.4
Rejecting common language phrases, %	3.2	2.2	2.9	3.4	2.9
Total, %	13.8	12.8	9.7	16.6	13.2

Table 3. Number of candidates in case of minimal length of clone is 1 and 5

Number of candidates	LKD	Zend	SVN	DocBook
Number of single clone groups	12819/1034	33400/5213	27847/3119	8228/870
Number of pairs	351/108	1400/613	616/249	232/50
Total	13170/1254	34800/5826	28463/3368	8460/920

Let us consider **question 3**. We assessed the question using the metric called amount of reuse, which tracks percentages of reused text [30]. We calculate the metric by dividing the amount of reusable text by the total size of documentation. We take all refactoring candidates as reusable text and calculate the amount as $\sum_{C \in (\text{all candidates})} length(C)$, where $length(C)$ is the number of symbols in a clone or a clone pair multiplied by the number of clones in the group (see Sect. 4.5). We measure documentation/text fragments size in symbols. It would be better to measure it in tokens but we had some technical problems with that. The average amount of reusable text for all tested documents is between 48 % and 52.9 %. The results show that when refactoring is carried out in an automatic (straightforward) way, reuse happens to be quite significant. But it is hard to estimate real reuse amount because, as it has been mentioned, technical writer performs additional semantic filtering of candidates for refactoring. To estimate the quality of refactoring more precisely, additional experiments with real project documentation are necessary.

7   Conclusions

Our experiments have shown that even after filtering we have a lot of insignificant clones. Some of them are easy to remove with improved filtering, but others can only be filtered manually. The precision of the algorithm is a baseline for our future work. Support of adaptive reuse should be also extended, e.g. proving extraction of information elements with n extension points, where $n > 1$.

During our experiments, it became clear that our tool should be improved to be more convenient in operating with clone groups, e.g. providing more facilities for construction of information elements.

The proposed approach can be useful in software product line documentation management environment to extract reusable document fragments for documentation of different product line members and organize reusable document structure. It simplifies document maintenance process and, of course, it is meaningful only if maintenance (product line member or/and its documentation) is significant. Our approach can also be used in the context of variability management [31] in software product line development.

Supporting semantic reuse can allow to integrate our approach with various software traceability techniques [32,33], and mapping document fragments into other software artifacts: code, requirements, model entities, etc. In this case, reuse can improve the quality of this mapping, and semantic-oriented adaptive reuse could increase the granularity of the mapping.

Apart from software engineering, the proposed approach could also be used in such areas as Ontology Engineering [34] or Enterprise Architecture Modeling [35]: usually, models are stored in XML format, and irregular repetitions are also possible here, taking into account that a number of analysts can work with a large volume of information, and a lot of information is unstructured (documents and comments applied to models, long names of model entities, etc.).

Acknowledgements. The authors thank the students Artem Shutak, Dmitry Kopin, Mikhail Smarzhevskij and Adeel Khan, who implemented the draft versions of selected parts of the solution, and participated in discussions.

References

1. Garousi, G., Garousi, V., Moussavi, M., Ruhe, G., Smith, B.: Evaluating usage and quality of technical software documentation: an empirical study. In: Proceedings of EASE 2013, pp. 24–35 (2013)
2. Watson, R.: Developing best practices for API reference documentation: creating a platform to study how programmers learn new APIs. In: Proceedings of IPCC 2012, pp. 1–9 (2012)
3. Parnas, D.L.: Precise documentation: the key to better software. In: Nanz, S. (ed.) The Future of Software Engineering, pp. 125–148. Springer, Heidelberg (2011)
4. Holmes, R., Walker, R.J.: Systematizing pragmatic software reuse. ACM Trans. Softw. Eng. Methodol. **21**(4), 20:1–20:44 (2013)
5. Czarnecki, K.: Software reuse and evolution with generative techniques. In: Proceedings of the IEEE/ACM International Conference on Automated Software Engineering, p. 575 (2007)
6. Jarzabek, S., Bassett, P., Zhang, H., Zhang, W.: XVCL: XML-based variant configuration language. In: ICSE 2003, pp. 810–811 (2003)
7. Bassett, P.: The theory and practice of adaptive reuse. SIGSOFT Softw. Eng. Notes **22**(3), 2–9 (1997)
8. Koznov, D., Romanovsky, K.: DocLine: a method for software product lines documentation development. Program. Comput. Softw. **34**(4), 216–224 (2008)
9. Romanovsky, K., Koznov, D., Minchin, L.: Refactoring the documentation of software product lines. In: Huzar, Z., Koci, R., Meyer, B., Walter, B., Zendulka, J. (eds.) CEE-SET 2008. LNCS, vol. 4980, pp. 158–170. Springer, Heidelberg (2011)
10. Akhin, M., Itsykson, V.: Clone detection: why, what and how? In: Proceedings of CEE-SECR 2010, pp. 36–42 (2010)

11. Rattan, D., Bhatia, R.K., Singh, M.: Software clone detection: a systematic review. Inf. Softw. Technol. (INFSOF) **55**(7), 1165–1199 (2013)
12. Walsh, N., Muellner, L.: DocBook: The Definitive Guide, p. 644. O'Reilly, Sebastopol (1999)
13. Basit, H.A., Smyth, W.F., Puglisi, S.J., Turpin, A., Jarzabek, S.: Efficient token based clone detection with flexible tokenization. In: Proceedings of ACM SIGSOFT International Symposium on the Foundations of Software Engineering, pp. 513–516. ACM Press (2007)
14. Linux Kernel Documentation, snapshot on 11 December 2013 (2013). https://github.com/torvalds/linux/tree/master/Documentation/DocBook/
15. Darwin Information Typing Architecture (DITA) Version 1.2 Specification (2012). http://docs.oasis-open.org/dita/v1.2/os/spec/DITA1.2-spec.pdf
16. Zhi, J., Garousi, V., Sun, B., Garousi, G., Shahnewaz, S., Ruhe, G.: Cost, benefits and quality of technical software documentation: a systematic mapping. J. Syst. Softw. **99**, 175–198 (2015)
17. Zhong, H., Zhang, L., Xie, T., Mei, H.: Inferring resource specifications from natural language API documentation. In: Proceedings of 24th ASE, pp. 307–318 (2009)
18. Zhong, H., Su, Z.: Detecting API documentation errors. In: Proceedings of SPASH/OOPSLA, pp. 803–816 (2013)
19. Wingkvist, A., Lowe, W., Ericsson, M., Lincke, R.: Analysis and visualization of information quality of technical documentation. In: Proceedings of the 4th European Conference on Information Management and Evaluation, pp. 388–396 (2010)
20. Wingkvist, A., Ericsson, M., Lowe, W.: A visualization-based approach to present and assess technical documentation quality. Electron. J. Inf. Syst. Eval. **14**(1), 150–159 (2011)
21. VizzAnalyzer Clone Detection Tool. http://www.arisa.se/vizz_analyzer.php
22. Cameron, H.G.: Wright: technical writing tools for engineers and scientists. Comput. Sci. Eng. **12**(5), 98–103 (2010)
23. Grigorev, S., Kirilenko, I.: GLR-based abstract parsing. In: Proceedings of the 9th Central & Eastern European Software Engineering Conference in Russia (2013)
24. Fowler, M., et al.: Refactoring: Improving the Design of Existing Code. Addison-Wesley, Reading (1999)
25. Document Refactoring Toolkit. http://www.math.spbu.ru/user/kromanovsky/docline/index_en.html
26. Zend PHP Framework documentation, snapshot on 24 April 2015 (2015). https://github.com/zendframework/zf1/tree/master/documentation
27. SVN Book, snapshot on 24 April 2015 (2015). http://sourceforge.net/p/svnbook/source/HEAD/tree/trunk/en/book/
28. DocBook Definitive Guide, snapshot on 24 April 2015 (2015). http://sourceforge.net/p/docbook/code/HEAD/tree/trunk/defguide/en/
29. Basili, V.R., Caldiera, G., Rombach, H.D.: The goal question metric approach. Encycl. Softw. Eng. **2**, 528–532 (1994). Wiley
30. Frakes, W., Terry, C.: Software reuse: metrics and models. ACM Comput. Surv. **28**(2), 415–435 (1996)
31. Krueger, C.W.: Variation management for software product lines. In: Proceedings of SPL 2002, San Diego, CA, USA, pp. 37–48 (2002)
32. Abadi, A., Nisenson, M., Simionovici, Y.: A traceability technique for specifications. In: Proceedings of ICPC 2008, pp. 103–112 (2008)
33. Terekhov, A.N., Sokolov, V.V.: Document implementation of the conformation of MSC and SDL diagrams in the REAL technology. Progra. Comput. Softw. **33**(1), 24–33 (2007)

34. Gavrilova, T.A.: Ontological engineering for practical knowledge work. In: Apolloni, B., Howlett, R.J., Jain, L. (eds.) KES 2007. LNCS, vol. 4693, pp. 1154–1161. Springer, Heidelberg (2007)
35. Grigoriev, L., Kudryavtsev, D.: ORG-Master: combining classifications, matrices and diagrams in the enterprise architecture modeling tool. In: Mouromtsev, D., Klinov, P. (eds.) KESW 2013. CCIS, vol. 394, pp. 250–257. Springer, Heidelberg (2013)

Modeling Actor Systems Using
Dynamic I/O Automata

Ilham W. Kurnia(✉) and Arnd Poetzsch-Heffter

University of Kaiserslautern, Kaiserslautern, Germany
{ilham,poetzsch}@cs.uni-kl.de

Abstract. Actor-based programming has become an important technique for the development of concurrent and distributed systems. This paper presents a new automaton model for actor systems and demonstrates how the model can be used for compositional verification. The model allows expressing the detailed behavior of actor components where components are built from actors and other components. It abstracts from internal and environment behavior, supports encapsulation of actors, and captures the dynamic aspects of actor creation and exposure of actor names to the component environment, which are crucial for verification. We handle these changes at the component interface by specializing dynamic I/O automata. The model can be used as a foundation of different verification techniques. We illustrate this by combining weakest precondition techniques on the actor level with simulation proofs on the component level.

1 Introduction

Actors [2] are a well studied programming model that gets more and more attention for developing concurrent and distributed systems (e.g., actors in Scala [19]). At runtime, an actor-based system consists of a dynamically changing set of actors. *Actors* are similar to objects: They have a unique name and a local state; they can create new actors and send messages to other actors addressing them by their name. As the sender does not wait for a reply, i.e., *messages are passed asynchronously*, message sending naturally leads to concurrent behavior of sender and receiver.

Our overall goal is the compositional verification of actor systems. More precisely, we want to verify the behavior of actor components independently of their environment and use component specifications to verify larger components. This goal entails the following requirements:

- A hierarchical component concept is needed that goes beyond single actors and allows to develop components by encapsulating other components.
- Components have to be handled in an *open* way, i.e., without knowing their environment (cf. [20]).
- Dynamic actor creation and the passing of actor names has to be captured.

M. Mazzara and A. Voronkov (Eds.): PSI 2015, LNCS 9609, pp. 186–202, 2016.
DOI: 10.1007/978-3-319-41579-6_15

The combination of these requirements is surprisingly challenging. In particular, a component consisting of several actors might expose some of its actors to the environment, thereby enabling the environment to interact with these actors. *Exposing actors* to the environment dynamically changes the component interface (as demonstrated in Sect. 2). Thus, it is important to precisely keep track of the exposed actors to capture the component behavior.

We use automaton models as they allow constructive specification techniques [27]. They can incorporate both notions of states and actions, making them flexible to integrate with various verification techniques. In particular, they are often compositional which allows for compositional reasoning. The challenge is to capture the dynamic behavior at the component interfaces. In our approach, we follow the ideas of the dynamic I/O automaton (DIOA) model [6,7]. As the high degree of dynamicity provided by DIOA is larger than needed for our purposes and as it would further complicate verification, we adapt DIOA to actor systems. In summary, the paper makes the following contributions:

- It formally develops an automaton model that faithfully captures the dynamic semantics of actors and components (Sect. 3).
- It combines a verification technique for actor programs and a simulation-based proof technique to a two-tier verification approach for actor components (Sect. 4).

The paper closes with a discussion on related work and a conclusion.

Notation. We use abstract data structures sequence, set, multiset and map. The sequence data structure is represented by $Seq\langle T \rangle$, with T denoting the type of the sequence elements. An empty sequence is denoted by [] and a sequence concatenation is simply juxtaposition. The set data structure $Set\langle T \rangle$ is a container of values of type T while a multiset is denoted by $\mathcal{M}\langle T \rangle$. Standard notations for sets are used. The map data structure $Map\langle S, T \rangle$ is an associative container that maps unique keys of type S to values of type T. An empty map is denoted by {}. If m is a map, $m[x \mapsto y]$ represents the insertion or update of the key x with value y to m. The value y of key x is represented by $m(x)$. If x is not associated to any value, then $m(x) = \mathsf{undef}$. The predicate $diffOn(m_1, m_2, X)$ for a set of keys X is true if m_1 may differ from m_2 with respect to the values of keys in X and other keys are mapped to the same value.

2   Class-Based Actor Programming

Our techniques have been developed for the verification of ABS programs [23]. ABS is a class-based actor language with futures, subtyping and recursive data types. In this paper, we only consider a core fragment of ABS, called αABS. As illustrated in Listing 1.1, the syntax of αABS is similar to Java. Actor creation is like object creation using the new expression. The state of an actor consists of creation parameters and attributes (e.g., a Session-actor has the creation parameter c and an attribute w). A class defines the messages that are understood by its actors. The body of a message definition is a statement that is executed when the message is processed. Messages may have parameters, but do not have a return value. Syntactically, sending a message is similar to calling a method in Java. Semantically, a send is executed by adding the message to the buffer of the receiver actor. Actors retrieve messages from the buffer one by one and execute them until completion[1].

```
1 class Server(DB db) {                 11 class Session(Client c, DB db) {
2   reqSess(Client c) {                 12   Worker w = null;
3     Session ss = new Session(c, db);   13   perform(Query q) {
4     c.provSess(ss);                    14     if (w == null)
5 } }                                    15       w = new Worker(c, db);
6 class Worker(Client c, DB db) {        16     w.do(q);
7   do(Query q) {                        17   }
8     Value v = compute(q, db);          18 }
9     c.response(v);                     19
10 } }                                   20
```

Listing 1.1. Server implementation in αABS

The program in Listing 1.1 realizes a tiny server. Clients can request sessions from the server and then use the session actors to perform a query. The session actors internally use workers to execute the query and to send the response to the client. The domain of queries and results are represented by the data types `Query` and `Value`, respectively. Details of these types and of how queries are computed are not of interest here. The example is not meant to be realistic; rather it is designed to illustrate three important aspects:

– The server component is used in an unknown environment. The only information about the environment is that there are clients and that these clients accept the messages `provSess` and `response`. In particular, we do not known what the clients do with the session actors.
– At runtime, the server consists of a server actor, a set of session actors, and sets of workers. The session actors are dynamically created and exposed to the environment. Thus, they are part of the behavioral interface of the server. The worker actors are encapsulated and can never be accessed from the environment. They all use the server's database that can only be accessed via the session interface.
– The sessions run concurrently[2].

Inspired by component frameworks like OSGi [35], a *component* consists of a set of classes **C** with a designated *activator class* $C_0 \in \mathbf{C}$ [26]. The idea is that a *component instance* is created by creating an actor of class C_0. All actors transitively created by this activator belong to the component instance. Consequently, we require **C** to contain all classes of actors that might transitively be

---

[1] αABS does not support suspension of tasks or wait statements.
[2] For simplicity, we have only one worker per session. It is easy to extend the example to support pools of workers.

created by actors of class C_0. In the example, the Server class is the activator for a component consisting of {Server, Session, Worker}. A *subcomponent* contains less classes and a different activator class; e.g., {Session, Worker} with activator class Session is a subcomponent of the server component. Based on this notion, we can verify the Server properties from the properties of the Session component in a hierarchical way.

A safety property of the server is that its sessions correctly respond to the queries. In the following sections, we show how to accurately represent such systems using the DIOA model and verify that the implementation satisfies the desired behavior.

3   Automaton Model

The DIOA model [7] is a two-tier automaton model based on *signature automata* (SA)[3], formalized in Definition 1. On top of the standard elements of transition systems: the set of (initial) states and the labeled transition relation, SA also have *state signatures*: a description of its input, output and internal actions parameterized by the state. The state-based classification of actions (of the universe **Act**) not only allows us to explicitly distinguish the externally observable behavior represented by the automata, but also to have the interaction possibilities dependent on the states. The two-tier aspect and the state signatures are what are extended from I/O automata (IOA) [29]. SA retain an important property of IOA: they are input-enabled.

Definition 1 (Signature Automata). A *signature automaton* $\mathcal{A} = \langle states(\mathcal{A}), start(\mathcal{A}), sig(\mathcal{A}), steps(\mathcal{A}) \rangle$ is a 4-tuple where

- $states(\mathcal{A})$ is a set of states,
- $start(\mathcal{A}) \subseteq states(\mathcal{A})$ is a non-empty set of initial states,
- $sig(\mathcal{A})$ is a signature mapping where for each $s \in states(\mathcal{A})$, $sig(\mathcal{A})(s) = \langle in(\mathcal{A})(s), out(\mathcal{A})(s), int(\mathcal{A})(s) \rangle$ where $in(\mathcal{A})(s), out(\mathcal{A})(s), int(\mathcal{A})(s) \subseteq$ **Act** such that $in(\mathcal{A})(s) \cap out(\mathcal{A})(s) = in(\mathcal{A})(s) \cap int(\mathcal{A})(s) = out(\mathcal{A})(s) \cap int(\mathcal{A})(s) = \emptyset$,
- $steps(\mathcal{A}) \subseteq states(\mathcal{A}) \times acts(\mathcal{A}) \times states(\mathcal{A})$ is a transition relation, such that
  - $\forall (s, l, s') \in steps(\mathcal{A}) : l \in \widehat{sig}(\mathcal{A})(s)$,
  - $\forall s \in states(\mathcal{A}) : \forall l \in in(\mathcal{A})(s) : \exists s' \in states(\mathcal{A}) : s \xrightarrow{l} s'$, and
  - $acts(\mathcal{A}) = \bigcup_{s \in states(\mathcal{A})} \widehat{sig}(\mathcal{A})(s)$,

where the $\widehat{}$-operator represents the union of sets of the signature tuple.

Behavior can be represented by an SA in terms of *executions* and *traces*. An execution is a sequence of alternating sequence $s_0 l_1 s_1 \ldots$ of states and actions such that s_0 is an initial state and $s_{i-1} \xrightarrow{l_i} s_i$ is a transition in SA. A trace is

---

[3] We use abbreviations for automata to also represent "a single automaton". The usage is apparent from the context.

the *observable* variant of an execution, i.e., the projection of the execution to the sequence of its actions. The overall behavior of an entity represented by an SA is captured by a set of executions (traces). We further define an *external* trace to be a trace derived from an execution where each action l_i is either an input or output action at state s_{i-1}. The external traces describe the observable interaction between the entity and its environment.

The state signatures of SA are very flexible, such that an action may be an input action in one state and output in another, for example. This flexibility is excessive for representing actor systems, so we define in the following how to restrict them.

3.1   First Tier Model

The first tier of a DIOA model for actors is populated by actor automata (AA): SA that are enriched with the characteristics of (groups of) actors. This means:

- An actor can only send messages to other actors and pass these actors' names as parameters when they have been exposed to that actor.
- An actor must be able to accept any possible message sent by its environment.
- A newly created actor always has a fresh name.
- An actor processes one incoming message to completion at a time.

Before we show how to enrich SA to represent these characteristics, we first introduce several elementary building blocks. We shortly define a notion of components based on the creation dependency between classes. This notion allows for a definition of AA that covers both actors and component instances.

The universes of *actor(name)s*, *classes*, *messages*, and *data values* are represented by $a, b \in \mathbf{A}$, $C \in \mathbf{CL}$, $m \in \mathbf{M}$, and $d \in \mathbf{D}$, respectively. We say "actor a" to refer to an actor of some unique name a. The behavior of each actor is represented by a class C. A class also determines what kind of messages an actor of that class can process, represented by $aMsg(C) \subseteq \mathbf{M}$. This function states which messages are allowed to be sent to the actor and which messages the actor can send to other actors. We overload this function with an extra parameter $type \in \{in, out, int\}$ to distinguish respectively which messages are part of the input interface of the class, which messages can be sent by the actor to another actor, and which messages the actor can send to itself, e.g., to trigger internal computations. The function $class(a)$ represents the class of actor a and the parameterized universe $\mathbf{A}(C)$ defines the set of actors of class C. The component with activator class C is denoted by $[C]$.

A message m can be an actor creation message $\mathbf{new}\ C(\overline{p})$ or a message send $mtd(\overline{p})$. A parameter can either be a data value d or an actor name. As with actors, the universe of a data type D can be represented by $\mathbf{D}(D)$.

From these universes we build the set of events $\mathbf{E}$ which replaces the domain of actions $\mathbf{Act}$ for AA. An event $e \in \mathbf{E}$ represents the occurrence of a message $m = msg(e)$ being sent from the *sender* actor $a = sender(e)$ to the *target* actor $b = target(e)$ or being reacted to by b. If m is a creation message, b will be the name of the newly created actor while a is its creator. The actor creation event is written as $a \rightarrow b : \mathtt{new}\ C(\overline{p})$. We assume that actors are named hierarchically, so that we can say whether b is transitively created by a by checking that a is an ancestor of b (written $a \in ancestors(b)$). For message sends, we distinguish between the *emittance* of the message $(a \rightarrow b : mtd(\overline{p}))$ and its *reaction* $(a \twoheadrightarrow b : mtd(\overline{p}))$. The function $param(e)$ extracts the parameters of the message $msg(e)$, while the function $acq(e)$, short for acquaintance, extracts the actors exposed in e.

Adapting SA to represent actors and component instances (together we call them *entities*) based on the context described above requires two ingredients: enriched states and some constraints placed on the initial states, the state signatures and the transition relation. Definition 2 describes the states and constraints utilizing the function *isLocal* that identifies whether an actor is represented by the AA:

$$isLocal(a, a', kind) \stackrel{\text{def}}{=} (kind = TAct \implies a = a')$$
$$\wedge\ (kind = TComp \implies a' \in ancestors(a))$$

Definition 2 (Actor Automata). A parameterized SA $\mathcal{A}(this, kind) = \langle states(\mathcal{A}), start(\mathcal{A}), sig(\mathcal{A}), steps(\mathcal{A}) \rangle$ with the following description:

1. $states(\mathcal{A})$ is a map with a fixed domain $V \subseteq \mathbf{V}$ denoting the variables stored by the entity. V includes the following variables: buf, $known$, $expActors$, $ready$, $nameGen$, and t_{gen}, representing an event bag (of type $\mathcal{M}\langle\mathbf{E}\rangle$), the set of known actors ($2^{\mathbf{A}}$), the set of exposed actors ($2^{\mathbf{A}}$), whether the entity is at a ready point ($\mathbf{B}$), the actor name generator ($2^{\mathbf{A}}$), and the traces generated by the entity ($Seq\langle\mathbf{E}\rangle$), respectively. The read-only class parameters are stored under the variable $params$. Other variables are internal and grouped together under $ints$.
2. A non-empty set of initial states $start(\mathcal{A}) \subseteq states(\mathcal{A})$.
3. A signature mapping $sig(\mathcal{A})$ where for each state $s \in states(\mathcal{A})$, $sig(\mathcal{A})(s) = \langle in(\mathcal{A})(s), out(\mathcal{A})(s), int(\mathcal{A})(s) \rangle$, where $in(\mathcal{A})(s), out(\mathcal{A})(s), int(\mathcal{A})(s) \subseteq \mathbf{E}$.
4. A transition relation $steps(\mathcal{A}) \subseteq states(\mathcal{A}) \times acts(\mathcal{A}) \times states(\mathcal{A})$.

is an *actor automaton* representing an entity (with the initial actor) of kind "actor" (*TAct*) or "component instance" (*TComp*) of name *this* of class/component D when it satisfies the following constraints:

A1. $\forall s \in start(\mathcal{A}) : s(buf) = s(nameGen) = \emptyset \wedge this \in s(known) \wedge s(ready)$
$$\wedge\ s(expActors) = \{this\} \wedge s(t_{gen}) = [].$$

A2. $\forall s \in states(\mathcal{A}) : in(\mathcal{A})(s) =$
$$\left\{ e \,\middle|\, \begin{array}{l} isEmit(e) \wedge msg(e) \in aMsg(D, in) \\ \wedge\ isLocal(target(e), this, kind) \wedge \neg isLocal(sender(e), this, kind) \end{array} \right\}.$$

A3. $\forall s \in states(\mathcal{A}) : out(\mathcal{A})(s) =$
$$\left\{ e \,\middle|\, \begin{array}{l} isEmit(e) \wedge acq(e) \subseteq s(known) \wedge msg(e) \in aMsg(D, out) \\ \wedge\ (isSend(e) \implies isLocal(sender(e), this, kind) \\ \qquad\qquad \wedge\ \neg isLocal(target(e), this, kind)) \\ \wedge\ (isCreate(e) \implies target(e) \notin s(nameGen) \wedge sender(e) = this) \end{array} \right\}.$$

A4. $\forall s \in states(\mathcal{A}) : int(\mathcal{A})(s) =$
$$\left\{ e \left| \begin{array}{l} (isReact(e) \implies emitOf(e) \in s(buf)) \\ \wedge \ (isEmit(e) \implies isSend(e) \wedge acq(e) \subseteq s(known) \\ \qquad \wedge isLocal(sender(e), this, kind) \wedge isLocal(target(e), this, kind)) \end{array} \right. \right\}.$$

A5. $\forall (s, e, s') \in steps(\mathcal{A}) : e \in in(\mathcal{A})(s) \implies s' = s[buf \mapsto s(buf) \cup \{e\}].$

A6. $\forall (s, e, s') \in steps(\mathcal{A}) : isReact(e) \implies s(ready)$
$\wedge \ diffOn(s, s', \{buf, known, ready, t_{gen}, ints\}) \wedge s'(t_{gen}) = s(t_{gen})$ e
$\wedge \ s'(buf) = s(buf) - \{emitOf(e)\} \wedge s'(known) = s(known) \cup acq(e).$

A7. $\forall (s, e, s') \in steps(\mathcal{A}) : isEmit(e) \wedge e \in out(\mathcal{A})(s) \cup int(\mathcal{A})(s) \implies$
$\wedge \ diffOn(s, s'', \{expActors, ready, t_{gen}, ints\}) \wedge s'(t_{gen}) = s(t_{gen})$ e
$\wedge \ (isCreate(e) \implies s'(known) = s''(known) \cup \{target(e)\}$
$\qquad\qquad\qquad \wedge \ s'(nameGen) = s''(nameGen) \cup \{target(e)\})$
$\wedge \ (e \in int(\mathcal{A})(s) \implies s'(buf) = s''(buf) \cup \{e\}).$

Definition 2 describes how SA are transformed to AA. AA are parameterized with the (initial) actor (of the component instance) *this*, mimicking how classes are behavior templates of actors, and *kind*, the kind of the entity. The events used in a particular AA are parameterized accordingly by *this*. The states consist of predefined variables governing the local event buffer, the exposure knowledge of non-local and local actors from and to the environment, whether the actor is ready to process the next incoming message or whether the component instance is ready to execute the next message, the actor name generator, and the trace the entity has generated. These variables allow the construction of Constraints A1 to A7 that regulate over the state signatures and the transition relation to represent the actor characteristics.

Constraint A1 defines the initial states, where the buffer is still empty, the entity knowledge is still at its minimum, the entity is ready to process an incoming message and no actor has been generated yet. For a component instance, the last aspect means that no locally created actor is exposed to the environment.

Constraints A2 to A4 describe how the state signatures are derived from the state. The input and output state signatures are restricted by the allowed messages of the class/component and message direction. Only emittance events are part of these signatures. The internal state signatures are either reaction events to events stored in the buffer or emittance events where both sender and target actors are local.

Constraints A5 to A7 describe the effect of all transitions on the state variables. All incoming messages are put into the buffer without otherwise changing the state. The entity can only react to a message when it is ready to do so. Executing a reaction event causes the corresponding emittance event to be removed from the buffer and the set of known actors is updated by the newly received acquaintance. When an output or internal event can be emitted, we allow the set of exposed actors, the values of the ready flag and the internal variables to be changed. If the event is an actor creation event, the entity knows the created actor. To ensure fresh names, the name generator keeps the name of the created actor. If it is an internal event, then the event is directly added to the entity's buffer.

We drop the parameters *this* and *kind* from an AA when they are irrelevant to the discussion. The name(s) of the (set of) actor(s) is retrieved by the function *names*:

$$names(\mathcal{A}(this, kind)) \stackrel{\text{def}}{=} \begin{cases} \{this\}, & \text{if } kind = TAct \\ \{a \mid this = ancestors(a)\}, & \text{if } kind = TComp \end{cases}$$

For AA representing component instances, the function returns an over-approximation of the set of actors that are local to the instance.

More specific behavior of an AA that goes beyond the constraints is expressed by so-called AA specifications. We illustrate such specifications by an example.

Example 1. The behavior of an AA representing the server component (i.e., the system) can be specified in three parts: the *provided* and *required* interfaces, which form the set of allowed messages, the internal state, and the actions taken by a server component instance. As a component, the server's provided interface consists not only of the server actor's own interface (where it provides the **reqSess** method), but also of the interface of the associated session actors (where they provide the **perform** method). The required interface consists of the **provSess** and **response** methods. The component's specification does *not* include the internal communication, because they are not *observable* by the environment.

The internal states of the server component need to capture the created sessions, to which client each session is mapped to, and the queries the component instance is currently processing. The states of this component are populated when the component instance reacts to a message of the provided interface. This reaction is marked by the execution of an event $cl \twoheadrightarrow srv : \text{reqSess}(cl)$ or $cl \twoheadrightarrow sess : \text{perform}(q)$. In response, the server component sends back a fresh session $srv \rightarrow cl : \text{provSess}(sess)$ or the computed query $sess \rightarrow cl : \text{response}(\text{compute}(q))$, respectively.

The specifications for AA that represent classes can be further optimized because each actor processes one incoming message at a time. The actions executed by the **Server** class can be represented by the AA using the following event sequence:

$$cl \twoheadrightarrow srv : \text{reqSess}(cl) \quad srv \rightarrow sess : \text{new Session}(cl, db) \quad srv \rightarrow cl : \text{provSess}(sess).$$

The AA definition allows this event sequence to be portrayed accurately.

Important to note is that AA does not utilize the full flexibility of SA with regards to the state signature. An input event will always be an input event, and similarly to output and internal event. The lemma formalizes this fact.

Lemma 1. *Let $\mathcal{A}$ be an AA. We define $in(\mathcal{A})$ to be $\bigcup_{s \in states(\mathcal{A})} in(\mathcal{A})(s)$, and similarly for $out(\mathcal{A})$ and $int(\mathcal{A})$. Then $in(\mathcal{A}) \cap out(\mathcal{A}) = in(\mathcal{A}) \cap int(\mathcal{A}) = out(\mathcal{A}) \cap int(\mathcal{A}) = \emptyset$.*

Proof. Follows from Constraints A2 to A4.

This lemma implies that AA are essentially more flexible IOA and verification procedures for IOA are reusable. This lemma is also carried over to the second tier which handles the dynamic creation aspect.

3.2   Second Tier Model

Missing from the first tier is the effect of creating an actor or a component instance. Attie and Lynch [7] model this effect by defining configuration automata (CA). CA are based on the notion of configurations: the set of $\mathbb{A}$ of alive SA and a mapping $\mathbb{S}$ that maps each SA in $\mathbb{A}$ to a particular state. The configuration information allow CA, the main semantic model, to represent open systems that feature dynamic creation. Here we present the tweaked CA for actor systems.

For an actor system, on top of the set of alive AA and the state information, a configuration needs to store the information of actors that have been exposed to the environment $\mathbb{E}$. We set some sanity conditions on the alive AA such that they are pairwise representing distinct entities and it is impossible for AA to create entities that are already alive. Definition 3 formalizes this requirement using the *names* function and the output state signature of each AA in the configuration.

Definition 3 (Configurations). A *configuration* $\mathbb{C}$ is a triple $\langle \mathbb{A}, \mathbb{S}, \mathbb{E} \rangle$ where $\mathbb{A}$ is a set of AA, $\mathbb{S}$ maps each AA $\mathcal{A} \in \mathbb{A}$ to a state $s \in states(\mathcal{A})$, and $\mathbb{E} \subseteq names(\mathbb{C})$ is the set of actor(name)s that have been exposed to the environment such that

$$\forall \mathcal{A}, \mathcal{B} \in \mathbb{A} : \mathcal{A} \neq \mathcal{B} \implies (names(\mathcal{A}) \cap names(\mathcal{B}) = \emptyset$$
$$\wedge \ out(\mathcal{A})(\mathbb{S}(\mathcal{A})) \cap \{e \mid isCreate(e) \wedge target(e) \in names(\mathcal{B})\} = \emptyset).$$

The *names* function is lifted to configurations: $names(\mathbb{C}) = \bigcup_{\mathcal{A} \in \mathbb{A}} names(\mathcal{A})$.

Important to CA is that they are *derived* from configurations. That is, the signatures and the available transitions in a CA are fully dictated by the AA present in the configurations and their state mapping. The following definition precisely provides how to derive the signature of a configuration. It is based on the observation that an event is always observable by at most two actors: the sender and the target.

Definition 4 (Signatures of a Configuration). Let $\mathbb{C} = \langle \mathbb{A}, \mathbb{S}, \mathbb{E} \rangle$ be a configuration. Let *commonEv* be the set of common events between actors represented within the configuration: $commonEv = \{ e \mid sender(e), target(e) \in names(\mathbb{C}) \}$. Let *envEv* be the set of bogus events generated by the environment:

$$envEv = \left\{ e \left| \begin{array}{l} isSend(e) \wedge acq(e) \cap (\{a \mid ancestors(a) \cap names(\mathbb{C}) = \emptyset\} \cup \mathbb{E}) \neq \emptyset \\ \wedge \ sender(e) \notin names(\mathbb{C}) \end{array} \right. \right\}.$$

Then, the signature of $\mathbb{C}$ is $sig(\mathbb{C}) = \langle in(\mathbb{C}), out(\mathbb{C}), int(\mathbb{C}) \rangle$, where

- $in(\mathbb{C}) = (\bigcup_{\mathcal{A} \in \mathbb{A}} in(\mathcal{A})(\mathbb{S}(\mathcal{A}))) - commonEv - envEv,$
- $out(\mathbb{C}) = (\bigcup_{\mathcal{A} \in \mathbb{A}} out(\mathcal{A})(\mathbb{S}(\mathcal{A}))) - commonEv,$
- $int(\mathbb{C}) = \bigcup_{\mathcal{A} \in \mathbb{A}} (int(\mathcal{A})(\mathbb{S}(\mathcal{A}))) \cup (\bigcup_{\mathcal{A} \in \mathbb{A}} in(\mathcal{A})(\mathbb{S}(\mathcal{A})) \cap \bigcup_{\mathcal{A} \in \mathbb{A}} out(\mathcal{A})(\mathbb{S}(\mathcal{A}))),$

The signature of a configuration is the aggregation of the state signatures of each AA in the configuration. All events sent by and to actors in the configuration are clumped together as internal events. These *common events* from each actor's perspective are external events, but from the system's perspective they occur within the system. A special attention is needed for the input events, where due to the lack of information of the system on the AA stage, each AA is modeled as open as possible. This openness, however, include events that can never be generated by the environment (and the system at the current configuration): messages coming from an actor not represented by an AA in the configuration whose parameters include actors of the configuration that are not yet exposed. To retain input-enabledness, they must be removed from the configuration's input signature.

For each event in the signature of a configuration, we can derive the effect of executing that event from the involved AA. This transition from the pre-configuration to the post-configuration can be seen as an aggregate of the transitions of the participating AA. If the event creates another entity, the AA representing that entity is added to the configuration, such that the AA is mapped to some initial state. All AA that can participate in executing that event must perform the corresponding transition. The post-state of each transition is recorded in the post-configuration. The post-configuration also takes note of which actors become exposed to the environment after executing the event. Definition 5 formalizes this description.

Definition 5 (Intrinsic Transitions). Let $\mathbb{C} = \langle \mathbb{A}, \mathbb{S}, \mathbb{E} \rangle$, $\mathbb{C}' = \langle \mathbb{A}', \mathbb{S}', \mathbb{E}' \rangle$ be configurations and e an event. Let $\mathcal{A}'(target(e))$ be an AA of class $class(e)$ or component $[class(e)]$, if e is a creation event (i.e., $isCreate(e)$). There is an *intrinsic transition* from $\mathbb{C}$ to $\mathbb{C}'$ labeled by e, written $\mathbb{C} \stackrel{e}{\Rightarrow} \mathbb{C}'$, iff

1. $e \in \widehat{sig}(\mathbb{C})$,
2. $\mathbb{A}' = \mathbb{A} \cup \{\mathcal{A}'(target(e)) \mid isCreate(e)\}$,
3. for all $\mathcal{A} \in \mathbb{A}' - \mathbb{A} : \mathbb{S}'(\mathcal{A}) \in start(\mathcal{A}) \wedge \mathbb{S}'(\mathcal{A})(params) = param(e)$,
4. for all $\mathcal{A} \in \mathbb{A}$: if $e \in \widehat{sig}(\mathcal{A})(\mathbb{S}(\mathcal{A})) \wedge \mathbb{S}(\mathcal{A}) \stackrel{e}{\rightarrow}_{\mathcal{A}} s$, then $\mathbb{S}'(\mathcal{A}) = s$, otherwise $\mathbb{S}'(\mathcal{A}) = \mathbb{S}(\mathcal{A})$, and
5. $\mathbb{E}' = \mathbb{E} \cup \left\{ a \; \middle| \; \begin{array}{l} isSend(e) \wedge target(e) \notin names(\mathbb{C}) \\ \wedge \; a \in acq(e) - \{a \mid ancestors(a) \cap names(\mathbb{C}) = \emptyset\} \end{array} \right\}$.

The following definition assembles the configurations, signatures, and transitions into a CA. More precisely, all configurations are taken from AA that are deemed alive (Definition 3), whose signatures and possible transitions are exactly as stated in Definitions 4 and 5, respectively. For simplicity, we restrict ourselves to CA where initially only one entity is present in the configuration. Initial configurations that contain more than one entity can be simulated by having a main actor that creates the other entities and sends a start message to them in a non-deterministic order.

Definition 6 (Configuration Automata). A *configuration automaton* $\mathcal{C}$ is a pair $\langle sa(\mathcal{C}), config(\mathcal{C}) \rangle$ where

– $sa(\mathcal{C})$ is an SA; (the parts of this SA are abbreviated to $states(\mathcal{C}) = states(sa(\mathcal{C}))$, $start(\mathcal{C}) = start(sa(\mathcal{C}))$, etc. for brevity)
– a configuration mapping $config(\mathcal{C})$ with domain $states(\mathcal{C})$ such that for all $x \in states(\mathcal{C})$, $config(\mathcal{C})(x)$ is a configuration;

such that the following constraints are satisfied:

1. If $x \in start(\mathcal{C})$ and $(\mathcal{A}, s) \in config(\mathcal{C})(x)$, then $s \in start(\mathcal{A})$.
   Additionally, $\forall x \in start(\mathcal{C}) : \langle \mathbb{A}, \mathbb{S}, \mathbb{E} \rangle = config(\mathcal{C})(x) \wedge |\mathbb{A}| = 1 \wedge \mathbb{E} \subseteq names(\mathbb{A})$.
2. If $(x, e, x') \in steps(\mathcal{C})$ then $config(\mathcal{C})(x) \stackrel{e}{\Rightarrow} config(\mathcal{C})(x')$.
3. If $x \in states(\mathcal{C})$ and $config(\mathcal{C})(x) \stackrel{e}{\Rightarrow} \mathbb{C}$ for some event e and a configuration $\mathbb{C}$, then $\exists x' \in states(\mathcal{C})$ such that $config(\mathcal{C})(x') = \mathbb{C}$ and $(x, e, x') \in steps(\mathcal{C})$.
4. $\forall x \in states(\mathcal{C}) : in(\mathcal{C})(x) = in(config(\mathcal{C})(x))$
   $$\wedge\, out(\mathcal{C})(x) = out(config(\mathcal{C})(x)) \wedge int(\mathcal{C})(x) = int(config(\mathcal{C})(x)).$$

4   Verification

The automaton model can be used for verifying the correctness of an implementation of an actor system. We follow a two-tier approach proposed by, e.g., Misra and Chandy [30] to perform this task. The first tier is verifying that the class implementation satisfies the class specification, represented by an AA. In this tier, we follow an approach by Dovland et al. [15], where the class implementations are checked against desired trace-based *class invariants*. First, a trace-based class invariant is extracted from the AA. Then, the class implementation is translated into a simple sequential language in the spirit of the transformational approach by Olderog and Apt [34]. The verification takes place by, e.g., taking the weakest-liberal precondition of the translated implementation and deducing that the weakest-liberal precondition holds. This technique allows the verification of safety properties. The second tier is done by constructing a simulation relation from the CA representing the implementation of the component to the CA representing the component specification. This relation checks whether the component specification is fulfilled by the activator class and subcomponent specifications. We use a specialized simulation relation called the *possibility map* [29,33], which synchronizes only on external events. This tier allows the verification of liveness properties on top of the safety properties.

In the following subsections, we sketch how verification on each tier works. More details including a soundness proof for a more complex setting and the model's congruence to an actor-based language are available [24]. The reference also contains an application of the verification technique to components with recursive unbounded actor creation of a single chain.

4.1   Class Verification

Verifying the class implementation is done in two parts. First, we encode the AA representing the class specification as a class invariant. The class invariant reflects what needs to remain true at an actor before and after executing a method in response of an incoming message. Furthermore, it also ensures whenever an actor is in the middle of a computation, that computation is part of a response of the actor to an incoming message. To support the verification effort on this tier, we include a user-defined relation $\rho(\overline{f}, s)$ which links the class parameters used in the implementation and the state variables used in the AA. It is typically given during the verification process as the implementation is available and only the internal variables of the specification are compared to the class parameters.

Definition 7 (Class Invariants). Let $\mathcal{A}$ be an AA. Given a predicate $\rho(\overline{f}, s)$ over the class parameters $\overline{f}$ and a state s of the $\mathcal{A}$, the class invariant $\mathtt{I}(\overline{f}, \mathtt{t})$ of $\mathcal{A}$ over $\overline{f}$ and the trace $\mathtt{t}$ is defined as follows:

$$\mathtt{I}(\overline{f}, \mathtt{t}) \stackrel{\text{def}}{=} \exists s \in states(\mathcal{A}) : s(ready) \wedge s(t_{gen}) = \mathtt{t} \wedge \rho(\overline{f}, s)$$

Following the idea of Dovland et al. [15], we encode the class implementation into a simple sequential language SEQ with non-deterministic assignments [5]. This language consists of the typical sequential statement constructs, such as conditional, skip and sequential composition, enriched with a non-deterministic assignment, an assume statement, and a procedure construct. The non-deterministic assignment is used to assign the names of newly created actors, while the assume statement is used to establish that the invariant holds before and after the method execution, respectively. The procedure construct is used to represent the methods of a class.

Encoding the implementation in SEQ has the advantage of using well-established semantics such as the weakest liberal precondition semantics. This means we can introduce the following verification condition of class C with the invariant $\mathtt{I}(\overline{f}, \mathtt{t})$:

$$\forall m, \mathtt{t}, \overline{f}, \overline{x} : \mathtt{wf}(\mathtt{t}) \wedge \mathtt{I}(\overline{f}, \mathtt{t}) \implies wlp(m(\overline{x}) \ body_m, \mathtt{I}(\overline{f}, \mathtt{t}))$$

where $\mathtt{wf}(\mathtt{t})$ maintains the well-formedness of trace $\mathtt{t}$, $m(\overline{x}) \ body_m$ is a method definition in C populated by parameters $\overline{x}$, and $wlp(s, Q)$ is the weakest liberal precondition that ensures that postcondition Q holds after executing statement s.

Example 2. The class invariant of the Server class is derived from its AA $\mathcal{A}$ (Example 1) by setting the predicate ρ as *true*: $\mathtt{I}(db, \mathtt{t}) \stackrel{\text{def}}{=} \exists s \in states(\mathcal{A}) : s(ready) \wedge s(t_{gen}) = \mathtt{t}$. Assuming $e_1 = cl \twoheadrightarrow this : \mathtt{reqSess}(cl)$, $e_2 = this \rightarrow sess : \mathtt{new} \ \mathtt{Session}(db)$ and $e_3 = this \rightarrow cl : \mathtt{provSess}(sess)$, the verification condition for the implementation in Listing 1.1 is

$$\forall \mathtt{t}, db, cl : \mathtt{wf}(\mathtt{t}) \wedge \mathtt{I}(db, \mathtt{t}) \implies \forall sess : \mathtt{wf}(\mathtt{t} \ e_1 \ e_2) \implies \mathtt{wf}(\mathtt{t} \ e_1 \ e_2 \ e_3) \implies \mathtt{I}(\mathtt{t} \ e_1 \ e_2 \ e_3).$$

The verification proceeds by first-order logic deduction rules.

4.2 Component Verification

The second tier deals with verifying components and ultimately the whole system. The main verification method is the *possibility map* [29,33], a specialized simulation relation that allows an implementation to synchronize with its specification only on external events. That is, an implementation may conduct an arbitrary number of internal transitions to fulfill its desired observable behavior.

Definition 8 (Possibility Maps). Let C_1, C_2 be CA and $E_{ext} \subseteq Act(C_1)$ a set of events. A map $r = Map\langle states(C_1), states(C_2)\rangle$ is a *possibility map* from C_1 to C_2 with respect to E_{ext} if the following conditions hold.

1. If $x \in start(C_1)$ then $r(x) \neq$ undef and $r(x) \in start(C_2)$.
2. If $x \xrightarrow{e}_{C_1} x' \wedge r(x) \neq$ undef then $r(x') \neq$ undef and either $e \notin E_{ext} \wedge r(x) = r(x')$ or $r(x) \xrightarrow{e}_{C_2} r(x')$.

This verification method is defined for IOA and in general does not work for DIOA due to the dynamic state signatures. Actor systems have the advantage that the set of external events can be over-approximated (Lemma 1). This set is defined by the following function given the initial actor of the component instance:

$$extEv(a) = \{e \mid isMethod(e) \wedge isEmit(e) \wedge (\{sender(e), target(e)\} \cap ancestors(a) \neq \emptyset)\}$$

In addition to the external events, the component specification utilizes the reaction events of the input events which are captured by the following function.

$$E_{cmp}(a) = extEv(a) \cup \{e \mid emitOf(e) \in extEv(a)\}$$

If we can find a possibility map with respect to E_{cmp} between the CA containing the AA of the component specification and the CA containing the AA of the class specification, then the component specification is satisfied by its implementation.

Theorem 1. *Let $C_{[C]}$ be a CA whose initial configurations consist of a component instance of component $[C]$ and C_C a CA whose initial configurations consist of an actor this of class C. Let $r = Map\langle states(C_C), states(C_{[C]})\rangle$ be a possibility map from C_C to $C_{[C]}$ with respect to $E_{cmp}(this)$. Given the set of external traces $xtraces(C)$ of CA C, then,*

$$xtraces(C_C) \subseteq xtraces(C_{[C]}).$$

Proof. Follows from [33] for IOA and Lemma 1.

Example 3. Assume we have a verified specification of the [Session] component, where it represents the **perform** and the **response** of each query from the environment. The internal state of the [Session] component is the set of queries the component instance is currently processing. Using the specifications of the [Session] component and the **Server** class (Example 1), we can construct a possibility map between them and the AA of the **Server** component by:

- equating the event bag of the [Server] component instance to the event bags of the [Session] component instances and the Server actor,
- equating the queries of the [Server] component instance to the queries of the [Session] component instance, and
- mapping the correct [Session] component instance to each client, as stored in the internal state of the [Server] component instance.

5 Related Work

There are several automaton models for representing actors, but they either do not consider actor creation or all actors are assumed to be present in the system from the start. Belonging to the former approach are the translation of actor programs to constraint automata [37] and the modeling of timing aspects of actor programs by timed automata [22]. An example of the latter is the work by Leo [28] where actor systems are modeled by the composition of an infinite number of IOA, each of which has a flag indicating whether the represented actor has been created.

Automaton models that accurately capture dynamic creation need to store the created names. History-dependent automata [31,32] provide a generalized means to encode systems with dynamic creation, but without a separation of concerns between the behavior of the system's individual entities and the collective, instantiated behavior. Similar to DIOA [6,7], dynamic communicating automata (DCA) [8,9] and dynamic register automata [1] provide this separation, where a template automaton is used to describe the generic behavior of each process in the system. Instantiations of the template automaton (i.e., the processes) is collected in a configuration (for DCA, message sequence charts [21]). These models need a composition operator to avoid packing the behavior of every system component into one template automaton. Callable timed automata [10] represent behavioral templates for calls and the (timed) systems are represented using timed transition systems. An adaptation for actor systems is not straightforward, as the semantics are based on the calls instead of entities such as actors. Dynamic reactive modules [17] model process classes as transition systems that use logical formulas to describe the transition relations. This framework is more suitable for systems whose entities share variables.

Logics can be used to model actor systems. Some models based on temporal logic have been pursued [11,16,36], but they carry the drawback that the implementation has to be encoded in full together with the specification's formula. A promising approach is the use of trace-based dynamic logic [4,12,13], which can handle actor systems with more complex features such as futures. The modularity of the verification of this approach is up to the method level, with the integration of a (static) component notion as defined in this paper is still to be investigated. We have investigated a generalized Hoare logic based on the splitting of traces into input and output traces [25]. Implementation verification using this approach is an open challenge.

Models based on process algebra [3,18] require the construction of a (bi)simulation relation to compare the implementation and the specification, unless abstractions are applied [14,40] which allow automatic model checking at the loss of some precision. A translation from the expressive Specification Diagram for actor systems [38] to process algebra has been worked out [39].

6   Conclusion

In this paper we presented an automaton model based on DIOA for representing actor systems. The automaton model provides an explicit support for dynamic creation and dynamic topology. It enables accurate representation of the complete observable behavior of the actor systems, while allowing abstractions to be built based on a simple hierarchical component notion. The integration with the component notion enables a hierarchical end-to-end verification approach. We illustrate it using a transformational approach to a sequential language to verify the implementation and a simulation relation to verify the components.

We envision several directions of further research. First, a full support for futures in the model is still not yet established. One way to support this is by introducing a special kind of SA that only represent futures. An interesting question is how the futures generated by the environment can be handled by the model. Another direction is to investigate other verification techniques applicable to this model. Some preliminary work on adapting temporal logic for DIOA exists, but the logical rules and their soundness are not yet fully investigated.

References

1. Abdulla, P.A., Atig, M.F., Kara, A., Rezine, O.: Verification of dynamic register automata. In: FSTTCS, pp. 653–665 (2014)
2. Agha, G.: Actors: A Model of Concurrent Computation in Distributed Systems. MIT Press, Cambridge (1986)
3. Agha, G., Thati, P.: An algebraic theory of actors and its application to a simple object-based language. In: Owe, O., Krogdahl, S., Lyche, T. (eds.) From Object-Orientation to Formal Methods. LNCS, vol. 2635, pp. 26–57. Springer, Heidelberg (2004)
4. Ahrendt, W., Dylla, M.: A system for compositional verification of asynchronous objects. Sci. Comput. Program. **77**(12), 1289–1309 (2012)
5. Apt, K.R.: Ten years of Hoare's logic: a survey part II: nondeterminism. Theor. Comput. Sci. **28**, 83–109 (1984)
6. Attie, P.C., Lynch, N.A.: Dynamic Input/Output automata: a formal model for dynamic systems. In: Larsen, K.G., Nielsen, M. (eds.) CONCUR 2001. LNCS, vol. 2154, pp. 137–151. Springer, Heidelberg (2001)
7. Attie, P.C., Lynch, N.: Dynamic Input/Output automata: a formal and compositional model for dynamic systems. Inf. Comput. (2015) (To appear)
8. Bollig, B., Cyriac, A., Hélouët, L., Kara, A., Schwentick, T.: Dynamic communicating automata and branching high-level MSCs. In: Dediu, A.-H., Martín-Vide, C., Truthe, B. (eds.) LATA 2013. LNCS, vol. 7810, pp. 177–189. Springer, Heidelberg (2013)

9. Bollig, B., Hélouët, L.: Realizability of dynamic MSC languages. In: Ablayev, F., Mayr, E.W. (eds.) CSR 2010. LNCS, vol. 6072, pp. 48–59. Springer, Heidelberg (2010)

10. Boudjadar, A., Vaandrager, F., Bodeveix, J.-P., Filali, M.: Extending UPPAAL for the modeling and verification of dynamic real-time systems. In: Arbab, F., Sirjani, M. (eds.) FSEN 2013. LNCS, vol. 8161, pp. 111–132. Springer, Heidelberg (2013)

11. Dam, M., Fredlund, L., Gurov, D.: Toward parametric verification of open distributed systems. In: de Roever, W.-P., Langmaack, H., Pnueli, A. (eds.) COMPOS 1997. LNCS, vol. 1536, pp. 150–185. Springer, Heidelberg (1998)

12. Din, C.C., Dovland, J., Johnsen, E.B., Owe, O.: Observable behavior of distributed systems: component reasoning for concurrent objects. J. Log. Algebr. Program. **81**(3), 227–256 (2012)

13. Din, C.C., Owe, O.: Compositional and sound reasoning about active objects with shared futures. Research report 437 (2014)

14. D'Osualdo, E., Kochems, J., Ong, C.-H.L.: Automatic verification of erlang-style concurrency. In: Logozzo, F., Fähndrich, M. (eds.) Static Analysis. LNCS, vol. 7935, pp. 454–476. Springer, Heidelberg (2013)

15. Dovland, J., Johnsen, E.B., Owe, O.: Verification of concurrent objects with asynchronous method calls. In: SwSTE, pp. 141–150 (2005)

16. Duarte, C.H.C.: Proof-theoretic foundations for the design of actor systems. Math. Struct. Comput. Sci. **9**(3), 227–252 (1999)

17. Fisher, J., Henzinger, T.A., Nickovic, D., Piterman, N., Singh, A.V., Vardi, M.Y.: Dynamic reactive modules. In: Katoen, J.-P., König, B. (eds.) CONCUR 2011. LNCS, vol. 6901, pp. 404–418. Springer, Heidelberg (2011)

18. Gaspari, M., Zavattaro, G.: An algebra of actors. In: Ciancarini, P., Fantechi, A., Gorrieri, R. (eds.) FMOODS. Springer, New York (1999)

19. Haller, P., Odersky, M.: Scala actors: unifying thread-based and event-based programming. Theor. Comput. Sci. **410**(2–3), 202–220 (2009)

20. International Telecommunication Union - Telecommunication Standardization. Open distributed processing - reference models parts 1–4. Technical report, ISO/IEC (1995)

21. International Telecommunication Union - Telecommunication Standardization. Recommendation Z.120: Message Sequence Chart (MSC). Technical report, ISO/IEC (2011)

22. Jaghoori, M.M., Chothia, T.: Timed automata semantics for analyzing Creol. In: FOCLASA, pp. 108–122 (2010)

23. Johnsen, E.B., Hähnle, R., Schäfer, J., Schlatte, R., Steffen, M.: ABS: a core language for abstract behavioral specification. In: Aichernig, B.K., de Boer, F.S., Bonsangue, M.M. (eds.) Formal Methods for Components and Objects. LNCS, vol. 6957, pp. 142–164. Springer, Heidelberg (2011)

24. Kurnia, I.W.: An automata-theoretic approach to open actor system verification. Ph.D. thesis, University of Kaiserslautern, January 2015

25. Kurnia, I.W., Poetzsch-Heffter, A.: A relational trace logic for simple hierarchical actor-based component systems. In: AGERE! 2012, pp. 47–58. ACM (2012)

26. Kurnia, I.W., Poetzsch-Heffter, A.: Verification of open concurrent object systems. In: Giachino, E., Hähnle, R., de Boer, F.S., Bonsangue, M.M. (eds.) Formal Methods for Components and Objects. LNCS, vol. 7866, pp. 83–118. Springer, Heidelberg (2013)

27. Lamport, L.: What good is temporal logic? In: IFIP Congress, pp. 657–668 (1983)

28. Leo, J.: Dynamic process creation in a static model. Master's thesis, MIT (1990)

29. Lynch, N., Tuttle, M.R.: Hierarchical correctness proofs for distributed algorithms. In: PODC, pp. 137–151 (1987)
30. Misra, J., Mani Chandy, K.: Proofs of networks of processes. IEEE Trans. Software Eng. **7**(4), 417–426 (1981)
31. Montanari, U., Pistore, M.: Ugo Montanari and Marco Pistore. ENTCS **10**, 170–188 (1997)
32. Montanari, U., Pistore, M.: History-dependent automata: an introduction. In: Bernardo, M., Bogliolo, A. (eds.) SFM-Moby 2005. LNCS, vol. 3465, pp. 1–28. Springer, Heidelberg (2005)
33. Nipkow, T., Slind, K.: I/O automata in Isabelle/HOL. In: Dybjer, P., Nordström, B., Smith, J. (eds.) TYPES. LNCS, vol. 996, pp. 101–119. Springer, Heidelberg (1994)
34. Olderog, E.-R., Apt, K.R.: Fairness in parallel programs: the transformational approach. ACM TOPLAS **10**(3), 420–455 (1988)
35. OSGi core release 5 (2012). http://www.osgi.org
36. Schacht, S.: Formal reasoning about actor programs using temporal logic. In: Agha, G., De Cindio, F., Rozenberg, G. (eds.) APN 2001. LNCS, vol. 2001, pp. 445–460. Springer, Heidelberg (2001)
37. Sirjani, M., Jaghoori, M.M., Baier, C., Arbab, F.: Compositional semantics of an actor-based language using constraint automata. In: Ciancarini, P., Wiklicky, H. (eds.) COORDINATION 2006. LNCS, vol. 4038, pp. 281–297. Springer, Heidelberg (2006)
38. Smith, S., Talcott, C.L.: Specification diagrams for actor systems. High.-Order Symb. Comput. **15**(4), 301–348 (2002)
39. Thati, P., Talcott, C., Agha, G.: Techniques for executing and reasoning about specification diagrams. In: Rattray, C., Maharaj, S., Shankland, C. (eds.) AMAST 2004. LNCS, vol. 3116, pp. 521–536. Springer, Heidelberg (2004)
40. Zufferey, D., Wies, T., Henzinger, T.A.: Ideal abstractions for well-structured transition systems. In: Kuncak, V., Rybalchenko, A. (eds.) VMCAI 2012. LNCS, vol. 7148, pp. 445–460. Springer, Heidelberg (2012)

RSSA: A Reversible SSA Form

Torben Ægidius Mogensen[(⊠)]

DIKU, University of Copenhagen,
Universitetsparken 5, 2100 Copenhagen O, Denmark
torbenm@di.ku.dk

Abstract. The SSA form (Static Single Assignment form) is used in compilers as an intermediate language as an alternative to traditional three-address code because code in SSA form is easier to analyse and optimize using data-flow analysis such as common-subexpression elimination, value numbering, register allocation and so on.

We introduce RSSA, a reversible variant of the SSA form suitable as an intermediate language for reversible programming languages that are compiled to reversible machine language. The main issues in making SSA reversible are the unsuitability for SSA of the reversible updates and exchanges that are traditional in reversible languages and the need for φ-nodes on both joins and splits of control-flow. The first issue is handled by making selected uses of a variable destroy the variable and the latter by adding parameters to labels.

We show how programs in the reversible intermediate language RIL can be translated into RSSA and discuss copy propagation, constant propagation and register allocation in the context of RSSA.

1 Introduction

We start this paper by a brief summary of the traditional SSA form and a description of a (non-SSA) reversible intermediate language RIL [6]. We will then modify RIL to RSSA by adding the static-single-assignment property and a variant of the φ-nodes from the SSA form. The key insight is that a reversible SSA form needs for each variable not only a unique definition point, but also a unique undefinition (destruction) point.

We show that RSSA greatly simplifies optimisations such as copy propagation and constant propagation and discuss how RSSA can help solve the for reversible languages tricky problem of register allocation.

2 Static Single Assignment Form (SSA)

The SSA form is a type of intermediate language used in several compilers, most notably the LLVM compiler framework [3]. The SSA form was introduced by Wegman, Zadeck, Alpern and Rosen [1,8] to facilitate data-flow analysis such as value numbering and conditional constant propagation, because the SSA form makes definition-use chains trivial.

© Springer International Publishing Switzerland 2016
M. Mazzara and A. Voronkov (Eds.): PSI 2015, LNCS 9609, pp. 203–217, 2016.
DOI: 10.1007/978-3-319-41579-6_16

The main property of SSA form is that there is exactly one assignment or definition to each variable in the program. Unlike in functional languages, this assignment can be executed several times in a loop, changing the value of the variable, hence the term *Static* Single Assignment.

Converting traditional three-address code to SSA form involves three steps:

1. Add an index to each *defining* occurrence of a variable, i.e., when the variable is assigned a new value.
2. Add ϕ-nodes where differently indexed versions of the same variable meet in a control-flow join.
3. Add indices to variable *uses*, so a variable is given the index it has in the unique defining occurrence that reaches this use of the variable.

We will illustrate this by a short example. Consider the flow-chart program below:

$$
\begin{aligned}
&\textbf{begin} \\
&\qquad x := 0 \\
&loop: \\
&\qquad x := x + 1 \\
&\qquad \textbf{if}\ \ x < 10\ \ \textbf{then}\ \ loop\ \ \textbf{else}\ \ exit \\
&exit: \\
&\qquad x := x + 3 \\
&\textbf{end}
\end{aligned}
$$

In phase 1, we add indices to definitions of x:

$$
\begin{aligned}
&\textbf{begin} \\
&\qquad x_1 := 0 \\
&loop: \\
&\qquad x_2 := x + 1 \\
&\qquad \textbf{if}\ \ x < 10\ \ \textbf{then}\ \ loop\ \ \textbf{else}\ \ exit \\
&exit: \\
&\qquad x_3 := x + 3 \\
&\textbf{end}
\end{aligned}
$$

We next note that the use of x inside the loop can come from either the definition of x_1 or the definition of x_2. To ensure that the use of x after the join-point comes from a unique definition, we define x by a ϕ-node at the start of the loop:

$$
\begin{aligned}
&\textbf{begin} \\
&\qquad x_1 := 0 \\
&loop: \\
&\qquad x_4 := \phi(x_1,\, x_2) \\
&\qquad x_2 := x + 1 \\
&\qquad \textbf{if}\ \ x < 10\ \ \textbf{then}\ \ loop\ \ \textbf{else}\ \ exit \\
&exit: \\
&\qquad x_3 := x + 3 \\
&\textbf{end}
\end{aligned}
$$

The ϕ function chooses one of its arguments depending on which predecessor the control-flow came from. It is, strictly speaking, not a real function, as its implementation needs additional control-flow information, but for the purposes of data-flow analysis it can be seen as a function.

The use of x in the last assignment has only one possible definition (x_2), so no ϕ-node is needed there. The last step is adding indices to uses of variables:

```
begin
        x₁ := 0
    loop :
        x₄ := φ(x₁, x₂)
        x₂ := x₄ + 1
        if  x₂ < 10  then  loop  else  exit
    exit :
        x₃ := x₂ + 3
end
```

It is now trivial to see which (unique) definition defines a use of a variable, which makes data-flow analysis easy. Determining where ϕ-nodes are needed can be efficiently computed using dominance frontiers [2]. We define the basic concepts below.

- A *basic block* is a piece of code that starts with a label (or begin), ends with a jump, a fall-through to another label, or end and has no labels and jumps between these.
- A basic block B *dominates* a basic block C if all paths from begin to C goes through B. A basic block dominates itself, so B may be C itself. B can also be the basic block starting with begin.
- A basic block B *strictly dominates* a basic block C if B dominates C and $B \neq C$.
- The *dominance frontier* of a basic block B is the set of basic blocks C such that B dominates one of the immediate predecessors of C, but does not strictly dominate C itself. It is possible that B is in its own dominance frontier.

If a basic block B contains a definition of a variable used in a basic block C and C is in the dominance frontier of B, then C must have a ϕ-node for x. Note that a ϕ-node for x is also a definition of x, so this criterion is iterated until no more ϕ-nodes need to be added. When ϕ-nodes have been added, every use of a variable x is given the index of the unique definition of x that reaches the use of x. If the use of x is as an argument to a ϕ-function in a basic block C, this definition must go through the corresponding immediate predecessor of C.

See [2] for more details and efficient methods for computing the dominance frontier, inserting ϕ-nodes and adding indices to uses of variables.

A variant notation for the SSA form splits the ϕ-nodes between the join-point and the jumps to the join point. Labels used in join points are given parameters, and fall-through to join points are made into explicit jumps, so parameters can be added. In this variant, the example program above looks like this:

```
begin
        x1 := 0
        goto loop(x1)
loop(x4) :
        x2 := x4 + 1
        if  x2 < 10  then  loop(x2) else  exit
exit :
        x3 := x2 + 3
end
```

Note that this notation clears the potential confusion about which predecessor of a ϕ-node corresponds to which argument of the ϕ-function, but the notation is farther from traditional three-address code than the assignment-style ϕ-nodes. We will use this variant for our reversible SSA form, since we need to deviate from three-address code anyway.

3   The Reversible Intermediate Language RIL

We describe the reversible intermediate language RIL [6]. RIL is inspired by Janus [4], using unstructured jumps in the style of the Janus variant described in [5]. RIL has a formal semantic definition [6], but in this paper we will just describe it informally.

A RIL program consists of an unordered set of basic blocks, each consisting of an entry point followed by either updates and exchanges or a single subroutine call and is terminated by an exit point. We will describe each of these below.

3.1   Entry and Exit Points

An entry point has one of the forms

$l \leftarrow$ where l is a label,
$l_1 ; l_2 \leftarrow c$ where c is a condition and l_1 and l_2 are labels, or
begin l where l is a label.

An exit point has one of the forms:

$\rightarrow l$ where l is a label,
$c \rightarrow l_1 ; l_2$ where c is a condition and l_1 and l_2 are labels, or
end l where l is a label.

Each label in the program must occur in exactly one entry point and exactly one exit point. Furthermore, a label that occurs in a **begin** entry point must also occur in an **end** exit point.

Conditions are of the form $L \bowtie R$, where a left-value L is either a named variable x or of the form $M[x]$, representing the memory location pointed to by a variable x, and a right-value R is either a left-value or a signed constant, and $\bowtie$ is an operator from the set ==, <, >, !=, <=, >= and &, using notation from the programming language C. We use the value 0 to represent false and any non-zero value to represent true.

begin and **end** represent beginnings and ends of subroutines. The start and end of the entire program are entry and exit points with the label **main**. An exit point of the form $\rightarrow l$ constitutes an unconditional jump to the (unique) entry point where l occurs. An exit point of the form $c \rightarrow l_1; l_2$ constitutes a conditional jump: If c is true, the jump goes to l_1, otherwise to l_2. An entry point of the form $l \leftarrow$ unconditionally accepts incoming jumps. An entry point of the form $l_1; l_2 \leftarrow c$ conditionally accepts incoming jumps: Jumps to l_1 are accepted if c is true and jumps to l_2 are accepted if c is false. If the incoming jump is not accepted, a run-time error occurs.

3.2 Updates and Exchanges

A basic block can hold a (possibly empty) sequence of updates and exchanges.

An update is of the form $L \oplus= R_1 \odot R_2$, where L is a left-value, R_1 and R_2 are right-values and $\oplus=$ is one of the update assignments +=, -= or ^= with the same semantics as in the programming language C. $\odot$ is an infix arithmetic operation that can be either +, -, ^, &, |, >>, or <<, again with the same semantics as in C.

An exchange is of the form $L_1 \leftrightarrow L_2$, where L_1 and L_2 are left-values. The effect is that the values in the two specified locations are swapped.

In order to ensure reversibility, the following restrictions apply to updates and exchanges:

– In an update of the form $L \oplus= R_1 \odot R_2$, the same named variable can not occur both to the left and to the right of the update operator $\oplus=$.
– In an update of the form $L \oplus= R_1 \odot R_2$, memory accesses (left-values of the form $M[x]$) can not be used on both sides of the update operator $\oplus=$.
– In an exchange of the form $L_1 \leftrightarrow L_2$, the same named variable can not occur both to the left and to the right of the exchange operator $\leftrightarrow$.

3.3 Subroutine Calls

Instead of containing a sequence of exchanges and updates, a basic block can hold a single subroutine call. A subroutine call is done using the instructions **call** l and **uncall** l. There can be several calls to the same subroutine. We use an implicit stack to store return information.

A subroutine call must be in a basic block of the form $l_1 \leftarrow$ **call** $l \rightarrow l_2$ or $l_1 \leftarrow$ **uncall** $l \rightarrow l_2$.

In such a block, **call** l stores l_2 on the implicit stack and jumps to the entry point **begin** l until it reaches **end** l, at which point it pops the stack and jumps to the label l_2 that is stored on the top of the stack.

RIL (like Janus) also supports running subroutines backwards: **uncall** l stores l_2 on the implicit stack, and then runs the subroutine l backwards, starting from the exit point **end** l and ending with **begin** l, again returning via the stack to l_2.

3.4 Shorthands

To make code more readable, we introduce a number of shorthands when displaying RIL code in the paper.

We will use $L \oplus= R$ as an abbreviation of $L \oplus= R + 0$.

Two blocks $E\ I_1\ \rightarrow\ l$ and $l\ \leftarrow\ l\ I_2\ X$, where E in an entry point, X is an exit point and I_1 and I_2 are sequences of updates, exchanges or calls, can be abbreviated to a single extended basic block $E\ I_1\ I_2\ X$.

4 Combining SSA and RIL to RSSA

We illustrate the design of RSSA by rewriting the example program in Sect. 2 to RIL and then discuss the issues in converting this to a form that has the single-assignment property while retaining reversibility. Conversion to RIL is fairly simple:

$$\textbf{begin}\ main$$
$$x\ \texttt{+=}\ 0$$
$$\rightarrow entry$$
$$entry;\ loop \leftarrow x\ \texttt{==}\ 0$$
$$x\ \texttt{+=}\ 1$$
$$x < 10 \rightarrow loop;\ exit$$
$$exit \leftarrow$$
$$x\ \texttt{+=}\ 3$$
$$\textbf{end}\ main$$

The first update of x has no effect and is superfluous, as all variables are considered to be initialised to 0. It is added here to make the RIL version more similar to the three-address version from Sect. 2. Note that we have added a test to the join-point at the loop entry, which is required for reversibility.

The first step in SSA conversion (adding indices to variable definitions) is easy enough:

$$\textbf{begin}\ main$$
$$x_1\ \texttt{+=}\ 0$$
$$\rightarrow entry$$
$$entry;\ loop \leftarrow x\ \texttt{==}\ 0$$
$$x_2\ \texttt{+=}\ 1$$
$$x < 10 \rightarrow loop;\ exit$$
$$exit \leftarrow$$
$$x_3\ \texttt{+=}\ 3$$
$$\textbf{end}\ main$$

We need a ϕ-node to the join point at the loop entry. We use the variant notation, so we just add a parameter to the labels in the join point and in the jumps to the join point. Since the two labels in the join point share the incoming parameter, we place this between the two labels:

$$\begin{aligned}
&\textbf{begin } main \\
&x_1 \mathrel{+}= 0 \\
&\rightarrow entry(x) \\
&entry(x_4)loop \leftarrow x == 0 \\
&x_2 \mathrel{+}= 1 \\
&x < 10 \rightarrow loop(x)exit \\
&exit \leftarrow \\
&x_3 \mathrel{+}= 3 \\
&\textbf{end } main
\end{aligned}$$

Note that the parameter to the *loop* label in the conditional jump is shared with the *exit* label, so we must also give the entry point for *exit* a parameter:

$$\begin{aligned}
&\textbf{begin } main \\
&x_1 \mathrel{+}= 0 \\
&\rightarrow entry(x) \\
&entry(x_4)loop \leftarrow x == 0 \\
&x_2 \mathrel{+}= 1 \\
&x < 10 \rightarrow loop(x)exit \\
&exit(x_5) \leftarrow \\
&x_3 \mathrel{+}= 3 \\
&\textbf{end } main
\end{aligned}$$

Note the symmetry, which will be a rule: The two labels in a conditional entry point or in a conditional exit point will share a list of parameters (corresponding to a list of ϕ-nodes), and the other occurrences of these labels must have corresponding parameters. Parameters to labels in entry points are defining instances, so they are given indices, while parameters to labels in exit points are (as yet) not given indices.

The last step is adding indices to uses of x. Here, we have a problem: The update $x_2 \mathrel{+}= 1$ has an implicit use of x, but this use is not of x_2 but of x_4, which is not used afterwards. Similarly, the update $x_3 \mathrel{+}= 3$ has a hidden use of x_5, which is not used afterwards. Hence, we replace the updates by assignments with explicit uses of variables, but with the semantics that the first occurrence of a variable on the right-hand side of an assignment destroys that variable. The update to x_1 is now turned into a definition that introduces the variable x_1. The (almost) final RSSA form of the program is

$$\begin{aligned}
&\textbf{begin } main \\
&x_1 := 0 \\
&\rightarrow entry(x_1) \\
&entry(x_4)loop \leftarrow x_4 == 0 \\
&x_2 := x_4 + 1 \\
&x_2 < 10 \rightarrow loop(x_2)exit \\
&exit(x_5) \leftarrow \\
&x_3 := x_5 + 3 \\
&\textbf{end } main
\end{aligned}$$

We note the following:

1. An assignment to a variable introduces a new indexed version of the variable which is previously undefined, and so does a parameter to a label in an entry point.
2. The first variable used on the right-hand side of an assignment is destroyed by that use. Uses of variables as parameters to labels in exit points also destroy these variables.
3. An assignment of the form $x := y \oplus R_1 \odot R_2$ is reversely executed as $y := x \ominus R_1 \odot R_2$, where $\ominus$ is the semi-inverse of $\oplus$. For example, $x := y + 1$ is reversely executed as $y := x - 1$.
4. A definition like $x := 0$ must be reversible, so we introduce a form $0 := x$, which defines no variable but destroys x after verifying that it is equal to 0. We will generalise this notion of destroying variables by equality testing in Sect. 5.
5. Variables that are inputs to the program are added as parameters to the label $main$ in **begin** $main$. Similarly, outputs of the program are added as parameters to $main$ in **end** $main$. This means that the last line of the program above must be changed to **end** $main(x_3)$, but since the program has no input, no parameter is added to **begin** $main$.
6. All variables that are not part of the input should explicitly be initialised to 0 (like x is in the example above) and all variables y that are not part of the output should explicitly be destroyed using an assignment of the form $0 := y$.

The example above does not use variable exchanges, memory accesses or subroutine calls, so we will below discuss how these are handled.

A variable exchange of the form $x \leftrightarrow y$ uses and defines two variables, so we rewrite it to a simultaneous assignment $x, y := y, x$, so uses and definitions of the variables are explicitly separated. After adding indices, the two assignments are independent, and we can remove them by copy propagation (see Sect. 6.5).

Unlike variables, memory is not restricted to single assignment, so we can keep a memory update of the form $M[x] \oplus= e$ unchanged (except for adding indices to variable uses). Note that e can not use memory, so e must be of the form $y \oplus z$, where y and z are either variables or constants.

An exchange $M[x] \leftrightarrow M[y]$ can, likewise, be kept unchanged (except for adding indices to x and y), as no variable is defined.

To handle exchanges between a variable and a memory location (such as $x \leftrightarrow M[y]$), we introduce a new form $x := M[y] := z$, which defines x to be the value of $M[y]$ and overwrites $M[y]$ with the value of z, which is destroyed. The exchange $x \leftrightarrow M[y]$ is rewritten to $x := M[y] := x$, which will later have indices added, so the two occurrences of x will become different variables.

An entry of the form **begin** l is a join point, as there can be several calls to this. So, like in conditional entry points, we add parameters to the label. Similarly, **end** l is a split point, so we add parameters to the label here also. A subroutine will, hence, start with an entry point **begin** $l(x, \ldots)$ and end with an exit point **end** $l(y, \ldots)$. A call to l will have one of the forms $(y', \ldots) := $ **call** $l(x', \ldots)$

or $(x', \ldots) := \texttt{uncall } l(y', \ldots)$. The argument variables are destroyed and the result variables are created. We have essentially turned parameter-less subroutines into functions with parameter and result lists, but since the parameters are indexed versions of global variables, there will at any time only be one live copy of such a parameter, even if the procedure is called recursively.

5   Definition of RSSA

The syntax and informal semantics of RSSA is shown in Fig. 1.

In the syntax, we use atoms, R-values and conditions:

- An atom x is either a variable or a constant.
- An R-value R is either an atom or of the form $M[a]$, where a is an atom.
- A condition is of the form $R_1 \bowtie R_2$, where R_1 and R_2 are R-values.

Note that we allow a constant in all places where a variable can occur, even on the left-hand side of an assignment. This is both to make it possible to invert all instructions and to allow unlimited constant propagation. A general rule is that if a constant k occurs where a variable would otherwise be created and given a value v, it is instead verified that $k = v$. No new variable is created, but if the check fails, the program stops with an error message. If a constant is used where a variable would be destroyed, no variable is destroyed. We will, for reasons of brevity, in Fig. 1 not repeat explaining this behaviour every time a constant can be used in place of a variable.

A variable can (after indices are added) not both be defined and used by the same assignment. This is true also of the inverses of assignments.

A basic block consists of an entry point, a call or sequence of assignments, and an exit point. A program is a set of basic blocks. Every label in the program must occur in exactly one entry point and exactly one exit point, a label occurring in a **begin** must also occur in an **end**, and the program must contain an entry point **begin** *main*.

We use x, where x is an atom, as a shorthand for both $x + 0$ and $x \oplus 0 \odot 0$, noting that $0 \odot 0 = 0$ for all the operators $\odot$ that we allow, and $x \oplus 0 = x$ for all the operators $\oplus$ we allow. For example, $x := 0$ is a shorthand for $x := 0 + 0 + 0$, $0 := x$ is a shorthand for $0 := x + 0 + 0$, and $x := y + 3$ is a shorthand for $x := y + 3 + 0$. The syntactic context makes it clear if a variable x is used as a shorthand and what for.

Semantically, running a subroutine backwards is done by running it in the inverted program. Rules for inversion are shown in Fig. 2. We use the notation $A \rightleftharpoons B$ to say that A inverts to B and vice-versa. We assume that the entire program is inverted, so a **call** inverts to a **call** (as it calls an inverted subroutine) rather than to an **uncall**, swapping the argument and result lists. We use $\ominus$ to denote the semi-inverse of $\oplus$, so if $\oplus$ is +, $\ominus$ is − and so on.

Table 1. Converting assignments and calls from RIL to RSSA

RIL	RSSA
$x \oplus= R_1 \odot R_2$	$x_i := x \oplus R_1 \odot R_2$
$M[x] \oplus= R_1 \odot R_2$	$M[x] \oplus= R_1 \odot R_2$
$x \leftrightarrow y$	$x_i, y_j := y, x$
$M[x] \leftrightarrow M[y]$	$M[x] \leftrightarrow M[y]$
$x \leftrightarrow M[y]$	$x_i := M[y] := x$
$M[y] \leftrightarrow x$	$x_i := M[y] := x$
call l	$() := $ call $l()$
uncall l	$() := $ uncall $l()$

6   Converting RIL to RSSA

We will now give a complete description of how RIL programs are converted to
RSSA. We will do this in a sequence of mostly simple steps:

1. Add initialisers and finalisers to variables.
2. Convert individual assignments and calls from RIL to RSSA
3. Add indices to defining instances of variables.
4. Add parameters to labels in entry and exit nodes and add parameter and
   result lists to calls and subroutine entries and exits.
5. Add indices to uses of variables.
6. Clean up.

We will describe these in more detail below.

6.1   Adding Initialisers and Finalisers

Add the list of input-variables as parameters to **begin** *main* and add the list of
output-variables as parameters to **end** *main*.

A variable x that is not part of the input is explicitly initialised to 0 using an
assignment $x := 0$ that is added to the beginning of the program, and a variable
y that is not part of the output is explicitly destroyed by adding an assignment
$0 := y$ at the end of the program.

6.2   Converting Individual Assignments and Calls and Adding Indices

We convert assignments and calls as shown in Table 1. We add indices to variables
while we convert, which we indicate by subscripts i or j in the table. Each x_i
and y_j introduced by the conversion in the table is unique.

Note that parameter and result lists to calls are initially empty, as parameters
will not be added until the next step.

Entry points:

$l \leftarrow$ where l is a label. This is an unconditional entry point.

$l_1(x, \ldots)l_2 \leftarrow c$ where c is a condition, l_1 and l_2 are labels and the xs are atoms. If x is a variable, it is created and given the value of the corresponding parameter of the incoming label. If entered through a jump to l_1, the condition c is evaluated and verified to be true. If entered through a jump to l_2, the condition c is evaluated and is verified to be false.

begin $l(x, \ldots)$ where l is a label and the xs are atoms. This is a subroutine entry point. If an x is a variable, it is created and given the value of the corresponding incoming argument.

Exit points:

$\rightarrow l$ where l is a label. This is an unconditional jump.

$c \rightarrow l_1(y, \ldots)l_2$ where c is a condition, l_1 and l_2 are labels and the ys are atoms. First, the condition is evaluated. If this is true, l_1 is given the values of $(y, \ldots)$ as parameters and a jump to l_1 is made. If c is false, l_2 is given the values of $(y, \ldots)$ as parameters and a jump to l_2 is made.

end $l(y, \ldots)$ where l is a label and the ys are atoms. This is a subroutine exit point. The values of $(y, \ldots)$ are passed back to the caller.

Assignments and calls:

$x := y \oplus R_1 \odot R_2$ where x and y are atoms and R_1 and R_2 are R-values. The value w of $R_1 \odot R_2$ is calculated and the value v of y is fetched. If y is a variable, it is destroyed. If x is a variable, it is created and given the value $u = v \oplus w$.

$x, y := z, w$ The variables z and w are destroyed and their values given to the variables x and y, which are created.

$M[x] \oplus= y \odot z$ where x, y and z are atoms. The value w of $y \odot z$ is calculated, the value a of x is fetched and the contents v of memory at address a is fetched. The contents of memory at address a is then given the value $u = v \oplus w$.

$M[x] \leftrightarrow M[y]$ where x and y are atoms. The values a and b of x and y are fetched, and the contents of memory at addresses a and b are interchanged.

$x := M[y] := z$ where x, y and z are atoms. Read the value v of z. If z is a variable, destroy it. Read the value a of y and the contents u of the memory at address a. Store v at address a. If x is a variable, create it and give it the value u.

$(y, \ldots) := \text{call } l(x, \ldots)$ where l is a label and the xs and ys are atoms. The subroutine labelled l is called. The values of the xs are passed as arguments to the subroutine. If an x is a variable, it is destroyed. At return, the variables y are created and given the values passed back by the subroutine.

$(x, \ldots) := \text{uncall } l(y, \ldots)$ Run the subroutine l backwards, starting at end $l(y', \ldots)$ and finishing at begin $l(x', \ldots)$. Semantically, this corresponds to performing $(x, \ldots) := \text{call } l(y, \ldots)$ in the *inverted* program.

Fig. 1. Syntax and semantics of RSSA

Entry and exit points:

$$l \leftarrow \; \rightleftharpoons \; \rightarrow l$$
$$l_1; (x, \ldots)l_2 \leftarrow c \; \rightleftharpoons \; c \rightarrow l_1(x, \ldots)l_2$$
$$\texttt{begin } l(x, \ldots) \; \rightleftharpoons \; \texttt{end } l(x, \ldots)$$

Assignments and calls:

$$x := y \oplus R_1 \odot R_2 \; \rightleftharpoons \; y := x \ominus R_1 \odot R_2$$
$$x, y := z, w \; \rightleftharpoons \; z, w := x, y$$
$$M[x] \oplus= y \odot z \; \rightleftharpoons \; M[x] \ominus= y \odot z$$
$$M[x] \leftrightarrow M[y] \; \rightleftharpoons \; M[x] \leftrightarrow M[y]$$
$$x := M[y] := z \; \rightleftharpoons \; z := M[y] := x$$
$$(y, \ldots) := \texttt{call } l(x, \ldots) \; \rightleftharpoons \; (x, \ldots) := \texttt{call } l(y, \ldots)$$
$$(y, \ldots) := \texttt{uncall } l(x, \ldots) \; \rightleftharpoons \; (x, \ldots) := \texttt{uncall } l(y, \ldots)$$

Basic blocks:

$$N \; A \; X \; \rightleftharpoons \; X' \; A' \; N' \quad \text{if } N \rightleftharpoons N', A \rightleftharpoons A', \text{ and } X \rightleftharpoons X'.$$

Inverting a program is done by inverting its basic blocks. Inverting a sequence of assignments is done by inverting each assignment and reversing the sequence.

Fig. 2. Inverting RSSA programs

6.3 Adding Parameters to Labels and Calls

We use the dominance-frontier criterion described in Sect. 2 to determine if a variable x should be a parameter to a label.

We use the $RSSA$ definition of basic blocks and consider a call to have a path to the entry point of the called subroutine, and the exit point of a subroutine to have paths to all its callers.

If the criteria described in Sect. 2 prescribes a ϕ-node for a variable x at an entry point, the label(s) at the entry point get an indexed x as a parameter and all jumps and calls to these labels get non-indexed x added as arguments.

To add parameters to exit points, we invert the program and repeat the above process. If the criteria prescribe adding a parameter to an entry-point label in the inverted program, we add the parameter to the corresponding exit-point label in the original program. Even if both the forwards and backwards criteria prescribe adding a variable to a label, it is added only once.

6.4 Add Indices to Uses of Variables

To add an index to a use of a variable x, we must find the unique defining instance of x that reaches this use. We can do that by following all paths backwards from the use until we reach a definition, keeping track of basic blocks we have already visited, so we don't get stuck in a loop. Even though we follow multiple alternative paths back from the use, the criterion for adding parameters to labels ensures that there will be a unique reaching definition.

6.5   Clean up

A simultaneous assignment $x, y := z, w$ can be removed by replacing all uses of x by uses of z and all uses of y by uses of w. This simplified form of *copy propagation* is safe to do because of the single-assignment property of the RSSA form. After this clean up, the resulting RSSA program will contain no simultaneous assignments.

7   Optimisations on the RSSA Form

We discuss a few optimisations that are made simpler by the properties of the RSSA form.

7.1   Copy Propagation

As mentioned in Sect. 6.5, copy propagation is trivial. Copy propagation can remove all copy instructions from the program. Note that, excepting simultaneous assignments, copy instructions are of the form $x := y \oplus 0 \odot 0$.

7.2   Constant Propagation

An assignment of the form $x := k$, where k is a constant, is a shorthand for $x := k \oplus 0 \odot 0$. It can be removed by replacing all uses of x by k. This is similar to copy propagation and can be done at the same time.

Variable destructions $k := x$ can be propagated by first inverting the program, doing constant propagation as described above, and then inverting the program back.

This will eliminate the initialisations and finalisations of non-input and non-output variables that were introduced when converting RIL to RSSA. Applying constant propagation to the example program will yield

$$
\begin{aligned}
&\textbf{begin } main \\
&\rightarrow entry(0) \\
&entry(x_4)loop \leftarrow x_4 == 0 \\
&x_2 := x_4 + 1 \\
&x_2 < 10 \rightarrow loop(x_2)exit \\
&exit(x_5) \leftarrow \\
&x_3 := x_5 + 3 \\
&\textbf{end } main(x_3)
\end{aligned}
$$

7.3   Register Allocation

In RIL, register allocation is non-trivial, as all variables are either outputs or must be verified to be 0 at exit from the program, and all variables are either inputs or initialised to 0 at entry to the program. This makes all variables live throughout the program, so traditional register allocation based on liveness does not work for RIL.

In RSSA, variables are explicitly introduced and consumed, so they have limited life times. This can enable register allocation based on liveness. Liveness analysis is simplified by the fact that destruction of variables is explicit in RSSA, so a variable is live on all paths from its unique definition to its unique destruction, i.e., in all basic blocks that are dominated by the definition of the variable and post-dominated by its destruction (where post-domination is domination in the inverse program). These paths are often quite short, especially if initialisations of non-inputs and finalisations of non-outputs are constant-propagated.

On the flip side, RSSA conversion adds indices to variables, so a single variable in the RIL form becomes many variables in the RSSA form. This may potentially increase the need for registers, but as several versions of the same variable are rarely live at the same time (though it can happen after copy propagation and other optimisations), this is in practice not a problem.

If there are insufficient registers to hold all simultaneously-live variables, spill is needed. This is done in the traditional way by giving the spilled variable x a location a_x in memory. It is assumed that a_x holds the value 0 both before the definition of x and after it is destroyed. x is defined normally, but is then immediately swapped with the memory location using the instruction $0 := M[a_x] := x$, which verifies that the contents of memory at a_x was 0. Immediately before a consuming use of x, it is fetched from memory using the instruction $x := M[a_x] := 0$, which clears the memory location. Non-consuming uses of x can sometimes simply be replaced by $M[a_x]$, but in some cases this breaks the syntax, for example if $M[x] \leftrightarrow M[y]$ is replaced by $M[M[a_x]] \leftrightarrow M[y]$. In these cases, x is swapped in from memory before the use and swapped back again afterwards. For example, $M[x] \leftrightarrow M[y]$ would be replaced by the sequence

$$x' := M[a_x] := 0$$
$$M[x'] \leftrightarrow M[y]$$
$$0 := M[a_x] := x'$$

To preserve the RSSA property, x' must be an otherwise unused variable.

8   Conclusion and Discussion

We have defined a reversible variant of the SSA form called RSSA. We have shown how programs in the reversible intermediate language RIL can be transformed into RSSA, and we have sketched a few optimisations, including register allocation, that are simplified by the properties of RSSA. The main insight is that a variable should not only have a unique definition point but also a unique destruction point. Using a notation where labels have parameters simplifies the transformation, especially of subroutine calls.

By adding paths from an exit point of a subroutine to all callers when calculating dominators, we have included unfeasible paths: From one call to a subroutine back to the return point of an unrelated call. This makes the dominance property imprecise, and can cause parameters to be added where not strictly necessary. We can use context-free reachability to avoid these unfeasible paths and get more precise reachability results [7], but since CF reachability requires $O(n^3)$ time, this is rather costly. Alternatively, we can keep subroutines separate and SSA-convert each individually. This requires that all variables used by a subroutine are either entirely local to the subroutine or passed as parameters. This, actually, requires more parameters to be passed than added by our current approach, but it simplifies the treatment of subroutines. A subroutine in RIL consists of the basic blocks that are dominated by the entry point of the subroutine and post-dominated by its exit point (not considering paths along calls and returns), so it is easy enough to extract subroutines and add parameters and results for all variables that are used both inside the subroutine and outside it.

References

1. Alpern, B., Wegman, M.N., Zadeck, F.K.: Detecting equality of variables in programs. In: Proceedings of the 15th ACM SIGPLAN-SIGACT Symposium on Principles of Programming Languages, POPL 1988, pp. 1–11. ACM, New York (1988)
2. Cytron, R., Ferrante, J., Rosen, B.K., Wegman, M.N., Kenneth Zadeck, F.: Efficiently computing static single assignment form and the control dependence graph. ACM Trans. Program. Lang. Syst. **13**(4), 451–490 (1991)
3. Lattner, C., Adve, V.: LLVM: a compilation framework for lifelong program analysis & transformation. In: Proceedings of the International Symposium on Code Generation and Optimization: Feedback-directed and Runtime Optimization, CGO 2004, p. 75. IEEE Computer Society, Washington, DC (2004)
4. Lutz, C.: Janus: a time-reversible language. A letter to Landauer (1986). http://www.tetsuo.jp/ref/janus.pdf
5. Mogensen, T.Æ.: Partial evaluation of Janus part 2: assertions and procedures. In: Clarke, E., Virbitskaite, I., Voronkov, A. (eds.) PSI 2011. LNCS, vol. 7162, pp. 289–301. Springer, Heidelberg (2012)
6. Mogensen, T.Æ.: Garbage collection for reversible functional languages. In: Krivine, J., Stefani, J.-B. (eds.) RC 2015. LNCS, vol. 9138, pp. 79–94. Springer, Heidelberg (2015)
7. Reps, T., Horwitz, S., Sagiv, M.: Precise interprocedural dataflow analysis via graph reachability. In: Proceedings of the 22nd ACM SIGPLAN-SIGACT Symposium on Principles of Programming Languages, POPL 1995, pp. 49–61. ACM, New York (1995)
8. Rosen, B.K., Wegman, M.N., Zadeck, F.K.: Global value numbers and redundant computations. In: Proceedings of the 15th ACM SIGPLAN-SIGACT Symposium on Principles of Programming Languages, POPL 1988, pp. 12–27. ACM, New York (1988)

Checking Several Requirements
at once by CEGAR

Vitaly Mordan$^{(\boxtimes)}$ and Vadim Mutilin

Institute for System Programming
of the Russian Academy of Sciences, Moscow, Russia
{mordan,mutilin}@ispras.ru

Abstract. At present static verifiers, which are based on Counterexample Guided Abstraction Refinement (CEGAR), can prove correctness of a program against a specified requirement, find its violation in a program and stop analysis or exhaust the given resources without producing any useful result. If we use this approach for checking several requirements at once, then finding a first violation of some requirement or exhausting resources for some requirement will prevent checking the program against other requirements. In particular we may miss violations of some requirements. That is why in practice each requirement to the program is usually checked separately. However, static verifiers perform similar actions during checking of the same program against different requirements and thus a lot of resources are wasted. This paper presents a new CEGAR-based method for software static verification, that is aimed at checking programs against several requirements at once and getting the same result as basic CEGAR, which checks requirements one by one. In order to do it the suggested method divides resources among requirements equally and continues analysis after finding violation of requirement excluding that requirement. We used Linux kernel modules to conduct experiments, in which implementation of the suggested method reduced total verification time by 5 times. The total number of divergent results in comparison with CEGAR was about 2 %.

Keywords: Static verification · Counterexample guided abstraction refinement · Aspect

1 Introduction

Static verification is a formal means for checking program source code without its execution by exploring all possible program paths. The main benefit of static verification is that it aims at proving correctness of the software instead of simply finding frequent bugs. The main disadvantage, which makes it much less applicable in practice, is a large amount of required resources such as CPU time

---

The research was carried out with funding from the Ministry of Education and Science of Russia (the project unique identifier is RFMEFI61614X0015).

M. Mazzara and A. Voronkov (Eds.): PSI 2015, LNCS 9609, pp. 218–232, 2016.
DOI: 10.1007/978-3-319-41579-6_17

and memory especially for large software systems. Currently static verification tools (static verifiers), based on Counterexample Guided Abstraction Refinement (CEGAR), are appropriate for large software systems which is demonstrated in annual Competitions on Software Verification [1,2].

At the same time every program in a big software system may contain any number of different bugs, which are violations of requirements to that program. In order to find them static verifiers check the program against all specified requirements. The CEGAR approach checks the program against only one requirement at a time, because it stops after finding a bug (and thus other requirements will not be checked) and checking the program against some requirement may exhaust all given resources. Thus large amount of required resources for verification further increases depending on the number of requirements.

Let us consider an example which demonstrates this problem. Linux Driver Verification Tools (LDV Tools) are an open source toolset for checking correctness of Linux kernel modules against rule specifications (i.e. specifications of rules for correct usage of the kernel API) with help of different static verifiers [3]. It has already helped to find more than 190 bugs in Linux kernel modules [4]. The process of verification of all Linux kernel modules with help of LDV Tools against a single rule specification by static verifiers BLAST [5,6] or CPAchecker [7] takes about 2 days, whereas verification of 17 basic rule specifications takes about 40 days. But the number of rule specifications is 50 and a few new rule specifications are under development.

This paper presents a new static verification method which can significantly reduce required time even if the number of requirements to be checked is growing. The suggested method extends CEGAR in order to check more than one requirement at once. The main demand to this method is to prove correctness of programs against specified requirements and to find their violations as well as CEGAR do, but faster. This method was implemented as extensions of LDV Tools [3] and the CPAchecker [7] static verifier and was evaluated on verification of Linux kernel modules.

We make the following contributions:

- We propose a new method for static verification which extends the CEGAR approach for checking a program against several requirements at once.
- We implement this method as extensions of LDV Tools and the CPAchecker static verifier.
- We experimentally show that the suggested method reduces total verification time by 5 times on verification of Linux kernel modules, the total number of negative results, in which the suggested method requires more resources than CEGAR in order to prove correctness of a program against specified requirement or to find its violation, is about 2 %.

Next Section describes the CEGAR approach and introduces definitions which are used in the paper. Section 3 presents related work. In Sect. 4 the new method is suggested. Section 5 presents its implementation. In Sect. 6 the results of experiments are described.

2   Background

2.1   Definitions

In the paper we refer to an **aspect** as a formal representation of a checked requirement to a program [8]. Aspects represent what we intend to check in the program. For example: *allocated resources should be correctly freed*. Indeed, specifications of rules for correct usage of the kernel API are aspects.

Error location is a location in a program, which corresponds to an aspect violation (for example, predefined function *error()* or predefined label *ERROR*).

Verification task is a program source code, built on a program under analysis, which contains specific checks for an aspect. In CEGAR verification tasks usually are reachability tasks, their main goal is to prove that an error location cannot be reached from specified entry point in the program (for example, from function main).

Error trace is a sequence of operations in program source files that leads from a specified entry point to an error location (i.e. an aspect violation).

Verdict is a result of solving a verification task by a static verifier. Usually there are 3 possible verdicts:

- *Safe*: a program is correct against a specified aspect;
- *Unsafe*: a program violates a specified aspect, a corresponding violation is represented as an error trace;
- *Unknown*: a static verifier cannot solve a given verification task.

2.2   Counterexample Guided Abstraction Refinement

Since it is usually impossible to analyze a precise model of a program in a reasonable time, CEGAR operates with an abstract model of the program.

Concrete state consists of assignments of specific values to relevant variables at particular program locations [6].

Abstract state is a set of concrete states of a program [6].

Abstract Reachability Graph (ARG) is an abstraction of a program, in which nodes correspond to abstract states and edges correspond to program statements [6].

Verification fact is a result (possibly intermediate) of the verification process, that is necessary for proving correctness of the program against a given aspect [9].

Abstraction precision (precision) is a verification fact, that instructs the analysis which information should be tracked and which information should be omitted in abstraction of the program [9]. For example, in the predicate analysis [10] precisions define tracking predicates, in the explicit value analysis [11] precisions define tracking variables. Thus a precision defines the current level of abstraction in ARG.

The CEGAR algorithm is presented in Fig. 1 [12,13]. At the beginning CEGAR builds ARG based on an initial precision (for example, an empty precision). If a specified error location is not reached, then the algorithm terminates with the verdict *Safe*. Otherwise CEGAR checks a found counterexample for feasibility. If it is feasible then an error trace is built for the found counterexample and the algorithm terminates with the verdict *Unsafe*. Otherwise the precision is refined based on the infeasible counterexample and the CEGAR loop is continued.

Since static verification is an undecidable problem in general case, static verifiers, which implement the CEGAR approach, operate with limited resources (such as CPU time and memory) in practice and terminate their analysis with the verdict *Unknown* in case of resources exhaustion.

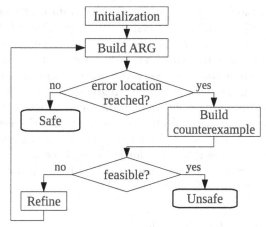

Fig. 1. The CEGAR loop.

2.3 Example

Let us consider an example. There are three aspects:

Aspect 1: *all allocated resources by usb_alloc_urb() should be freed by usb_free_urb().*

Aspect 2: *the same mutexes should not be acquired or released twice in the same process.*

Aspect 3: *an offset should not be greater than a size of an array.*

In order to get verdicts for all specified aspects with the basic CEGAR approach we need to prepare 3 different verification tasks and run the CEGAR algorithm 3 times. Each verification task is created based on program source code and a specified aspect. In a verification task a selected aspect corresponds to specific error location. For example, **Aspect_i** can correspond to error label *ERROR_i*, i = 1,2,3. Thus **Aspect_3** may be represented by the following checks in the verification task:

```
if (offset > size)
  ERROR_3 : goto ERROR_3;
```

3   Related Work

The idea of modifying the CEGAR algorithm in order to reduce verification time is not new. By adding auxiliary actions at different steps of the CEGAR algorithm (Fig. 1) it is possible to solve specific verification tasks faster.

3.1   Regression Verification

Even if a program is absolutely correct, it always can be modified. Every modification of the program potentially may add new bugs. Such bugs are called regressions. Regression verification is aimed at verifying program revisions in order to find regressions. One of the approaches to do it efficiently is to reuse verification results [9]. Verification facts, which were obtained during analysis, are stored as results and then are used on the *Initialization* step of the CEGAR algorithm (Fig. 1) to start analysis with the known level of abstraction, for example, to verify the next revision of that program. Experiments confirm [9], that reuse of verification facts reduces time for regression verification. At the same time in some cases reuse of verification results may increase time of analysis. For example, abstraction may become too accurate for the new revision (for some verification tasks precision reuse increased time almost twice [9]). Regression verification approaches are useful for reducing time for verification, but it is unclear whether verification facts can be reused between different aspects as well as between program revisions or not.

3.2   Conditional Model Checking

The verdict *Unknown* means that a static verifier fails to solve a verification task. It is still unclear whether the given program correct or not and thus resources were spent for nothing. In order to solve this problem the conditional model checking approach was suggested [14]. A static verifier saves its result even if it cannot solve the whole verification task. This result describes which parts of the program (e.g., abstract states in ARG) were successfully verified and which were not. Then another static verifier (or the same with another configuration) takes this result at the *Initialization* step of the CEGAR algorithm (Fig. 1) and verifies only those parts of the program which were not verified. Conditional model checking helps to solve problems which cannot be solved by a single launch of a static verifier [14]. Conditional model checking can be useful for resolving verdicts *Unknown*.

3.3   Method for Finding All Violations of an Aspect

Any program can contain any number of bugs for a given aspect. The basic CEGAR algorithm stops after it finds a first bug. In practice it significantly increases time for finding and fixing different bugs of the same kind. In order to solve this problem the method for finding all violations of an aspect was suggested [15]. Its main idea is to continue analysis after finding a bug. Obviously, this method requires more time for analysis (in comparison with the basic CEGAR), but it also reduces time for finding and fixing different bugs of the same kind. Nevertheless, analysis may be terminated abnormally after finding several bugs, for example, it may exhaust resources that means that there may be more bugs. That is why this method cannot be used directly for checking several aspects at once.

4   Multi-aspect Verification

Multi-aspect Verification (MAV) is aimed at configurable checking of several aspects for a given verification task at once. In this paper MAV is suggested as an extension of the CEGAR algorithm, but potentially the same ideas can be applied to other static verification approaches.

It is supposed that the verification task has already been built for the selected aspects (for more details see Sect. 5). The main requirement to MAV is to get the same result for all aspects (i.e. prove correctness or find error traces) as basic CEGAR for each aspect, but faster.

The first problem that must be resolved, is that basic CEGAR checks for a single error location, which corresponds to a single aspect. It is possible to check for several error locations (for example, check for several error labels at once), but those error locations do not correspond to specific aspects. Thus, if we intend to check for several error locations, each of them should get link to a corresponding aspect (for example, to determine which aspect is violated in a found error trace).

Second, checking of some aspect may interfere with checking of another one. The basic CEGAR approach stops after it finds a first error trace, thus violation of a single aspect leads to analysis termination for all aspects. Also it is impossible to limit resources for some aspect separately, thus if CEGAR cannot check a single aspect (for example, it exhausts time limit), then analysis of all aspects will be terminated.

So, the MAV method should satisfy the following requirements:

– to differ one aspect from another (in terms of error locations);
– to continue analysis after finding an error trace (the verdict *Unsafe*);
– to identify the verdicts *Unknown* and to continue analysis after them;
– to get the same verdicts for aspects as basic CEGAR;
– to consume less resources (in comparison with basic CEGAR).

4.1   The Multi-aspect Verification Method

The MAV algorithm was designed to meet the mentioned above requirements (Fig. 2). It extends the basic CEGAR algorithm and checks for several error locations.

In terms of MAV each **aspect** contains the following attributes: an unique identifier, a corresponding error location identifier (for example, specific error

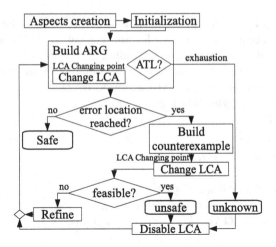

Fig. 2. The MAV algorithm.

label name), an aspect verdict, consumed resources (CPU time, wall time, etc.), corresponding verification facts. At the *Aspects creation* step (Fig. 2) links between aspects and error locations are created, attributes for each aspect get initial values.

Aspect verdict is an internal verdict of an aspect. Aspect verdict takes all common verdict values (which were defined in Sect. 2) and auxiliary value *Checking*, which means that this aspect is currently being checked.

In order to know, which aspect is being checked (to change aspect verdicts, to keep records of consumed resources, etc.), the notion of **Latest Checked Aspect (LCA)** is suggested. LCA is the latest aspect, which was checked during analysis. But during the ARG construction more than one aspect can be checked at once (i.e. ARG can be built based on several aspects at once). The following approximation is suggested: *only one aspect is being checked at the moment of time and the latest checked aspect is LCA.*

At the start of the algorithm LCA is unset. Then all time of analysis can be divided by **LCA changing points**, which are moments of time, when LCA changes. Current checked aspect is considered equal to LCA until the next LCA changing point. The main idea of these points is that they should represent that the algorithm builds ARG for the selected aspect. Since counterexample always contains reached error location, it is always possible to determine which aspect it violates and to add LCA changing point after the *Build counterexample* step. In general case LCA changing points can be added at the *Build ARG* step.

After that it is possible to divide an analysis time line for the **LCA intervals**, which are time intervals between two LCA changing points. Thus we can use the LCA intervals to calculate time, consumed by each aspect. In order to do it we add time of the interval to LCA time at the *Change LCA* step.

In general case verification facts for each aspect are obtained after the *Change LCA* step for LCA. For example, if verification facts are represented as precisions, we can obtain them for every infeasible counterexample after the *Refine* step. They define a current level of abstraction for LCA.

Tracking aspect time gives us the possibility for **Aspect Time Limit (ATL)** for each aspect. ATL is aimed at limiting total time for aspect. In case of ATL exhaustion, LCA will be disabled on the *Disable LCA* step (Fig. 2). Since in general case the LCA interval can exceed ATL by itself, ATL should be checked asynchronously inside the LCA interval (i.e. during the *Build ARG* step).

Therefore aspect verdicts are changed during analysis in the following way. At the *Aspects creation* step every aspect gets the aspect verdict *Checking*. In case of finding an error trace for some aspect, its aspect verdict changes to *Unsafe*. In case of ATL exhaustion, the corresponding aspect verdict changes to *Unknown*. If the algorithm has finished with the verdict *Safe*, then all aspects with the aspect verdict *Checking* change to *Safe*.

The *Disable LCA* step consists of the following operations: (1) stop checking error location, which corresponds to LCA, (2) remove verification facts relevant to LCA and (3) unset LCA. Verification facts, which correspond to some aspect, could both be useful for the others and interfere with the others (for more details see Sect. 6). It is possible to remove abstract states, relevant to LCA, from ARG as well, but we should take into account that any operation with full ARG may not be efficient (since ARG can consist of millions abstract states). Therefore we need options to determine, which verification facts we intend to track and where we intend to remove them.

The *Disable LCA* step unsets LCA, thus, for the next interval we do not have LCA until the next LCA changing point. We call such interval the **Interval without LCA** (except the first one). In terms of current approximation such intervals means that analysis does not check any aspect and thus time is wasted. It leads to extending the idea of ATL for the notion of **Internal Time Limit (ITL)**. The main idea of any ITL is to limit time for some operation (or sequence of operations) and then execute predetermined action in case of its exhaustion. Thus ATL is ITL, which limits total time for the aspect and in case of its exhaustion that aspect will be disabled. Potentially we can also limit the LCA interval, the first interval, the interval without LCA, etc.

The suggested approximation can be extended for more general case, in which more than one LCA can be at a time. In that case the notion of **Set of Latest Checked Aspects (SLCA)** is suggested. This approximation is more close to reality (since MAV may actually check for several aspects at a time), but cannot solve problem of tracking time and verification facts for each aspect as clearly as LCA approximation.

4.2   The Conditional Multi-aspect Verification Method

The main disadvantage of MAV is that it cannot continue analysis if the algorithm was somehow terminated. ATL helps to find time limit exhaustion for

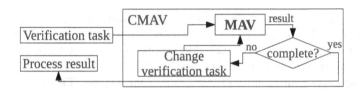

Fig. 3. The CMAV schema.

specific aspect, but memory limit exhaustion and abnormal termination of static verifiers are still remain as unresolved problems. In such cases all aspects with the aspect verdict *Checking* get the aspect verdict *Unknown*. But if only one aspect exceeds memory limit we could expect that MAV isolates it. In order to achieve this, MAV was extended based on ideas of Conditional model checking [14]. The main idea is to launch the MAV method a few times, passing intermediate results between each launch, until all aspects get verdicts. We call this extension **Conditional MAV (CMAV)**. The schema of CMAV is presented in Fig. 3.

In order to save all actual information about verification process we suggest common format, which keeps aspect attributes (an aspect identifier, an aspect verdict, a consumed time, an error trace identifier, a reason of *Unknown*) and LCA identifier. This intermediate result in common format is stored into the specified file. At the *Change LCA* step, the *Disable LCA* step and analysis termination information in this file is updated. Thus in case of any abnormal termination this file will contain all relevant information, including LCA, which might cause the termination.

We call each launch of the MAV algorithm an **iteration** of CMAV. After each iteration CMAV determines if analysis have been completed based on the file with intermediate results. If the algorithm was terminated abnormally, CMAV finds the reason of its termination and the aspect (or aspects), which caused it. In case of global problems (such as incorrect verification task), all aspects get the aspect verdict *Unknown* and CMAV terminates its analysis. Otherwise only those aspects which caused termination get the aspect verdict *Unknown* (for example, in case of memory limit exhaustion, while all aspect verdicts are still *Checking*, LCA gets the aspect verdict *Unknown*). If analysis is not completed, CMAV starts new iteration, which checks aspects with the aspect verdict *Checking*. In any case next iteration gets at least one less aspect to check. Thus, number of all iterations is less or equal than the number of all aspects. After the completion of the last iteration CMAV unites intermediate information from all iterations and presents it as the final result for the given verification task.

Also CMAV helps to resolve problem with the long intervals without LCA, the main reason of which is too complex ARG. Such intervals are possible only after the *Disable LCA* step, i.e. at least one aspect have already got the aspect verdict *Unsafe* or *Unknown*. In order to limit such intervals we suggest **Idle Interval Time Limit (IITL)**. IITL is ITL, which limits the interval without LCA. In case of IITL exhaustion CMAV starts new iteration, which gets at least one aspect less to check, since at least one aspect got its aspect verdict on the previous iteration (before the *Disable LCA* step).

5 Implementation

We have implemented the suggested method as extensions of LDV Tools and the CPAchecker static verifier. LDV Tools prepare verification tasks, based on multiple aspects, and launch CMAV iterations with processing results in the CMAV common format. The CPAchecker static verifier executes the MAV algorithm.

5.1 LDV Tools Extension

LDV Tools take multiple aspects as input and join them into a Combined aspect. The Combined aspect contains references to the original aspects, for example, each error location corresponds to some original aspect. For the preparation of the Combined aspect LDV Tools were equipped with the new component merging aspects.

The CPAchecker input configuration includes references to original aspects. Therefore we can choose the set of original aspects to check while passing verification task prepared with help of the Combined aspect.

The wrapper inside LDV Tools which launches CPAchecker reads CPAchecker output in the CMAV common format to determine whether analysis is completed or the next CMAV iteration is needed. In the later case the wrapper changes verification task by removing references to corresponding aspects from the CPAchecker input configuration. Thus on the next iteration CPAchecker ignores original aspects for which we have already got verdicts.

If the analysis is completed then LDV Tools prepare final report containing information for every original aspect (its verdict, consumed time, error trace, reason of *Unknown*), so it can be easily compared with CEGAR final reports.

5.2 CPAchecker with MAV

We extended the CPAchecker static verifier in order to support the MAV method based on its description in Sect. 4. Here implementation details are presented.

Aspect. In CPAchecker the notion of error location is extended for the notion of property, which is represented by automaton. In automaton there is a state (or states) specified as an error state and the task is to prove that the error state cannot be reached. LDV Tools pass to CPAchecker such automata with references to the original aspects with verification task. Such references represent different error labels in program source code, thus automata check that corresponding error labels cannot be reached.

In order to check a few properties at once we suggest automaton composition. In automaton composition every automaton gets a unique name and can be disabled. The *Aspects creation* step creates aspects for every passed automaton, aspects identifiers are equal to corresponding automaton names. The *Disable LCA* step disables corresponding automaton.

In general case every error location can correspond to some part of the automaton (for example, each error location corresponds to some automaton transition). Then such automaton parts should get unique names at the *Aspects creation* step and can be disabled at the *Disable LCA* step.

LCA. We implemented approximation, in which only one aspect is being checked at a time. LCA changing points happen only after the *Build counterexample* step.

Adjustable Precision. We extended abstraction precision based on set theory. At the start precision is empty, which corresponds to an empty set. We added operations of addition and subtraction between two precision and operation of clearing precision. We called such extended precision as adjustable precision. Thus every used type of precision in analysis are adjustable precision.

Furthermore only adjustable precision is used as verification fact. At the *Aspects creation* step each aspect gets empty precision as corresponding verification fact. After finding infeasible counterexample it is possible to get new precision (from the *Refine* step) and add it to precision of LCA.

ITLs. In addition to suggested above ITLs (ATL for MAV and IITL for CMAV) we implemented 2 heuristic ITLs. **Basic Interval Time Limit (BITL)** limits each LCA interval, in case of its exhaustion LCA is disabled with the aspect verdict *Unknown*. **First Interval Time Limit (FITL)** limits the first interval, in case of its exhaustion CPAchecker terminates its analysis, all *Checking* aspects get the aspect verdict *Unknown*. The main reason of additional ITLs is to find the aspect verdict *Unknown* faster (since it means that we neither could prove aspect correctness nor find its violation). Any of those ITLs can be unset.

Cleaning Adjustable Precision. Since we use only adjustable precision as verification facts, only adjustable precision should be cleaned at the *Disable LCA* step. We can remove corresponding adjustable precision from every abstract state (the whole ARG) or only from not yet processed abstract states (so called waitlist). Moreover, we can subtract precision, which corresponds to LCA, or clear it. In general case 5 different strategies are possible: (1) **None** (do not remove anything); (2) **WL/Subtract** (subtract from each precision in waitlist precision, that correspond to LCA); (3) **ARG/Subtract** (subtract from each precision in ARG precision, that correspond to LCA); (4) **WL/Clear** (clear all precisions in waitlist) and (5) **ALL** (clear all precisions in ARG).

The suggested strategies represent different techniques to precision reuse effect between different aspects (up from full precision reuse in **None** strategy to not using this effect at all in **All** strategy). In general case there are examples, in which some strategy is better, than the others. All strategies were implemented, experiments with their comparison are presented in Sect. 6.

6   Results of the Experiments

In order to evaluate the suggested method we conducted the following experiments. Verification tasks were prepared with help of LDV Tools based on Linux kernels 3.16-rc1 and 4.0-rc1. All experiments were performed on machines with 3.4 GHz Quad Core CPU (Intel Core i7-2600), 16 Gb of RAM and Ubuntu 12.04

(64-bit). 17 LDV Tools basic aspects [16] were used for all experiments. For basic CEGAR we used CPAchecker revision 14998 with *ldv* configuration, which includes predicate analysis [10] and explicit value analysis [11], each launch of the CEGAR algorithm was limited to 900 s of CPU time and 15 Gb of RAM. For CMAV we used LDV Tools branch *cmav* and CPAchecker branch *cmav* (revision 15941), each iteration of CMAV was limited to 1200 s of CPU time and 15 Gb of RAM, ATL = 900 s (same as time limit for CEGAR), IITL = 20 s, BITL = 100 s, FITL = 100 s.

6.1   Cleaning Adjustable Precision Strategies

The first experiment is meant to compare different strategies of cleaning adjustable precision. In order to do it 1000 verification tasks were prepared based on Linux kernel modules 3.16-rc1, which violate at least one aspect. The results of this experiment are presented in Table 1.

Table 1. Cleaning adjustable precision strategies comparison (l is an average number of iterations/launches for one verification task).

Strategy	CPU time (hours)	Error traces	Iterations/Launches	l
None	140	543	2084	2.084
WL/Subtract	118	610	1984	1.984
WL/Clear	127	599	1580	1.58
ARG/Subtract	122	590	2005	2.005
ALL	120	605	1451	1.451
CEGAR	389	604	17000	17

Experiment results revealed the features of the suggested strategies. **None** strategy shows the best result only in case of nested error traces (i.e. there are two error traces for different aspects and the first one is contained in the second), but their numbers are low (about 20 in the experiment). **ARG/Subtract** is aimed at preventing negative precision reuse effect at all, but the operation itself is slow (it may exhaust the iteration time limit). **WL/Subtract** strategy minimizes such negative precision reuse effect for most cases and thus finds the maximal number of error traces. **WL/Clear** strategy is better than the others only in particular cases, in which precision in ARG helps to other aspects, but precision in waitlist (even for other aspects) does not. **ALL** strategy is unexpectedly fast (it also requires the lowest number of CMAV iterations) since it fully removes negative precision reuse effect with minimal number of additional operations. At the same time **ALL** strategy loses so called positive precision reuse effect, which allows to solve verification tasks that were not solvable in CEGAR (that is demonstrated in the next experiment). In comparison with basic CEGAR all strategies are faster in about 3 times, since CEGAR always requires 17 launches per one verification task, whereas CMAV requires only about 2 launches to solve one verification task. In the next experiments we use **WL/Subtract** strategy as the best strategy of this experiment, since it minimizes the negative precision reuse effect in most cases, keeps positive precision reuse effect and requires reasonable resources.

6.2 Verification of All Linux Kernel Modules

In order to evaluate the suggested method all Linux kernel modules of version 4.0-rc1 were verified with the help of CEGAR and CMAV. LDV Tools prepare 6021 verification tasks for that Linux kernel version. The basic CEGAR approach total time is 1047 h (CPU time), LDV Tools total time (together with CEGAR) is about 960 h (wall time), the total number of found error traces is 623.

Time. CPAchecker with CMAV total time is 360 h (CPU time), which is 3 times less than for CEGAR, LDV Tools total time (together with CMAV) is 200 h (wall time), which is 5 times less than with CEGAR. Average time for one iteration is 155 s (it is limited to 1200 s). Maximal time for a verification task is 8165 s (time of all iterations). Analysis of experimental results revealed, that aspect time in CMAV (which is total LCA intervals time) is less than corresponding time in CEGAR on average at 6 times, because of similar actions in CEGAR during checking of different aspects. But we should take into account, that CMAV contains the intervals without LCA for performing common or auxiliary actions, so the full CPU time of CMAV is 3 times less than for CEGAR.

Verdicts. CMAV verdicts are the same as in CEGAR in 97.61 %. The number of CMAV negative transitions (*Safe* or *Unsafe* in CEGAR and *Unknown* in CMAV) is 2.17 %. The number of CMAV positive transitions (*Unknown* in CEGAR and *Safe* or *Unsafe* in CMAV) is 0.22 %. There are no missed bugs (transitions from *Unsafe* to *Safe*) or additional false alarms (transitions from *Safe* to *Unsafe*) in CMAV in comparison with CEGAR. Table 2 contains more detailed comparison of verdicts in CEGAR and CMAV.

Table 2. Comparison of verdicts in CEGAR and CMAV for verification of all Linux kernel modules of version 4.0-rc1 (6021 verification tasks) against 17 aspects.

Algorithm		Safe		Unsafe		Unknown
CEGAR		98651		623		3083
CMAV	*negative*	96654	−2195 (2.15 %)	624	−22 (0.02 %)	5079
	positive		+ 198 (0.20 %)		+23 (0.02 %)	

The first reason of negative transitions in CMAV is more complex verification tasks, which may require more time. For example, in order to find the verdict *Unsafe* in module *drivers/isdn/i4l/isdn.ko* against aspect 08_1a CEGAR requires about 830 s, but in CMAV it exhausts ATL (900 s). They still can be found if we increase ATL (in case of *drivers/isdn/i4l/isdn.ko* for about 1200 s). The second reason of negative transitions in CMAV is heuristic ITLs in CMAV.

For example, up to 48 % of the lost verdicts *Safe* for each aspect could be found in case of unsetting FITL. At the same time, total time of analysis also increases in almost 1.3 times. Thus by changing ITLs it is possible to change balance between verification time and possible inaccurate results.

The main reason of positive transitions in CMAV is reusing precision and ARG between different aspects, which may decrease time for finding error traces or proving correctness. For example, in module *fs/gfs2/gfs2.ko* CMAV could find 4 new error traces, which are *Unknown* in CEGAR. In the CMAV method corresponding error traces are found for about 700–800 s. The CEGAR algorithm also can find them, but for about 1400–1500 s. Thus CMAV solves verification tasks, that cannot be resolved in basic CEGAR with the same resource limitation.

Iterations. Total number of CMAV iterations is 8395, and thus the ration between iterations and verification tasks is $l = 1.39$. CMAV solves 5511 verification tasks (almost 92 %) by the first iteration (i.e. for 92 % of all tasks the MAV method is enough, 8 % needs the CMAV method). Maximal number of iterations for one verification task is 15 (all aspect verdicts are *Unknown*).

7   Conclusion

The suggested method extends the CEGAR approach and provides a means to check several requirements at once. Experiments showed that its implementation in the CPAchecker static verifier and LDV Tools worked 5 times faster than LDV Tools with the CEGAR approach, CPAchecker time was reduced by 3 times. More than 90 % of all verification tasks require only one launch of the CPAchecker static verifier to check program against all requirements. At the same time verdicts for verification tasks are the same for about 97.61 % of all verification tasks. Some verification tasks (about 2.17 %) need more resources than in basic CEGAR. At the same time positive effect of precision reuse helps to solve some tasks (about 0.22 %), that cannot be resolved in basic CEGAR with the same resource limitation, and even the total number of found error traces in CMAV is greater than in CEGAR.

The main benefit of the suggested method is more optimal usage of resources. Also it can be configured by using different options (for example, internal time limits) for specific verification task and user demands, it is possible to determine balance between verification time and quality of analysis.

The suggested method was presented and implemented as the CEGAR extension, but potentially the same ideas could be used for the other static verification approaches. One of the perspective area of the future development is integration of the suggested method with the method for finding all violations of an aspect, which will allow to find all violations of several aspects at once.

References

1. Beyer, D.: Competition on software verification. In: Flanagan, C., König, B. (eds.) TACAS 2012. LNCS, vol. 7214, pp. 504–524. Springer, Heidelberg (2012)

2. Beyer, D.: Software verification and verifiable witnesses. In: Baier, C., Tinelli, C. (eds.) TACAS 2015. LNCS, vol. 9035, pp. 401–416. Springer, Heidelberg (2015)

3. Khoroshilov, A., Mutilin, V., Novikov, E., Shved, P., Strakh, A.: Towards an open framework for C verification tools benchmarking. In: Clarke, E., Virbitskaite, I., Voronkov, A. (eds.) PSI 2011. LNCS, vol. 7162, pp. 179–192. Springer, Heidelberg (2012)

4. Website: problems found in Linux kernels. http://linuxtesting.org/results/ldv

5. Shved, P., Mandrykin, M., Mutilin, V.: Predicate analysis with BLAST 2.7. In: Flanagan, C., König, B. (eds.) TACAS 2012. LNCS, vol. 7214, pp. 525–527. Springer, Heidelberg (2012)

6. Beyer, D., Henzinger, T., Jhala, R., Majumdar, R.: The software model checker BLAST. Int. J. Softw. Tools Technol. Transf. 9(5–6), 505–525 (2007)

7. Beyer, D., Keremoglu, M.E.: CPACHECKER: a tool for configurable software verification. In: Gopalakrishnan, G., Qadeer, S. (eds.) CAV 2011. LNCS, vol. 6806, pp. 184–190. Springer, Heidelberg (2011)

8. Novikov, E.: An approach to implementation of aspect-oriented programming for C. Program. Comput. Softw. 39(4), 194–206 (2013)

9. Beyer, D., Löwe, S., Novikov, E., Stahlbauer, A., Wendler, P.: Precision reuse for efficient regression verification. In: Proceedings of the 9th Joint Meeting of the European Software Engineering Conference and the ACM SIGSOFT Symposium on Foundations of Software Engineering (ESEC/FSE 2013), St. Petersburg, Russia, 18–26 August 2013, pp. 389–399. ACM (2013)

10. Beyer, D., Keremoglu, M., Wendler, P.: Predicate abstraction with adjustable-block encoding. In: Formal Methods in Computer-Aided Design, FMCAD 2010 (2010)

11. Beyer, D., Löwe, S.: Explicit-state software model checking based on CEGAR and interpolation. In: Cortellessa, V., Varró, D. (eds.) FASE 2013 (ETAPS 2013). LNCS, vol. 7793, pp. 146–162. Springer, Heidelberg (2013)

12. Clarke, E., Grumberg, O., Jha, S., Lu, Y., Veith, H.: Counterexample-guided abstraction refinement. In: Emerson, E.A., Sistla, A.P. (eds.) CAV 2000. LNCS, vol. 1855, pp. 154–169. Springer, Heidelberg (2000)

13. Mandrykin, M., Mutilin, V., Khoroshilov, A.: Vvedenie v metod CEGAR - utochnenie abstraktsii po kontrprimeram [Introduction to CEGAR - Counter-Example Guided Abstraction Refinement]. Trudy ISP RAN [Proc. ISP RAS] 24, 219–292 (2013)

14. Beyer, D., Henzinger, T.A., Keremoglu, M.E., Wendler, P.: Conditional model checking: a technique to pass information between verifiers. In: Proceedings of the 20th ACM SIGSOFT International Symposium on the Foundations of Software Engineering, FSE 2012, Cary, NC, 10–17 November 2012. ACM (2012)

15. Mordan, V., Novikov, E.: Minimizing the number of static verifier traces to reduce time for finding bugs in Linux kernel modules. In: Proceedings of the Spring/Summer Young Researchers Colloquium on Software Engineering, vol. 8 (2014)

16. Zakharov, I., Mandrykin, M., Mutilin, V., Novikov, E., Petrenko, A., Khoroshilov, A.: Configurable toolset for static verification of operating systems kernel modules. Program. Comput. Softw. 41(1), 49–64 (2015)

Unifying Requirements and Code: An Example

Alexandr Naumchev[1]([⊠]), Bertrand Meyer[1,2], and Victor Rivera[1]

[1] Software Engineering Laboratory, Innopolis University, Innopolis, Russia
{a.naumchev,b.meyer,v.rivera}@innopolis.ru
[2] ETH Zürich, Zurich, Switzerland
http://university.innopolis.ru/

Abstract. Requirements and code, in conventional software engineering wisdom, belong to entirely different worlds. Is it possible to unify these two worlds? A unified framework could help make software easier to change and reuse. To explore the feasibility of such an approach, the case study reported here takes a classic example from the requirements engineering literature and describes it using a programming language framework to express both domain and machine properties. The paper describes the solution, discusses its benefits and limitations, and assesses its scalability.

Keywords: Software engineering · Requirements specifications · Multirequirements · Eiffel

1 Introduction

According to the standard view in software engineering, the tasks of requirements, design and implementation require distinct techniques and produce different artifacts.

What if instead of focusing on the differences we recognized the fundamental unity of the software construction process through all its stages? The principle of seamlessness (see e.g. [1]) follows from this assumption that the commonalities are more fundamental than the differences, and that it pays to use the same set of concepts, notations and tools throughout the development, from the most general and user-oriented initial steps down to the most technical tasks.

A consequence of the seamlessness principle is that requirements are just another software artifact, susceptible to many of the same techniques as code and design. In particular, assuming a modern programming language with powerful abstraction facilities, the requirements can be written in the same notation as the program.

The notion of multirequirements [2] adds to this principle the idea of using several interleaved descriptions: natural language, graphical, and formal (Eiffel text) serving as the reference.

How realistic is the seamless multirequirements approach, what are its limits, and what benefits does it bring? To help answer this question, the present article takes the example used in a classic paper of the requirements literature, Jackson's

© Springer International Publishing Switzerland 2016
M. Mazzara and A. Voronkov (Eds.): PSI 2015, LNCS 9609, pp. 233–244, 2016.
DOI: 10.1007/978-3-319-41579-6_18

and Zave's zoo control system, and describes it entirely in a seamless style, including the formal constraints that form a key part of the original article.

The goal of the paper is not advocacy but experimentation. The advocacy is present in the earlier references cited above. We practice a seamless approach to software construction and consider it fruitful, but the present discussion does not attempt to establish its superiority; rather it starts from the seamlessness hypothesis - in particular, the hypothesis that a single notation, Eiffel, is applicable to requirements analysis just as much as to programming - and applies this hypothesis fully and consistently to a significant example. While we draw some conclusions, the important part is the result of the experiment as presented here, enabling readers to form their own conclusions as to the benefits and limits of the approach.

Section 2 briefly explains why it is interesting to put into question the traditional separation between software development tasks. Section 3 proposes an approach to unify software development tasks by combining the approaches described in [2,3]. Section 4 introduces some theoretical and technical background. Section 5 presents the approach applied to an example. Finally, Sect. 6 concludes and mentions future work.

1.1   Summary of Contributions

Experimentation mentioned at the end of Sect. 1 resulted in the following key outcomes.

- An evidence suggesting that it is possible to use Multirequirements approach [2] for describing cyber-physical systems like zoo turnstile controller. At the same time, different types of exemplar statements goes far beyond just the relational statements used in [2].
- An evidence suggesting that a real programming language notation may be even more expressive than most of the popular formal notations. Section 5.5 contains all the details.
- An example showing how object orientation helps to effectively manage complexity in specifications. The approach used in [3], where the specification is basically a linear list of statements, does not scale to the case of large systems, when the number of requirements is too big. Object orientation provides a way to relate the conceptual objects so that the resulting specification will be scattered across the classes in an intuitive way.

2   The Drawbacks of Too Much Separation of Concerns

Historically, there was a reason for emphasizing the distinction between development tasks. The goal was to highlight the specific needs of requirements and design, moving away from the "code first, think later" way of building software. But as the precepts of software engineering have gained wide acceptance and programming languages have moved from low-level machine-coding notations to descriptive formalisms with high expressive power, the reverse approach is worth exploring: instead of emphasizing the differences, show the fundamental unity of the software process.

The traditional approach is subject to five criticisms.

(i) Insufficient information. Requirements analysts do not know what details are important for developers. They are good at expressing customer needs in a form the customer is ready to sign, but they typically do not know what is implementable and what is not. [4] discusses some typical flaws of natural language requirements specifications.

(ii) Lack of communication. When developers see ambiguous or contradictory elements in the requirements, they will not always go back and ask, but will often interpret the requirement according to their own understanding, which may or may not coincide with user wishes.

(iii) Impedance mismatches [1]. The use of different formalisms at different stages requires translations and creates risks of mistakes.

(iv) Impediment to change. With different formalisms, it is difficult [1] to ensure that a change at one level is reflected at other levels.

(v) Impediment to reuse. The presence of requirements as a document specific to each project may mask the commonality between projects and make the team miss potential reuse of existing developments.

3   A Seamless Approach

3.1   Unifying Processes

Consideration of the problems listed above leads to trying a completely different approach, which recognizes that beyond the obvious differences between tasks of software development they share fundamental needs, concepts, principles, techniques. In particular, they can be addressed through a common notation. Modern programming languages are not just coding tools to talk to a machine, but powerful tools for expressing abstract concepts and modeling complex systems. The Eiffel notation used in the present work uses object-oriented principles of classes, genericity, polymorphism and inheritance, which have proved adept at describing sophisticated systems (independently of their technical programming aspects) in a modular, flexible, reusable and evolutionary way. Thanks to the presence of Design by Contract mechanisms, it can describe not only the structure of systems but their abstract semantics.

3.2   The Hypothesis

The hypothesis explored in this paper, in light of the above analysis, is that it is possible to design a software development process that:

(i) Uses for requirements the same notation and tools as for design and implementation.

(ii) Links the resulting documents (requirements, design, code) together, ensuring a major goal of software engineering: traceability.

(iii) Makes it possible to prove, formally, the correctness of the implementation against the specification.

(iv) Supports extendibility by ensuring that small changes in the requirements will cause a proportionally small change in the design and the implementation.

3.3   How to Test the Hypothesis

The present work relies on the following scenario for testing the preceding hypothesis at least in part:

(i) Propose a candidate process.
(ii) Select examples and apply the process.
(iii) Analyze the outcome.

[2] sketches such a process, based on using object orientation for representing the relationships between the conceptual objects in the requirements document. The basic idea was to have an object-oriented code along with the natural language description of a requirement. It is also possible to represent each code fragment graphically as a BON diagram [5].

[2], however, uses as example the very notion of requirements process. In other words, it is self-referential. This confers (we hope) a certain elegance to the example, but makes it look artificial. In the present paper we take a more standard example, coming from a classic requirements paper by Jackson and Zave [3].

More precisely, the requirements from the example are represented using the model-based [6] contracts-equipped [7] object-oriented [1] notation (Eiffel).

4   Theoretical and Technical Background

4.1   Design by Contract

Work [7] gives a comprehensive description of Design By Contract. Design By Contract integrates Hoare-style assertions [8] within object-oriented programs [1] constraining the data that run time objects hold. This approach equips each class feature (member) with a predicate expression, that specify its behavior, in the form of pre- and postcondition. The postcondition has to hold whenever the precondition held and the feature finished its computation before the program execution process invokes the next feature. Design By Contract equips the class itself with an invariant predicate expression which holds in all states of the corresponding objects.

4.2 Model-Based Contracts

If classical contracts are for constraining the data that run time objects actually hold, model-based contracts are "meta" contracts for constraining the objects as mathematical entities (sets, sequences, bags, relations etc.), and an execution process does not instantiate the corresponding mathematical representations at run time as parts of the objects. Model-Based Contracts are useful when it is not possible to capture all the nuances by means of classical contracts. The PhD thesis [6] gives some examples of such situations and a comprehensive description of the concept.

4.3 AutoProof

The AutoProof [9] tool is capable of formally proving the correctness of contract-equipped object-oriented programs, both classical and model-based. AutoProof proves for every routine that the conjunction of the precondition and the class invariant before invocation ensures the conjunction of the postcondition and the class invariant after invocation. The class is verified if and only if all the class features are verified.

5 Unifying the Two Worlds: An Example

Avoiding the problems analyzed in Sect. 2 means unifying the worlds of requirements and code in a unified framework. This section illustrates the approach. It takes the example from the work [3] and shows how to express requirements of various types in the style of work [2] - namely, using Eiffel as a formal specification language for expressing each requirement. Originally the authors used this example to demonstrate the process of deriving specifications from requirements, and the unified approach captures all the nuances of this process.

5.1 Example Overview

The authors of [3] start with giving the overall context: *"...Our small example concerns the control of a turnstile at the entry to a zoo. The turnstile consists of a rotating barrier and a coin slot, and is fitted with an electrical interface..."* This small paragraph mostly describes the relationships between the conceptual objects. Figure 1 contains specification of the context in the style of work [2].

Translating the specification from Fig. 1 back to natural language using the object-oriented semantics results in almost the same initial description: "A ZOO has a TURNSTILE turnstile; a TURNSTILE has a COINSLOT coinslot and a BARRIER barrier so that coinslot has Current TURNSTILE as turnstile and barrier has Current TURNSTILE as turnstile..." COINSLOT and BARRIER hold references to the TURNSTILE instances in order to capture the *"electrical interface"* phenomena: the word "interface" means something over which the parties are able to communicate with each other; communicating means sending

```
class ZOO                              class COINSLOT
feature                                feature
   turnstile : TURNSTILE                  turnstile : TURNSTILE
end                                    invariant
                                          turnstile.coinslot = Current
class TURNSTILE                        end
feature
   coinslot : COINSLOT                 class BARRIER
   barrier : BARRIER                   feature
invariant                                 turnstile : TURNSTILE
   coinslot.turnstile = Current        invariant
   barrier.turnstile = Current            turnstile.barrier = Current
end                                    end
```

Fig. 1. Expressing the context formally

messages to each other, and to send message to someone in the object-oriented world is to take a reference to the object and perform a qualified call on it. So at the very least the parties should hold references to each other to be able to communicate in two directions.

5.2 The Designation Set

After stating the problem context the authors of [3] describe the *designation set*. Each designation basically corresponds to a separate type of events observed in the problem area. The authors give the designations as a set of predicates as in Fig. 2. Figure 3 is an Eiffel implementation of each designation set described in Fig. 2. The implementation uses Eiffel features names as labels for the events types. The natural language descriptions from Fig. 2 provide heuristics on which feature should be added to which class (Fig. 2 highlights the correspondence with **bold**). Each event type has an associated history - a sequence of moments in time when the events of this particular type occurred. For example, *enters* : $MML\_SEQUENCE[INTEGER\_64]$ (in Fig. 3) is a sequence of moments in time expressed in milliseconds when events of type *enter* took place. $MML\_SEQUENCE$ is a class from the MML (Mathematical Modeling Library) and denotes mathematical sequence. MML contains special classes for expressing model-based contracts. Although it is possible to instantiate some simple objects from these classes (like a sequence containing one element), the instances will not be modifiable. The *model* annotation is the Eiffel mechanism to represent model-based contracts (introduced in Sect. 4.2). For instance, expres-

- **Push**(e): In event e a visitor pushes the **barrier** to its intermediate position
- **Enter**(e): In event e a visitor pushes the barrier fully home and so gains entry to the **zoo**
- **Coin**(e): In event e a valid coin is inserted into the **coin slot**
- **Lock**(e): In event e the **turnstile** receives a locking signal
- **Unlock**(e): In event e the **turnstile** receives an unlocking signal

Fig. 2. The Zoo Turnstile example designation set

```
note
  model:  enters
deferred class ZOO
feature
  enter
  deferred
  ensure
    enters.but_last ~ old enters
    enters.last > old enters.last
  end
  enters : MML_SEQUENCE[INTEGER_64]
end

note
  model:  locks, unlocks
deferred class TURNSTILE
feature
  lock
  deferred
  ensure
    locks.but_last ~ old locks
    locks.last > old locks.last
  end
  unlock
  deferred
  ensure
    unlocks.but_last ~ old unlocks
    unlocks.last > old unlocks.last
  end
  locks : MML_SEQUENCE[INTEGER_64]
  unlocks : MML_SEQUENCE[INTEGER_64]
end
```

```
note
  model:  coins
deferred class COINSLOT
feature
  coin
  deferred
  ensure
    coins.but_last ~ old coins
    coins.last > old coins.last
  end
  coins : MML_SEQUENCE[INTEGER_64]
end

note
  model:  pushes
deferred class BARRIER
feature
  push
  deferred
  ensure
    pushes.but_last ~ old pushes
    pushes.last > old pushes.last
  end
  pushes : MML_SEQUENCE[INTEGER_64]
end
```

Fig. 3. Specifying the designation set formally

sion *model* : *enters* in Fig. 3 gives a hint that *enters* feature will be used for expressing the model-based part of the contract.

The *deferred* keyword states that the specification gives only formal definitions of the events (in terms of pre- and postconditions [8]) and does not give the corresponding operational reactions of the machine on the events. The *ensure* clause is the postcondition of the feature. It describes how the system changes after reacting on an event of the corresponding type. These specifications are intuitively plausible: an event occurrence should result in extending the corresponding history with the moment in time when the event took place, and the time of the new event should be strictly bigger than the time of the previous event, as shown, for instance, by the postcondition in feature *unlock* of Fig. 3. The keyword **old** is used to indicate expressions that must be evaluated in the pre-state of the routine, and ~ makes a comparison by value.

5.3   Shared Phenomena

The authors of [3] introduce the notion of shared phenomena - that is, the phenomena visible to both the world (the environment) and the machine (the notions of the world and the machine were introduced by Jackson in [10]). In the present approach this notion is covered by using the "has a" relationships between the *ZOO* and the *TURNSTILE* classes, accompanied with the model-based contracts. Namely, since a *ZOO* has a turnstile as its feature, it can see

```
deferred class ZOO
feature
  turnstile : TURNSTILE
  enters :  MML_SEQUENCE[INTEGER_64]
invariant
  enters.count <= turnstile.coinslot.coins.count
end
```

Fig. 4. Entries should never exceed payments

any phenomena hosted by the turnstile: $locks, unlocks, coins, pushes$; since a $TURNSTILE$ does not hold any references to a ZOO, it can not observe nor control the $enter$ events modeled by ZOO.

5.4 Specifying the System

Work [3] introduces a set of criteria by means of which it is possible to identify whether the machine is specified or not. One of the criteria states that all requirements should be expressed in terms of shared phenomena only. Requirements refinement is the process of converting the requirements stated in terms of both shared and non-shared phenomena to the form in which they are expressed in terms of shared phenomena only. Refinement process consists of identifying some laws, which hold in the environment regardless of the machine behaviour, and constraining the machine behaviour. The resulting constraints imposed on the machine together with the laws of the environment should logically imply the requirements stated in the beginning.

The authors of [3] state that the laws of the environment are always expressed in the indicative mood, while the restrictions imposed on the machine behavior are expressed in the optative mood.

All properties of the problem derived in [3] - be they optative or indicative descriptions - can be conceptually divided into the two main categories.

Properties Which Hold at Any Moment in Time: An example of such property is the $OPT1$ requirement (expressed in Fig. 4) saying that entries should never exceed payments (the authors of [3] use $OPT*$ for labeling properties expressed in an optative mood). Within the present approach this requirement can be expressed in the following way. The "something always holds" semantics fits perfectly into the semantics of Eiffel invariant: "something holds in all states of the object", as expressed in Fig. 4.

Properties Which Hold Depending on the Type of the Next Event to Occur: The indicative property $IND2$ saying that it is impossible to push the barrier if the turnstile is locked will serve as an example (the authors of [3] use $IND*$ for labeling properties expressed in the indicative mood). Figure 5 depicts the corresponding specification. The initial description is divided into the two different claims: first, the turnstile should be unlocked at least once, and second,

```
deferred class BARRIER
feature
  push
  require
    not turnstile.unlocks.is_empty
    (not turnstile.locks.is_empty) implies (turnstile.unlocks.last >
                                            turnstile.locks.last)
  deferred
  end
end
```

Fig. 5. It is impossible to use locked turnstile

```
deferred class BARRIER
feature
  turnstile: TURNSTILE
  push
  deferred
  ensure
    ((old turnstile.unlocks.last > old turnstile.locks.last) and
     (pushes.count = turnstile.coinslot.coins.count))
      implies (turnstile.locks.last > pushes.last and
               (turnstile.locks.last − pushes.last) < 760)
  end
  pushes: MML_SEQUENCE[INTEGER_64]
end
```

Fig. 6. The machine locks the turnstile timely

if the turnstile has ever been locked, the last unlock should have occurred later than the last lock.

Real Time Properties: The authors of [3] derive several timing constraints on the events processing. For example, the $OPT7$ requirement says that the amount of time between the moment when the number of the barrier pushes becomes equal to the number of coins inserted and the moment when the machine locks the turnstile should be less than 760 ms. This is basically a constraint for the reaction on the *push* event: if the next *push* event uses the last coin, the machine should ensure that the turnstile is locked in a timely fashion, so that a human being will not have time to enter without paying. The 760 quantity reflects the fact that it takes at least 760 ms for a human being to rotate the barrier completely and enter the Zoo.

Taking this reasoning into consideration, the present specification approach handles the timing constraint by putting it into the *push* feature postcondition (as depicted in Fig. 6). The antecedent of the implication assumes the situation when before the *push* event the turnstile was locked (*oldturnstile.unlocks.last* > *oldturnstile.locks.last* expression in Fig. 6), and after the event occurrence the number of barrier pushes became equal to the number of coins inserted (*pushes.count = turnstile.coinslot.coins.count* expression in Fig. 6). The consequent reflects the requirement that, having in place the situation that the antecedent describes, there should be a *lock* event which is more late than the last *push* event (*turnstile.locks.last* > *pushes.last* expression in Fig. 6), and

```
deferred class ZOO
feature
    turnstile : TURNSTILE_ABSTRACT
    enter
    deferred
    end
    enters : MML_SEQUENCE[INTEGER_64]
invariant
    turnstile.coinslot.coins.count > enters.count implies
        (agent enter).precondition
end
```

Fig. 7. The turnstile let people who pay enter

the distance between them should be less than 760 ms ($(turnstile.locks.last - pushes.last) < 760$ expression in Fig. 6).

5.5 Specifying the "Unspecifiable"

One of the requirements mentioned in [3] was $OPT2$ saying that the visitors who pay are not prevented from entering the Zoo. The authors give only informal statement of this requirement: $\forall v, m, n \bullet ((Enter\#(v, m) \wedge Coin\#(v, n) \wedge (m < n)) \implies$ '*The machine will not prevent another Enter event*'.

The antecedent of this implication should be read like "the number of entries is less than the number of coins inserted". The authors of [3] do not formalize the consequent and leave it in the natural language form. The present specification approach handles this requirement using standard Eiffel mechanism called *agents* (see Fig. 7).

The *agent* clause treats a feature (the *enter* feature in this particular case) as a separate object so that the feature precondition becomes one of the boolean-type features of the resulting object.

6 Conclusion

Software construction involves different activities. Typically these activities are performed separately. For instance, requirements and code, as developed nowadays, seem to belong to different worlds. The case study reported in this paper shows the feasibility of unifying requirements and code in a single framework.

This paper takes the classic Zoo Turnstile example [3] and implements it using Eiffel programming language. Eiffel is used not just to express the domain properties but also the properties of the machine [10], enabling users to combine requirements and code in a single framework. This paper does not present the complete implementation of the example due to limited space. Full implementation can be reached in the GitHub project [11].

The specification approach presented in this work is suitable not only for formalizing the statements that [3] formalizes, but also for formalizing those which are not possible to formalize with classical instruments like predicate or temporal logic (like $OPT2$ requirement, see Fig. 7).

The present approach is not only expressively powerful - it enables smooth transition to design and implementation. GitHub project [11] contains a continuation of the present work in the form of a complete implementation of the Zoo Turnstile example.

In order to understand the benefits of the present approach better it seems feasible to evaluate it against the hypothesis stated in Sect. 3.2:

(i) Unity of software development tasks: indeed, all the code fragments corresponding to different specification items merged together will bring a complete design solution available at [11] (the classes ending with "_abstract").

(ii) Traceability between the specification and the implementation: the classes ending with "_concrete" available at [11] contain the implementation and relate to the specification classes by means of inheritance.

(iii) Provability of the classes: the AutoProof system [9] is capable of formally proving both classical and model-based contracts in Eiffel. However, it is not yet capable of proving "higher-level" agents-based contracts like the one used in Fig. 7 for expressing requirement $OPT2$ from the work [3]. Adding this functionality to AutoProof is one of the next work items.

(iv) Extendibility of the solution: since Eiffel artifacts used in the formalizations of the requirements items correspond to their natural language counterparts directly, it is visible right away how a change in one representation will affect the second.

Speaking about scalability of the approach, a formal representation of a requirements item specified with Eiffel is as big as the scope of the item and its natural language description are, so the overall complexity of the final document should not depend on the size of the project. Anyway, this is something to test by applying the approach to a bigger project.

6.1 Future Work

The future actions plan include:

(i) to prove formally that the specifications are consistent. In particular to ensure that the features specifications preserve the invariants of their home classes; to ensure that the invariants are self-consistent. For example it should not be possible for $P(x)$ and $\neg P(x)$ to hold at the same time.

(ii) to extend the BON notation [5] so that it will be capable of expressing model-based contracts.

(iii) to design machinery for translating model-based contract-oriented requirements to their natural language counterpart so that the result will be recognizable by a human being.

(iv) to apply the approach to a bigger project.

(v) to extend AutoProof technology [9] so that it will be able to handle agents in specifications (like in Fig. 7).

It seems feasible to utilize AutoProof technology [9] for achieving goal (i). AutoProof is already capable of proving that a feature implementation preserves its specification (except specifications with agents), and it seems logical to empower it with the capabilities for working solely on the specifications level. Work [12] contains a formal proof that it is possible to achieve goal (v).

As a result of implementing the plan a powerful framework for expressing all possible views on the software under construction should emerge. The threshold of success includes the possibility to generate the specification classes (their names end with "_abstract") available at [11] automatically, using requirements documents produced according to the present process as input.

Acknowledgment. This work has been supported by the Russian Ministry of education and science with the project "Development of new generation of cloudy technologies of storage and data control with the integrated security system and the guaranteed level of access and fault tolerance" (agreement: 14.612.21.0001, ID: RFMEFI61214X0001). Also, the authors would like to thank their colleagues Alexander Chichigin and Dr. Manuel Mazzara from the Innopolis University Software Engineering Laboratory for their invaluable feedback.

References

1. Meyer, B.: Object-Oriented Software Construction, vol. 2. Prentice Hall, New York (1988)
2. Meyer, B.: Multirequirements. In: Seyff, N., Koziolek, A. (eds.) Modelling and Quality in Requirements Engineering (Martin Glinz Festscrhift). MV Wissenschaft (2013)
3. Jackson, M., Zave, P.: Deriving specifications from requirements: an example. In: Proceedings of the 17th International Conference on Software Engineering, pp. 15–24. ACM (1995)
4. Meyer, B.: On formalism in specifications. IEEE Softw. **2**(1), 6–26 (1985)
5. Waldén, K., Nerson, J.M.: Seamless Object-Oriented Software Architecture. Prentice-Hall, Upper Saddle River (1995)
6. Polikarpova, N.: Specified and verified reusable components. Ph.D. thesis, Diss., Eidgenössische Technische Hochschule ETH Zürich, Nr. 21939, 2014 (2014)
7. Meyer, B.: Touch of Class: Learning to Program Well with Objects and Contracts. Springer, Heidelberg (2009)
8. Hoare, C.A.R.: An axiomatic basis for computer programming. Commun. ACM **12**(10), 576–580 (1969)
9. Tschannen, J., Furia, C.A., Nordio, M., Meyer, B.: Automatic verification of advanced object-oriented features: the autoproof approach. In: Meyer, B., Nordio, M. (eds.) LASER 2011. LNCS, vol. 7682, pp. 133–155. Springer, Heidelberg (2012)
10. Jackson, M.: The world and the machine. In: 17th International Conference on Software Engineering, ICSE 1995, pp. 283–283. IEEE (1995)
11. Naumchev, A.: Jackson-zave zoo turnstile implementation (2015). https://github.com/anaumche/Zoo-Turnstile-Multirequirements
12. Nordio, D.M.: Proofs and proof transformations for object-oriented programs. Ph.D. thesis, Citeseer (2009)

Program Schemata Technique to Solve Propositional Program Logics Revised

Nikolay Shilov[✉]

A.P. Ershov Institute of Informatics Systems, Russian Academy of Sciences,
Lavren'ev av. 6, 630090 Novosibirsk, Russia
shilov@iis.nsk.su

Abstract. Propositional program (dynamic, temporal and process) logics are basis for logical specification of program systems (including parallel, distributed and multiagent systems). Therefore development of efficient algorithms (decision procedures) for validation, provability and model checking of program logics is an important research topic for the theory of programming.

The essence of a program schemata technique consists in the following. Formulas of a program logic to be translated into uninterpreted nondeterministic monadic flowcharts (so called Yanov schemata) so that the scheme is total (i.e. terminates) in all special interpretations if and only if the initial formula is a tautology (i.e. is identically true). Since this generalized halting problem is solvable (with an exponential complexity), it implies the decidability of initial program logic (and leads to a decidability upper bound).

The first version of the technique was developed by Nikolay V. Shilov and Valery A. Nepomnjaschy in 1983–1987 for variants of Propositional Dynamic Logic (PDL). In 1997 the technique was expanded on the propositional μ-Calculus. In both cases a special algorithm was used to solve the generalized halting problem.

A recent development of program schemata technique consists in revised decision procedure for the halting problem. A new decision procedure consists in model checking of a special fairness property (presented by some fixed μ-Calculus formula) in finite models presented by Yanov schemata flowcharts. Exponential lower bound for transformation of μ-Calculus formulas to equivalent guarded form is a consequence of the new version of the decision procedure.

1 Propositional μ-Calculus

Let us define syntax and semantics of the propositional μ-Calculus (μC) [8], one of the most expressive propositional program logics.

Definition 1. *Let $Con = \{true, false\}$ be Boolean constants and Var and Act be disjoint (countable) alphabets of propositional and program variables. Syntax of μC consists of formulas to be defined by structural induction.*

This work is supported by the RFBR-grant # 13-01-00645-a.

M. Mazzara and A. Voronkov (Eds.): PSI 2015, LNCS 9609, pp. 245–259, 2016.
DOI: 10.1007/978-3-319-41579-6_19

- *All constants in Con and variable in Var are formulas.*
- *Any propositional combination of formulas is a formula:* negation $\neg\phi$, conjunction $(\phi \wedge \psi)$ *and* disjunction $(\phi \vee \psi)$ *are formulas for any formulas ϕ and ψ.*
- *For any program variable $a \in Act$ and formula ϕ modal constructs* sometimes $(\langle a \rangle \phi)$ *and* always $([a]\phi)$ *are formulas.*
- *For any propositional variable $x \in Var$ and formula ϕ without negative[1] and bound[2] instances of x, the least fix-point $(\mu x.\phi)$ and the greatest fix-point $(\nu x.\phi)$ are formulas too[3].*

Let us drop the top-level parenthesis around formulas as well as those parenthesis inside formulas that may be restored according to the standard precedence rules for the propositional connectives: negation precedes conjunction that precedes disjunction

For any syntactic expression r and any two expressions of same kind[4] s and t let $r_{t/s}$ be the result of instantiation of t instead of all instances of s in r; also let $r_{t/s}^0$ denote the expression t itself, and for every $n \geq 0$ let $r_{t/s}^{n+1}$ be $r_{r_{t/s}^n/s}$ i.e. $r_{t/s}^m$ stays for m-times substitution of t instead of s in ϕ. For example, if ϕ is a formula $\psi \vee \langle a \rangle x$ (where $x \in Var$ and $a \in Act$ are propositional and program variables) then[5]

- $\phi_{true/x}^0 \equiv true$,
- $\phi_{true/x}^1 \equiv (\psi \vee (\langle a \rangle true))$,
- $\phi_{true/x}^2 \equiv (\psi \vee (\langle a \rangle(\psi \vee (\langle a \rangle true))))$, etc.

μC semantics is defined in models that are called *labeled transition systems* (LTS) in Computer Science and *Kripke systems/structures* in Logic and Philosophy; let us just use term *model* instead of both in this paper.

Definition 2. *Each model M is a triple (D, R, E) where*

- *the* domain $D \neq \varnothing$ *is a set of* states;
- *the* interpretation $R : Act \to 2^{D \times D}$ *is a function that assigns a binary relation $R(a) \subseteq D \times D$ to each $a \in Act$;*
- *the* valuation $E : Var \to 2^D$ *is a function that assigns a unary predicate $E(x) \subseteq D$ to each $x \in Var$.*

If $M = (D, R, E)$ is a model, $S \subseteq D$ is a set of states, and $x \in VAR$ is a propositional variable then let $M_{S/x}$ denote a model $(D, R, E_{S/x})$ where[6] valuation

---

[1] An instance of a subformula is said to be negative if it is in the scope of odd number of negations; otherwise the instance is said to be positive.

[2] An instance of a variable x is said to be bound if it is in the scope of μx or νx; otherwise it is said to be free.

[3] The definition implies that all bound variable within a formula must be different.

[4] i.e. both are simultaneously propositional variables, program variables, formulas, etc.

[5] Hereafter we use '$\equiv$' for syntax identity, but '$=$' for (set-theoretic) equality.

[6] Acronym *upd* stays for *update*, i.e. the following second-order function modifier: for any function $f : X \times Y$, elements $x \in X$ and $y \in Y$ let $upd(f, x, y) = \lambda z \in X.$ *if* $z = x$ *then* y *else* $f(y)$.

$E_{S/x}$ is $upd(E, x, S)$ i.e. a valuation that may differ from E for propositional variable x only: $E_{S/x}(x) = S$.

Definition 3. μC semantics in may be defined by extending valuations (provided by models) from propositional variables onto all formulas by structural induction as follows. For any model $M = (D, R, E)$ let

- $M(true) = D$, $M(false) = \varnothing$, and $M(x) = E(x)$ for every $x \in Var$;
- $M(\neg\phi) = D \setminus M(\phi)$, $M(\phi \wedge \psi) = M(\phi) \cap M(\psi)$, $M(\phi \vee \psi) = M(\phi) \cup M(\psi)$;
- $M(\langle a \rangle \phi) = \{s \in D \ : \ \exists t \in D((s,t) \in R(a) \text{ and } t \in M(\phi))\}$,
- $M([a]\phi) = \{s \in D \ : \ \forall t \in D((s,t) \in R(a) \text{ implies } t \in M(\phi))\}$;
- $M(\mu x.\phi)$ is the least (w.r.t. $\subseteq$) set of states $S \subseteq D$ that $M_{S/x}(\phi) = S$;
- $M(\mu x.\phi)$ is the greatest (w.r.t. $\subseteq$) set of states $S \subseteq D$ that $M_{S/x}(\phi) = S$.

Satisfiability $\models$ is a ternary relation between states, models and formulas defined as follows: $s \models_M \phi$ iff $s \in M(\phi)$.

The above definition needs some justification since it refers to existence of the set-theoretic least and greatest fix-points $M_{S/x}(\phi) = S$ over 2^D. Correctness of this definition follows from monotonicity of a function $\lambda S \subseteq D.M_{S/x}(\phi) : 2^D \to 2^D$ (assuming ϕ hasn'tt negative instances of x) and Knaster-Tarski fix-point theorem [8,13,15]. We skip full details of this justification (due to space limitations) but formulate a corollary that follows from the proof of the theorem[7].

Corollary 1. For any propositional variable $x \in Var$, μC-formula ϕ without bound and negative instances of x, for every $n \geq 0$ and every model M the following inclusions hold: $M(\phi^n_{false/x}) \subseteq M(\mu x.\phi)$ and $M(\nu x.\phi) \subseteq M(\phi^n_{true/x})$.

Definition 4. Let ϕ be any μC-formula.

- ϕ is said to be valid in a model M ($\models_M \phi$), if $M(\phi) = D_M$ where D_M is the domain of the model; ϕ is said to be valid ($\models \phi$), if it is valid in all models.
- ϕ is said to be satisfiable in a model M, if there exists a state s such that $s \models_M \phi$; ϕ is said to be satisfiable if it is so in some model.

The following definition just recalls some general logic concepts.

Definition 5.

- Calculus is a formal language provided with syntax-driven inference system; if the inference system has axioms (i.e. premise-free inference rules) then provable sentences are those of the language that may be inferred from axioms. A calculus with axioms is called axiomatic system.
- A formal language provided with model-base concept of validity (for its sentences) is
  - decidable if there exists an algorithm to solve the set of valid sentences;
  - axiomatizeable if there exists an algorithm to enumerate all valid sentences.

---

[7] We need the corollary for justification of some statements in the paper.

- A calculus (or axiomatic system) provided with model-base validity is
  - sound *if all provable sentences are valid;*
  - complete *if all valid sentences are provable.*
- A formal language provided with model-base validity is said to be syntactical-ly-axiomatizable *if it has a sound and complete axiomatic system.*

In the original paper [8] D. Kozen defined syntax, Kripke semantics (i.e. model-based validity) and axiomatic system (i.e. a calculus itself) for μ-Calculus and proved soundness of the axiomatic system. The first sound and complete axiomatization for μC was built 10 years later by I. Walukiewicz [14]; I. Walukiewicz proved completeness of the original axiomatization next 7 years later in [15].

μ-Calculus was proved to be decidable with exponential upper bound 15 years after the original paper [8] independently by N.V. Shilov in [11] and by E.A. Emerson and C.J. Jutla [3]. E.A. Emerson and C.J. Jutla proved exponential upper bound by reduction of the satisfiability problem to the emptiness problem for Büchi automata; furthermore they also proved $EXP - Time$ completeness of the satisfiability problem. In contrast, N.V. Shilov suggested linear time translation of μC-formulas to non-deterministic Yanov[8] schemata [9,11] such that reduces validity problem to a so-called generalized halting problem for schemata; it had been shown earlier by V.A. Nepomniaschij and N.V. Shilov [9,11] that the generalized halting problem is decidable for Yanov schemata in exponential time.

2   Special Classes of Models and Formulas

Definition 6. *μC-formulas ϕ and ψ are said to be equivalent in a class of models $\mathbb{M}$ if $M(\phi) = M(\psi)$ for every model M in this class. In particular, when $\mathbb{M}$ is the class of all models then the formulas are said equivalent. If a class $\mathbb{M}$ consists of a single model M then formulas are said to be equivalent in this model M.*

Definition 7. *μC-formula is said to be* normal *if all instances of negation are at literal level (i.e. $\neg$ may appear only in front of propositional variables in the formula).*

According to the following very standard statement each μC-formula may be transformed in linear time into an equivalent normal formula.

Proposition 1. *For any propositional variable x and program variable a, for any μC-formulas ϕ and ψ the equivalences in the Table 1 are valid.*

Definition 8. *An instance of a propositional variable in a formula is said to be* guarded *if it occurs in the range of any modality $[\dots]$ or $\langle\dots\rangle$. A propositional variable is said to be* guarded *in a formula if all its instances are guarded in the formula. μC-formula is said to be* guarded *if all its bound variables are guarded.*

---

[8] Alternative spelling: Ianov.

Table 1. Normalization equivalences

$\neg(\neg\phi)$ is equivalent to ϕ	
$\neg(\phi \wedge \psi)$ is equivalent to $(\neg\phi) \vee (\neg\psi)$	$\neg(\phi \vee \psi)$ is equivalent to $(\neg\phi) \wedge (\neg\psi)$
$\neg(\langle a\rangle\psi)$ is equivalent to $[a](\neg\psi)$	$\neg([a]\psi)$ is equivalent to $\langle a\rangle(\neg\psi)$
$\neg(\mu x.\psi)$ is equivalent to $\nu x.(\neg\psi_{\neg x/x})$	$\neg(\nu x.\psi)$ is equivalent to $\mu x.(\neg\psi_{\neg x/x})$

One can read in papers [14,15] that every μC-formula can be converted into equivalent guarded one in *polynomial* time. But recently it was proved that *"known guarded transformations can cause an exponential blowup in formula size, contrary to existing claims of polynomial behavior"* [1].

Proposition 2. *Every μC-formula is equivalent to some guarded μC-formula that may be constructed from the input formula in exponential time and space.*

Proof. First, if a formula ϕ has no instances of a propositional variable x then $\mu x.\phi$ and $\nu x.\phi$ are both equivalent to ϕ.

Next, let x be a propositional variable and ϕ be a formula without negative instances of x; let us classify instances of x in ϕ as follows:

- guarded instances or instances in the scope of any *alien* fix-point construct[9];
- unguarded instances that are out of scope of any alien fix-point construct;

let us refer instances of the first type by x_{fp} and instances of the second type by x_{os}; then following equivalences hold:

- $\mu x.\phi$ is equivalent to $\mu x.\phi_{false/x_{os}}$, i.e. the same formula where all unguarded instances of x are replaced by $false$;
- $\nu x.\phi$ is equivalent to $\nu x.\phi_{true/x_{os}}$, i.e. the same formula where all unguarded instances of x are replaced by $true$.

Using these equivalences one can eliminate all unguarded bound instances of variables that are out of scope of any alien fix-point construct.

Finally, for any propositional variables x and y, any μC-formulas $\phi(x,y)$ and $\psi(x,y)$ without negative and bound instances of x and y, for any fix-point constructs $\pi, \rho \in \{\mu, \nu\}$, any fresh[10] propositional variable z and t, the following formulas are equivalent:

- $\pi x.\phi(x, \rho y.\psi(x,y))$,
- $\pi x.\phi(x, \rho y.\psi(\pi z.\phi(z, \rho t.\psi(z,t)), y))$,
- $\pi x.\phi(x, \rho y.\psi(\pi z.\phi(z,y), y))$.

Observe, that if formula $\psi(x,y)$ has no unguarded instances of y, then the formula $\pi x.\phi(x, \rho y.\psi(\pi z.\psi(z,y), y))$ has no unguarded instances of neither x, nor y, nor z in the scope of an alien fix-point construct ρy or πz. ∎

---

[9] i.e. a construct that bounds another variable.
[10] i.e. that are not in use neither in ϕ nor in ψ.

Definition 9. *A model $M = (D, R, E)$ is said to be* strict *if every program variable $a \in Act$ is interpreted as a total function $R(a) : D \to D$. A variant of μ-Calculus (with same syntax as μC) based on (i.e. that uses) strict interpretations only, is called* strict μ-Calculus (μ-Strict *or* μS).

Let us remark that Propositions 1 and 2 are true for μ-Strict. But strict μ-Calculus also has some specifics: for every program variable $a \in Act$ and any μS-formula ϕ the following μS-formulas $[a]\phi$ and $\langle a \rangle \phi$ are equivalent due to interpretation of program variables by total functions. This observation implies the following corollary.

Corollary 2. *Every μS-formula is equivalent to some normal guarded box-free[11] μS-formula that may be constructed from the input formula in exponential time and space.*

Definition 10. *Formulas (in different languages maybe) are said to be* equally valid *if they all are simultaneously valid (according to their semantics) or all simultaneously are not valid. Similarly, formulas are said to be* equally satisfiable *if they all are simultaneously satisfiable (according to their semantics in different models maybe) or all simultaneously are not satisfiable.*

Let us introduce (classical propositional) implication $\to$ and equivalence $\leftrightarrow$ in the standard manner as macros legal to use in *non-normal* formulas: for any formulas ϕ and ψ let $\phi \to \psi$ stays for $(\neg \phi) \vee \psi$, and $\phi \leftrightarrow \psi$ stays for $(\phi \to \psi) \wedge (\psi \to \phi)$.

Next let us introduce few more macros inspirited by Propositional Dynamic Logic (PDL) [5]: for any program variables a and b, any formulas ϕ and ψ let

- $[(a; \phi?)^*; b]\psi$ stays for $\nu x.([b]\psi \wedge [a](\phi \to x))$,
- $\langle (a; \phi?)^*; b \rangle \psi$ stays for $\mu x.(\langle b \rangle \psi \vee \langle a \rangle (\phi \wedge x))$.

It is possible to say that ';' is *sequential composition* of programs, '*' is non-deterministic *iteration* of a program, and '?' is a *test* construct that converts a 'property' to a guard. Thus formula $[(a; \phi?)^*; b]\psi$ suggests to iterate a any (non-deterministic) number of times (while ϕ holds after each iteration), then apply b and check that at the end ψ is always true; in contrast, formula $\langle (a; \phi?)^*; b \rangle \psi$ suggests to iterate a some (non-deterministic) number of times (with care about ϕ after each iteration), then apply b and eventually ψ should be true.

The following proposition has been proved in [11].

Proposition 3. *Let ϕ be a μC-formula. For every program variable $a \in Act$ that occurs in ϕ, let f_a, g_a and p_a be fresh (disjoint) program variables and propositional variable (individual for each a). Let μS-formula ψ be result of replacement in ϕ of all instances of each program variable $a \in Act$ by an instance of expression $(f_a; p_a?)^*; g_a$; then μC-formula ϕ is equally valid/satisfiable with μS-formula ψ. It implies that every μC-formula is equally valid/satisfiable with some μS-formula that may be constructed from the input formula in linear time.*

---

[11] i.e. a formula without instances of modality [...].

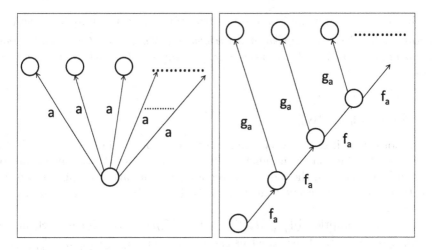

Fig. 1. Simulation of a countable μC-model by μS-model

Proof. Firstly let us remark that ϕ is valid iff it is valid in all *tree-based* countable models. Here a tree-based countable model is any model (D, R, E) where D as the set of nodes and $\{R(a) : a \in Act\ occurs\ in\ \phi\}$ as the set of edges form a directed tree. One can think about a tree-based model for ϕ as a labeled directed tree where nodes are states, edges are graphs of interpreted program variables that occur in ϕ; edges of this tree are marked by corresponding program variables and nodes are marked by propositional variables occurring in ϕ that are evaluated as valid in these nodes. A tree-based model that "emulates" a given model for ϕ can be constructed as follows: for each state glue together all its successor states that are indistinguishable by any formula of μC, and then unfold this reduced model into an infinite tree (starting from any desired state). Let us remark that gluing indistinguishable states and coping by unfolding don't change validity of any formula in states and their copies. Remark also that after gluing together all indistinguishable states the reduced model is (not more than) countable; hence unfolded tree-based model is also countable.

Next, we can transform a countable tree-based model for ϕ into a countable tree-based μS-model for μS-formula ψ, by "simulating" interpretation of each program variable $a \in Act$ (that occurs in ϕ) as specified below and illustrated on Fig. 1: for each state s

- let us introduce a countable set of auxiliary states,
- let f_a enumerates all the auxiliary states in some order,
- let p_a be valid as many times on auxiliary states as is the number of a-successors of s,
- let g_a returns a corresponding a-successor of s for each of auxiliary states.

In the resulting μS-model the validity of the formula ψ in the states of the original μC-model coincides with the validity of ϕ in the original μC-model. ∎

The following statement is a corollary from Knaster-Tarski fix-point theorem.

Corollary 3. *For any propositional variable $x \in Var$, any μC-formula ϕ that has no negative or bound instances of x, for any strict model M the following holds:*

- $M(\mu x.\phi) = \bigcup_{n \geq 0} M(\phi^n_{false/x})$,
- $M(\nu x.\phi) = \bigcap_{n \geq 0} M(\phi^n_{true/x})$.

Proof. Both equalities are very similar, so let us prove the first one only by simultaneous induction by number of fix-point constructs in ϕ; since proof of the induction basis and the induction step are very similar, let us just sketch the induction basis, i.e. to prove that $M(\mu x.\phi) = \bigcup_{n \geq 0} M(\phi^n_{false/x})$ for a fix-point-free formula ϕ.

Firstly, subsumption $\bigcup_{n \geq 0} M(\phi^n_{false/x}) \subseteq M(\mu x.\phi)$ is valid in each model according to Corollary 1. Next, let us assume (in contrary) $\bigcup_{n \geq 0} M(\phi^n_{false/x}) \neq M(\mu x.\phi)$. Then let us denote $\bigcup_{n \geq 0} M(\phi^n_{false/x})$ by S. Due to the assumption, $M_{S/x}(\phi) \neq S$. Hence there exists a state $s \in D_M$ such that $s \in (M_{S/x}(\phi) \setminus S)$. Since ϕ is fix-point-free and M is strict, then there exists a finite set $S_{fin} \subseteq S$ such that $s \in M_{S_{fin}/x}(\phi)$. It implies that $s \in \bigcup_{n \geq 0} M(\phi^n_{false/x})$ due to finiteness of S_{fin}. — Contradiction. Hence $M_{S/x}(\phi) = S$. ∎

Definition 11. *A model (D, R, E) is called Herbrand model [9] (or free model in Russian tradition [4, 7]) if the domain D is the set Act^* of all finite words constructed from program variables (including the empty word θ) and interpretation R is defined as follows: $R(a)(w) = wa$ for any program variable $a \in Act$ and any word $w \in Act^*$.*

If to analyze the proof of Proposition 3 above then it is possible to prove the following statement.

Proposition 4. *μC-formula is valid/satisfiable iff it is valid/satisfiable in every/some Herbrand model.*

3   Non-deterministic Yanov Schemata

Yanov schemata [4, 6, 10] is one of classical program models that enjoys decidability of many algorithmic problems like (functional) equivalence, emptiness and totality (halting) [4, 7]. The term *Yanov scheme* was introduced by Andrey P. Ershov; he also developed graphical flowchart notation and complete graphical axiomatization for the equivalence problem [4, 10].

Non-deterministic Yanove schemata were introduced in [9] and then were used in [11]. Let us repeat below basic syntax and semantics definitions for non-deterministic Yanov schemata.

Definition 12. *Let us use natural numbers (including 0) as labels[12]. Assignment (or labeled assignment operator) is any expression of the form "l : f goto L" where l is a label, f is a program variable, and L is a finite set (the empty set maybe) of labels[13]. Choice (or labeled choice operator) is any expression of the form "l : if p then L^+ else L^-" where l is a label, p is a propositional variable, L^+ and L^- are finite sets of labels (each may be empty). Non-deterministic Yanov scheme is a finite set of labeled operators.*

According to the definition above, a label may mark several operators in a non-deterministic Yanov scheme. Definition of syntax of the classical Yanov schemata results from the above definition by imposing the following additional constraints:

– a label may mark a single operator in a scheme;
– all sets L, L^+ and L^- in operators are singletons.

Let us reserve term *Yanov scheme* (or simply *scheme*) for non-deterministic Yanov scheme, but use term *standard* Yanov scheme when we discuss the classical case.

Semantics of Yanov schemata is defined in strict models. Speaking informally, *run* of a scheme in a model may start from any state but the first operator to fire must be marked by label 0 (zero); then run consists of firings of operators according to control flow that is defined by labels; run halts when control is passed to any label that does not mark any operator within the scheme[14].

Definition 13. *Let S be an arbitrary fixed Yanov scheme and $M = (D, R, E)$ be any fixed strict model. Configuration is any pair of the form (l, s) where l is a label (that occurs in S) and s is a state (of the model). Firing of an operator is a pair of configurations $(l, s)(l', s')$ as defined below:*

– *firing of an assignment operator "l : f goto L" (that occurs in S) is a pair of configurations $(l, s)(l', s')$ where $s' = R(f)(s)$ and $l' \in L$;*
– *firing of a choice operator "l : if p then L^+ else L^-" (that occurs in S) is a pair of configurations $(l, s)(l', s')$ where $s' = s$ and $l' \in \begin{cases} L^+ & \text{if } s \in E(p) \\ L^- & \text{otherwise.} \end{cases}$*

A run *is any sequence of configurations $(l_0, s_0) \ldots (l_k, s_k)(l_{k+1}, s_{k+1}) \ldots$ such that each neighbor pair $(l_k, s_k)(l_{k+1}, s_{k+1})$ within this sequence is a firing of some operator (of S of course). A complete run starts with a configuration with label 0 and is either infinite or ends with a configuration with a final label (in S).*

Let us recall some facts and concept about the standard Yanov schemata. Every standard Yanov scheme in any strict model for any initial state has a single complete run that starts in this state. A standard Yanov scheme is said

---

[12] Let us assume that notation for number representation is fixed.
[13] Let us use the standard representation for finite sets: ∅ for the empty set and elements enumerated in a pair of curly parenthesis '{' and '}'.
[14] These labels are called final labels of the scheme.

to be *total*, if it hasn't any infinite complete run in any strict model. The *halting (totality) problem* for standard Yanov schemata is to decide for an input scheme whether it is total or not. It is well-known that the problem is decidable, and a scheme is total iff in every Herbrand model starting in configuration[15] $(0, \theta)$ the scheme always halts[16] [7].

Definition 14. *Let $Fin \subseteq Var$ be a finite set of propositional variables. Let us say that a Herbrand model $M = (D, R, E)$ fits Fin, if for every propositional variable $p \in Fin$ its evaluation $E(p)$ is a finite set. A scheme S is said to be total with respect to Fin, if in every Herbrand model that fits Fin, scheme S has a finite complete run starting in configuration $(0, \theta)$.*

Definition 15. *Generalized halting (totality) problem for non-deterministic Yanov schemata is to decide for an input scheme S and input finite set of propositional variables Fin whether S is total with respect to Fin.*

Generalized halting problem has been proven to be decidable [9,11] with upper bound $\exp(n_A + n_C)$ where n_A and n_C are numbers of assignments and choices in the input scheme. Below we will present a new decision procedure for the problem in a sub-class of *guarded schemata* inspirited by a decision procedure for a special class of automata [12].

Definition 16. *Yanov scheme is said to be guarded if any non-empty path on flow-chart of the scheme that starts in a choice operator with some propositional variable as the condition, and ends in a choice operator[17] with the same condition, has an instance of an assignment operator.*

It is well-known that functional equivalence is decidable for the standard Yanov schemata [4,7]. This equivalence may be expanded onto non-deterministic Yanove schemata by considering input-output relations augmented by looping, and can been proven to be decidable since every scheme can be effectively transformed to appropriate equivalent canonical guarded scheme [9]. These equivalence and transformation were very helpful for proving decidability of Propositional Dynamic Logic [9] but aren't so helpful in study of decidability of μ-Calculus.

Nevertheless we are interested in guarded non-deterministic schemata since such schemata may be converted to models for μ-Calculus.

Definition 17. *Let S be a guarded scheme. For each propositional variable p that occurs in S, let $+p$ and $-p$ be a pair of new (fresh) program variables. Let M_S be the following model (D_S, R_S, E_S).*

- *D_S is union of the following three sets:*
  - *$\{(l, f) : l$ is a label, f is a program variable such that S has an assignment "$l : f$ goto . . . " $\}$;*

---

[15] Recall that θ is the empty word.

[16] i.e. it has a *finite complete* run.

[17] maybe the same operator where the path starts.

- $\{(l, +p), (l, -p) : l$ is a label, p is a propositional variable such that S has a choice "l : if p then ... else ... "$\}$;
- $\{(l, stop) : l$ is a final label in $S\}$.
- R_S interprets old and new program variables as follows:
  - for each program variable f that occurs in S, $R_S(f) = \{((l, f), (k, m)) : (l, f), (k, m) \in D_S$ and S has an assignment "l : f goto L", where $k \in L\}$;
  - for each propositional variable p in S, $R_S(+p) = \{((l, p), (k, m)) : (l, f), (k, m) \in D_S$ and S has a choice "l : if p then L^+ else ... "$, where $k \in L^+\}$;
  - for each propositional variable p in S, $R_S(-p) = \{((l, p), (k, m)) : (l, f), (k, m) \in D_S$ and S has a choice "l : if p then ... else L^-"$, where $k \in L^-\}$.
- For each propositional variable p in S, $E_S(p) = \{(l, +p) : (l, +p) \in D_S\}$.

Any state of D_S in the form $(0, \dots)$ is called initial.

Definition 18. Let $Fun \subseteq Act$ be a finite set of program variables, ϕ be μC-formula, $M = (D, R, E)$ be a model, and $s \in D$ be a state. An infinite sequence of states $s_0, s_1, \cdots \subseteq D$ is generated by Fun from s in M, if $s_0 = s$ and for all $k \geq 0$ there is a program variable $a \in Fun$ that $(s_k, s_{k+1}) \in R(a)$. Let us say that

- formula ϕ is inevitable for Fun in M from s, if every infinite sequence of states $s_0, s_1, \cdots \subseteq D$ generated by Fun from s in M has a state $s_j \models_M \phi$;
- program variables Fun are fair for (or with respect to) ϕ in M from s, if every infinite sequence of states $s_0, s_1, \cdots \subseteq D$ generated by Fun from s in M has an infinite subsequence $t_0, t_1, \dots$ that $t_j \models_M \phi$ for all $j \geq 0$.

Proposition 5. Let S be a guarded scheme, Fin be a set of propositional variables, M_S be model constructed from S as specified in the Definition 17, and Fun be the set of all program variables that correspond to propositional variables in Fin according to this definition. Then the following clauses are equivalent:

- S is total with respect to Fin;
- Fun is fair with respect to $\bigvee_{p \in Fin} p$ in M_S from every initial state.

Proof. A path $l_0, \dots l_k, \dots$ in a flowchart is said to be valid if there exists a strict model M and sequence of states $s_0, \dots s_k, \dots$ (with same length as the path) such that $(l_0, s_0) \dots (l_k, s_k) \dots$ is a run in this model. A scheme is said to be *free* [7,11] if any path on its flowchart is a valid. It is easy to see that every guarded scheme is free. Due to this freedom of S and finiteness of Fin we have: S isn't total with respect to $Fin \Leftrightarrow$ there exists an infinite path in M_S where formula $\bigvee_{p \in Fin} p$ is valid an infinitely often. ∎

Definition 19. Let $Fun \subseteq Act$ be a finite set of program variables, and ϕ be any μC-formula. Let us introduce two more macros:

- let[18] $AF(Fun, \phi)$ stays for $\mu y.(\phi \vee \bigwedge_{a \in Fun} [a]y)$,

---

[18] AF means *Always in Future* is a modality from Computation Tree Logic CTL [2].

– and $fair(Fun, \phi)$ stays for $\nu x.AF(Fun, \phi \wedge x)$.

Proposition 6. *For every model $M = (D, R, E)$, for every state $s \in D$, every finite set of program variables Fun, and every μC-formula ϕ the following equivalences hold:*

- $s \models_M AF(Fun, \phi) \Leftrightarrow \phi$ *is inevitable for Fun in M from s;*
- $s \models_M fair(Fun, \phi) \Leftrightarrow Fun$ *is fair for ϕ in M from s.*

Proof. The first equivalence is trivial and well-know from Computational Tree Logic [2]. To prove the second equivalence, let us pickup an arbitrary infinite sequence of states $s_0, s_1, \cdots \subseteq D$ generated by Fun from s in M such that $s_0 \models_M fair(Fun, \phi)$; according to the first equivalence, the sequence has a state $t_0 \models_M \phi \wedge AF(Fun, fair(Fun, \phi))$, i.e. $t_0 \models_M \phi$ and $t_0 \models_M AF(Fun, fair(Fun, \phi))$; it implies that the sequence has another state t_1 (somewhere after t_0) where $t_1 \models_M \phi \wedge AF(Fun, fair(Fun, \phi))$; due the same argument we can find states t_2, t_3 and so on. ∎

The following proposition is a corollary from Propositions 5 and 6.

Proposition 7. *Let S be a guarded scheme, Fin be a set of propositional variables, M_S be model constructed from S as specified in the Definition 17, and Fun be the set of all program variables that correspond to propositional variables in Fin according to this definition. Then S is total with respect to Fin if and only if $(0, m) \models_{M_S} fair(Fun, \bigvee_{p \in Fin} p)$ for all m such that $(0, m)$ is a state in D_S.*

Definition 20. *Global model checking [2] for a program logic (a variant of μ-Calculus in particular) in a class of models for this logic is an algorithmic problem to compute (to construct) the set $M(\phi)$ for input model M (in this class) and input formula ϕ (of this logic).*

Proposition 8. *Generalized halting problem for guarded non-deterministic Yanov schemata is decidable in quadratic time $O(n_A + n_C)^2$ where n_A and n_C are numbers of assignments and choices in the input scheme.*

Proof. The upper bound $O(|\phi| \times |M|^{alt(\phi)})$ for model checking μC in finite models is well-known [2]; here

- $|\phi|$ is the total number of Boolean connectives and modalities in the input formula,
- $alt(\phi)$ is the maximal number of *alternations* of nesting μ/ν-constructs in the formula,
- $|M|$ is the overall size of the input model (i.e. the total number of states and edges).

Let S be a guarded scheme, Fin be a set of propositional variables, M_S be model constructed from S as specified in the Definition 17. According to Proposition 7, we have to model check formula $fair(Fun, \bigvee_{p \in Fin} p)$ in the finite model M_S. It suffices to remark that $|fair(Fun, \bigvee_{p \in Fin} p)|$ is some fixed constant, $alt(fair(Fun, \bigvee_{p \in Fin} p)) = 1$ and $|M_S| = O(n_A + n_C)^2$. ∎

4 Main Results

4.1 Translation Algorithm

Let us define below a recursive algorithm $F2S$ (*Formulas To Schemata*) to translate normal guarded μS-formulas into guarded non-deterministic Yanov schemata. We would like to use in the definition the following standard control-flow constructs:

- $S'; S''$ for sequential composition of two schemata,
- *if* q *then* S' *else* S'' for deterministic choice in two schemata,
- $S' \cup S''$ for non-deterministic choice in two schemata;

all these control-flow constructs are easy to define formally in terms of non-deterministic Yanov schemata. Let us also use some macro-notations:

- *stop* for all final labels of a scheme under consideration (i.e. labels that occur in the scheme but don't mark any operator),
- *loop* for a fixed scheme that always loops (e.g., $\{0 : if\ p\ then\ \{0\}\ else\ \{0\}\}$).

    Algorithm $F2S$:

- For any propositional variable
    - $F2S(p) = \{0 : if\ p\ then\ stop\ else\ loop\}$;
    - $F2S(\neg p) = \{0 : if\ p\ then\ loop\ else\ stop\}$;
- $F2S(\phi \wedge \psi) = if\ q\ then\ F2S(\phi)\ else\ F2S(\psi)$, where q is a new (fresh) propositional variable;
- $F2S(\phi \vee \psi) = F2S(\phi) \cup F2S(psi)$;
- for any program variable
$$F2S([a]\phi) = F2S(\langle a \rangle \phi) = \{0 : a\ goto\ stop\}; F2S(\phi).$$
- $F2S(\mu x.\phi)$ results from $F2S(\phi)$ by replacement instead of every choice operator (with condition x) "*if* x *then* $stop$ *else* $loop$" the unconditional operator "*goto* $\{0\}$".
- $F2S(\nu x.\phi)$ results from $F2S(\phi)$ by replacement instead of every choice operator (with condition x) "*if* x *then* $stop$ *else* $loop$" the choice operator "*if* x *then* $\{0\}$ *else* $stop$".

Proposition 9. *Algorithm $F2S$ translates normal guarded μC-formulas into guarded non-deterministic Yanov schemata in linear time.*

Definition 21. *Let $M = (D, R, E)$ and $M' = (D', R', E')$ be two models with same domain (i.e. $D = D'$) and interpretation of program variables (i.e. $R = R'$), let Fin be a set of propositional variables; we say that M' is a modification of M on Fin, if valuations E and E' differs on variable in Fin only (i.e. $E(p) = E'(p)$ for every $p \notin Fin$).*

Proposition 10. *Let M be any Herbrand model, ϕ be a normal guarded formula of the strict μ-Calculus, Gfp (Greatest fix points) be the set of all propositional variables that are bound by ν in this formula, and Cnj be the set of all new propositional variables q that are introduce for conjunctions in an exercise of $F2S(\phi)$. Then μS-formula ϕ is valid in M if and only if the non-deterministic Yanov scheme $F2S(\phi)$ halts in every M' that fits Gfp and is a modification of M on $Gfp \cup Cnj$.*

Proof. Induction on formula structure. Induction base is the case when a formula is a literal (i.e. a propositional variable or its negation); in this case proof is trivial due to explicit definition of $F2S$ in these cases.

Induction step in case of disjunction $\vee$ and modalities $[\ldots]$ or $\langle \ldots \rangle$ is straightforward due to simplicity of definition of $F2S$ in these cases.

Let us consider conjunction. Since $F2S(\phi \wedge \psi) = if\ q\ then\ F2S(\phi)\ else\ F2S(\psi)$, where q is a variable in Cnj, and since q has instances neither in $F2S(\phi)$ nor in $F2S(\psi)$, then we can interpret this variable arbitrary and (by this) test both $F2S(\phi)$ and $F2S(\psi)$ for halting.

Let us discuss an idea that is behind the induction step in case of $\mu p.\phi$. According to Corollary 3, $M(\mu x.\phi) = \bigcup_{n \geq 0} M(\phi^n_{false/x})$. Recall that $F2S(\mu x.\phi)$ results from $F2S(\phi)$ by substitution of unconditional "goto $\{0\}$" instead of "*if x then stop else loop*", i.e. $F2S(\mu x.\phi)$ is equivalent to $F2S(\bigvee_{n \geq 0} \phi^n_{false/x})$.

Finally, an idea behind induction step for $\nu p.\phi$ follows. Again, according to Corollary 3, $M(\nu x.\phi) = \bigcap_{n \geq 0} M(\phi^n_{true/x})$. Since $F2S(\nu x.\phi)$ results from $F2S(\phi)$ by substitution of "*if x then $\{0\}$ else stop*" instead of "*if x then stop else loop*" (where $x \in Gfp$) then $F2S(\nu x.\phi)$ is equivalent to $F2S(\bigwedge_{n \geq 0} \phi^n_{true/x})$ because x can be true only finite number of times. ∎

4.2   Results and Conclusion

Main Theorem follows from Propositions 1–4 and 8–10.

Theorem 1. *The propositional μ-Calculus is decidable with exponential upper bound (on formula size).*

Since it is known that μ-Calculus is $EXP - Time$ complete [3], Propositions 1–4 and 8–10 imply the following corollary.

Corollary 4. *Any algorithm that transforms μ-Calculus formulas into equivalent guarded formulas, must be exponential in fix-point nesting depth of the input formula.*

Concluding Remarks. To the best of our knowledge, the lower bound from Corollary 4 is a very new result [1]. Study of implications from this result (for parity games [15] for instance) may be a topic for further research. Another possible research topic may be complete axiomatization of the propositional μ-Calculus in a manner similar to the complete axiomatization for the Propositional

Linear Temporal Logic in [12]. Research on a new approach to axiomatization may be interesting since completeness proof in [14,15] uses reduction to guarded fragment.

References

1. Bruse, F., Friedmann, O., Lange, M.: Guarded Transformation for the Modal mu-Calculus (2013). arXiv:1305.0648v2, http://arxiv.org/abs/1305.0648
2. Clarke, E.M., Grumberg, O., Peled, D.: Moedel Checking. MIT Press, Cambridge (1999)
3. Emerson, E.A., Jutla, C.J.: The complexity of tree automata and logics of programs. SIAM J. Comput. **29**, 132–158 (1999)
4. Ershov, A.P.: Origins of Programming: Discourses on Methodology. Springer, New York (1990)
5. Harel, D., Kozen, D., Tiuryn, J.: Dynamic Logic. MIT Press, Cambridge (2000)
6. Ianov, Y.I.: The logical schemes of algorithms. In: Lyapunov, A.A., Goodman, R., Booth, A.D. (eds.) Problems of Cybernetics, vol. I, pp. 82–140. Pergamon Press, New York (1960)
7. Kotov, V.E., Sabelfeld, V.K.: Theory of Program Schemata. Nauka Publeshers, Moscow (1991). (In Russian)
8. Kozen, D.: Results on the propositional Mu-calculus. Theoret. Comput. Sci. **27**, 333–354 (1983)
9. Nepomniaschy, V.A., Shilov, N.V.: Non-deterministic program schemata, their relation to dynamic logic. In: International Conference on Mathematical Logic and its Applications, pp. 137–147. Plenum Press, New York (1987). (Revised version: Cybernetics **24**(3), 285–293 (1988)
10. Podlovchenko, R.I.: A.A. Lyapunov and A.P. Ershov in the theory of program schemes and the development of its logic concepts. In: Bjørner, D., Broy, M., Zamulin, A.V. (eds.) PSI 2001. LNCS, vol. 2244, pp. 8–23. Springer, Heidelberg (2001)
11. Shilov, N.V.: Program schemata vs. automata for decidability of program logics. Theoret. Comput. Sci. **175**, 15–27 (1997)
12. Shilov, N.V.: An approach to design of automata-based axiomatization for propositional program, temporal logics (by example of linear temporal logic). In: Logic, Computation, Hierarchies. Ontos Mathematical Logic, vol. 4, pp. 297–324. Ontos-Verlag/De Gruyter, Germany (2014)
13. Tarski, A.: A lattice-theoretical fixpoint theorem and its applications. Pac. J. Math. **5**, 285–309 (1955)
14. Walukiewicz, I.: A complete deductive system for the mu-calculus. In: Proceedings of IEEE LICS 1993, pp. 136–147 (1993)
15. Walukiewicz, I.: Completeness of Kozen's axiomatisation of the propositional Mu-calculus. Inf. Comput. **157**, 142–182 (2000)

Automated Two-Phase Composition
of Timed Web Services

Maciej Szreter[(✉)]

Institute of Computer Science, Polish Academy of Sciences, Warsaw, Poland
mszreter@ipipan.waw.pl

Abstract. The paper extends PlanICS web services composition system by augumenting services with an explicit notion of time, and evolution of variables as a function of time. Its distinguishing feature is focusing not only on time constraints in services, but covering the whole service definition and composition process: providing an ontology with a strong type system on which definitions of typed stateless timed services are based, timed user queries, offers from service providers corresponding to instances of service types, and searching for services and offers matching the user query. A novel idea is that services express their timed behavior by producing timed automata as a part of their output. Abstract and concrete planning is described, dealing respectively with service types (including time dependencies), and with offer sets corresponding to these types.

1 Introduction

Composition of web services is an area of intensive research being performed in several directions. These are, among others, improving the scalability in order to deal with very big numbers of services, extending the semantic part of the composition process, adding new features to service definitions, which enable the finer and more precise composition of services. Introducing explicit time to services is yet another active research direction, however most papers focus on searching for satisfying time constraints by services put together in an ad-hoc manner, rather than published, discovered and composed in a way analogous to untimed services. The key aim of this paper is to tackle this problem. The distinguishing features of our approach are:

- the complete planning process, starting from services registration in an ontology, with abstract descriptions being a basis for the search of a plan. Our method performs the two-phase (abstract and concrete) planning, what is the distinguishing feature of PlanICS web service composition system [1],
- strong type system, extending the PlanICS way of modeling, and making it easier to separate timed and untimed aspects of a service activity. This significantly simplifies modeling, as a service provider can apply the time automata

This work has been supported by the National Science Centre under the grant No. 2011/01/B/ST6/01477.

M. Mazzara and A. Voronkov (Eds.): PSI 2015, LNCS 9609, pp. 260–275, 2016.
DOI: 10.1007/978-3-319-41579-6_20

(which is the formalism we use) only for representing the timed part of the service behavior,

- instantaneous services execution model based on the IOPR rule (Inputs, Outputs, Preconditions and Results). Services produce time automata describing how they change *dynamic variables* they control, depending possibly on time and values of other variables,
- introducing offers (i.e., instances of service types), what means that several providers would send their offers for each service type, and either the best (or just acceptable) combination of offers is then chosen, consistent with the abstract plan dealing with service types. Offers provide concrete values for abstract typed variables defined in the respective service type. Services instead of modifying all their (possibly complex) type definitions in the ontology each time they are queried, may prepare their customized offers.

Taking out a loan in a bank is an example of a scenario modeled by time automata produced by services. When a loan is approved, a customer can perform (and complete) other related activities (for example, buying a house) while paying off the loan can take years to come. As the running example shows, our approach allows for modeling services inspired by real-world scenarios: we are able to easily model several aspects from the area of finance: loans, delayed payments, savings accounts, buying and selling bonds, discounts for bigger buyers, etc. It also allows for modeling durations of events, what is the focus of the most papers about composing timed services, as well as untimed relations between variables. The proposed approach is integrated into Planics web service composition system.

There exist many web service composition tools. Planics is similar to [2] in the general idea of semantic description of services, but is focused more on efficiency issues. Below we restrict to work for timed web services. To the best of our knowledge, no solution exists covering the complete process starting from the level of an ontology and automated composition. [3] deals with timing aspects of BPEL composition, adding additional mechanisms for specifying durations and timeouts. A translation to NuSMV verifier is provided. It uses a low level modeling lacking of a semantic description. The composition is simple, and agents have their partners hard-coded into automata modeling them. [4] models timed services at the level of BPEL. Services are translated to a formalism based on timed automata. Care is taken to precisely define semantics of timed activities, but the paper focuses on automated testing and not on composition. [5] models services in WS-BPEL, and translates the problem to a planning domain. Services are stateful and the effort is directed on improving the communication efficiency. A complex resolution algorithm based on binary decision graphs is developed. [6] models web services as timed automata, with mediators fixing compositions where timed constraints cannot be satisfied. The service composition problem is translated to Uppaal verification. It is not described how services are selected for composition. [7] is yet another paper modeling timed web services as timed automata and translating the composition problem to a model checking problem. The automata modeling services are customized by hand for the composition

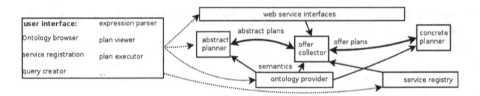

Fig. 1. PlanICS overview. The rectangles stand for the software components of the system. The bold arrows correspond to computation of a plan, the thin arrows model the planner infrastructure, the dotted arrows represent the user interaction.

scenario, for example by using ad-hoc variable instances without proper typing. [8] focuses on the minimal and maximal durations of executing services, without modeling time into their internal structure. [9] describes how an interface is added to web services in order to define a translation to Uppaal automata and verify some time properties. [10] is maybe the most advanced solution of service composition using timed automata (as well as Constraint Logic Programming). It uses Orc orchestration language which is related to WS-BPEL. Compared to our approach, it is single-stage and focuses mostly on fixing timing issues in services rather then orchestrating services satisfying a query.

The paper is organized as follows. Section 2 describes the internals of PlanICS. Section 3 introduces timed automata and merges them into PlanICS web services, rending them timed in this way. Section 4 extends abstract and concrete planning to these timed services. Section 5 provides experimental evaluation for the concrete planning, and Sect. 6 concludes the paper.

2   Introduction to PlanICS

PlanICS is a system implementing an original approach which solves the service composition problem in some clearly separated stages. Figure 1 shows the system overview. The formalism behind PlanICS is defined very precisely. We describe it in a general way, formalizing only the parts relevant to the described work, and pointing at [11] for the complete references.

2.1   Basic Syntax and Semantics of Objects and Services

The basic building blocks of PlanICS are objects and (web) services. The services transform the objects, and the objects are composed from other objects, called attributes. We denote by $\mathbb{I}$ the set of all identifiers, and by $\mathbb{A}$ the set of all the attributes, with $\mathbb{A} \subset \mathbb{I}$.

An *object type* is a pair $(t, Attr)$, where $t \in \mathbb{I}$ and $Attr \subseteq \mathbb{A}$. $\mathbb{P}$ is the set of all object types. The object types are composed of typed attributes with domains. In this paper we restrict our quantitative analysis to the domain of real numbers. Note that boolean values and character strings can be reduced to this domain. An *object* is a pair $(id, type)$, where $id \in \mathbb{I}$ and $type \in \mathbb{P}$. We denote by $id : type$ assigning *type* to the object *id*.

The services process objects, and have attribute lists *in, out, inout* referring to the objects read by a service (this does not mean being discarded), produced by it, or both read and produced, respectively. Moreover, abstract formulas, in disjunctive normal form without negations, are defined over the attributes, built from predicates *isNull(a)* and *isSet(a)* stating that attribute *a* is not set or set. An *user query* expresses what is the input and what the output of the composition, and is technically modeled similarly to a service. For a service *s* or a user query *q*, a *specification* is $spec_x = (in_x, out_x, inout_x, pre_x, post_x)$, where $x \in \{s, q\}$, with meaning of attribute lists described above, and pre_x and $post_x$ are abstract formulas over attributes from lists.

Types of services and objects (called *classes*) are organized in an inheritance tree rooted in the abstract type *Thing* (abstract types cannot be instantiated). All the services and objects are derived from the abstract types *Service* and *Artifact*, respectively. The types are stored in an *ontology*. We define a transitive, irreflexive, and antisymmetric *inheritance* relation $Ext \subseteq \mathbb{P} \times \mathbb{P}$, such that $((t_1, A_1), (t_2, A_2)) \in Ext$ iff $t_1 \neq t_2$ and $A_1 \subseteq A_2$. That is, a subtype contains all the attributes of a base type and optionally introduces more attributes.

Having defined the syntax, we now move towards the Planics semantics. For an abstract formula α, a *valuation of object attributes* is a partial function assigning, for every object, to every its attribute *a* a value *true* or *false* if *isSet(a)* or *isNull(a)* predicates occur in a clause in α, respectively, or is undefined otherwise. By an *object state* we mean an object with the assigned valuation. A *world* is a pair consisting of a set of objects, and a valuation function for them.

From the semantic point of view, the service types and user queries are defined by their *interpretations*, which are pairs of worlds. In the first one, called *input world set* for services and *initial world set* for a query, there are objects belonging to in_x or $inout_x$, and the valuation is the family of the valuation functions over pre_x. In the second one, called *output world set* for services and *expected world set* for a query, there are objects from sets $inout_x$ or out_x, and the valuation is the family of the valuation functions over $post_x$.

2.2   Abstract Planning

An interpretation of a specification, as defined above, determines the pair of worlds transformed by a service or a query. In planning, we want to combine several services, modifying (parts of) consecutive worlds so that the query would be satisfied. We now present how this is done in Planics.

Two valuations for two objects are *compatible* if the types of both objects are the same, or one of them is a subtype of the another one, and the valuations agree for every attribute. Similar worlds are identified by the notion of *world compatibility*: worlds *w* and *w'* are compatible if they contain the same number of objects, and for every object state from *w* there exists a compatible object state from *w'*, and vice versa. Worlds with different numbers of objects are compatible if there exist a sub-world in the bigger world compatible with the smaller one.

The key idea of the abstract planning is transforming worlds by services in order to satisfy the user query. A *context function* describes a mapping of objects from the initial, expected and intermediate worlds into the attributes of user query and services. Then, for two worlds $w, w' \in W$, referred to as *world before* and *world after*, respectively, a *world transformation* for service s transforms w into w' in a context ctx, if these worlds can be mapped into the attribute list of s, and the additional requirements are met. Let IN be a ctx context image of the set in_s. The world before contains a sub-world built over IN, compatible with a sub-world of some input world of the service s, built over the objects from in_s. The state of the objects from IN is consistent with pre_s. The objects from IN and those not involved in the transformation do not change their states in the world after. The conditions for images of *inout* and *out* sets are given in [11].

A *transformation sequence seq* is a sequence of worlds transformed by services in a context. For a user query $q = (W_{init}^q, W_{exp}^q)$, seq is a *user query solution* of q if there exists a world $w \in W_{init}^q$ and some world w' such that seq leads from w to w', and w' is compatible with some $w_{exp}^q \in W_{exp}^q$.

Finally, we want to abstract away the ordering of services where it is irrelevant. We introduce an equivalence relation of solutions: two solutions are equivalent if the number of occurrence for every service type are equal in them. For a sequence *seq*, a *context abstract plan (CAP)* is the set of all the solutions equivalent to *seq* w.r.t. the relation defined above.

2.3   Collecting Offers and Concrete Planning

In the second planning stage CAP is used by an *offer collector* (OC) [12], i.e., a tool which queries real-world services in cooperation with the service registry (see Fig. 1), which keeps an evidence of real-world web services, registered accordingly to the service type system from the ontology. During the registration the service provider defines a mapping between input/output data of the real-world service and the object attributes processed by the declared service type.

OC communicates with the real-world services of the types present in a CAP, sending the constraints on the data, which can potentially be fed to the service in an inquiry, and on the data expected to be received in an offer in order to keep on building a potential plan. The constraints are constructed from the *pre* and *post* conditions. Usually, each service type represents a set of real-world services. Moreover, querying a single service can produce several offers. Thus, we define an offer set as a result of the offer collecting planning stage.

Definition 1 (Offer, offer set). *Assume that the n-th instance of a service type from a CAP processes some number of objects having in total m attributes. A single offer collected by OC is a vector $P = [v_1, v_2, \ldots, v_m]$, where v_j is a value of a single object attribute from the n-th intermediate world of the CAP.*

An offer set O^n is a $k \times m$ matrix, where each row corresponds to a single offer and k is the number of offers in the set. The element $o_{i,j}^n$ is the j-th value of the i-th offer collected from the n-th service type instance from the CAP.

The detailed translation of a PLANICS query to a set of constraints is beyond the scope of this paper, because it would require describing the whole inference process inside OC. More details on constraints can be found in [12].

Finally, the *concrete planning* consists in finding an assignment of offers to the CAP (a *concrete plan*), possibly satisfying some optimality criteria.

3   Dynamic (timed) Services

In this section the definition of a PLANICS service, introduced above, will be extended to the timed case. Let $\mathbb{N}$ denote the set of natural numbers (including 0), $\mathbb{Z}$ - the set of integers, and $\mathbb{R}$ ($\mathbb{R}_+$) - the set of (non-negative) reals.

Example 1. Let us now sketch the running example. The query can be described as follows: a user will have some money available, and wants to get apple juice. The amount of money available will change over time, and also there are requirements concerning the delivery schedules and quantities. In particular, it is acceptable either to deliver a smaller amount earlier, or a bigger amount later.

3.1   Ontology - Dynamic Variables as Object Attributes

We introduce *dynamic* variables as object attributes to the ontology, possibly modeling some physical quantities. Let denote by $\mathbb{A}_d \subseteq \mathbb{A}$ the set of dynamic variables. One of them is time, flowing globally at a constant rate. We set the domain of dynamic variables to the real numbers. If an object o has only one dynamic attribute a and the object identifier is clear from the context, we refer to this attribute by o instead of $o.a$.

Example 2. An example ontology contains the following object types (the dynamic attributes are shown in bold):

- $w : Ware$ - a ware, something that can be sold or bought. It has the attributes *owner : Owner, location : Location,*
- $o : Owner$ - an owner of a ware,
- $m : Money$ - money, inherits from $Ware$, with the dynamic attribute q: **quantity**, the inherited attributes $o : Owner$ and $l : Location$, and the attribute $c : Currency$,
- $a : Apples$, inherits from $Ware$, with the dynamic attribute q: **quantity** and the inherited attributes $o : Owner$ and $l : Location$,
- $j : Juice$, inherits from $Ware$, with the dynamic attribute q: **quantity** and the attributes $o : Owner$ and $l : Location$.

3.2   Timed Automata, Dynamic Automata

In our approach, a dynamic variable can be watched or modified by a service over a period of time. Services refer to dynamic variables by producing *dynamic automata*, which are timed automata with discrete data [13], defined over the dynamic variables. Below we provide the precise definitions.

Let IV be a finite set of the integer variables. The set of *arithmetic expressions* over IV, denoted $Expr(IV)$, is defined by the following grammar: $expr = c \mid v \mid v \otimes c \mid c \otimes v \mid v \otimes v$, where $c \in \mathbb{Z}$, $v \in IV$ and $\otimes \in \{+, -, *\}$.

The set of *boolean expressions* over IV are defined as follows: $\beta = $ **true** $\mid expr \sim expr \mid \beta \sim \beta \mid \neg\beta$ where $expr \in Expr(IV)$ and $\sim \in \{=, \neq, <, \leq, \geq, >\}$. The set of *instructions* over IV, denoted by $Ins(IV)$, is given by $\alpha := \epsilon \mid v := expr \mid \alpha\alpha$, with $v \in IV$, $expr \in Expr(IV)$, and ϵ denotes an empty sequence. Thus, an instruction over IV is either an *atomic instruction* over IV $v := expr$, or a (possibly empty) sequence of atomic instructions. Moreover, by $Ins^L(IV)$ we denote the set consisting of all these $\alpha \in Ins(IV)$, in which any $v \in IV$ appears on the left-hand side of every assignment at most once. Let by $IV^L \subseteq IV$ denote the variables of A occurring in left-hand side of at least one assignment, and by IV^R the set of the variables appearing only on the right-hand sides of assignments. A *variable valuation* is a total function $\mathbf{v} : IV \to \mathbb{Z}$. We extend it to expressions of $BoE(IV)$ in an usual way.

Let $\mathcal{X}$ be a set of real-valued variables, called *clocks*. The set of *clock constraints* over $\mathcal{X}$, denoted $\mathcal{C}(\mathcal{X})$, is defined by the grammar $cc := true \mid x_i \sim c \mid x_i - x_j \sim c \mid cc \wedge cc$, where $x_i, x_j \in \mathcal{X}$, $c \in \mathbb{N}$, and $\sim \in \{\leq, <, =, >, \geq\}$. Let $\mathcal{X}^+$ denote the set $\mathcal{X} \cup x_0$, where $x_0 \notin \mathcal{X}$ is a fictitious clock representing the constant 0. An assignment over $\mathcal{X}$ is a function $a : \mathcal{X} \to \mathcal{X}^+$. $Asg(\mathcal{X})$ denotes the set of all the assignments over $\mathcal{X}$.

A *clock valuation* is a total function $\mathbf{c} : \mathcal{X} \to \mathbb{R}_+$. Given a valuation $\mathbf{c}$ and $d \in \mathbb{R}_+$, by $\mathbf{c} + d$ we denote a clock valuation $\mathbf{c}'$ such that $\mathbf{c}' = \mathbf{c}(x) + d$ for every clock $x \in \mathcal{X}$. Moreover, for some $\mathbf{c}$ and an assignment $a \in Asg(\mathcal{X})$, by $\mathbf{c}(a)$ we denote a clock valuation $\mathbf{c}'$ such that for all $x \in \mathcal{X}$ it holds $\mathbf{c}'(x) = \mathbf{c}(a(x))$ if $a(x) \in \mathcal{X}$, and $\mathbf{c}'(x)$ otherwise.

The satisfaction relations $\models$ for a clock constraint $cc \in \mathcal{C}(\mathcal{X})$ and $\mathbf{c}$, and for a Boolean expression $\beta \in BoE(IV)$ and $\mathbf{v}$, are defined in the usual way [13].

Definition 2 (Timed automaton). *A timed automaton is a tuple* $(L, l_0, IV, \mathcal{X}, Act, \mathcal{E}, I)$, *where L is a set of locations, $l_0 \in L$ is an initial location, IV is a set of integer variables, $\mathcal{X}$ is a set of clocks, Act is a set of actions, $\mathcal{E} \subseteq L \times Act \times BoE(IV) \times \mathcal{C}(\mathcal{X}) \times 2^{\mathcal{X}} \times L$ is a set of edges between locations with an action, a guard, and a set of clocks to be reset, $I : L \to \mathcal{C}(\mathcal{X})$ assigns invariants to locations.*

Every element $e = (l, a, \beta, cc, \alpha, aa, l') \in \mathcal{E}$ represents a transition from the location l to l', labeled with a, β and cc are the enabling conditions for e w.r.t. variables and clocks, respectively, α is the instruction to be performed, and aa are clocks to be reset.

Because of the space restrictions we skip the definitions of the semantics of timed automata and their parallel composition, adopting the standard approach. The semantics defines the behaviour of a timed automaton as a transition system, with two types of transitions, corresponding either to time flow or executing an action, observing the guards and possibly resetting some clocks. Invariants need to be satisfied for every run. A parallel composition of automata is an automaton, executing either timed transitions in all the components, or synchronizing over shared action labels. Standard definitions of automata runs, labeling locations with variables, and reachability of states satisfying boolean formulas over these variables are also assumed.

Given a subset $J = \{j_1, \ldots, j_m\}$ of $\{1, \ldots, n\}$, and the instructions $\{\alpha_j \in Ins^L(IV) \mid j \in J\}$, define $\bigsqcup_{j \in J} \alpha_j$ as a sequence $\alpha_{j_{k_1}}, \ldots, \alpha_{j_{k_m}}$ with $j_{k_1} \in J$ and $j_{k_i} < j_{k_{i+1}}$ for each $i = 1, \ldots, m-1$. Define by $Act(a) = \{1 \le i \le n \mid a \in Act_i\}$ the set of indices corresponding to automata containing the action a.

It is also necessary to fix the ordering of instructions. The conditions specified in [13] hold for all the automata presented in the paper. We will refer by automata to the networks of automata, possibly consisting of a single automaton.

Given a set of dynamic variables $\mathbb{A}_d \subseteq \mathbb{A}$, a *dynamic automaton A* is a timed automaton where $IV(A) \subseteq \mathbb{A}_d$.

Because we want the dynamic automata to be variables in the attribute lists of web services, a type needs to be assigned to each of them. For an automaton A, we define the type signature $\mathcal{T} = [type(d) \mid d \in \mathbb{A}_d \cap IV(A)]$, where $type(d)$ is a type of a dynamic variable, with a fixed ordering, and denote the resulting type by $\mathcal{A}^{\mathcal{T}}$. For two type signatures $\mathcal{T}_1$ and $\mathcal{T}_2$, $\mathcal{T}_1$ is a supertype of $\mathcal{T}_2$ if it contains at most the variables occurring in $\mathcal{T}_2$. For simplicity, the information which variables are constant is not added to type signatures, so this issue needs to be taken into account at the run-time level. To save space, we refer to the types by first letters of their names, so $\mathcal{A}^{M,T}$ is an abbreviation for the type $\mathcal{A}^{Money,Time}$. There are no types with names beginning with the same letter in the paper, so it causes no confusion. For example, $\mathcal{A}^{M,T}$ is a supertype of $\mathcal{A}^{J,M,T}$.

3.3 Ontology - Dynamic Services

In addition to plain PlanICS services, not referring to time, we introduce *dynamic services*. Each dynamic service has a set of dynamic variables in its attribute list. It can observe and modify these variables. For non-dynamic attributes, the rules defined for untimed PlanICS apply. The dynamic variables are treated in a different way. All the services, both dynamic and non-dynamic, execute immediately, and the former produce dynamic automata defined over these variables. These automata describe how every service plans to react to the dynamic variables, and possibly change them. All the automata start at a certain point of global time and execute for a finite period, until each of them reaches one of its final locations. The product of automata describes the behavior of all the services participating in the composition. The dynamic automata from the user query are added to the product, determining the initial and final worlds.

A dynamic service extends a PlanICS service and is a basic building block of the timed extension.

Definition 3 (Dynamic service specification). *A dynamic service is a service s which:*

- *has a nonempty set of dynamic variables in its attribute lists,*
- *produces a vector of dynamic automata $V = [A_1, \ldots, A_n]$ in list out (called dynamic service description). Every automaton $A \in V$ has a single initial state, a final state, and two actions $\{start_s, end_s\} \subseteq Act(A)$ such that only transitions labeled with $start_s$ leave from the initial state, and only transitions labeled with end_s lead to the final state,*
- *for every automaton A, a predicate $isSet(a)$ is added to each clause of the post formula for every instance of a dynamic variable a occurring in $type(A)$.*

The types of dynamic automata do not distinguish between the dynamic variables modified by an automaton, and those being only read. This is to simplify the type system and avoid introducing additional rules. Instead, the information about the variables modified by a service is determined by its attribute lists in the following way: for variable v referred to by service s, and for every automaton $A \in out_s$ such that $v \in IV(A)$ we have:

- $v \in in_s$ - $v \in IV^R(A) \cap \mathbb{A}_d$ (it is read-only),
- $v \in inout_s \cup out_s$ - $v \in IV(A) \cap \mathbb{A}_d$ (it can be read and changed),

We also restrict the write operations performed over dynamic variables to adding or subtracting some values. Dynamic automata for different services do not communicate by ways other than by the dynamic variables specified explicitly in the attribute lists.

We assume that there is always present in the ontology a read-only single-instance object of class $Time$, with a single clock t measuring global time, accessible implicitly to all the dynamic services.

Example 3. Below are shown the type specifications of the services in our ontology: (empty attribute lists are skipped)

- $BankLoan : out = \{m : Money, A_{BL} : \mathcal{A}^{M,T}\}$
- $BankDeposit\ inout = \{m : Money\}, out = \{A_{BD} : \mathcal{A}^{M,T}\}$
  Note that $BankDeposit$ assumes that there are some money in its input world. It will not be applied to worlds where there are no money at all.
- $SellApples\ inout = \{m : Money\}, out = \{a : Apples, A_{SA} : \mathcal{A}^{A,M,T}\}$
- $SellJuice\ inout = \{m : Money\}, out = \{j : Juice, A_{SJ} : \mathcal{A}^{J,M,T}\}$
- $ProduceJuice\ inout = \{m : Money, a : Apples\}, out = \{j : Juice, A_{PJ} : \mathcal{A}^{A,J,M,T}\}$. Placing $Apples$ in the $inout$ list shows at the type level that the service can change the quantity of apples. Should this variable occur in in, the value could be only read.

The information about the types of produced dynamic automata should be as detailed as possible, in order to facilitate planning. For example, producing automata of types $\mathcal{A}^{J,T}$ and $\mathcal{A}^{M,T}$ is not equivalent to generating $\mathcal{A}^{J,M,T}$, as the latter asserts that dynamic variables of types $Money$ and $Juice$ directly depend on each other.

3.4 Dynamic User Query

A *dynamic user query* is essentially a timed service: dynamic variables can occur in its attribute lists, and dynamic automata in the list *out*. These automata define which values of dynamic variables are expected in the initial and final world, and possibly also in the intermediate worlds. As all the dynamic automata start their execution at the same time instance, the initial locations with possible invariants determine the initial world for the plan. We require that only the variables from the lists *in* and *inout* can be used in this scheme. Locations labeled with *goal* determine the expected world. Let by A_q denote the network of automata composed of all the automata occurring in the user query.

Example 4. The specification of the user query is: $inout = \{m : Money\}$, $out = \{j : Juice, A_j : \mathcal{A}^{J,M,T}, A_m : \mathcal{A}^{M,T}\}$, $pre : isSet(m) \wedge m.Owner = $ 'myName', $post : isSet(j) \wedge isSet(m) \wedge j.Location = $ 'myCity' $\wedge j.Owner = $ 'myName'.

The argument lists declare the qualitative information: money must be "real" (i.e. instantiated) in the initial and final world, and juice in the final world. The lists and the dynamic automata (Fig. 2, left) add some quantitative information, the former about setting the new owner and location, and the latter about expected values of the dynamic variables. In particular, $A_m : \mathcal{A}^{M,T}$ declares that the amount of money available grows in the consecutive periods, what is modeled by the invariants and guards constraining money and time, respectively. $A_j : \mathcal{A}^{J,M,T}$ adds no requirements over the initial state, but expresses that the composition will be successful if either more than 80 units or 120 units are be provided in 60 or 90 days, respectively.

3.5 Dynamic Offers

Dynamic offers are PlanICS offers produced by dynamic services. In addition to non-dynamic attributes, in their attribute lists there are variables of dynamic automata types:

Definition 4 (Dynamic Offer). *Assume that the n-th instance of a service from a CAP processes some number of objects, having in total m attributes, and also m^d dynamic attributes. A single dynamic offer collected by OC is a vector $P = [v_1, \ldots, v_m, A_1, \ldots, A_{m^d}]$, where v_j is a value of a single object attribute and A_j is a value of a dynamic automaton attribute from the n-th intermediate world of the CAP.*

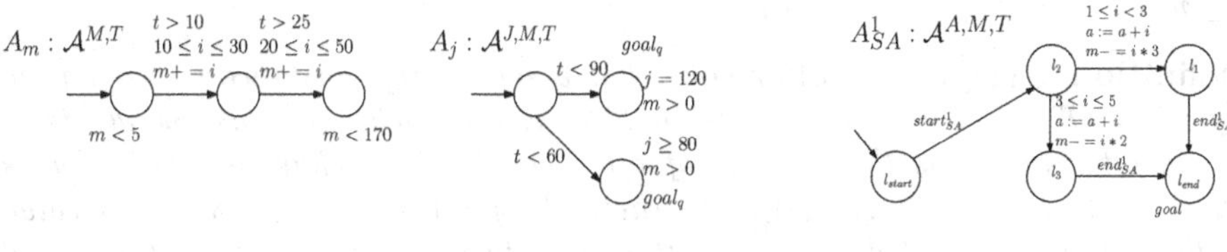

Fig. 2. Automata for the user query (left), an offer for *SellApples* service (right).

Example 5. A (simple) offer definition for type *SellApples* is shown in Fig. 2, right. The amount of apples to be sold is modeled by a variable i, and there are two prices depending on i. There is no reference to time.

4   Planning in Dynamic Services and Offers

In this section it will be shown how Planics planning works for dynamic services.

4.1   Abstract Planning

Given the requirements expressed in the user query and the service specifications in the ontology, the Planics abstract planner either finds the abstract plan(s), or states that none exists. Introducing the dynamic extensions does not require modifying the abstract planner, because at this stage, for an attribute of any type, it is relevant only whether its value is set or not. Dynamic automata appear in the attribute lists, but the abstract planner does not analyze their internal structure, and only deals with their types.

Example 6. The result of the abstract planning, as described in [11], is a feasible plan (Fig. 3). Note that although the abstract plans have been defined as sequences of service types, we present them as graphs corresponding to ordering of services. We also show the context objects for dynamic variables, for clarity named accordingly with service attributes. CAP_1 is a simple one: buy apple juice, invest some money as a bank deposit, to (hopefully) make the acquisition feasible.

4.2   Dynamic Concrete Planning Problem

An input is an abstract plan CAP to be concretized, either selected automatically or chosen by the user. The concrete planning described in Sect. 2 needs to be extended. Now, offers assign not only real values to the non-dynamic variables, but also concrete instances of the dynamic automata to the attributes with dynamic automata types. Intuitively, a concrete plan is satisfied if the non-dynamic variables satisfy all the respective constraints, and the goal locations of the user query automata are reachable in their product with automata from a sequence of dynamic offers, matching the types of the services from CAP.

The above description is formalized by the following definitions. For CAP, let $DS(CAP)$ denote a set of dynamic service indices, i.e. $DS(CAP) = \{i \mid 1 \leq i \leq n \land i\text{-th service is dynamic}\}$.

Definition 5 (Dynamic offer set). *For a service type instance s, a dynamic offer set O^n is a $k \times (m + m^d)$ matrix, where each row corresponds to a single offer and k is the number of offers in the set. Thus, the j-th row is $P_j = [v^n_{i,1}, \ldots, v^n_{i,m}, A^n_{i,1}, \ldots, A^n_{i,m^d}]$, where $v^n_{i,j}$ for $1 \leq j \leq m$ is the j-th value of the i-th offer collected from the n-th service type instance from the CAP, and A^n_{i,j^d} for $1 \leq j^d \leq m^d$ is a dynamic automaton being a service dynamic attribute.*

Moreover, for every automaton A_{i,j^d}^n representing the service s and indexed with i in CAP, the actions $start_s, end_s$ are renamed to $start_i, end_i$.[1]

Definition 6 (Dynamic concrete planning problem). *Let CAP be an abstract plan to be concretized, and $\mathbb{O} = (O^1, \ldots, O^n)$ the vector of dynamic offer sets collected by OC such that for every $i = 1, \ldots, n$ and $j = 1, \ldots, k_i$, the j-th row of O^i is $P_j^i = [v_{j,1}^i, \ldots, v_{j,m_i}^i A_{j,1}^i, \ldots, A_{j,m_i^d}^i]$. Let $\mathbb{P}$ denote the set of all sequences $(P_{j_1}^1, \ldots, P_{j_i}^i, \ldots, P_{j_n}^n)$, such that $j_i \in \{1, \ldots, k_i\}$ and $i \in \{1, \ldots, n\}$. The Dynamic Concrete Planning Problem (DCPP) is defined as finding $S \in \mathbb{P}$ such that the following conditions hold:*

1. *$\mathbb{C}(S)$ is satisfied, where $\mathbb{C}(S) = \{C_j(S) \mid j = 1, \ldots, c$ for $c \in \mathbb{N}\}$ is a set of constraints over non-dynamic attributes, derived from offer pre- i post-conditions and from optimality criteria (conditions for the untimed case),*
2. *given the network of timed automata:*
   $A_{DCPP} = A_q \| (\prod_{i \in DS(CAP)} \prod_{1 \leq m \leq m_i^d}$ for $P_{j_i}^i \in S(A_{j,m}^i))$, *a state satisfying the property $\varphi_C = (\bigwedge_{i \in DS(CAP)} goal_i \wedge goal_q)$ is reachable in A_{DCPP}.*

We say that S is a solution of DCPP for CAP and $\mathbb{O}$.

For simplicity, we do not require solutions to be optimal, as opposed to the untimed case. Any solution satisfying the criteria is accepted. Note also that the type information, concerning both dynamic and non-dynamic attributes, is used in concrete planning only to ensure that offers match service specifications. For $i \notin DS(CAP)$ there are no dynamic automata, so $m_i^d = 0$.

4.3 Solving DCPP

First we focus on the point 2. from the definition of DCPP given above. We comment on point 1. at the end of this Section.

Checking the reachability of the goal state in A_{DCPP} directly would require testing every combination of offers, rending it clearly ineffective. We thus construct the automata network A_C, containing, for every dynamic service s with index $i \in DS(CAP)$, the automata for all the offers and the control automaton A_i^{ctrl}, enforcing that only automata for a single offer execute completely and all the other remain in their initial states. We show that reachability properties with respect to DCPP for A_{DCPP} and A_C are equivalent. A_i^{ctrl} has locations l_{start}, l_{end}, and l_j, for every $1 \leq j \leq m_i^d$, and we add the transitions from l_{start} to l_j (labeled with $start_s$), and from l_j to l_{end} (labeled with end_s^j). This ensures that only A_i^j, corresponding to the j-th offer of type s executes, by synchronizing with A_i^{ctrl}. All the automata for the remaining offers for this type will not leave their initial locations. Additionally, in every automaton $A_{j,m}^i$, representing the j-th offer for service s, the action labels $start_s$ and end_s are renamed to $start_s^j$ and end_s^j, respectively. The resulting network of automata is:

---

[1] For simplicity, we use type names rather than indices in the example. This is correct because there is only a single service of every type in CAP.

$A_C = \prod_{i \in DS(AP)} (A_i^{ctrl} \| \prod_{1 \leq k \leq k_i} \prod_{1 \leq j \leq m_i^d} A_{k,j}^i) \| A_q$, and the property to be checked is φ_C. If a solution is found, the concrete plan contains the offers for which the dynamic automata reached their final locations.

Lemma 1. *For every vector of offer sets $\mathbb{O}$, we have that $S \in \mathbb{P}(\mathbb{O})$ is a solution of A_{DCPP} iff is a solution of A_C.*

Proof. The runs of both automata networks are different, as A_{DCPP} encodes only a single sequence, while A_C all the sequences of $\mathbb{P}$. Moreover, there are control automata in A_C. However, the construction guarantees, by synchronizing with the control automata, that for every service type only one offer executes completely, and all the remaining offers remain in their initial locations.

Condition 1. From the definition of DCPP corresponds to the non-dynamic case. Because dynamic and non-dynamic variables do not influence each other, a concrete PlanICS planner can be used for selecting offers satisfying 1., and this solution (if it exists) can be then checked for condition 2. This procedure can be repeated iteratively until finding a solution satisfying both conditions, or determining that none exist. It can be conjectured that the latter algorithm will be much less efficient w.r.t the number of offers than the former one. Testing non-dynamic requirements can be also encoded into time automata for simple cases.

5   Experimental Results

This section provides the experimental evaluation of the dynamic concrete planning. We show no results for the abstract phase, because none of the PlanICS abstract planners fully implements the nested types (e.g. objects being parts of other objects) necessary to formalize our type system. One can however expect that plans of the complexity presented in Fig. 3 could be computed in very short times. Abstract solvers were described in many papers and proved to be fast for huge of services and offers. We focus on concrete planning for dynamic services.

We used BMC [13] and Uppaal [14] tools for reachability checking for timed automata. BMC (Bounded Model Checking) translates the problem to checking satisfiability, using an efficient SAT solver for increasing depths of model unwinding. If a satisfiable formula is found, the algorithm stops. Otherwise, it continues until the full model is searched or the solver gives up. Uppaal is an explicit-state tool, what means that locations of stored states are kept in a hash table.

In Table 1 we show the results generated for abstract plan CAP_2, which extends CAP_1 in the following way: money can be deposited in a bank or borrowed from a bank, and juice can be either acquired or produced from apples. Helper services sum instances of dynamic variables: money and juice, which occur in more than none instance. The modeled offers are similar to those shown in Fig. 2 with respect to the conditions and size, but we cannot present all of them because

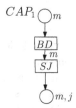

Fig. 3. Example abstract plan. Rectangles correspond to the services, circles to the initial and final worlds. Contexts map the objects from worlds to the service attributes. *BD* denotes *BankDeposit*, *SJ* − *SellJuice*.

Table 1. Experimental results - verification times in seconds. k - number of offers for each service type, FULL - automaton A_o, SIMPLE - the simplified translation, YES/NO - existence of a solution, U - Uppaal, B - BMC, to - timeout ($> 60[s]$)

	FULL				SIMPLE			
	YES		NO		YES		NO	
k	U	B	U	B	U	B	U	B
1	2	5	to	6	5	9	54	5
2	3	16	to	8	9	12	to	5
3	6	17	to	10	3	13	to	6
4	4	19	to	9	5	12	to	7

of the space restrictions. Different constants in guards and invariants determine whether there exists a concrete plan or not.

For some examples, where each offer is represented by a single automaton, the presented translation can be done more efficiently. Instead of defining separate automata for every offer, for every service types the offers can be represented by branches in a single automaton, starting in the initial state and leading to the final state. Only a single instance of clocks is then used. This optimization can be applied to our examples, and it answers how the number of clocks and components influences the efficiency.

The results show that the tools perform differently, depending on the structure of the task. Uppaal finds counterexamples fast if they exist, but checking the whole model takes very long time. The performance strongly depends on the verification options. For example, breadth-first-search is much less efficient than depth-first-search. BMC is sensitive mostly to the depth of the model (i.e., to which depth the model is unwound). Numbers of components, clocks and variables, and the truth of the property, influence the effectiveness to the much smaller degree. The negative results are produced faster.

In general, verification times seem to be long, given that our automata are relatively simple (timeouts are set to 60 s, because service composition require quick answers). The explanation is that our reachability problem is rather untypical from the perspective of the existing tools. The automata modeling service types do not have shared actions, what contributes to the big number of executions with many possible orderings of local actions. Moreover, in the non-simplified model, only a single automaton executes for every service type, while the remaining offers add clocks, variables and components. For realistic scenarios, the tools would need to solve this issue, what could be an interesting research problem related to several possible semantics of timed concurrent systems.

6   Final Remarks and Future Work

The paper presents a new way of modeling timed web services following the IOPR approach, and their composition, providing service ontology, strong typing system and two-phase composition algorithm. The key feature is expressing timing behavior as timed automata produced by services. The proposed solution is compatible with PlanICS web services composition system. Dynamic automata can be accessible by software interfaces or pre-defined for simple scenarios should they appear too sophisticated for the offer providers.

There are several possible directions of the future work. Services could not only produce, but also take dynamic automata as an input, specified as a part of their interface. For example, when applying for a loan, a customer shows the received incomes during the last year. Another extension would be optimization of dynamic variables, making use of features provided by verification tools for timed automata. The novel idea of services representing their behavior by timed automata sent and received as a part of their communication with other services can be extended beyond stateless services presented in this paper. For example, services could run and communicate continuously in a single composition task, instead of executing only once. This would provide the semantics for emerging Internet of Things ad-hoc networks, with the agents modeled by web services.

References

1. Doliwa, D., Horzelski, W., Jarocki, M., Niewiadomski, A., Penczek, W., Polrola, A., Szreter, M., Zbrzezny, A.: PlanICS - a web service composition toolset. Fundam. Inform. **112**, 47–71 (2011)
2. Roman, D., de Bruijn, J., Mocan, A., Lausen, H., Domingue, J., Bussler, C.J., Fensel, D.: WWW: WSMO, WSML, and WSMX in a nutshell. In: Mizoguchi, R., Shi, Z.-Z., Giunchiglia, F. (eds.) ASWC 2006. LNCS, vol. 4185, pp. 516–522. Springer, Heidelberg (2006)
3. Kazhamiakin, R., Pandya, P., Pistore, M.: Timed modelling and analysis inweb service compositions. In: Proceedings of the First International Conference on Availability, Reliability and Security. ARES 2006, pp. 840–846 (2006)
4. Lallali, M., Zaidi, F., Cavalli, A.: Timed modeling of web services composition for automatic testing. In: Proceedings of the of SITIS 2007, pp. 417–426 (2007)
5. Bertoli, P., Pistore, M., Traverso, P.: Automated composition of web services via planning in asynchronous domains. Artif. Intell. **174**, 316–361 (2010)
6. Guermouche, N., Godart, C.: Composition of web services: from qualitative to quantitative timed properties. In: Bouguettaya, A., Sheng, Q.Z., Daniel, F. (eds.) Web Services Foundations, pp. 399–422. Springer, Heidelberg (2014). Rapport LAAS nr 14012
7. Stöhr, D., Glesner, S.: Automated composition of timed services by planning as model checking. In: Proceedings of ZEUS-12, pp. 34–41 (2012)
8. Du, Y., Tan, W., Zhou, M.: Timed compatibility analysis of web service composition: a modular approach based on Petri Nets. IEEE T. Autom. Sci. Eng. **11**, 594–606 (2014)
9. Jingjing, H., Zhu Wei, Z.X., Dongfeng, Z.: Web service composition automation based on timed automata. (Applied Mathematics and Information Sciences)

10. Dong, J., Liu, Y., Sun, J., Zhang, X.: Towards verification of computation orchestration. Formal Aspects of Comput. **26**, 729–759 (2014)
11. Niewiadomski, A., Penczek, W.: SMT-based abstract temporal planning. In: Proceedings of the International Workshop on Petri Nets and Software Engineering, Tunis, Tunisia, June 23–24, 2014, pp. 55–74 (2014)
12. Niewiadomski, A., Skaruz, J., Penczek, W., Szreter, M., Jarocki, M.: SMT versus genetic and OpenOpt algorithms: concrete planning in the PlanICS framework. Fundam. Inform. **135**, 451–466 (2014)
13. Zbrzezny, A., Półrola, A.: SAT-based reachability checking for timed automata with discrete data. Fundam. Inform. **70**(1–2), 579–593 (2007)
14. Behrmann, G., David, A., Larsen, K., Håkansson, J., Pettersson, P., Yi, W., Hendriks, M.: UPPAAL 4.0. In: QEST. IEEE Computer Society 125–126 (2006)

Equivalence of Finite-Valued Symbolic Finite Transducers

Margus Veanes[⊠] and Nikolaj Bjørner

Microsoft Research, Redmond, USA
{margus,nbjorner}@microsoft.com

Abstract. Symbolic Finite Transducers, or SFTs, is a representation of finite transducers that annotates transitions with logical formulas to denote sets of concrete transitions. This representation has practical advantages in applications for web security analysis, where it provides ways to succinctly represent web sanitizers that operate on large alphabets. More importantly, the representation is also conducive for efficient analysis using state-of-the-art theorem proving techniques. Equivalence checking plays a central role in deciding properties of SFTs such as idempotence and commutativity. We show that equivalence of finite-valued SFTs is decidable, i.e., when the number of possible outputs for a given input is bounded by a constant.

1 Introduction

State machines, such as automata and transducers typically use finite alphabets. This is both helpful when formulating the main algorithms and it is realistic when considering applications from text processing. Furthermore, implementations can apply compression algorithms on the transition functions when the alphabet is large. In symbolic analysis of automata, however, there are practical advantages to formulating transitions directly as predicates, and sometimes it is beneficial to use character types possibly even with an infinite domain, e.g., integers. We are interested in transducers that arise from applications such as web sanitizers and string encoders [1], that work over large alphabets like Unicode. The focus here is on the class of SFTs that, for a given input sequence, can output a finite number of possible outputs sequences.

A concrete example is an Html sanitizer that may either use a decimal or a hexadecimal encoding of characters codes, see Fig. 1. Other typical parameters are, whether to use a "safe list" (of characters not to be encoded) or not, or whether to use shorthands such as "&" for encoding "&" and other common characters. Viewed as an SFT, a given input string such as "=" may be encoded as "=" or as "=", corresponding to the value of the second parameter of EncodeHtml, but there is an upper bound on how many different outputs an input sequence may be mapped into (two in this case), i.e., the underlying SFT is *finite-valued*. Our main result is that equivalence of SFTs is decidable in the finite-valued case. This is a nontrivial extension of decidability of SFT

© Springer International Publishing Switzerland 2016
M. Mazzara and A. Voronkov (Eds.): PSI 2015, LNCS 9609, pp. 276–290, 2016.
DOI: 10.1007/978-3-319-41579-6_21

```
 1: static string EncodeHtml(string strInput, bool useDecimal = false)
 2: {
 3:    if (strInput == null) return null;
 4:    if (strInput.Length == 0) return string.Empty;
 5:    StringBuilder b = new StringBuilder();
 6:    foreach (char c in strInput)
 7:      if ((('a' <= c) && (c <= 'z')) || (c == ',') ||
 8:          (('A' <= c) && (c <= 'Z')) || (c == ' ') ||
 9:          (('0' <= c) && (c <= '9')) || (c == '.') ||
10:          (c == '-') || (c == '_') || (c == ';'))
11:        b.Append(c);
12:      else {
13:        b.Append(string.Format(useDecimal ? "&#{0}" : "&#x{0:X}",(int)c));
14:        b.Append(";");
15:      }
16:    return b.ToString();
17: }
```

Fig. 1. Html sanitizer with decimal or hexadecimal formatting.

equivalence in the *single-valued* case [2] and enables analysis scenarios that are, in general, not expressible with single-valued SFTs. SFTs do not have a notion of parameters other than the actual input. Instead, the use of parameters can be abstracted by considering finite-valued transducers.

2 Examples and an Application to Web Sanitizers

We here illustrate the use of SFT analysis on web security analysis. *Cross site scripting (XSS) attacks* are a major concern in web applications, and happen as a result of untrusted data leaking across web sites. Part of data may be interpreted as code (e.g. JavaScript) by a browser, that may end up being executed in the browser of another user. The first line of defense against XSS attacks is the use of *sanitizers* in web servers, that escape or remove potentially harmful strings. Although sanitizers are typically small programs, in the order of tens of lines of code, writing them correctly is difficult [3]. We represent a sanitizer program as a symbolic finite transducer. It uses transduction functions.

*Example 1 (*Transduction Functions). In most modern programming languages, *strings* correspond to character sequences where characters use Unicode (UTF16) encoding. Assume that there is a sort BV_k, for $k \geq 1$, and that $\mathcal{U}^{\mathrm{BV}_k}$ is the domain of k-bit bit-vectors. The elements of $\mathcal{U}^{\mathrm{BV}_k}$ correspond to k-bit binary encodings of nonnegative integers from 0 to $2^k - 1$. A natural representation of Unicode characters for symbolic analysis is as elements in $\mathcal{U}^{\mathrm{BV}_{16}}$. Assume the following operations, where $k = 16$:

$$<: \mathrm{BV}_k \times \mathrm{BV}_k \rightarrow \mathrm{BOOL},$$
$$\pi_m^n : \mathrm{BV}_k \rightarrow \mathrm{BV}_k, \text{ for } 0 \leq m < n \leq k,$$
$$\oplus : \mathrm{BV}_k \times \mathrm{BV}_k \rightarrow \mathrm{BV}_k,$$

where $<$ corresponds to the underlying integer order and matches the lexicographic order over characters; π_m^n projects bits m through $n-1$ and pads the result with $k - n + m$ zeros; $\oplus$ is addition modulo 2^k. Then

$$\mathbf{h}_j(c) \overset{\text{def}}{=} Ite(9 < \pi_{4j}^{4j+4}(c),\ \pi_{4j}^{4j+4}(c) \oplus 55,\ \pi_{4j}^{4j+4}(c) \oplus 48)$$

extracts the j'th nibble (half-byte) of c, $0 \le j \le 3$, and maps it to its hexadecimal representation ('0','1',...,'9','A',...,'F').

The transduction function allows defining a symbolic transducer.

Example 2 (Transducer Guards). The SFT below represents a so-called "string sanitizer", where certain characters c in the input string, not satisfying the condition

$$\varphi(c) : (\text{'a'} \le c \wedge c \le \text{'z'}) \vee (\text{'A'} \le c \wedge c \le \text{'Z'})$$
$$\vee\ (\text{'0'} \le c \wedge c \le \text{'9'})\ \vee c = \text{' '} \vee c = \text{'.'}$$
$$\vee\ c = \text{','} \vee c = \text{'-'} \vee c = \text{'\_'} \vee c = \text{';'}$$

are in the output string replaced by their hexadecimal representation:

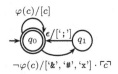

where $\ulcorner c \urcorner$ is the (up-to) four-character encoding of c:

$$\ulcorner c \urcorner \overset{\text{def}}{=} Ite(\mathbf{h}_3(c) \neq \text{'0'}, [\mathbf{h}_3(c), \mathbf{h}_2(c), \mathbf{h}_1(c), \mathbf{h}_0(c)],$$
$$Ite(\mathbf{h}_2(c) \neq \text{'0'}, [\mathbf{h}_2(c), \mathbf{h}_1(c), \mathbf{h}_0(c)],$$
$$Ite(\mathbf{h}_1(c) \neq \text{'0'}, [\mathbf{h}_1(c), \mathbf{h}_0(c)], [\mathbf{h}_0(c)])))$$

with $\mathbf{h}_j$'s as defined in Example 1. It is also straight-forward to rewrite the conditions into four transitions with simple guards and a fixed number of outputs each.

The work in [1] introduces a domain specific language BEK based on SFTs for writing and analyzing sanitizers. The main application of SFTs in the context of BEK is to formally verify key security properties of sanitizers. Two examples of such properties are *idempotence* (to determine if applying the same sanitizer twice matters) and *commutativity* (to determine if the order of applying different sanitizers matters). Since sanitizers are functions that take arbitrary input strings and (other optional parameters) the corresponding SFTs are consequently finite-valued and often *total*, i.e., produce at most some bounded number of output strings for each input string and accept all input strings.

3   Preliminaries

We recall the definition of a finite transducer [4]. Intuitively, a finite transducer is a generalization of a Mealy machine that may omit inputs and outputs and may be nondeterministic. We use ϵ as a special symbol denoting the empty word.

Definition 1. A *finite transducer* (*FT*) A is a six-tuple $(Q, q^0, F, I, O, \delta)$, where Q is a finite set of *states*, $q^0 \in Q$ is the *initial state*, $F \subseteq Q$ is the set of *final states*, I is the *input alphabet*, O is the *output alphabet*, and δ is a finite *transition function* from $Q \times (I \cup \{\epsilon\})$ to $2^{Q \times O^*}$.

There exist several alternative definitions of FTs. By using the *standard form theorem* of FTs [4, Theorem 2.17], Definition 1 is easily seen to be equivalent to those definitions.

We indicate a component of an FT A by using A as a subscript. We often use the technically more convenient view of δ_A as a set of transitions Δ_A and write $p \xrightarrow{a/v}_A q$ for $(q, v) \in \delta_A(p, a)$. We omit the subscript A when it is clear from the context.

$$\Delta_A \stackrel{\text{def}}{=} \Delta_A^\epsilon \cup \Delta_A^{\bar{\epsilon}}$$
$$\Delta_A^{\bar{\epsilon}} \stackrel{\text{def}}{=} \{p \xrightarrow{a/v} q \mid (q, v) \in \delta_A(p, a), a \in I_A\}$$
$$\Delta_A^\epsilon \stackrel{\text{def}}{=} \{p \xrightarrow{\epsilon/v} q \mid (q, v) \in \delta_A(p, \epsilon)\}$$

Given a set V of elements, we write $v = [v_0, \dots, v_{n-1}]$, for $v \in V^*$. For $v, w \in V^*$, $v \cdot w$ denotes the concatenation of v with w. (Both $[]$ and ϵ denote the empty sequence.)

Given $q_i \xrightarrow{u_i/v_i}_A q_{i+1}$ for $i < n$ we write $q_0 \xrightarrow{u/v}_A q_n$ where $u = u_0 \cdot u_1 \cdot \dots \cdot u_{n-1}$ and $v = v_0 \cdot v_1 \cdot \dots \cdot v_{n-1}$. We write also $q \xrightarrow{\epsilon/\epsilon}_A q$.

Definition 2. An FT A induces the *transduction*,

$$T_A(u) \stackrel{\text{def}}{=} \{v \mid \exists q \in F_A (q_A^0 \xrightarrow{u/v} q)\}.$$

Two FTs A and B are *equivalent* if $T_A = T_B$.

We define $\mathbf{d}(A)$ as the underlying nondeterministic finite automaton with epsilon moves (ϵNFA) that is obtained from the FT A by eliminating outputs on all transitions. We write $L(B)$ for the language accepted by an ϵNFA B.

Definition 3. An FT A is *finite-valued* if there exists k such that for all $u \in I_A^*$, $|T_A(u)| \leq k$; A is *single-valued* if for all $u \in I_A^*$, $|T_A(u)| \leq 1$.

Definition 4. An FT A is a *generalized sequential machine* or *GSM*[1] if $\Delta_A^\epsilon = \emptyset$. We say A is *input-ϵ-free*.

Definition 5. An FT A is *deterministic* if $\mathbf{d}(A)$ is deterministic.

There exist single-valued FTs for which there exists no equivalent deterministic FT (e.g., an FT that removes all input symbols after the *last occurrence* of a given symbol.) Conversely, determinism does not imply single-valuedness, since several transitions with same input but distinct outputs may collapse into single transitions in $\mathbf{d}(A)$. Other definitions of deterministic FTs (allowing input-ϵ) are used by some authors [5]. Definition 5 is consistent with [4].

---

[1] Definition 4 is consistent with [4,5]. However, the definition of a GSM is not standardized in the literature. Some sources define GSMs without a dedicated set of final states [6].

3.1   Background Structure and Models

We work modulo a *background* structure $\mathcal{U}$ over a language $\Gamma_{\mathcal{U}}$ that is multi-sorted. We also write $\mathcal{U}$ for the universe (domain) of $\mathcal{U}$. For each sort σ, $\mathcal{U}^{\sigma}$ denotes a nonempty sub-domain of $\mathcal{U}$. There is a Boolean sort BOOL, $\mathcal{U}^{\text{BOOL}} = \{\mathbf{true}, \mathbf{false}\}$, and the standard logical connectives are assumed to be part of the background. *Terms* are defined by induction as usual and are assumed to be well-sorted. Function symbols with range sort BOOL are called relation symbols. Boolean terms are called formulas or predicates. A term without free variables is *closed*.

An *uninterpreted function symbol of arity* $n \geq 1$ is a function symbol $f \notin \Gamma_{\mathcal{U}}$ with a *domain sort* $\sigma_1 \times \cdots \times \sigma_n$ and a *range sort* σ. An *interpretation for* f is a function from $\mathcal{U}^{\sigma_1} \times \cdots \times \mathcal{U}^{\sigma_n}$ to $\mathcal{U}^{\sigma}$. An *uninterpreted constant* is a constant $c \notin \Gamma_{\mathcal{U}}$ of some sort σ. An *interpretation for* c is an element of $\mathcal{U}^{\sigma}$. By convention, a constant is also called a *function symbol of arity* 0.

We write $\Sigma(t)$ for the set of all uninterpreted function symbols that occur in a term t. Given a set of uninterpreted function symbols Σ, t is a *term over* Σ, or a Σ-*term* if $\Sigma(t) \subseteq \Sigma$. We say Σ-*model* for an expansion of $\mathcal{U}$ to $\Gamma_{\mathcal{U}} \cup \Sigma$. The interpretation of a closed Σ-term t in a Σ-model M, is denoted by t^M and is defined by induction as usual. There is a background function (symbol) Ite:BOOL $\times \sigma \times \sigma \to \sigma$ for each sort σ and $Ite(\varphi, t, f)^M = $ if φ^M then t^M else f^M Let φ be a closed Σ-formula. A Σ-model M *satisfies* φ or φ *is true in* M or $M \vDash \varphi$, if $\varphi^M = \mathbf{true}$; φ is *satisfiable* if it has a model, denoted by $IsSat(\varphi)$; φ is *true* if $\varphi^M = \mathbf{true}$ for all Σ-models M.

For each sort σ let c_σ stand for a *default fixed uninterpreted constant* of sort σ. We omit the sort σ when it is clear from the context. Let $\mathcal{T}^{\sigma}(\Sigma)$ denote the set of all closed terms of sort σ only using uninterpreted symbols from Σ, $\mathcal{T}^{\sigma}$ stands for $\mathcal{T}^{\sigma}(\Sigma)$ where Σ is an infinite set of uninterpreted constants of some fixed sort. Unless stated otherwise, we assume that $\mathcal{T}^{\sigma}$ is quantifier free, closed under substitutions, Boolean operations, and equality. $\mathcal{F}$ stands for $\mathcal{T}^{\text{BOOL}}$.

4   Symbolic Finite Transducers

Symbolic automata provide a representation of automata where several transitions from a given source state to a given target state may be combined into a single transition with a symbolic label denoting multiple concrete labels. This representation naturally separates the finite state graph from the character representation.

Definition 6. A *Symbolic Finite Transducer (SFT)* A *over* Γ *with input sort* ι *and output sort* o, or $A_\Gamma^{\iota/o}$, is a six-tuple $(Q, q^0, F, \iota, o, \Delta)$, where Q is a finite set of *states*, $q^0 \in Q$ is the *initial state*, $F \subseteq Q$ is the set of *final states*, ι is the *input sort*, o is the *output sort*, and $\Delta = \Delta^{\bar{\epsilon}} \cup \Delta^{\epsilon}$,

$$\Delta^{\bar{\epsilon}} : Q \times \mathcal{F}(c_\iota) \times (\mathcal{T}^o(c_\iota))^* \times Q$$
$$\Delta^{\epsilon} : Q \times \{\epsilon\} \times (\mathcal{T}^o)^* \times Q$$

is a finite *symbolic transition relation*.

A single transition $(p, \varphi, \mathbf{u}, q) \in \Delta_A$ is also denoted by $p \xrightarrow{\varphi/\mathbf{u}}_A q$ or $p \xrightarrow{\varphi/\mathbf{u}} q$ when A is clear from the context; φ is called the *input condition* or *guard* of the transition and $\mathbf{u}$ is called the *output sequence* of the transition. Let I_A denote the set of non-epsilon input conditions in Δ_A. Let O_A denote the set of output terms in Δ_A.

The definition of a *symbolic finite automaton* *(SFA)* is the special case of an SFT whose outputs are empty. A transition of an SFA A^ι is denoted by $p \xrightarrow{\varphi} q$ where $\varphi \in I_A \cup \{\epsilon\}$.

We lift the interpretation of terms to apply to sequences of terms. Given $\mathbf{u} = [u_i]_{i<n} \in (T^\gamma(\Sigma))^*$, for $n \geq 0$, and a Σ-model M, $\mathbf{u}^M \overset{\text{def}}{=} [u_i^M]_{i<n} \in (\mathcal{U}^\gamma)^*$.

Definition 7. An SFT $A^{\iota/o}$ denotes the *concrete FT*

$$[\![A]\!] \overset{\text{def}}{=} (Q_A, q_A^0, F_A, \mathcal{U}^\iota, \mathcal{U}^o, \Delta^{\bar\epsilon} \cup \Delta^\epsilon), \text{ where}$$
$$\Delta^{\bar\epsilon} = \{p \xrightarrow{c_\iota^M/\mathbf{u}^M} q \mid p \xrightarrow{\varphi/\mathbf{u}} q \in \Delta_A^{\bar\epsilon},\ M \vDash \varphi\},$$
$$\Delta^\epsilon = \{p \xrightarrow{\epsilon/\mathbf{u}^\iota} q \mid p \xrightarrow{\epsilon/\mathbf{u}} q \in \Delta_A^\epsilon\},$$

where M ranges over $\{c_\iota\}$-models. Let $T_A \overset{\text{def}}{=} T_{[\![A]\!]}$.

Example 3. Consider the SFT A in Example 2. Then $|\Delta^{\bar\epsilon}_{[\![A]\!]}| = 2^{16}$. For example, $[\![A]\!]$ has the following transitions:

$$q_0 \xrightarrow{\text{'b'}/[\text{'b'}]} q_0, \quad q_0 \xrightarrow{\text{'ö'}/[\text{'\&'},\text{'\#'},\text{'x'},\text{'F'},\text{'6'}]} q_1 \xrightarrow{\epsilon/[\text{';'}]} q_0$$

So $T_A(\text{"böb"}) = \{\text{"b\&\#xF6;b"}\}$.

The following basic property of SFTs is important in the context of algorithm design for SFTs.

Definition 8. An SFT A is *clean* if $IsSat(\varphi)$ for $\varphi \in I_A$.

Other properties of SFTs are defined in terms of their denotations as FTs: SFT A is *deterministic*, resp. *single-valued*, input-ϵ-free, if $[\![A]\!]$ is deterministic, resp. single-valued, input-ϵ-free. The following proposition follows from Definitions 5 and 7.

Proposition 1. *A is deterministic if and only if A is input-ϵ-free and for all $p \xrightarrow{\varphi/\mathbf{u}} q, p \xrightarrow{\psi/\mathbf{v}} r \in \Delta_A$, if $q \neq r$ then $\varphi \wedge \psi$ is unsatisfiable.*

4.1 Alphabets of SFTs

In order to base the definitions of SFTs on classical formal language theory, the concrete alphabets $\mathcal{U}^\iota$ and $\mathcal{U}^o$ need to be *finite*. For example, in Example 2, $|\mathcal{U}^{\text{BV16}}| = 2^{16}$. However, for the symbolic representation the main concern is decidability and complexity of the character theory, rather than *finiteness* of the underlying domain. This point becomes more transparent when we discuss algorithms for SFTs. When considering an input or output sort whose domain is *infinite*, e.g. integers, all algorithms on SFTs remain intact, while SFTs are in this case strictly more expressive than FTs.

Example 4. Consider the sort INT for integers and the following SFT $A^{\text{INT/INT}}$:

The image of T_A is $\{[n, n] \mid n \in \mathcal{U}^{\text{INT}}\}^*$ that is not accepted by any SFA, since infinitely many states are required, contrary to the image of a finite transduction (also called *rational transduction*) that is a regular language.

Example 4 is an instance of the general case when $A^{\iota/o}$ is a clean SFT where both $\mathcal{U}^\iota$ and $\mathcal{U}^o$ are infinite, A has a transition whose output sequence contains c_ι in other than the first output term and denotes infinitely many concrete transitions. In this case the image of T_A cannot be recognized using a finite number of states.

5 Equivalence

Our main theorem is Theorem 1, it builds on Lemma 5 as our main technical result. The theorem generalizes the decidability of equivalence of single-valued SFTs [1]. The main reason why the technique for checking equivalence of single-valued SFTs does not generalize to checking equivalence of finite-valued SFTs is that the dependency from inputs to outputs does not remain *functional* in the finite-valued case. In the single-valued case one can detect inequivalence during an incremental product construction using local satisfiability checks, by essentially detecting *non-single-valuedness* of the product [1, Lemma 2]; this is nonsensical in the finite-valued case.

We use several lemmas to prove Theorem 1. The main ones are Lemma 4 and Lemma 5. Lemma 4 is used to transform the SFTs into a normal form that considerably simplifies the proof of Lemma 5. The main construction used in Lemma 5 is a product construction of the given SFTs. The product construction uses multiple outputs. The number of states in the product is bounded by the product of the number of states of the component SFTs. The key idea is to exhaustively detect *conflict-states* that represent product states at which point we know that there exists an input element that will at some point cause different outputs be yielded by the SFTs.

Proposition 2. *Let A be a finite-valued SFT such that $T_A(\epsilon) = \emptyset$. There is an input-$\epsilon$-free SFT that is effectively equivalent to A.*

Proof. First, assume that A is clean, has no epsilon-loops, no dead-ends, and no unreachable states. Second, note that A cannot have *input-epsilon loops* $p \overset{\epsilon/\mathbf{u}}{\leadsto} p$, $\mathbf{u} \neq \epsilon$, because A is finite-valued.

Let $\Delta_A(p)$ denote the set of all transitions in Δ_A starting from p. Similarly for Δ_A^ϵ and $\Delta_A^{\bar{\epsilon}}$.

The idea is to transform A repeatedly, each time decreasing the number of states p, such that $\Delta_A^\epsilon(p) \neq \emptyset$, while preserving equivalence. The following transformation is repeated until $\Delta_A^\epsilon(p) = \emptyset$ for $p \in Q_A \setminus \{q_A^0\}$.

1. Choose a non-initial state q such that $\Delta_A^\epsilon(q) \neq \emptyset$.
2. For each transition $p \xrightarrow{\varphi/\mathbf{u}} q$ in A add the new transitions

$$\{p \xrightarrow{\varphi/\mathbf{u}\cdot\mathbf{v}} r \mid q \xrightarrow{\epsilon/\mathbf{v}} r \in \Delta_A^\epsilon(q)\}$$

to A. Note that $r \neq q$ and if $\varphi = \epsilon$ then $p \neq q$. Also, the semantics of $\mathbf{v}$ is not affected because $\Sigma(\mathbf{v}) = \emptyset$.
3. Remove the transitions $\Delta_A^\epsilon(q)$ from A.

Equivalence of the transformed A to the original one follows by using absence of input-epsilon loops and that $q \neq q_A^0$. Eliminate all dead-ends that were created.

Finally, transitions in $\Delta_A^\epsilon(q_A^0)$ are eliminated one by one as follows. Fix $q_A^0 \xrightarrow{\epsilon/\mathbf{u}} p$. Since $T_A(\epsilon) = \emptyset$ we know that $p \notin F_A$ and since p is not a dead-end $\Delta_A(p) \neq \emptyset$. We know also that $q_A^0 \neq p$. Replace the transition $q_A^0 \xrightarrow{\epsilon/\mathbf{u}} p$ by

$$\{q_A^0 \xrightarrow{\varphi/\mathbf{u}\cdot\mathbf{v}} r \mid p \xrightarrow{\varphi/\mathbf{v}} r \in \Delta_A(p)\}$$

Repeat the step until $\Delta_A^\epsilon(q_A^0) = \emptyset$. $\qquad\square$

Note that if A in Proposition 2 is not clean, then more transitions may be added during the transformations but whose guards remain unsatisfiable and the statement remains correct. If A is clean then the transformed SFT is also clean, since guards are not modified.

Example 5. Consider the SFT in Example 2. Input-epsilon elimination yields the following equivalent SFT:

where $\bar{c}$ stands for $['\&', '\#', 'x'] \cdot \ulcorner c \urcorner \cdot [';']$.

We say that a state of an SFT is *relevant* if it is reachable from the initial state and not a dead-end. We use the following pumping lemma over word equations.

Lemma 1. *For all $u_1, u_2, v_1, v_2, w_1, w_2, z_1, z_2$: if $u_1 \cdot u_2 = v_1 \cdot v_2$, $u_1 \cdot w_1 \cdot u_2 = v_1 \cdot z_1 \cdot v_2$ and $u_1 \cdot w_2 \cdot u_2 = v_1 \cdot z_2 \cdot v_2$ then $u_1 \cdot w_1 \cdot w_2 \cdot u_2 = v_1 \cdot z_1 \cdot z_2 \cdot v_2$.*

Lemma 2. *Let A be a finite-valued SFT. For all u, v, w, and relevant $p \in Q_A$, if $p \xrightsquigarrow{u/v}_A p$ and $p \xrightsquigarrow{u/w}_A p$ then $v = w$.*

Proof. Suppose there exist u, v, w, and p such that $p \xrightsquigarrow{u/v}_A p$ and $p \xrightsquigarrow{u/w}_A p$ and $v \neq w$. Then for any k, by Lemma 1, there exist u_1, u_2, v_1 and v_2 and m such that $T_A(u_1 \cdot u^m \cdot u_2) \geq k$, contradicting finite-valuedness of A. $\qquad\square$

Definition 9. An SFT A is a *component* if it is strongly connected and $F_A = \{q_A^0\}$, q_A^0 is called the *anchor* of A. An SFT A is a *sequence (of components)* if it consists of disjoint components A_i for $0 \leq i \leq n$ such that $q_A^0 = q_{A_0}^0$, $F_A = F_{A_n}$, and there is a single transition $q_{A_i}^0 \rightarrow q_{A_{i+1}}^0$ for $0 \leq i < n$.

Definition 10. The *union* of a set **A** of SFTs is an SFT with a new initial state and epsilon moves to the initial states of SFTs in **A**.

Definition 11. An SFT is in *sequence normal form (SNF)* if it is a union of pairwise disjoint sequences.

Lemma 3. *All SFTs have an effectively equivalent SNF.*

Proof. Let A be an SFT. The sequences are constructed by considering all loop-free paths from the initial state of A to some final state, possibly creating extra states if a strongly connected component of A is entered and exited through different states. $\square$

The following lemma is used to simplify the proof of Lemma 5 by normalizing the representation of SFTs.

Lemma 4. *Every finite-valued SFT has an effectively equivalent SNF with single-valued sequences.*

Proof. By using Lemma 3 we assume, without loss of generality, that the SFT is a single sequence. Moreover, by using Proposition 2, we assume that the SFT is input-ϵ-free.

We apply the following algorithm to transform the SFT into a set of single-valued sequences. First, note that if the SFT is a single component then it is already single-valued by Lemma 2. Next, we describe the algorithm for the case when the SFT has the form $A\alpha B$, where A and B are two components with anchors p and q and α is a nonempty path $p \leadsto q$. The case when either A or B have no transitions follows also from Lemma 2. So assume that both A and B contain nonempty paths $p \leadsto p$ and $q \leadsto q$. Different outputs may arise by ambiguous parses of an input sequence u through $A\alpha B$ that must allow paths:

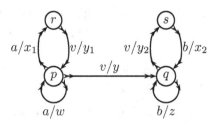

and u has the form $a^m \cdot a \cdot v \cdot v \cdot b \cdot b^n$ causing the conflict $x_1 \cdot y_1 \cdot y \cdot z \neq w \cdot y \cdot y_2 \cdot x_2$ in the output. We can rule out the case when $a = b = \epsilon$ or else there exist either unboundedly many different outputs for v^k, by increasing k, contradicting finite-valuedness, or just a single output, independent of the parse, e.g. when $y_1 = y_2 = \epsilon$. So assume $a \neq \epsilon$ (the case $b \neq \epsilon$ is symmetrical). The idea is to resolve the conflict by replacing AvB with $(A \setminus \{av, v\}^*)vB$, $AavvB$ and $AavB$.

In order to detect and resolve such conflicts symbolically, extract the sequence $\bar{\varphi}$ of guards on the path α and search for the corresponding symbolic paths in A and B by checking satisfiability of the corresponding guard sequences for which there exist different output sequences. The maximum length of the paths corresponding to a and b that need to be considered is $|Q_A||Q_B|$.

For example, let $\alpha = p \xrightarrow{\psi/t} q$. And suppose there exist transitions $p \xrightarrow{\varphi_1/u_1} p \xrightarrow{\varphi_1'/u_1'} r \xrightarrow{\psi_1/t_1} p$ in A and transitions $q \xrightarrow{\varphi_2/u_2} q \xrightarrow{\psi_2/t_2} s \xrightarrow{\varphi_2'/u_2'} q$ in B. Let $\theta_i = \{c \mapsto c_i\}$ where c_i is fresh. Assume the following formula is satisfiable:

$$\varphi_1\theta_1 \wedge \psi\theta_2 \wedge \psi_2\theta_3 \wedge \varphi_2'\theta_4 \wedge \varphi_1'\theta_1 \wedge \psi_1\theta_2 \wedge \psi\theta_3 \wedge \varphi_2\theta_4$$
$$\wedge u_1\theta_1 \cdot t\theta_2 \cdot t_2\theta_3 \cdot u_2'\theta_4 \neq u_1'\theta_1 \cdot t_1\theta_2 \cdot t\theta_3 \cdot u_2\theta_4$$

Then there exist u with different outputs. Construct the SFA D for the guard sequences $\{[\varphi_1 \wedge \varphi_1'], [\varphi_1 \wedge \varphi_1', \psi_1]\}^*$, in particular accepting $\{a, a \cdot v\}^*$ as above. Let $\bar{D}$ be the complement of D. Let $A' = A \upharpoonright \bar{D}$ (thus removing the conflicts from A). Let α_1 be the path $p \xrightarrow{\varphi_1 \wedge \varphi_1'/u_1} p_1 \xrightarrow{\psi/t} q$ and let α_2 be the path $p \xrightarrow{\varphi_1 \wedge \varphi_1'/u_1'} r_2 \xrightarrow{\psi_1/t_1} p_2 \xrightarrow{\psi/t} q$. Now replace $A\alpha B$ with the SFTs $A'\alpha B$, $A\alpha_1 B$ and $A\alpha_2 B$. Note that $A'\alpha B$ is now single-valued and can be transformed to SNF. It follows that the union of the new sequences is equivalent to $A\alpha B$. Repeat the transformation on $A\alpha_1 B$ and $A\alpha_2 B$. Termination follows from that both have fewer nonequivalent conflicts remaining and that the length of paths α causing conflicts is effectively bounded by the size of the original SFT. The proof can be generalized to the case of sequences of arbitrary length. $\qquad\square$

The following lemma is our main technical result. Some details of the proof have been omitted but can be found in [7]. It generalizes the decidability of equivalence of single-valued SFTs [1]. For a single-valued SFT A write $A(u) = v$ when $T_A(u) = \{v\}$.

Lemma 5. *Let $A^{\iota/\circ}, B_1^{\iota/\circ}, \ldots, B_k^{\iota/\circ}$ be input-ϵ-free single-valued SFTs for some $k \geq 1$ then the problem $\exists x \left(\bigwedge_{i=1}^{k} T_A(x) \neq T_{B_i}(x)\right)$ is decidable if $\mathcal{F}$ is decidable.*

Proof. Case $k = 1$ is [1, Theorem 2]. We prove the case for $k = 2$. Generalization to $k > 2$ is technically more involved but straightforward. Let $B = B_1$, $C = B_2$. We only need to consider inputs in $L = L(\mathbf{d}(A)) \cap L(\mathbf{d}(B)) \cap L(\mathbf{d}(C))$. For example, if $u \in L(\mathbf{d}(A)) \setminus L(\mathbf{d}(B))$ and $u \in L(\mathbf{d}(C))$ then $T_A(u) \neq T_B(u)$ and the problem reduces to equivalence of $A \upharpoonright \overline{\mathbf{d}(B)}$ and C, where the construction of $A \upharpoonright \overline{\mathbf{d}(B)}$ is effective. The other cases are similar.

For the case L construct the product $D = A \times B \times C$ that has states $Q_A \times Q_B \times Q_C$ and 3-output-transitions

$$(p, q, r) \xrightarrow{\varphi \wedge \psi_1 \wedge \psi_2/(u,v,w)} (p', q', r'),$$
$$\text{for} \quad p \xrightarrow{\varphi/u}_A p', \quad q \xrightarrow{\psi_1/v}_B q', \quad r \xrightarrow{\psi_2/w}_C r'$$

such that $IsSat(\varphi \wedge \psi_1 \wedge \psi_2)$. Note that $L(\mathbf{d}(D)) = L$. The unreachable states and the dead-ends are eliminated from D. $D(u) \stackrel{\text{def}}{=} (A(u), B(u), C(u))$, Let $p_0 = q_A^0$, $q_0 = q_B^0$ and $r_0 = q_C^0$. We write s_0 for (p_0, q_0, r_0) and s_f for some $(p_f, q_f, r_f) \in F_A \times F_B \times F_C$.

Given $u \in L$ and $D(u) = (\mathbf{a}, \mathbf{b}, \mathbf{c})$, there are two (possibly overlapping) cases for a B-*conflict* $\mathbf{a} \neq \mathbf{b}$ (symmetrically for a C-*conflict* $\mathbf{a} \neq \mathbf{c}$):

1. there is a *B-length-conflict*: $|\mathbf{a}| \neq |\mathbf{b}|$, or
2. there is a *B-character-conflict*: for some i, $\mathbf{a}[i] \neq \mathbf{b}[i]$.

We say that a state $s \in Q_D$ is a *B-length-conflict-state* if there exists a *simple loop* (a loop without nested loops) $s \overset{u/(v,w,\_)}{\rightsquigarrow} s$ such that $|v| \neq |w|$. The statements below make implicit use of the assumption that D contains no unreachable states and no dead-ends.

(*) There are two ways how a B-length-conflict can arise.
1.(a) There exists a B-length-conflict state s in D.
1.(b) There exists a loop-free path $s_0 \overset{u/(v,w,\_)}{\rightsquigarrow} s_f$ such that $|v| \neq |w|$.

  Proof of (*): We show that cases 1.a and 1.b are exhaustive. Consider any $u \in L$ such that $D(u) = (v, w, \_)$ and $|v| \neq |w|$ and suppose 1.b is false. Then there must exist $u_1, u', u_2, v_1, v', v_2, w_1, w', w_2$ such that

$$u = u_1 \cdot u' \cdot u_2, \quad v = v_1 \cdot v' \cdot v_2, \quad w = w_1 \cdot w' \cdot w_2,$$

and a loop $s \overset{u'/(v',w',\_)}{\rightsquigarrow} s$ where $|v'| \neq |w'|$, or else $|v| = |w|$ since 1.b is false. Now suppose the loop is not simple. Then there exist $u_1', u'', u_2', v_1', v'', v_2', w_1', w'', w_2'$ such that

$$u' = u_1' \cdot u'' \cdot u_2', \quad v' = v_1' \cdot v'' \cdot v_2', \quad w' = w_1' \cdot w'' \cdot w_2',$$

and a state s',

If $|v''| = |w''|$ then $|v_1' \cdot v_2'| \neq |w_1' \cdot w_2'|$ and

and repeat the argument for the shorter path if it is not simple. Otherwise, if $|v''| \neq |w''|$ and the loop through s' is not simple apply the argument for s'. □
  In the case of 1.a we have that for any path

$$s_0 \overset{u_1/(v_1,w_1,\_)}{\rightsquigarrow} s \overset{u_2/(v_2,w_2,\_)}{\rightsquigarrow} s_f$$

there exists u, v, w, $|v| \neq |w|$, and a large enough $m \geq 0$, such that, for all $n \geq m$,

$$D(u_1 \cdot u^n \cdot u_2) = (v_1 \cdot v^n \cdot v_2, w_1 \cdot w^n \cdot w_2, \_),$$
$$|v_1 \cdot v^n \cdot v_2| \neq |w_1 \cdot w^n \cdot w_2|$$

Note that the problems of deciding 1.a and 1.b are decidable. In order to decide if a state s is a B-length-conflict-state consider all the possible simple loops $s \rightsquigarrow s$: for each such path check if the outputs lengths for A and B are different. There are finitely many such paths. Similarly for 1.a.

Next, we proceed by case analysis, showing that we can effectively decide all the different combinations of possible B-conflicts and C-conflicts that can arise. We write B.1.a for the case when there exists a B-length-conflict-state, similarly for the other cases.

Case (B.1.a, C.1.a): Check if there exist s_B and s_C such that s_B is a B-length-conflict-state and s_C is a C-length-conflict state and $s_B \rightsquigarrow s_C$. Then there exists a path

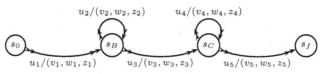

where $|v_2| \neq |w_2|$ and $|v_4| \neq |z_4|$. It follows that there exist m and n such that

$$|v_1 \cdot v_2^m \cdot v_3 \cdot v_4^n \cdot v_5| \neq |w_1 \cdot w_2^m \cdot w_3 \cdot w_4^n \cdot w_5|$$
$$|v_1 \cdot v_2^m \cdot v_3 \cdot v_4^n \cdot v_5| \neq |z_1 \cdot z_2^m \cdot z_3 \cdot z_4^n \cdot z_5|$$

Thus there exists $u = u_1 \cdot u_2^m \cdot u_3 \cdot u_4^n \cdot u_5 \in L$ such that $D(u)$ is a B-conflict and a C-conflict. There are finitely many such combinations. The case $s_C \rightsquigarrow s_B$ is symmetrical. No other simultaneous combinations of (B.1.a, C.1.a) are possible.

Case (B.1.a, C.1.b): Check if there exists a B-length-conflict-state s and a loop-free path $s_0 \rightsquigarrow s \rightsquigarrow s_f$ that causes a C-length conflict, i.e., there exists a path

$$u_1/(v_1, w_1, z_1) \qquad u_3/(v_3, w_3, z_3)$$
$$\boxed{s_0} \longrightarrow \boxed{s} \longrightarrow \boxed{s_f}$$

such that $|v_1 \cdot v_3| \neq |z_1 \cdot z_3|$. There exists u_2 such that $s \overset{u_2/(v_2, w_2, z_2)}{\rightsquigarrow} s$ where $|v_2| \neq |w_2|$. Thus, there exists m such that

$$|v_1 \cdot v_2^m \cdot v_3| \neq |w_1 \cdot w_2^m \cdot w_3|, \qquad |v_1 \cdot v_2^m \cdot v_3| \neq |z_1 \cdot z_2^m \cdot z_3|$$

Thus there exists $u = u_1 \cdot u_2^m \cdot u_3 \in L$ such that $D(u)$ is a B-conflict and a C-conflict. There are finitely many such combinations. No other simultaneous combinations of (B.1.a, C.1.b) are possible. The case (B.1.b, C.1.a) is symmetrical.

Case (B.1.b, C.1.b): Check if there exists a loop-free path $s_0 \rightsquigarrow s_f$ that causes both a B-length-conflict and and a C-length-conflict. Then there exists u such that $D(u)$ is a B-conflict and a C-conflict. There are finitely many such paths and no other simultaneous occurrences of (B.1.b, C.1.b) are possible.

Case (B.2, C.1): Assume, by previous cases, that (B.1, C.1) is not possible. Let ℓ be the length of the longest possible output from either A, B or C on any loop-free path. Clearly, ℓ can be computed effectively. Suppose there exists a C-length-conflict-state s. Consider all paths

$$\rho_m : \quad s_0 \rightsquigarrow (s \rightsquigarrow s)^m \rightsquigarrow s_f, \quad m \leq 2\ell$$

Since B.1.a is not possible, we know that for all loops $s \rightsquigarrow s$ the A-output and the B-output have the same length. For each ρ_m check if a simultaneous B-character-conflict and C-length-conflict exists.

If no such simultaneous conflicts exist it follows from the following argument that no such simultaneous conflicts exist in any longer paths. We may assume that all such loops have nonempty A (and thus B) outputs, since empty outputs neither cause nor remove any character conflicts.

- Suppose some ρ_m, $\ell \leq m < 2\ell$, contains a B-character conflict. Then, by choice of ℓ and since all the A and B-outputs are nonempty, there exist u_i, v_i, w_i, z_i, $1 \leq i \leq 2$, such that

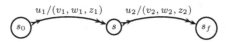

and either the character conflict occurs in the prefixes of v_1, w_1 or in the suffixes of v_2, w_2 (i.e., the conflict is not in the overlap). Thus, the B-character-conflict remains in

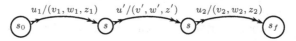

for any $s \xrightarrow{u'/(v',w',z')} s$, where $|v'| = |w'|$ and $|v'| \neq |z'|$. We now have a contradiction, because either ρ_m or ρ_{m+1} must cause a simultaneous C-length-conflict, i.e., either $|v_1 \cdot v_2| \neq |z_1 \cdot z_2|$ or $|v_1 \cdot v' \cdot v_2| \neq |z_1 \cdot z' \cdot z_2|$.
- Thus, in particular, ρ_ℓ and $\rho_{\ell+1}$ do not cause any B-character-conflicts. It now follows from Lemma 1 that for all $m \geq \ell$, in ρ_m the outputs of A and B will be equal.

There are finitely many symbolic paths in D that correspond to the concrete ρ_m's above. For each such path construct a formula in $\mathcal{F}$ that is satisfiable iff a B-character-conflict exists. For example, for a symbolic path

$$s_0 \xrightarrow{\varphi_1/(v_1, w_1, \_)} s \xrightarrow{\varphi_2/(v_2, w_2, \_)} s_f,$$

given substitution $\theta_i = \{c_\iota \mapsto c_i\}$ where c_i is a fresh uninterpreted constant the formula is:
$$\varphi_1 \theta_1 \wedge \varphi_2 \theta_2 \wedge v_1 \theta_1 \cdot v_2 \theta_2 \neq w_1 \theta_1 \cdot w_2 \theta_2$$

The case C.1.b is covered by considering all loop-free paths. It follows that the case (B.2, C.1) is decidable. The case (B.1, C.2) is symmetrical. Case (B.2, C.2) is proved in [7]. One can show that the above cases are exhaustive. Decidability follows for $k = 2$.   □

The proof of the lemma uses arbitrarily many uninterpreted constants of sort ι, i.e., it assumes decidability of $\mathcal{F}$ while the proof of the case for $k = 1$ uses at most two distinct constants of sort ι and assumes decidability of $\mathcal{F}(\{c : \iota, d : \iota\})$

Theorem 1. *Equivalence of finite-valued SFTs is decidable provided that $\mathcal{F}$ is decidable.*

Proof. Let A and B be finite-valued SFTs. Assume $D = L(\mathbf{d}(A)) = L(\mathbf{d}(B))$, or else A and B are not equivalent. By using Lemma 4 assume A and B are on SNF containing single-valued SFTs. Assume, without loss of generality that A and B do not accept the empty string and that all component sequences in A and B are input-ϵ-free. To decide $A \cong B$, we check that for all $v \in D$, $T_A(v) \subseteq T_B(v)$ and $T_B(v) \subseteq T_A(v)$. Conversely, $A \not\cong B$ iff either (1) or (2) holds for some $v \in D$:

1. for some A_1 in A and all B_1 in B, $T_{A_1}(v) \neq T_{B_1}(v)$.
2. for some B_1 in B and all A_1 in A, $T_{A_1}(v) \neq T_{B_1}(v)$.

Decidability of (1) and (2) follows now from Lemma 5. □

6 Related Work

Equivalence checking of FTs is undecidable in general [8], and is undecidable already for GSMs. The special case of equivalence checking of single-valued SFTs over decidable character background is shown to be decidable in [2]. This result is substantially generalized here (Theorem 1) to *finite-valued* SFTs. This result generalizes also the decidability of equivalence of finite-valued FTs [5,9–11]. Lemma 4 is a symbolic generalization of a decomposition technique studied in [11]. A fundamental simplifying assumption compared to SFTs is that the range of an FT is always regular. Equivalence of single-valued *extended* SFTs (SFTs with lookahead) is studied in [12], the motivation there is to analyze decoders, and it gives an orthogonal extension of decidability of equivalence of single-valued SFTs. Besides the work on BEK [1], finite state transducers have been used for dynamic and static analysis to validate sanitization functions in web applications in [3], by an over-approximation of the strings accepted by the sanitizer using static analysis of existing PHP code. Other security analysis of PHP code, e.g., SQL injection attacks, use string analyzers to obtain over-approximations (in form of context free grammars) of the HTML output by a server [13–15].

7 Conclusion

We studied equivalence of finite-valued Symbolic Finite Transducers. Although equivalence checking is in general undecidable the cause for undecidability is subtle, and this paper identifies a boundary based on whether the transducer is finite-valued (and satisfiability of guard formulas is decidable). The symbolic representation of transducers is both convenient for applications and allows for succinct representations. Basic automata algorithms lift in many cases in a straight-forward way to this representation, and it allows leveraging state-of-the-art theorem proving technology for analyzing the automata. Our main motivation behind this work originates from analysis of sanitizers.

References

1. Hooimeijer, P., Livshits, B., Molnar, D., Saxena, P., Veanes, M.: Fast and precise sanitizer analysis with Bek. In: USENIX Security, pp. 1–16 (2011)
2. Veanes, M., Hooimeijer, P., Livshits, B., Molnar, D., Bjorner, N.: Symbolic finite state transducers: Algorithms and applications. In: POPL 2012. ACM, pp. 137–150 (2012)
3. Balzarotti, D., Cova, M., Felmetsger, V., Jovanovic, N., Kirda, E., Kruegel, C., Vigna, G.: Saner: Composing static and dynamic analysis to validate sanitization in web applications. In: SP (2008)
4. Yu, S.: Regular languages. In: Rozenberg, G., Salomaa, A. (eds.) Handbook of Formal Languages, vol. 1, pp. 41–110. Springer, Heidelberg (1997)
5. Demers, A., Keleman, C., Reusch, B.: On some decidable properties of finite state translations. Acta Informatica **17**, 349–364 (1982)
6. Harrison, M.A.: Introduction to Formal Language Theory. Addison-Wesley, Reading (1978)
7. Bjørner, N., Veanes, M.: Symbolic transducers. Microsoft Research, Technical Report MSR-TR-2011-3 (2011)
8. Ibarra, O.: The unsolvability of the equivalence problem for Efree NGSM's with unary input (output) alphabet and applications. SIAM J. Comput. **4**, 524–532 (1978)
9. Schützenberger, M.P.: Sur les relations rationnelles. In: Brakhage, H. (ed.) Automata Theory and Formal Languages. LNCS, vol. 33, pp. 209–213. Springer, Heidelberg (1975)
10. Culic, K., Karhumäki, J.: The equivalence problem for single-valued two-way transducers (on NPDT0L languages) is decidable. SIAM J. Comput. **16**(2), 221–230 (1987)
11. Weber, A.: Decomposing finite-valued transducers and deciding their equivalence. SIAM J. Comput. **22**(1), 175–202 (1993)
12. D'Antoni, L., Veanes, M.: Equivalence of extended symbolic finite transducers. In: Sharygina, N., Veith, H. (eds.) CAV 2013. LNCS, vol. 8044, pp. 624–639. Springer, Heidelberg (2013)
13. Minamide, Y.: Static approximation of dynamically generated web pages. In: Proceedings of the 14th International Conference on the World Wide Web, WWW 2005, pp. 432–441 (2005)
14. Wassermann, G., Su, Z.: Sound and precise analysis of web applications for injection vulnerabilities. In: PLDI, pp. 32–41. ACM (2007)
15. Wassermann, G., Yu, D., Chander, A., Dhurjati, D., Inamura, H., Su, Z.: Dynamic test input generation for web applications. In: ISSTA (2008)

Relaxed Parsing of Regular Approximations of String-Embedded Languages

Ekaterina Verbitskaia$^{(\boxtimes)}$, Semyon Grigorev, and Dmitry Avdyukhin

Saint Petersburg State University, Saint Petersburg, Russia
kajigor@gmail.com, rsdpisuy@gmail.com, dimonbv@gmail.com

Abstract. We present a technique for syntax analysis of a regular set of input strings. This problem is relevant for the analysis of string-embedded languages when a host program generates clauses of embedded language at run time. Our technique is based on a generalization of RNGLR algorithm, which, inherently, allows us to construct a finite representation of parse forest for regularly approximated set of input strings. This representation can be further utilized for semantic analysis and transformations in the context of reengineering, code maintenance, program understanding etc. The approach in question implements *relaxed parsing*: non-recognized strings in approximation set are ignored with no error detection.

Keywords: String-embedded languages · String analysis · Parsing · Parser generator · RNGLR

Introduction

There is a broad class of applications which utilize the idea of *string embedding* of one language into another. In this approach a host program generates string representation of clauses in some external language which are then passed to a dedicated runtime component for analysis and execution. One significant example of string embedded language is embedded SQL [1]; among others, some frameworks such as JSP [2] and PHP mySQL interface[1] can be mentioned.

Despite providing a high level of expressiveness and flexibility, string embedding makes the behavior of the system less predictable and harder to reason about since a whole class of verification procedures is postponed until run time, which complicates development, testing and maintenance. To overcome this deficiency, it is desirable to perform syntax analysis of well-formedness of all generated clauses prior to execution. However, since the host language, as a rule, is Turing-complete, the precise analysis is undecidable; the common approach is to analyse an over-approximating set of strings represented in some constructive form. It's worth to mention that, similarly to regular syntax analysis, the analysis of string-embedded languages often follows two-level scheme: first a set of

---

[1] http://php.net/manual/en/mysqli.query.php.

© Springer International Publishing Switzerland 2016
M. Mazzara and A. Voronkov (Eds.): PSI 2015, LNCS 9609, pp. 291–302, 2016.
DOI: 10.1007/978-3-319-41579-6_22

strings is tokenized to provide an approximation for tokenized stream set, then this set is parsed by a syntax analyzer.

This paper contributes a generalization of RNGLR (Right-Nulled Generalized LR [3]) algorithm, which, instead of linear stream of tokens, analyzes a regular set of streams. Our algorithm can be considered as proper generalization since it provides exactly the same result as the original one on a trivial one-element set; moreover, our implementation reuses original RNGLR parse tables. The distinctive feature of our approach in comparison with other techniques for analysis of string-embedded languages is that it provides the set of parsing trees, encoded in the form of Shared Packed Parse Forest (SPPF) [4]. The choice of RNGLR looks quite natural in this regard since in its original form it already incorporates the technique to deal with multiple ways of parsing. On the other hand, our approach can be categorized as *relaxed* parsing since it silently ignores non-recognized part of the input; we do not consider this property as an essential drawback because it only means that, to provide best results, it has to be combined with some existing recognition-centric approaches.

1   Related Works

Our approach for syntax analysis of string-embedded languages borrows some common principles from existing techniques in this area. In addition, we reuse RNGLR syntax analysis algorithm and some accompanying constructs. In this section we provide a review and recollect some important notions which will be referred to later on.

1.1   String-Embedded Languages Analysis Techniques

The analysis of string-embedded languages, as a rule, requires a set of *hotspots* to be indicated in the host application source code. Hotspot is considered as some "point of interest", where the analysis of the set of possible string values is desirable. This task can be performed either in a user-assisted manner or automatically using some pragmatic considerations or knowledge of the framework being analyzed. The following logical steps include static analysis to construct an approximation for the set of all possible string values, lexical, syntax, and, perhaps, some kind of semantic analysis. These steps are not necessarily performed separately; some of them may be omitted.

A rather natural idea of *regular approximation* is to approximate the set of all possible strings by a regular expression. In recognition-centric formulation, this approach boils down to the problem of inclusion of approximating regular language into context-free reference language, which is decidable for a number of practically significant cases [5]. Many approaches follow this route. In [6], forward reachability analysis is used to compute regular approximation for all string values in the program. Further analysis is based on patterns detection in approximation set or generation of some finite subset of strings for analysis by standalone tools. Regular approximation in [7] is acquired by widening context-free approximation, initially built as a result of program analysis. Our approach is partially inspired by Alvor [8,9] which utilizes GLR-based technique for syntax analysis of regular approximation; this framework implements abstract lexical analysis to convert a regular language over characters into regular language over tokens, which simplifies syntax analysis.

Kyung-Goo Doh et al. in a series of papers [10–12] introduced an approach, based on implicit representation of the set of potential strings as a system of data-flow equations. Conventional LALR(1) is chosen for the basis of parsing algorithm; original parse tables are reused. Syntax analysis is performed as the system of dataflow equations is being solved iteratively in the space of abstract stacks. The problem of infinite stack growth, which appears in general case, is handled using abstract interpretation [13]. This approach later evolved to a certain kind of semantic processing in terms of attribute grammars which made it possible to analyze a wider class of languages, than LALR(1).

1.2 Right-Nulled Generalized LR Parsing Algorithm

RNGLR (Right-Nulled Generalized LR) is a modification of Generalized LR (GLR) algorithm, which was developed by Masaru Tomita [14] in the context of natural language processing. GLR was designed to handle ambiguous context-free grammars. Ambiguities in the grammar produce shift/reduce and reduce/reduce conflicts, speaking in terms of LR approach. The algorithm uses parse tables, similar to those for classical LR, each cell of which can contain multiple actions. The general approach is to carry out all possible actions during parsing using graph-based data structures to efficiently represent the set of stacks and derivation trees. Originally, Tomita's algorithm was unable to recognize all context-free languages. Elizabeth Scott and Adrian Johnstone presented RNGLR [3], which extends GLR with a certain way of handling *right nullable* rules (i.e. rules of the form A → $\alpha\beta$, where β reduces to an empty string).

To efficiently represent the set of all stacks produced during parsing, RNGLR uses Graph Structured Stack (GSS). GSS is a directed graph, whose vertices correspond to the elements of individual stacks and edges link successive stack elements. Each vertex can have multiple incoming and outgoing edges to merge multiple stacks together; thus stack element sharing is implemented. Each vertex is a pair (s, l), where s is a parser state and l is a *level* (position in the input string). Vertices in GSS are unique and there are no multi-edges.

According to RNGLR, an input is read left-to-right, one token at a time, and the levels of GSS are constructed sequentially for each input position: first, all possible reductions are applied, then the next input terminal is shifted and pushed to the GSS. When a reduction or pushing is performed, the algorithm modifies GSS in the following manner. Suppose an edge (v_t, v_h) has to be added to the GSS. By construction, the head vertex v_h is always already in the GSS. If the tail vertex is also in the GSS, then a new edge (v_t, v_h) is added (provided it is not yet there); otherwise both new tail vertex and new edge are created and added to the GSS. Every time a new vertex $v = (s, l)$ is created, the algorithm calculates the new parser state s' from s and the next terminal of the input. The pair (v, s'), called *push*, is added to the global collection $\mathcal{Q}$. The set of ϵ-reductions (i.e. reductions with length $l = 0$) is also calculated, when a new vertex is added to the GSS, and reductions from this set are added to the global queue $\mathcal{R}$. Reductions with length $l > 0$ are calculated and added to $\mathcal{R}$ each time a new (non-ϵ) edge is created.

An input string can have several derivation trees and, as a rule, they can have numerous identical subtrees. Shared Packed Parse Forest (SPPF) [4] is a directed graph designed for a compact representation of all possible derivation trees. SPPF has the following structure: the *root* (i.e. vertex with no incoming edges) corresponds to the starting nonterminal of the grammar; vertices with no outgoing edges correspond to terminals or derivation of ϵ-string; the rest of the vertices is divided into two classes: *nonterminal* and *production*. Each nonterminal vertex keeps a collection of production nodes, each of which represents one possible derivation of that nonterminal. Production vertices represent a right-hand side of the production and keep an ordered list of terminal or nonterminal nodes. The length of this list lies in the range $[l - k..l]$, where l is the length of production right-hand side, and k is the number of rightmost symbols which derive ϵ (nullable symbols are ignored to reduce memory consumption).

SPPF is constructed simultaneously with GSS. Each edge of the GSS is associated with either a terminal or nonterminal node. When a GSS edge is added with a push, a new terminal node is created and associated with the edge. Nonterminal nodes are associated with edges which were added, when reductions were performed: if the edge has already been in GSS, a production node is added to the family of nonterminal nodes, associated with the edge. All subgraphs from the edges of the reduction path are added as children to the production node. After the input is read to the end, all vertices with accepting states are searched and nodes associated with outgoing edges of such vertices are merged to form the resulting SPPF. All unreachable vertices are deleted from the SPPF graph, which leaves only the actual derivation trees for the input.

The detailed algorithm description in the form of pseudocode can be found in Appendix A.

2   Relaxed Parsing of Regular Sets

The input of our algorithm (see *parse* function in Algorithm 1) is a reference grammar G with alphabet of terminal symbols T and a finite non-deterministic automaton $(Q, \Sigma, \delta, q_0, q_f)$ with a single start state q_0, single final state q_f and no ϵ-transitions, where $\Sigma \subseteq T$ — alphabet of input symbols, Q — alphabet of states, δ — transition relation. RNGLR parse tables and some accessory information (called *parserSource* in pseudocode) are generated for the grammar G.

Algorithm 1. Parsing algorithm

```
 1: function PARSE(grammar, automaton)
 2:     inputGraph ← construct inner graph representation of automaton
 3:     parserSource ← generate RNGLR parse tables for grammar
 4:     if inputGraph contains no edges then
 5:         if parserSource accepts empty input then report success
 6:         else report failure
 7:     else
 8:         ADDVERTEX(inputGraph.startVertex, startState)
 9:         Q.Enqueue(inputGraph.startVertex)
10:         while Q is not empty do
11:             v ← Q.Dequeue()
12:             MAKEREDUCTIONS(v)
13:             PUSH(v)
14:             APPLYPASSINGREDUCTIONS(v)
15:         if ∃v_f : v_f.level = q_f and v_f.state is accepting then report success
16:         else report failure
17: function PUSH(innerGraphV)
18:     U ← copy innerGraphV.unprocessed
19:     clear innerGraphV.unprocessed
20:     for all v_h in U do
21:         for all e in outgoing edges of innerGraphV do
22:             push ← calculate next state by v_h.state and the token on e
23:             ADDEDGE(v_h, e.Head, push, false)
24:             add v_h in innerGraphV.processed
25: function MAKEREDUCTIONS(innerGraphV)
26:     while innerGraphV.reductions is not empty do
27:         (startV, N, l) ← innerGraphV.reductions.Dequeue()
28:         find the set of vertices X reachable from startV
29:         along the path of length (l − 1), or 0 if l = 0;
30:         add (startV, N, l − i) in v.passingReductions,
31:         where v is an i-th vertex of the path
32:         for all v_h in X do
33:             state_t ← calculate new state by v_h.state and nonterminal N
34:             ADDEDGE(v_h, startV, state_t, (l = 0))
35: function APPLYPASSINGREDUCTIONS(innerGraphV)
36:     for all (v, edge) in innerGraphV.passingReductionsToHandle do
37:         for all (startV, N, l) ← v.passingReductions.Dequeue() do
38:             find the set of vertices X,
39:             reachable from edge along the path of length (l − 1)
40:             for all v_h in X do
41:                 state_t ← calculate new state by v_h.state and nonterminal N
42:                 ADDEDGE(v_h, startV, state_t, false)
```

The general idea of the algorithm is to traverse the automaton graph and sequentially construct GSS, similarly as in RNGLR. However, as we deal with a graph instead of a linear stream, the next symbol turns into the *set of terminals* on all outgoing edges of current vertex. This results in a different semantics of pushing and reducing (see line 21, Algorithm 1, and lines 9 and 21, Algorithm 2). We use queue Q to control the order of automaton graph vertices processing. Every time a new GSS vertex is added, all zero-reductions have to be performed and then new tokens have to be shifted, so a corresponding graph vertex has to be enqueueed for further processing. Addition of new GSS edge can produce reductions to handle, so the graph vertex at the tail of the added edge has also to be enqueueed (see Algorithm 2). Reductions are applied along the paths in GSS, and if we add a new edge to some tail vertex, which was already presented in GSS, we also have to recalculate all *passing* reductions (see *applyPassingReductions* function in Algorithm 1).

Algorithm 2. GSS construction

1: **function** ADDVERTEX($innerGraphV, state$)
2:     $v \leftarrow$ find a vertex with state = $state$ in
3:     $innerGraphV.processed \cup innerGraphV.unprocessed$
4:     **if** v is not *null* **then**   ▷ The vertex have been found in GSS
5:         **return** $(v, false)$
6:     **else**
7:         $v \leftarrow$ create new vertex for $innerGraphV$ with state $state$
8:         add v in $innerGraphV.unprocessed$
9:         **for all** e in outgoing edges of $innerGraphV$ **do**
10:             calculate the set of zero-reductions by v
11:             and the token on e and add them in $innerGraphV.reductions$
12:         **return** $(v, true)$
13: **function** ADDEDGE($v_h, innerGraphV, state_t, isZeroReduction$)
14:     $(v_t, isNew) \leftarrow$ ADDVERTEX($innerGraphV, state_t$)
15:     **if** GSS does not contain edge from v_t to v_h **then**
16:         $edge \leftarrow$ create new edge from v_t to v_h
17:         $Q.Enqueue(innerGraphV)$
18:         **if** not $isNew$ and $v_t.passingReductions.Count > 0$ **then**
19:             add $(v_t, edge)$ in $innerGraphV.passingReductionsToHandle$
20:         **if** not $isZeroReduction$ **then**
21:             **for all** e in outgoing edges of $innerGraphV$ **do**
22:                 calculate the set of reductions by v
23:                 and the token on e and add them in $innerGraphV.reductions$

Like RNGLR, we associate GSS vertices with positions in the input, and, in our case, a position coincides with some state of input automaton. We construct some inner data structure (referred to as *inner graph*) by copying input automaton graph and extending each of its vertices with the following collections:

- *processed*: GSS vertices, for which all the pushes were processed. This set aggregates all GSS vertices, associated with inner graph vertex.
- *unprocessed*: GSS vertices, for which all the pushes are to be processed. This set is analogous to Q of original RNGLR.

– *reductions*: a queue, which is analogous to $\mathcal{R}$ of original RNGLR: all reductions to be processed.
– *passingReductionsToHandle*: pairs of GSS vertex and GSS edge to apply passing reductions along them.

Besides parser *state* and *level* (which is equal to the input automaton state), a collection of *passing reductions* is stored in a GSS vertex. Passing reduction is a triplet $(startV, N, l)$, representing reductions, whose path contains given GSS vertex. This triplet is similar to one describing reduction, where l is a remaining length of the path. Passing reductions are stored for every vertex of the path (except for the first and the last) during path search in *makeReductions* function (see Algorithm 1).

We inherit SPPF construction from the original RNGLR; in our case, derivation trees for strings, accumulated along the paths of the input automaton graph, are merged.

3   Example of Parsing and SPPF Construction

We demonstrate the application of our algorithm by the following example. The reference grammar is shown below:

$$(0)\ start\_rule\ ::=\ s$$
$$(1)\ \qquad s\ ::=\ \text{LBR}\ \ s\ \ \text{RBR}\ \ s$$
$$(2)\ \qquad s\ ::=\ \epsilon$$

The automaton for regular approximation after tokenization is shown on the Fig. 1; the SPPF, provided by our algorithm, is shown on the Fig. 2. To reduce clutter we omit in the SPPF right nullable symbols in the rules: thus there are no nodes for the last nonterminal s in the right-hand side of the rule (1).

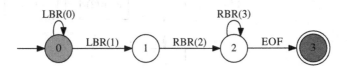

Fig. 1. Regular approximation for string-embedded code after tokenization

Nonterminal which have multiple possible derivations are colored in the figure. To extract a derivation tree for an input string one should choose one production node for each colored nonterminal node.

As it can be seen, some of the words from regular approximation do not belong to the reference language (for example, LBR LBR RBR). The algorithm ignores such strings and constructs SPPF, which contains derivation trees for all recognized strings w.r.t. reference grammar.

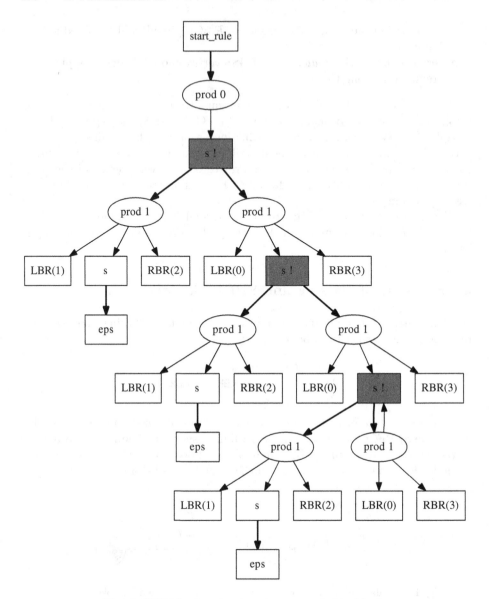

Fig. 2. SPPF for input automaton presented in Fig. 1

4   Correctness of the Algorithm

In this section we present a justification of termination and correctness of our algorithm.

STATEMENT 1. *Algorithm terminates for any input.*

PROOF. Each vertex of inner graph contains, at most, N GSS vertices, where N is the number of parser states. So, the total number of GSS vertices is, at most, $N \times n$, where n is the number of vertices in the inner graph. Since GSS has no multi-edges, the number of its edges is $O((N \times n)^2)$. The algorithm dequeues some vertex to process from $\mathcal{Q}$ in each iteration of the main loop. Vertices are enqueued to $\mathcal{Q}$ only when a new edge is added to GSS. Since the number of GSS edges is finite, the algorithm always terminates.   □

To prove correctness, we first introduce the following definition:

DEFINITION. *Correct tree* is an ordered tree with the following properties:

1. The root is the start nonterminal of the grammar G.
2. The leaf nodes are terminals of G. The sequence of the leaf nodes corresponds to some path in the inner graph.
3. The interior nodes are nonterminals of G. All children of nonterminal N correspond to the symbols of the right-hand side of some production for N in G.

Informally, a correct tree is a derivation tree (w.r.t. reference grammar) for some word in regular approximation. Now we have to prove that, first, SPPF contains only correct trees, and second, that for any recognized by the reference grammar string there is some correct tree in the SPPF.

LEMMA. For every GSS edge (v_t, v_h), $v_t \in V_t.processed$, $v_h \in V_h.processed$, the terminals of the associated subtree correspond to some path in the inner graph p from V_h to V_t.

PROOF. The proof is by induction on the height of derivation tree. The base case is either some ϵ-tree or a tree with a single leaf. An ϵ-tree corresponds to a path of zero length; the tail and the head of the edge associated with ϵ-tree are identical, thus the statement is true. A tree with the single leaf corresponds to a single terminal read from an edge (V_h, V_t) of the inner graph, thus the statement is true.

A tree of height k has a nonterminal N as its root. By third statement of correct tree definition, there is a production $N \to A_0, A_1, \ldots, A_n$ for children $A_0, A_1, \ldots, A_n$ of the root node. A subtree A_i is associated with GSS edge (v_t^i, v_h^i) and, as its height is $k - 1$, by inductive hypothesis, there is a path in the inner graph from V_h^i to V_t^i. $V_t^i = V_h^{i+1}$, since $v_t^i = v_h^{i+1}$, thus there is a path in the inner graph from V_h^0 to V_t^n, corresponding to the tree under consideration.   □

STATEMENT 2. *Every tree, generated from SPPF, is correct.*

PROOF. Consider arbitrary tree, generated from SPPF, and prove that it is correct. The first and the third statements of correctness definition immediately follow from SPPF definition. The second statement of the definition follows from LEMMA 1 by considering all edges from GSS vertices on the last level, labeled by accepting state, to the vertices on level 0.   □

STATEMENT 3. *For every path p in the inner graph, recognized w.r.t. reference grammar, a correct tree corresponding to p can be generated from SPPF.*

PROOF. Consider arbitrary correct tree and show it can be generated from SPPF. The proof follows the proof of correctness for RNGLR algorithm, except for the following moment. RNGLR constructs GSS layer-by-layer: it is guaranteed, that $\forall j \in [0..i-1]$ j-th level of the GSS would be fixed by the time, when i-th level is processed. In our case, this property does not hold, which leads to a possible generation of some paths for already applied reductions. The only possible way to actually add a new path is to add an edge (v_t, v_h), where v_t is already in the GSS and it has some incoming edges. Since the algorithm stores which reductions have passed through each vertex, to overcome this problem it is sufficient to continue passing reductions, stored in v_t, and this is exactly what *applyPassingReductions* function does.   □

5   Conclusion

We presented and proved the correctness of generalized RNGLR algorithm, designed for syntactic analysis of regular sets of tokens. The algorithm constructs a set of derivation trees for every recognized string of the input set in the form of SPPF, whereas non-recognized part of the input is ignored. The distinctive feature of our approach is that, unlike others, it delivers a set of all parse trees, encoded in the form of SPPF, for recognized part. We implemented our algorithm in F# as a part of YaccConstructor project[2] within the framework for string-embedded languages support [15]; host-language specific features were implemented using JetBrains ReSharper SDK[3], which potentially makes it possible to analyse multiple host languages (our experiments involved C# and Javascript).

Presented algorithm does not report incorrect strings from an input set. Nevertheless, the algorithm may still be used in the context of reengineering, when most of the analysed code is errorless. The examples of such tasks are DBMS migration or migration from string-embedding approach to new technologies, e.g. LINQ.

We can indicate some directions for future research. First, the complexity estimation of our algorithm is still unclear; existing literature say very little on this subject; in addition the contribution of SPPF construction has to be taken into account. Another direction concerns the utilization of SPPF for semantic analysis. While it is clear, that availability of SPPF is beneficial in general sense, the concrete ways of its utilization can be cumbersome since SPPF represents potentially infinite set of parse trees.

Acknowledgments. We thank Dmitri Boulytchev for the scientific guidance and the feedback on this work.

---

[2] https://github.com/YaccConstructor/YaccConstructor.
[3] https://www.jetbrains.com/resharper.

A   Appendix: RNGLR pseudocode

Algorithm 3. RNGLR algorithm

1: **function** PARSE($grammar, input$)
2:     $\mathcal{R} \leftarrow \emptyset$ ▷ Queue of tuples of GSS vertex, nonterminal, and reduction length
3:     $\mathcal{Q} \leftarrow \emptyset$ ▷ Collection of pairs of GSS vertex and parser state
4:     **if** $input = \epsilon$ **then**
5:         **if** $grammar$ accepts empty input **then** report success
6:         **else** report failure
7:     **else**
8:         ADDVERTEX($0, 0, startState$)
9:         **for all** i in $0..input.Length - 1$ **do**
10:             REDUCE(i)
11:             PUSH(i)
12:             **if** $i = input.Length - 1$ and there is a vertex in the last level of GSS which state is accepting **then**
13:                 report success
14:             **else** report failure
15: **function** REDUCE(i)
16:     **while** $\mathcal{R}$ is not empty **do**
17:         $(v, N, l) \leftarrow \mathcal{R}.Dequeue()$
18:         find the set $\mathcal{X}$ of vertices reachable from v along the path of length $(l - 1)$
19:         or length 0 if $l = 0$
20:         **for all** $v_h = (level_h, state_h)$ in $\mathcal{X}$ **do**
21:             $state_t \leftarrow$ calculate new state by $state_h$ and nonterminal N
22:             ADDEDGE($i, v_h, v.level, state_{tail}, (l = 0)$)
23: **function** PUSH(i)
24:     $\mathcal{Q}' \leftarrow$ copy $\mathcal{Q}$
25:     **while** $\mathcal{Q}'$ is not empty **do**
26:         $(v, state) \leftarrow \mathcal{Q}.Dequeue()$
27:         ADDEDGE($i, v, v.level + 1, state, false$)

Algorithm 4. GSS construction

1: **function** ADDVERTEX($i, level, state$)
2:     **if** GSS does not contain vertex $v = (level, state)$ **then**
3:         add new vertex $v = (level, state)$ to GSS
4:         calculate the set of shifts by v and the $input[i + 1]$ and add them to $\mathcal{Q}$
5:         calculate the set of zero-reductions by v and the $input[i + 1]$ and
6:         add them to $\mathcal{R}$
7:     **return** v
8: **function** ADDEDGE($i, v_h, level_t, state_t, isZeroReduction$)
9:     $v_t \leftarrow$ ADDVERTEX($i, level_t, state_t$)
10:     **if** GSS does not contain edge from v_t to v_h **then**
11:         add new edge from v_t to v_h to GSS
12:         **if** not $isZeroReduction$ **then**
13:             calculate the set of reductions by v and the $input[i + 1]$ and
14:             add them to $\mathcal{R}$

References

1. ISO. ISO/IEC 9075: 1992. Information Technology – Database Languages – SQL (1992)
2. Houglan, D., Tavistock, A.: Core JSP, p. 416. Upper Saddle River, Prentice Hall PTR (2000)
3. Scott, E., Johnstone, A.: Right nulled GLR parsers. ACM Trans. Program. Lang. Syst. **28**(4), 577–618 (2006)
4. Rekers, J.: Parser generation for interactive environments. Ph.D. thesis. University of Amsterdam, 174p (1992)
5. Asveld, P.R.J., Nijholt, A.: The inclusion problem for some subclasses of context-free languages. Theor. Comput. Sci. **230**(1–2), 247–256 (1999)
6. Fang, Y., Alkhalaf, M., Bultan, T., Ibarra, O.H.: Automata-based symbolic string analysis for vulnerability detection. Formal Methods Syst. Des. **44**(1), 44–70 (2014)
7. Christensen, A.S., Møller, A., Schwartzbach, M.I.: Precise analysis of string expressions. In: Proceedings of the 10th International Conference on Static Analysis, pp. 1–18 (2003)
8. Annamaa, A., Breslav, A., Kabanov, J., Vene, V.: An interactive tool for analyzing embedded SQL queries. In: Ueda, K. (ed.) APLAS 2010. LNCS, vol. 6461, pp. 131–138. Springer, Heidelberg (2010)
9. Annamaa, A., Breslav, A., Vene, V.: Using abstract lexical analysis and parsing to detect errors in string-embedded DSL statements. In: Proceedings of the 22nd Nordic Workshop on Programming Theory, pp. 20–22 (2010)
10. Doh, K.-G., Kim, H., Schmidt, D.A.: Abstract parsing: static analysis of dynamically generated string output using LR-parsing technology. In: Palsberg, J., Su, Z. (eds.) SAS 2009. LNCS, vol. 5673, pp. 256–272. Springer, Heidelberg (2009)
11. Doh, K.-G., Kim, H., Schmidt, D.A.: Abstract LR-parsing. In: Agha, G., Danvy, O., Meseguer, J. (eds.) Formal Modeling: Actors, Open Systems, Biological Systems. LNCS, vol. 7000, pp. 90–109. Springer, Heidelberg (2011)
12. Kim, H., Doh, K.-G., Schmidt, D.A.: Static validation of dynamically generated HTML documents based on abstract parsing and semantic processing. In: Logozzo, F., Fähndrich, M. (eds.) Static Analysis. LNCS, vol. 7935, pp. 194–214. Springer, Heidelberg (2013)
13. Cousot, P., Cousot, R.: Abstract interpretation: a unified lattice model for static analysis of programs by construction or approximation of fixpoints. In: Proceedings of the 4th Symposium on Principles of Programming Languages, pp. 238–252 (1977)
14. Tomita, M.: An efficient all-paths parsing algorithm for natural languages. Carnegie-Mellon University, Department of Computer Science (1984)
15. Grigorev, S., Verbitskaia, E., Ivanov, A., Polubelova, M., Mavchun, E.: String-embedded language support in integrated development environment. In: Proceedings of the 10th Central and Eastern European Software Engineering Conference in Russia, pp. 21:1–21:11 (2014)

Branching Processes of Timed Petri Nets

Irina Virbitskaite[1,2(✉)], Victor Borovlyov[1,2], and Louchka Popova-Zeugmann[3]

[1] A.P. Ershov Institute of Informatics Systems,
SB RAS, 6, Acad. Lavrentiev avenue, 630090 Novosibirsk, Russia
virb@iis.nsk.su
[2] Novosibirsk State University, 2, Pirogov avenue, 630090 Novosibirsk, Russia
[3] Humboldt University of Berlin, Unter den Linden 6, 10099 Berlin, Germany

Abstract. The intention of this note is to spread the Couvreur et al.'s semantic framework of branching processes [9], suitable for describing the behavior of general Petri nets with interleaving semantics, to timed general Petri nets with step semantics in order to characterize unfolding as the greatest element of a complete lattice of branching processes. In case of maximal step semantics of timed Petri nets, we impose some restrictions on the model behavior and define a new class of branching processes and unfoldings under the name of apt ones which are shown to satisfy the complete lattice properties.

1 Introduction

In recent years there has been a growing interest in the development and use of unfolding-based approaches. Originally introduced in the setting of Petri nets, unfolding can be seen as a specification formalism that is able to describe the intrinsic parallelism of the modeled systems, as well as a semantics providing in a single structure explicit information concerning causality, conflict and concurrency of events in systems computations.

The unfolding (occurrence net with forward branched places) semantics was firstly introduced by Nielsen, Plotkin and Winskel in [17] for safe Petri nets. Engelfriet in [10] characterized the unfolding as the greatest element of a complete lattice of occurrence nets embedding into initially one marked Petri nets without arc weights. Meseguer et al. [16] extended this to cover also arc weights. More recently, Couvreur et al. [9] proposed a new structure, the faithful unfolding of a Petri net, which allows for the good algebraic properties identified by Engelfriet [10], and which is applicable to general nets, without any finiteness or safeness assumption.

Whilst the unfolding can be infinite, McMillan identified the possibility of a finite prefix that contains enough information to reason about all the reachable markings of the original Petri nets. The approach has gained the interest of researchers in verification (see e.g. [2,5,7,11]), diagnosis [3,4] and planning [6,14].

This work is supported in part by DFG-RFBR (project CAVER, grants BE 1267/ 14-1 and 14-01-91334).

M. Mazzara and A. Voronkov (Eds.): PSI 2015, LNCS 9609, pp. 303–313, 2016.
DOI: 10.1007/978-3-319-41579-6_23

We especially emphasize the expansion of the finite prefix approach towards time(d) extensions of Petri nets [8,12,13]. Besides, an infinite branching process semantics has been proposed for hierarchical timed safe Petri nets, where time intervals of duration are attached to each transition. It is also worth mentioning the papers [1,19] where causal net process semantics have been put forward for time safe Petri nets and timed bounded Petri nets, respectively.

The intention of this note is to spread the Couvreur et al.'s semantic framework of branching processes [9], suitable for describing the behavior of general Petri nets with interleaving semantics, to timed general Petri nets with step semantics in order to characterize unfolding as the greatest element of a complete lattice of branching processes. In case of maximal step semantics (all enabled non-conflicting transitions are fired) of timed Petri nets, we impose some restrictions on the model structure and behavior and define a new class of branching processes and unfoldings under the name of apt ones which are shown to satisfy the complete lattice properties.

2   Preliminaries

Multisets. Let $\mathbb{N}$ be the set of non-negative integers. A *multiset* over X is a function $\mu : X \to \mathbb{N}$, i.e. $\mu \in \mathbb{N}^X$. The number $\mu(x) \in \mathbb{N}$ is the *coefficient* of $x \in X$. The *support* of the multiset μ is the set $\overline{\mu} = \{x \in X \mid \mu(x) > 0\}$. Note that the support of a multiset may be infinite. Let $\emptyset$ denote the empty multiset. Multisets are often represented as vectors in $\mathbb{N}^X$ or as sums of the form $\sum_{x \in X} \mu(x)x$. The operations of addition and subtraction of multisets over X are defined componentwise, as on vectors (note however that negative coefficients are not allowed). Multisets are partially ordered by letting $\mu \leq \nu$ if $\mu(x) \leq \nu(x)$ for each $x \in X$. An infinite sum $\sum_{i \in I} \mu_i$ of multisets is said to be *well-defined* if $\sum_{i \in I} \mu_i(x) \in \mathbb{N}$, for any $x \in X$. If X and Y are sets, a mapping $h : X \longrightarrow Y$ can be extended to multisets, $h : \mathcal{N}^X \longrightarrow \mathcal{N}^Y$, by letting $h(\mu) = \sum_{x \in X} \mu(x)h(x)$ if the sum is well-defined.

Graphs. Let $(X, \to)$ be a graph. We denote by $\xrightarrow{*}$ ($\xrightarrow{+}$) the reflexive and transitive closure (transitive closure) of $\to$. We use the following notions: for $Y \subseteq X$, ${}^\bullet Y = \{x \in X \mid \exists y \in Y, x \to y\}$, $Y^\bullet = \{x \in X \mid \exists y \in Y, y \to x\}$, ${}^*Y = \{x \in X \mid \exists y \in Y, x \xrightarrow{*} y\}$, $Y^* = \{x \in X \mid \exists y \in Y, y \xrightarrow{*} x\}$. If $Y = \{y\}$, we write simply ${}^\bullet y$, $y^\bullet$, ${}^*y$ and y^*. When the graph $(X, \to)$ is *acyclic* (i.e., $x \xrightarrow{+} x$ never holds, for any $x \in X$), the relation $\xrightarrow{*}$ forms a partial order on X. In this case, the graph $(X, \to)$ is *finitary* if $|\{y \in X \mid y \xrightarrow{*} x\}| < \infty$, i.e. every vertex is preceded by a finite number of vertices.

Lattices. For a partially ordered set $(X, \leq)$ and a subset $Y \subseteq X$, we say that $x \in X$ is a *lower (respectively, upper) bound* of Y if $x \leq y$ (respectively, $y \leq x$) for each element $y \in Y$. The greatest lower bound (respectively, least upper bound) of Y, if it exists, is denoted by $inf(Y)$ (respectively, $sup(Y)$). If any two-element subset of X admits a greatest lower bound and a least upper bound, X is called a *lattice*. It is a *complete lattice*, if any subset of X admits a greatest lower and a least upper bound.

3   Timed Petri Nets

In this section we introduce the syntax and (maximal) step semantics of timed Petri nets whose transitions are labeled over a set of actions with time durations.

Let $\mathbb{N}$ be a set of natural numbers, and $\mathcal{A}$ a set of actions.

Definition 1. *A (labeled) timed Petri net (over $\mathcal{A}$) (TdPN) is a 7-tuple $\mathcal{N}_\mathcal{A} = (P, T, Pre, Post, m_0, L, \Delta)$ such that*

1. *$N(\mathcal{N}_\mathcal{A}) = (P, T, Pre, Post, m_0)$ is a Petri net consisting of: two disjoint (finite or infinite) sets P and T whose elements are called places and transitions, respectively, two multisets Pre and $Post$ over $P \times T^1$ called flow functions, and a multiset m_0 over P called the initial marking. A marking m of $N(\mathcal{N}_\mathcal{A})$ is a multiset over P^2. The pre-condition of a transition $t \in T$ (denoted $Pre(t)$) is the marking $Pre(\cdot, t)$, and the post-condition of t (denoted $Post(t)$) is the marking $Post(\cdot, t)$. Moreover, $\sum_{t \in T'} Pre(t)$ and $\sum_{t \in T'} Post(t)$ are the markings[3] of $N(\mathcal{N}_\mathcal{A})$, for all $T' \subseteq T$,*
2. *$L : T \longrightarrow \mathcal{A}$ is a labeling function associating an action from $\mathcal{A}$ with each transition from T,*
3. *$\Delta : \mathcal{A} \longrightarrow \mathbb{N}$ is a timing function associating a natural number from $\mathbb{N}$ with each action from $\mathcal{A}$. Let $sup(\mathcal{N}_\mathcal{A}) = \sup\{\Delta(L(t)) \mid t \in T\}$.*

Notice that a TdPN is a timed Petri net as specified in [18] in case if the sets P and T are finite, $\mathcal{A} = T$, and L is the identical function.

Example 1. Figure 1 shows a graphical representation of a labeled timed Petri net $\mathcal{N}_\mathcal{A}$ over the set $\mathcal{A} = \{a_1, a_2, a_3, a_4\}$ of actions. Here, places and transitions are depicted as circles and as rectangles, respectively; pre- and post-conditions

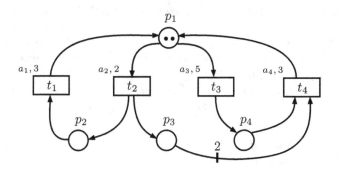

Fig. 1. A graphical representation of the TdPN $\mathcal{N}_\mathcal{A}$

---

[1] The number of arcs between each place and each transition is a natural number.

[2] A marking contains a natural number of tokens in each net place.

[3] The number of arcs between each place and each subset of transitions is a natural number.

of the transitions are indicated by labels on arcs, if the corresponding coefficients are greater than 1; the initial marking is shown by the corresponding numbers of tokens in the places; each transition is labeled by an action with the corresponding time duration, indicated near the transition.

For TdPNs $\mathcal{N}_\mathcal{A} = (P, T, Pre, Post, m_0, L, \Delta)$ and $\mathcal{N}'_\mathcal{A} = (P', T', Pre', Post', m'_0, L', \Delta')$, a mapping $h : P \cup T \rightarrow P' \cup T'$ is a *homomorphism* from $\mathcal{N}_\mathcal{A}$ to $\mathcal{N}'_\mathcal{A}$ iff

- $h(P) \subseteq P'$, $h(T) \subseteq T'$,
- $m'_0 = h(m_0)$,
- $\Delta' = \Delta$,
- for each transition $t \in T$, it holds:
  - $Pre'(h(t)) = h(Pre(t))$,
  - $Post'(h(t)) = h(Post(t))$,
  - $L'(h(t)) = L(t)$.

Notice that in this definition, $h(m_0)$, $h(Pre(t))$ and $h(Post(t))$ must be well-defined.

We now move to considering the behavior of TdPNs. A *state* of a TdPN $\mathcal{N}_\mathcal{A}$ is a triple $z = (m, ft, u)$, where m is a marking of $N(\mathcal{N}_\mathcal{A})$, ft is a set of the firing transitions, and $u : \mathcal{A} \longrightarrow \mathbb{N}$ is a *dynamic timing function* such that $u(a) \leq \Delta(a)$, for all $a \in \mathcal{A}$. The *initial state* z_0 is a triple $(m_0, \emptyset, u_0)$, where m_0 is the *initial marking* and $u_0(a) = 0$, for all $a \in \mathcal{A}$. A non-empty subset $R \subseteq T$ is a *step in a state* z if it holds: (i) $\sum_{t \in R} Pre(t) \leq m$, (ii) $\forall t \in R : u(L(t)) = 0$, (iii) $\forall t, t' \in R : t' \neq t \longrightarrow L(t) \neq L(t')$; a *maximal step in* z, if R is a step in z and, moreover, the following property holds: for all $\hat{t} \in T \setminus R$, $(Pre(\hat{t}) \leq m \wedge u(L(\hat{t})) = 0 \wedge \forall t \in R : L(\hat{t}) \neq L(t)) \longrightarrow (\sum_{t \in R} Pre(t) + Pre(\hat{t}) \not\leq m)$.

Definition 2. *Let* $z = (m, ft, u)$ *be a state of a TdPN* $\mathcal{N}_\mathcal{A}$ *and* $R \subseteq T$. *Then,*

- *R can fire in z (denoted $z \xrightarrow{R}_{(max)}$) iff R is a (maximal) step in z,*
- *after the firing of the (maximal) step R in z, the TdPN moves to the state $z' = (m', ft', u')$ (denoted $z \xrightarrow{R}_{(max)} z'$), where*
  1. *$m' := m - \sum_{t \in R} Pre(t) + \sum_{\substack{t \in R, \\ \Delta(L(t)) = 0}} Post(t)$,*
  2. *$ft' := ft \cup \{t \in R \mid \Delta(L(t)) \neq 0\}$,*
  3. *$u'(a) := \begin{cases} \Delta(a), & \text{if } t \in R \wedge a = L(t), \\ u(a), & \text{otherwise,} \end{cases}$*
- *the elapsing of one time unit in step semantics (denoted $z \xrightarrow{1}$) is always possible in z; the elapsing of one time unit in maximal step semantics (denoted $z \xrightarrow{1}_{max}$) is possible in z iff $u(L(t)) = 0 \longrightarrow Pre(t) \not\leq m$, for all $t \in T$,*
- *after the elapsing of one time unit in (maximal) step semantics in z, the TdPN moves to the state $z' = (m', ft', u')$ (denoted $z \xrightarrow{1}_{(max)} z'$), where*

1. $m' := m + \sum\limits_{\substack{t \in ft \\ u(L(t))=1}} Post(t)$,

2. $ft' := \{t \in ft \mid u(L(t)) > 1\}$,

3. $u'(a) := \begin{cases} u(a) - 1, & \text{if } u(a) > 1, \\ 0, & \text{otherwise.} \end{cases}$

Lemma 1. *Given a homomorphism h from a TdPN $\mathcal{N}_A$ to a TdPN $\mathcal{N}'_A$, and a state (m, ft, u) of $\mathcal{N}_A$ such that $h(m)$ is well-defined, h is injective on ft, and $u = h(u)$,*

(i) *if $(m, ft, u) \xrightarrow{R} (m', ft', u')$ in $\mathcal{N}_A$, then $h(m')$ is well-defined, h is injective on R, and $h(m, ft, u) \xrightarrow{h(R)} h(m', ft', u')$ in $\mathcal{N}'_A$,*

(ii) *$(m, ft, u) \xrightarrow{1} (m', ft', u')$ in $\mathcal{N}_A$, then $h(m')$ is well-defined, h is injective on ft', and $h(m, ft, u) \xrightarrow{1} h(m', ft', u')$ in $\mathcal{N}'_A$.*

For a TdPN $\mathcal{N}_A$, $\sigma := z_0 = z_0^0 \xrightarrow{R_1}_{(max)} z_1^0 \xrightarrow{1}_{(max)} z_1^1 \ldots z_1^{j_1-1} \xrightarrow{1}_{(max)} z_1^{j_1}$
$\ldots z_{n-1}^{j_{n-1}} \xrightarrow{R_n}_{(max)} z_n^0 \xrightarrow{1}_{(max)} z_n^1 \ldots z_n^{j_n-1} \xrightarrow{1}_{(max)} z_n^{j_n}$ such that $z_i^k \neq z_i^{k+1}$ for all $1 \leq i \leq n$ and $0 \leq k < j_i$ ($n \geq 0$, $j_i \geq 0$) is a *firing sequence in (maximal) step semantics*. A state z of $\mathcal{N}_A$ is *reachable in (maximal) step semantics* if there is a firing sequence in (maximal) step semantics containing z.

We say that $\mathcal{N}_A$ is

- *plainly labeled* iff the labeling function L is injective,
- *time progressive* iff $\sum\limits_{i>0} \Delta(L(t_i)) \geq sup(\mathcal{N}_A)$ for each infinite set $\{t_1, t_2, \ldots\}$ of transitions such that $\forall i > 0 : t_i^\bullet \cap {}^\bullet t_{i+1} \neq \emptyset$,
- *possessing the non-multiple enabling property in (maximal) step semantics* iff for each state (m, ft, u) reachable in (maximal) step semantics, for each (maximal) step R in (m, ft, u), and for each transition $t \in R$, there is a place $p \in {}^\bullet t$ such that $m(p) - \sum\limits_{t' \in R} Pre(p, t') < Pre(p, t)$,
- *proper* iff $\mathcal{N}_A$ is plainly labeled, time progressive, and possessing the non-multiple enabling property in maximal step semantics,
- *quasi-live in (maximal) step semantics* iff for all $t \in T$ there exists a (maximal) step R in a state (m, ft, u) reachable in (maximal) step semantics of $\mathcal{N}_A$ such that $t \in R$.

Example 2. Consider the behavior of the TdPN $\mathcal{N}_A$ shown in Fig. 1. The initial state of $\mathcal{N}_A$ is $z_0 = (2p_1, \emptyset, 0)$. The sets $\{t_2\}$, $\{t_3\}$ and $\{t_2, t_3\}$ are steps in z_0, and, moreover, $\{t_2, t_3\}$ is the only maximal step in z_0. After the firing of the step $\{t_2\}$ in z_0, $\mathcal{N}_A$ moves to the state $z_1 = (p_1, \{t_2\}, u(a_1) = u(a_3) = u(a_4) = 0; u(a_2) = 2)$, and after the elapsing of one time unit in step semantics in z_1, we get the state $z_1^1 = (p_1, \{t_2\}, u(a_1) = u(a_3) = u(a_4) = 0; u(a_2) = 1)$. Furthermore,

$\sigma = z_0 \xrightarrow{\{t_2,t_3\}}_{(max)} z_1^0 \xrightarrow{1}_{(max)} z_1^1 \xrightarrow{1}_{(max)} z_1^2 \xrightarrow{\{t_1\}}_{(max)} z_2^0 \xrightarrow{1}_{(max)} z_2^1 \xrightarrow{1}_{(max)}$
$z_2^2 \xrightarrow{1}_{(max)} z_2^3 \xrightarrow{\{t_2\}}_{(max)} z_3^0 \xrightarrow{1}_{(max)} z_3^1 \xrightarrow{1}_{(max)} z_3^2 \xrightarrow{\{t_1,t_4\}}_{(max)} z_4^0$ is a firing

sequence in (maximal) step semantics of $\mathcal{N}_\mathcal{A}$, where $z_1^0 = (\emptyset, \{t_2, t_3\}, u(a_1) = u(a_4) = 0; u(a_2) = 2; u(a_3) = 5), z_1^1 = (\emptyset, \{t_2, t_3\}, u(a_1) = u(a_4) = 0; u(a_2) = 1; u(a_3) = 4), z_1^2 = (p_2 + p_3, \{t_3\}, u(a_1) = u(a_2) = u(a_4) = 0; u(a_3) = 3), z_2^0 = (p_3, \{t_1, t_3\}, u(a_2) = u(a_4) = 0; u(a_1) = 3; u(a_3) = 3), z_2^1 = (p_3, \{t_1, t_3\}, u(a_2) = u(a_4) = 0; u(a_1) = 2; u(a_3) = 2), z_2^2 = (p_3, \{t_1, t_3\}, u(a_2) = u(a_4) = 0; u(a_1) = 1; u(a_3) = 1), z_3^3 = (p_1 + p_3 + p_4, \emptyset, u(a_1) = u(a_2) = u(a_3) = u(a_4) = 0), z_3^0 = (p_3 + p_4, \{t_2\}, u(a_1) = u(a_3) = u(a_4) = 0; u(a_2) = 2), z_3^1 = (p_3 + p_4, \{t_2\}, u(a_1) = u(a_3) = u(a_4) = 0; u(a_2) = 1), z_3^2 = (p_2 + 2p_3 + p_4, \emptyset, u(a_1) = u(a_2) = u(a_3) = u(a_4) = 0), z_4^0 = (\emptyset, \{t_1, t_4\}, u(a_2) = u(a_3) = 0; u(a_1) = 3; u(a_4) = 3)$. Then, we can conclude that the TdPN $\mathcal{N}_\mathcal{A}$ is quasi-live in (maximal) step semantics. It is not difficult to check that $\mathcal{N}_\mathcal{A}$ is a proper TdPN.

4   Branching Processes and Unfoldings of TdPNs

Following traditions, we consider a branching process of a TdPN as a pair consisting of an occurrence net being a TdPN with the acyclic and finitary bipartite graph whose nodes are called conditions (instead of places) and events (instead of transitions) and a homomorphism from the occurrence net to the TdPN, satisfying some additional restrictions.

A TdPN $\mathcal{O}_\mathcal{A} = (B, E, In, Out, q_0, l, \delta)$ is a *(labeled) occurrence net (over $\mathcal{A}$) (TdON)* in (maximal) step semantics iff

 – $|{}^\bullet b| \leq 1$, for each condition $b \in B$,
 – the support of q_0 is exactly the set $\{b \in B \mid |{}^\bullet b| = 0\}$,
 – $\mathcal{O}_\mathcal{A}$ is quasi-live in (maximal) step semantics.

According to the definition above, the graph of any TdON $\mathcal{O}_\mathcal{A}$ is acyclic and finitary.

Given two TdONs $\mathcal{O}_\mathcal{A} = (B, E, In, Out, q_0, l, \delta)$ and $\mathcal{O}'_\mathcal{A} = (B', E', In', Out', q'_0, l', \delta')$, we say that $\mathcal{O}_\mathcal{A}$ is a *subnet* of $\mathcal{O}'_\mathcal{A}$ (denoted $\mathcal{O}_\mathcal{A} \sqsubseteq \mathcal{O}'_\mathcal{A}$), if $B \subseteq B'$, $E \subseteq E'$, $q_0 = q'_0$, $\delta = \delta'$, and $In(e) = In'(e)$, $Out(e) = Out'(e)$, $l(e) = l'(e)$, for all $e \in E$. A subnet $\mathcal{O}_\mathcal{A}$ of $\mathcal{O}'_\mathcal{A}$ is a *prefix* of $\mathcal{O}'_\mathcal{A}$ if $x \in B \cup E$ whenever $x \xrightarrow{*} y$ for some $y \in B \cup E$. It is not difficult to see that any subnet $\mathcal{O}_\mathcal{A}$ of $\mathcal{O}'_\mathcal{A}$ is a TdON iff $\mathcal{O}_\mathcal{A}$ is a prefix of $\mathcal{O}'_\mathcal{A}$.

Definition 3. *Given a TdPN $\mathcal{N}_\mathcal{A} = (P, T, Pre, Post, m_0, L, \Delta)$, a pair $\beta = (\mathcal{O}_\mathcal{A} = (B, E, In, Out, q_0, l, \delta), h)$ is a* branching process in (maximal) step semantics *of $\mathcal{N}_\mathcal{A}$ iff $\mathcal{O}_\mathcal{A}$ is a TdON in (maximal) step semantics and $h : B \cup E \to P \cup T$ is a homomorphism from $\mathcal{O}_\mathcal{A}$ to $\mathcal{N}_\mathcal{A}$ such that:*

(i) h is injective on $\overline{q}_0$, and on the post-set $e^\bullet$, for all $e \in E$, and
(ii) whenever $In(e) = In(e')$ and $h(e) = h(e')$, then $e = e'$, for all $e, e' \in E$.

For branching processes $\beta = (\mathcal{O}_\mathcal{A}, h)$ and $\beta' = (\mathcal{O}'_\mathcal{A}, h')$ in (maximal) step semantics of a TdPN $\mathcal{N}_\mathcal{A}$, a homomorphism g from $\mathcal{O}_\mathcal{A}$ to $\mathcal{O}'_\mathcal{A}$ is a *homomorphism from β to β'* if $h = h' \circ g$.

Lemma 2. *Given branching processes $\beta = (\mathcal{O}_\mathcal{A}, h)$ and $\beta' = (\mathcal{O}'_\mathcal{A}, h')$ in (maximal) step semantics of a TdPN $\mathcal{N}_\mathcal{A}$, there is at most one homomorphism g from β to β' and, moreover, g is injective, if it exists.*

For a branching process $\beta = (\mathcal{O}_\mathcal{A}, h)$ in maximal step semantics of $\mathcal{N}_\mathcal{A}$, a state (q, fe, u) reachable in maximal state semantics of $\mathcal{O}_\mathcal{A}$ is called *finishing* iff in each firing sequence σ containing (q, fe, u), there is no maximal step in (q, fe, u) and in each state following (q, fe, u) in σ.

A branching process $\beta = (\mathcal{O}_\mathcal{A}, h)$ in (maximal) step semantics of $\mathcal{N}_\mathcal{A}$ is called *apt* iff for each state (q, fe, u) reachable in (maximal step semantics) of $\mathcal{O}_\mathcal{A}$, it holds: whenever $(q, fe, u) \xrightarrow{R}_{(max)}$ in $\mathcal{O}_\mathcal{A}$, then $h(q, fe, u) \xrightarrow{h(R)}_{(max)}$ in $\mathcal{N}_\mathcal{A}$, and whenever $(q, fe, u) \xrightarrow{1}_{(max)}$ in $\mathcal{O}_\mathcal{A}$ (and (q, fe, u) is a non-finishing state), then $h(q, ft, u) \xrightarrow{1}_{(max)}$ in $\mathcal{N}_\mathcal{A}$. Notice that every branching process in step semantics of $\mathcal{N}_\mathcal{A}$ is apt but it is not the case for branching processes in maximal step semantics of $\mathcal{N}_\mathcal{A}$.

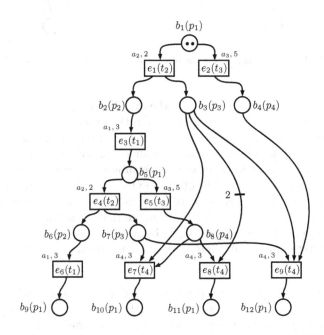

Fig. 2. The branching process β in step semantics of the TdPN $\mathcal{N}_\mathcal{A}$

Example 3. First, consider Fig. 2 with the branching process $\beta = (\mathcal{O}_\mathcal{A}, h)$ in step semantics of the TdPN $\mathcal{N}_\mathcal{A}$ shown in Fig. 1. Here, the corresponding values of the homomorphism h are indicated in parentheses near by the events and conditions. However, β is not a branching process in maximal step semantics of $\mathcal{N}_\mathcal{A}$ because it is impossible to find a maximal step in some state reachable

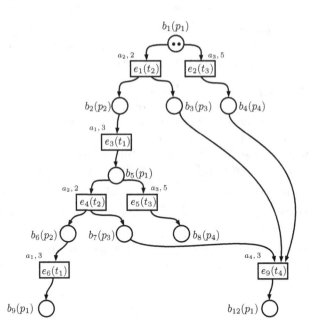

Fig. 3. The branching process β' in maximal step semantics of the TdPN $\mathcal{N}_A$

in maximal step semantics, containing the event e_7 or the event e_8, i.e. $\mathcal{O}_A$ is not quasi-live in maximal step semantics. On the other hand, Fig. 3 shows the branching process $\beta' = (\mathcal{O}'_A, h')$ in maximal step semantics of $\mathcal{N}_A$. Moreover, it not difficult to become convinced that β' is an apt branching process in maximal step semantics of $\mathcal{N}_A$. Further, examine the subnet $\mathcal{O}''_A$ consisting of the event e_1 and the conditions b_1, b_2 and b_3 of the TdON $\mathcal{O}'_A$ and the restriction h'' of h' to the elements of $\mathcal{O}''_A$. Clearly, $\beta'' = (\mathcal{O}''_A, h'')$ is a branching process in maximal step semantics of $\mathcal{N}_A$. However, it is easy to see that β'' is not an apt branching process in maximal step semantics of $\mathcal{N}_A$ because $R^{O''} = \{e_1\}$ is a maximal step in the initial state of $\mathcal{O}''_A$ but $h''(R^{O''})$ is not a maximal step in the initial state of $\mathcal{N}_A$.

Lemma 3. *Given an (apt) branching process $(\mathcal{O}_A, h)$ in (maximal) step semantics of a TdPN $\mathcal{N}_A$, if (q, fe, u) is a (non-finishing) state reachable in (maximal) step semantics of $\mathcal{O}_A$, then $h(q, fe, u)$ is a state reachable in (maximal) step semantics of $\mathcal{N}_A$.*

Lemma 4. *Given an (apt) branching process $(\mathcal{O}_A, h)$ in (maximal) step semantics of a TdPN $\mathcal{N}_A$ possessing the non-multiple enabling property, $\mathcal{O}_A$ is a TdON possessing the non-multiple enabling property.*

We extend the natural partial order $\sqsubseteq$ on TdONs in (maximal) step semantics to a quasi-order $\preceq$ on branching processes in (maximal) step semantics of $\mathcal{N}_A$ as follows: $\beta \preceq \beta'$ iff there exists a homomorphism from β to β'. We say that β

and β' are *isomorphic* iff $\beta \preceq \beta'$ and $\beta' \preceq \beta$. A $\preceq$-maximal branching process in (maximal) step semantics of $\mathcal{N}_A$ is called an *unfolding* in (maximal) step semantics of $\mathcal{N}_A$.

Consider a characterization of (apt) unfoldings in (maximal) step semantics of TdPNs.

Proposition 1. *An (apt) branching process $\beta = (\mathcal{O}_A, h)$ in (maximal) step semantics of a (proper) TdPN $\mathcal{N}_A$ is its (apt) unfolding in (maximal) step semantics iff the following property holds:*

(*) whenever (q, fe, u) is a state reachable in (maximal) step semantics of $\mathcal{O}_A$, R is a (maximal) step in $h(q, fe, u)$ of $\mathcal{N}_A$, containing a transition t, such that $Pre(t) = h(\widetilde{q})$ for some marking $\widetilde{q} \leq q$, then there exists a (maximal) step R^O in (q, fe, u), containing an event e, such that $h(R^O) = R$, $h(e) = t$, and $In(e) = \widetilde{q}$.

The following three results establish important properties of unfoldings of TdPNs.

Lemma 5. *Given an (apt) branching process $\beta = (\mathcal{O}_A, h)$ and an (apt) unfolding $\beta' = (\mathcal{O}'_A, h')$ in (maximal) step semantics of a (proper) TdPN $\mathcal{N}_A$, there is a unique homomorphism g from β to β'.*

Lemma 6. *Given (apt) unfoldings β and β' in (maximal) step semantics of (proper) $\mathcal{N}_A$, such that $\beta \preceq \beta'$, β and β' are isomorphic.*

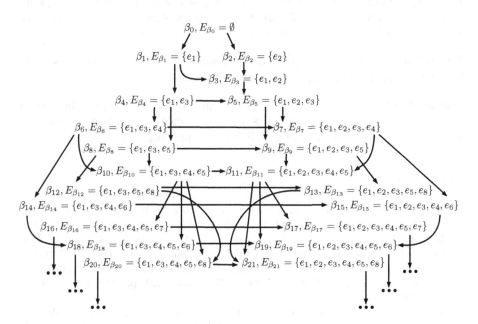

Fig. 4. An initial fragment of the complete lattice of branching processes in step semantics of the TdPN $\mathcal{N}_A$

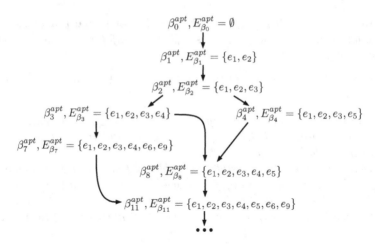

$$\beta_0^{apt}, E_{\beta_0}^{apt} = \emptyset$$

$$\beta_1^{apt}, E_{\beta_1}^{apt} = \{e_1, e_2\}$$

$$\beta_2^{apt}, E_{\beta_2}^{apt} = \{e_1, e_2, e_3\}$$

$$\beta_3^{apt}, E_{\beta_3}^{apt} = \{e_1, e_2, e_3, e_4\} \qquad \beta_4^{apt}, E_{\beta_4}^{apt} = \{e_1, e_2, e_3, e_5\}$$

$$\beta_7^{apt}, E_{\beta_7}^{apt} = \{e_1, e_2, e_3, e_4, e_6, e_9\}$$

$$\beta_8^{apt}, E_{\beta_8}^{apt} = \{e_1, e_2, e_3, e_4, e_5\}$$

$$\beta_{11}^{apt}, E_{\beta_{11}}^{apt} = \{e_1, e_2, e_3, e_4, e_5, e_6, e_9\}$$

$$\vdots$$

Fig. 5. An initial fragment of the complete lattice of apt branching processes in maximal step semantics of the TdPN $\mathcal{N}_\mathcal{A}$

Theorem 1. *Every (proper) TdPN $\mathcal{N}_\mathcal{A}$ has a unique up to isomorphism (apt) unfolding $\mathcal{U}_{(apt)}$ in (maximal) step semantics such that $\beta \preceq \mathcal{U}_{(apt)}$, for any (apt) branching process β in (maximal) step semantics of $\mathcal{N}_\mathcal{A}$.*

Theorem 1 and Lemma 2 imply that every (apt) branching process in (maximal) step semantics of a (proper) TdPN $\mathcal{N}_\mathcal{A}$ is isomorphic to a single prefix of the (apt) unfolding in (maximal) step semantics of $\mathcal{N}_\mathcal{A}$. So, we are ready to establish the following important fact.

Proposition 2. *The set of (apt) branching processes in (maximal) step semantics of a (proper) TdPN $\mathcal{N}_\mathcal{A}$ forms a complete lattice w.r.t. $\preceq$.*

Example 4. Figures 4 and 5 show initial fragments of the complete lattices of branching processes in step semantics and apt branching processes in maximal step semantics, respectively, of the TdPN $\mathcal{N}_\mathcal{A}$ depicted in Fig. 1.

References

1. Aura, T., Lilius, J.: Time processes for time Petri nets. In: Azéma, P., Balbo, G. (eds.) ICATPN 1997. LNCS, vol. 1248, pp. 136–155. Springer, Heidelberg (1997)
2. Baldan, P., Bruni, A., Corradini, A., Koenig, B., Rodriguez, C., Schwoon, S.: Efficient unfolding of contextual Petri nets. Theor. Comput. Sci. **449**, 2–22 (2012)
3. Baldan, P., Haar, S., König, B.: Distributed unfolding of Petri nets. In: Aceto, L., Ingólfsdóttir, A. (eds.) FOSSACS 2006. LNCS, vol. 3921, pp. 126–141. Springer, Heidelberg (2006)
4. Benveniste, A., Fabre, E., Jard, C., Haar, S.: Diagnosis of asynchronous discrete event systems, a net unfolding approach. IEEE Trans. Autom. Control **48**(5), 714–727 (2003)

5. Bergenthum, R., Mauser, S., Lorenz, R., Juhas, G.: Unfolding semantics of Petri nets based on token flows. Fundamenta Informaticae **94**(3–4), 331–360 (2009)
6. Bonet, B., Haslum, P., Hickmott, S.L., Thiébaux, S.: Directed unfolding of Petri nets. In: Jensen, K., Aalst, W.M.P., Billington, J. (eds.) Transactions on Petri Nets and Other Models of Concurrency I. LNCS, vol. 5100, pp. 172–198. Springer, Heidelberg (2008)
7. Bonet, B., Haslumb, P., Khomenko, V., Thiebauxb, S., Vogler, W.: Recent advances in unfolding technique. Theor. Comput. Sci. **551**, 84–101 (2014)
8. Chatain, T., Jard, C.: Time supervision of concurrent systems using symbolic unfoldings of time Petri nets. In: Pettersson, P., Yi, W. (eds.) FORMATS 2005. LNCS, vol. 3829, pp. 196–210. Springer, Heidelberg (2005)
9. Couvreur, J., Poitrenaud, D., Weil, P.: Branching processes of general Petri nets. Fundamenta Informaticae **122**, 31–58 (2013)
10. Engelfriet, J.: Branching processes of Petri nets. Acta Informatica **28**(6), 575–591 (1991)
11. Esparza, J.: Model checking using net unfoldings. Sci. Comput. Program. **23**(2–3), 151–195 (1994)
12. Fleischhack, H., Pelz, E.: Hierarchical timed high level nets and their branching processes. In: Aalst, W.M.P., Best, E. (eds.) ICATPN 2003. LNCS, vol. 2679, pp. 397–416. Springer, Heidelberg (2003)
13. Fleischhack, H., Stehno, C.: Computing a finite prefix of a time Petri net. In: Esparza, J., Lakos, C.A. (eds.) ICATPN 2002. LNCS, vol. 2360, pp. 163–181. Springer, Heidelberg (2002)
14. Hickmott, S., Rintanen, J., Thiebaux, S., White, L.: Planning via Petri net unfolding. In: Proceedings of 20th International Joint Conference on Artificial Intelligence. AAAI Press, pp. 1904–1911(2007)
15. Khomenko, V., Koutny, M., Vogler, W.: Canonical prefixes of Petri net unfoldings. Acta Informatica **40**(2), 95–118 (2003)
16. Meseguer, J., Montanari, U., Sassone, V.: On the semantics of place/transition Petri nets. Math. Struct. Comput. Sci. **7**(4), 359–397 (1997)
17. Nielsen, M., Plotkin, G.D., Winskel, G.: Petri nets, event structures and domains. part i. theor. comput. sci. **13**(1), 85–108 (1981)
18. Popova-Zeugmann, L.: Time and Petri Nets, pp. 1–209. Springer, Heidelberg (2013). I-XI
19. Valero, V., de Frutos, D., Cuartero, F.: Timed processes of timed Petri nets. In: DeMichelis, G., Díaz, M. (eds.) ICATPN 1995. LNCS, vol. 935, pp. 490–509. Springer, Heidelberg (1995)

Implementation and Evaluation of Contextual Natural Deduction for Minimal Logic

Bruno Woltzenlogel Paleo[1,2(✉)]

[1] Vienna University of Technology, Vienna, Austria
[2] Australian National University, Canberra, Australia
bruno.wp@gmail.com

Abstract. The *contextual* natural deduction calculus (**ND^c**) extends the usual natural deduction calculus (**ND**) by allowing the implication introduction and elimination rules to operate on formulas that occur inside contexts. It has been shown that, asymptotically in the best case, **ND^c**-proofs can be quadratically smaller than the smallest **ND**-proofs of the same theorems. In this paper we describe the first implementation of a theorem prover for minimal logic based on **ND^c**. Furthermore, we empirically compare it to an equally simple **ND** theorem prover on thousands of randomly generated conjectures.

1 Introduction

Natural deduction was introduced by Gentzen in [13] and one of its distinguishing features is that the meaning of a logical connective is determined by elimination and introduction rules, and not by axioms. As a result, formal natural deduction proofs are considered to be similar in structure to their informal counterparts and hence more *natural*. This subjective claim is corroborated by the observation that widely used proof assistants[1] follow a natural deduction style.

However, as exemplified in [21], the inference rules of natural deduction style calculi can be inconvenient, lengthy and ultimately unnatural for formalizing reasoning steps that modify a deeply located subformula of a formula, such as: Tseitin's transformation, skolemization, double negation elimination, quantifier shifting, prenexification... Because these deep reasoning steps are commonly used by automated deduction tools during preprocessing of the theorem to be proved, the resulting proofs may contain deep inferences [10]. Therefore, automatically replaying (i.e. reproving) these proofs in proof assistants (e.g. when an automated deduction tool is integrated within a proof assistant [2]) can be inefficient in terms of proving time and size of the generated shallow proof.

These challenges motivated the invention (in [21]) of the *contextual natural deduction calculus* (**ND^c**), which is a simple extension of the usual natural deduction calculus (here called **ND**) allowing introduction and elimination rules to operate on formulas occurring inside contexts. The goals in [21] were purely theoretical. It was shown that **ND^c** is sound and complete, that proofs can be

---

[1] e.g. Isabelle (www.cl.cam.ac.uk/research/hvg/Isabelle/) and Coq (http://coq.inria.fr).

© Springer International Publishing Switzerland 2016
M. Mazzara and A. Voronkov (Eds.): PSI 2015, LNCS 9609, pp. 314–324, 2016.
DOI: 10.1007/978-3-319-41579-6_24

normalized, and that some proofs can be quadratically smaller than the smallest proofs of the same theorem in the usual natural deduction calculus. In contrast, the main goal of the work reported in the present paper is to evaluate $\mathbf{ND^c}$ empirically. This is important, because asymptotic proof-complexity results can be misleading when the assymptotic behaviour they describe for particular worst cases or best cases is not observed in cases that occur most often in practice.

$\mathbf{ND^c}$ can be regarded not only from a theorem proving perspective but also from a *proof compression* point of view: a given $\mathbf{ND}$-proof ψ could be compressed by transforming it to a smaller $\mathbf{ND^c}$-proof. Since every $\mathbf{ND}$-proof is also an $\mathbf{ND^c}$-proof, a straightforward proof compression algorithm could simply try to reprove ψ's theorem using an $\mathbf{ND^c}$ theorem prover.

The implementation of prototypical theorem provers based on $\mathbf{ND}$ and $\mathbf{ND^c}$ within the Skeptik framework (https://github.com/Paradoxika/Skeptik) is discussed in Sect. 3. These provers are restricted to minimal logic (intuitionistic logic having only the implication connective). Although it would be straightforward to extend the contextual techniques to inference rules for other connectives as well, the restriction to minimal logic implies less implementation effort and is sufficient to estimate how promising the idea of contextual natural deduction might be in practice. An experimental infra-structure, including a random formula generator, also had to be implemented, as briefly described in Sect. 4. The experimental results are shown and analyzed in Sect. 5.

Related work: due to the increasing maturity of automated deduction tools, there has been a lot of recent work on proof production [11] and on the development of algorithms for simplifying the generated proofs in a post-processing phase. These methods have focused mostly on propositional resolution proofs output by SAT- and SMT-solvers so far [1,3,4,9,12,23], but generalizations to first-order resolution have been proposed as well [14]. There are also algorithms aimed at compressing and structuring sequent calculus proofs by eliminating or introducing cuts [17,22,25,26] or by extracting Herbrand sequents from proofs [18–20]. [21] is probably the first work considering, from a theoretical perspective, the compressibility of natural deduction proofs, and this paper reports the first realization of this idea in practice. Contextual inferences have a lot in common with the related idea of *deep inference*, which has been intensively investigated in the last decade, especially for classical logic (e.g. [5,7,8,16]) but also for intuitionistic logic [6,15,24]. Despite the technical differences, deep inference calculi were an inspiration for the development of contextual natural deduction.

2   Contextual Natural Deduction

In this paper a *derivation* is a tree of inferences (instances of the inference rules), operating on sequents of the form $\Gamma \vdash t : T$, where Γ is a (possibly empty) set of named *hypotheses* $h_1 : H_1, \ldots, h_n : H_n$, t is a (contextual) lambda term (whose free variables are among the names in Γ and whose bound variables are assumed to have unique names) and T is a minimal logic formula (or equivalently, by the Curry-Howard isomorphism, the type of t). A derivation ψ is a *proof* of a theorem

T if and only if its leaves are axiom inferences and it ends in $\vdash t : T$, for some term t. Figure 1 shows the rules of a natural deduction calculus for minimal logic (here called **ND**).

$$\overline{\Gamma, a : A \vdash a : A}$$

$$\frac{\Gamma, a : A \vdash b : B}{\Gamma \vdash \lambda a^A . b : A \to B} \to_I$$

$$\frac{\Gamma \vdash f : A \to B \qquad \Gamma \vdash a : A}{\Gamma \vdash (f\ a) : B} \to_E$$

Fig. 1. The natural deduction calculus **ND**

Figure 2 shows the inference rules of the *contextual natural deduction calculus* **ND^c** along with a corresponding extension of the lambda calculus. **ND^c** extends **ND** by allowing the inference rules to operate on subformulas located deeply inside the premises. The notation $\mathcal{C}_\pi[F]$ indicates a formula that has the subformula F in position π. $\mathcal{C}_\pi[\_]$ is called the *context* of F in the formula $\mathcal{C}_\pi[F]$. A *position* π is encoded as a binary string indicating the path from the root of $\mathcal{C}_\pi[F]$ to F in the tree structure of $\mathcal{C}_\pi[F]$; thus, a subformula at position π of a formula P, denoted $\mathrm{At}_\pi(P)$, can be retrieved by traversing the formula according to the following inductive definition:

$$\mathrm{At}_\epsilon(A) = A \qquad \mathrm{At}_{0\pi}(A \to B) = \mathrm{At}_\pi(B) \qquad \mathrm{At}_{1\pi}(A \to B) = \mathrm{At}_\pi(A)$$

A position is said to be *positive* (*negative*) if and only if it contains an even (odd) number of digits 1. In other words, in the tree structure of a formula, a node and its left (right) child always occupy positions with opposite (same) polarities, and the root position is positive. Moreover, a position is *strongly positive* if and only if it does not contain any digit 1. **ND^c** has two implication elimination rules (i.e. $\to_E^{\leftarrow}$ and $\to_E^{\rightarrow}$) because the contexts can be combined in two different ways, which are indicated by the superscript left and right harpoons. The natural deduction calculus **ND** can be considered a restriction of **ND^c** enforcing empty contexts. Examples of **ND^c**-proofs are available in [21].

3   Implementation

Implementation was done in `Scala`, leveraging and extending the `Skeptik` proof compression library. Although `Skeptik`'s original focus was on propositional resolution proofs, the addition of data structures for natural deduction was easy and required no refactoring, because `Skeptik` has always taken advantage of `Scala`'s object-orientation features to be agnostic with respect to proof systems.

Note: π, π_1 and π_2 must be positive positions.

$$\overline{\Gamma, a : A \vdash a : A}$$

$$\frac{\Gamma, a : A \vdash b : \mathcal{C}_\pi[B]}{\Gamma \vdash \lambda_\pi a^A.b : \mathcal{C}_\pi[A \to B]} \to_I (\pi)$$

Contextual Soundness Condition:
a is allowed to occur in b only if π is strongly positive.

$$\frac{\Gamma \vdash f : \mathcal{C}^1_{\pi_1}[A \to B] \qquad \Gamma \vdash a : \mathcal{C}^2_{\pi_2}[A]}{\Gamma \vdash (f\ a)_{\overrightarrow{(\pi_1;\pi_2)}} : \mathcal{C}^1_{\pi_1}[\mathcal{C}^2_{\pi_2}[B]]} \overrightarrow{\to}_E (\pi_1; \pi_2)$$

$$\frac{\Gamma \vdash f : \mathcal{C}^1_{\pi_1}[A \to B] \qquad \Gamma \vdash a : \mathcal{C}^2_{\pi_2}[A]}{\Gamma \vdash (f\ a)_{\overleftarrow{(\pi_1;\pi_2)}} : \mathcal{C}^2_{\pi_2}[\mathcal{C}^1_{\pi_1}[B]]} \overleftarrow{\to}_E (\pi_1; \pi_2)$$

Fig. 2. The contextual natural deduction calculus $\mathbf{ND^c}$

In `Skeptik`, inference rules are classes. In order to increase the confidence on the correctness of inference rules, each rule class includes correctness checking code and is kept as small as possible. The 3 classes for the **ND** rules are only 13 lines long. The single class `ImpElimC` for the two contextual implication elimination rules has 17 lines and the soundness condition for the `ImpIntroC` rule is a 10-line long trait. To the extent that these few lines of code are trusted, any proof constructed using these inference rules is correct. Any code that is not essential to the rule is written not in the class but in its companion object.

The class `SimpleProver` implements a theorem prover that is generic in the sense that it takes arbitrary (companion objects of) inferences rules and then performs bottom-up proof search using the given inference rules. For each open goal, the prover tries all inference rules in a bottom-up manner in parallel, generating all possible subgoals. Then it recursively tries to prove the subgoals in parallel. When returning from the recursion, the prover chooses the smallest subproof among all alternative subproofs returned by the recursive calls. This exhaustive search strategy is appropriate in the context of proof compression, where the goal is to find small proofs not necessarily as fast as possible. The depth of the recursion is bounded by the maximum proof height specified as a parameter of `SimpleProver`.

The companion objects of the inference rules implement a standard interface, which provides methods that generate subgoals as required by the prover and reconstruct the proof when the subgoals are proved. In the case of **ND**'s implication elimination rule, when generating subgoals for a goal of the form $\Gamma \vdash B$, it is necessary to guess a formula A in order to generate the subgoals $\Gamma_1 \vdash A \to B$ and $\Gamma_2 \vdash A$. Exhaustively guessing all possible formulas would be inefficient. Instead, the rule searches for hypotheses of the form $D_1 \to (\ldots \to (D_k \to B)\ldots)$ in Γ and then generates the subgoals $\Gamma \vdash (D_k \to B)$ and $\Gamma \vdash D_k$. The search Although proof search is still complete under this restriction, the proofs it finds are always normalized. Consequently, a proof found by this procedure is not necessarily the smallest possible proof, because sometimes non-normal proofs can be smaller.

Example 1. Let $t : T$ be a closed simply typed lambda term corresponding to a proof ψ_t of T with ℓ inferences. Then the term $(\lambda x^T.\lambda c^{T \to T \to Z}.((c\ x)\ x))\ t$ corresponds to a proof ψ of $(T \to T \to Z) \to Z$ with $(\ell + 8)$ inferences having ψ_t as a subproof. The proof search procedure described above, however, would never be able to construct ψ. To do so, it would have to start by applying implication elimination. But since there are no hypotheses, no application of implication elimination is possible according to the proof search procedure described above. Instead, the procedure will have to start with an application of implication introduction and will eventually construct the proof ψ' corresponding to the normalized term $\lambda c^{T \to T \to Z}.((ct)t)$. Because ψ' has $(2\ell + 4)$ inferences, ψ is smaller than ψ' and hence ψ' is not the smallest possible proof, for large enough ℓ.

In the case of $\mathbf{ND^c}$ rules, the generation of subgoals is complicated further by the need to take positions into account. For a goal of the form $\Gamma \vdash F$, the contextual implication elimination rule first searches for all positive positions π_1 and π_2 such that $F = \mathcal{C}_{\pi_1}[\mathcal{C}_{\pi_2}[B]]$ for some B. Then it searches for a hypothesis of the form $\mathcal{C}_{\pi_1}[D_1 \to (\ldots \to (D_k \to B)\ldots)]$ (or $\mathcal{C}_{\pi_2}[D_1 \to (\ldots \to (D_k \to B)\ldots)]$) and, if it succeeds, it generates the subgoals $\Gamma \vdash \mathcal{C}_{\pi_1}[(D_k \to B)]$ and $\Gamma \vdash \mathcal{C}_{\pi_2}[D_k]$ (or, respectively, $\Gamma \vdash \mathcal{C}_{\pi_2}[(D_k \to B)]$ and $\Gamma \vdash \mathcal{C}_{\pi_1}[D_k]$).

Example 2. Consider the goal $h : C \to (D \to B) \vdash (D \to (C \to B)$. There are the following possibilities of values for the pair (π_1, π_2): (ϵ, ϵ), $(\epsilon, 0)$, $(\epsilon, 00)$, $(0, \epsilon)$, $(0, 0)$, $(00, \epsilon)$. Consider the case when $\pi_1 = 0$ and $\pi_2 = 0$. In this case, $\mathcal{C}_{\pi_1}[] = D \to []$ and $\mathcal{C}_{\pi_2}[] = C \to []$. h is of the form $\mathcal{C}_{\pi_2}[D \to B]$. Therefore, for this case, the subgoals $h : C \to (D \to B) \vdash \mathcal{C}_{\pi_2}[D \to B]$ (i.e. $h : C \to (D \to B) \vdash C \to (D \to B)$) and $h : C \to (D \to B) \vdash \mathcal{C}_{\pi_1}[D]$ (i.e. $h : C \to (D \to B) \vdash D \to D$) are generated. The proof search procedure then continues trying to prove these subgoals. After the subgoals are proved, a proof of the original goal can be obtained with an application of contextual implication elimination. The other cases for (π_1, π_2) do not result in contexts that match the hypothesis h; therefore, no subgoals are generated for those other cases.

4   Experimental Setup

In order to evaluate the provers, a random formula generator was implemented. It takes a desired size s and a desired number of distinct atomic formulas q as input. Then it generates a list of length s containing q distinct atomic formulas. The list is grown recursively, and at each iteration, every atomic formula is equally likely to be selected. At this stage, care is taken to avoid generating formulas that are isomorphic modulo variable renaming (e.g. $A \to B$, $B \to A$, $A \to C$, ...; only $B \to A$ can be generated). Subsequently, the generator transforms this list into a minimal logic formula by recursively introducing implications at random positions in the list. The positions are equally likely to be selected (i.e. $A \rightarrow (A \rightarrow A)$ and $(A \rightarrow A) \rightarrow A$ are equally probable to be generated).

The experiments varied the value of s from 3 to 15 and the value of q from 1 to $s - 1$. For each pair of values (s, q), 1000 formulas were generated, except for small values of s and q, for which there are less than 1000 distinct formulas. In total, 76755 formulas were generated.

For each generated formula f, the **ND** prover with a timeout of 30 s and a maximum proof height of 20. The **ND^c** prover, on the other hand, had a timeout of 300 s and a maximum proof height of $h + 1$, where h is the height of proof of f found by the **ND** prover. The larger timeout was chosen because **ND^c**'s contextual rules clearly result in a larger search space, with more subgoals to try. With the larger timeout, it is possible to measure the impact of the larger search space in the proof search time.

5   Results of the Experiments

30127 formulas were proved by the **ND** prover. 46628 formulas were shown to be countersatisfiable by the **ND** prover, because it terminated before the timeout exhausting the proof search space without finding a proof. There was no case of timeout for the **ND** prover. There were 533 cases of timeout for the **ND^c** prover.

Among the 29594 formulas on which both provers were successful, 2557 (8.49 %) had shorter proofs in **ND^c** than in **ND**. The total length of the **ND^c**-proofs was 2.97 % lesser than the total length of the proofs found by the **ND** prover on all 29594 formulas. The total length of the **ND^c**-proofs was 27.8 % lesser than the total length of the **ND**-proofs on the 2557 proofs that admit shorter **ND^c** proofs.

In Fig. 3, each dot represents a generated formula and its position indicates the length of the proof found by each prover. Overlapped dots are shown as darker dots. In the standard box-whiskers plot of Fig. 4, formulas have been grouped by the length of their **ND**-proofs. For each group, the chart shows the median length of **ND^c**-proofs, as well as the quantiles, fences and outliers. This chart, together with the bar charts in Fig. 5 indicate a dependence of the compressibility of proofs on the length. Figure 5 shows that the proportion of formulas that admit shorter **ND^c**-proofs (i.e. whose **ND**-proofs could be compressed to shorter **ND^c**-proofs) tends to grow with the length of the **ND**-proofs. In a larger proof, the likelihood of an opportunity for compression is greater; however, the compression might be less significant in comparison to the proof length, as indicated by the decreasing trend in Fig. 6.

The 3D-charts in Fig. 7 shed further light on what influences the proportion of formulas that admit shorter **ND^c**-proofs and the total compression ratios (including all 29594 formulas). The proportion of formulas admitting shorter **ND^c**-proofs (and their total compression ratios) is higher the lower the number

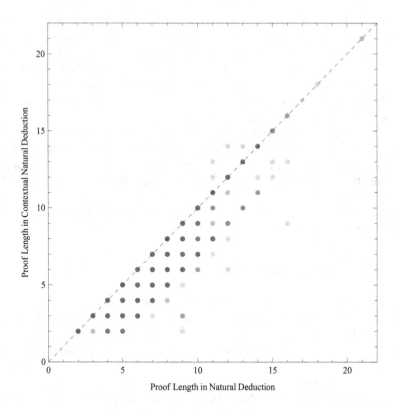

Fig. 3. Scatter Plot of Proof Lengths

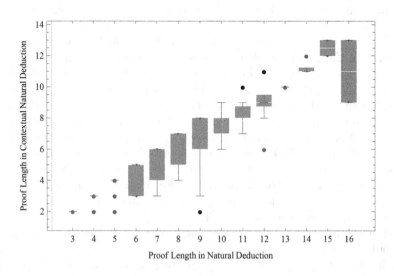

Fig. 4. Box-Whiskers Plot of Proof Lengths

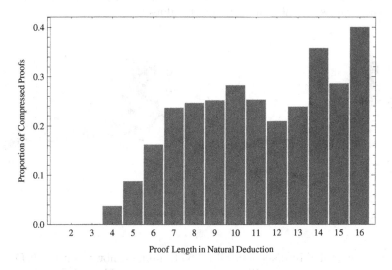

Fig. 5. Proportion of Compressed Proofs by Length

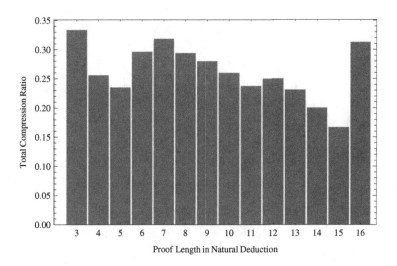

Fig. 6. Total Compression by Length

of distinct atoms they contain and the larger they are. The depths[2] of the formulas also seem to play a role, with greater compression proportions and total compression ratios for intermediary depth values.

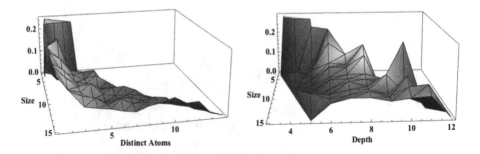

Fig. 7. Proportion of Compressed Proofs

Figure 8 (which takes into account all 76755 formulas) shows that the **ND** prover rarely took longer than 10 milliseconds on a formula. The **ND^c** prover was, as expected, significantly slower than the **ND** prover, because the search space for **ND^c** proofs is much larger. Nevertheless, the **ND^c** prover is surprisingly faster in a few cases, probably due to the stricter upper-bound on proof height.

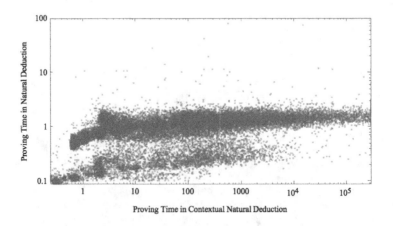

Fig. 8. Scatter Plot of Proving Time

---

[2] depth$(A) = 1$, for an atomic A; depth$(B \to C) = \max(\text{depth}(B), \text{depth}(C)) + 1$.

6   Conclusions

The empirical investigation reported in this paper confirms the expectation that ND^c can provide shorter proofs in a significant number of cases. Because the benchmarks were randomly generated, it is still an open question whether contextual natural deduction will perform well on real-world benchmarks. Nevertheless, the good performance on randomly generated benchmarks complements and the previous theoretical result of asymptotic best-case quadratic compression shown in [21]. Together, the experimental evaluation and the theoretical improved proof complexity constitute strong evidence that contextualization is worth pursuing for the sake of obtaining shorter proofs in natural deduction style.

The price to pay for shorter proofs is currently a much longer proving time. In this paper, proving time was restricted by bounding the proof height during proof search. Other more sophisticated techniques to restrict proof search should be investigated in the future, in order to improve the efficiency of theorem proving in ND^c.

To evaluate the benefit of contextual natural deduction on real-world benchmarks, it is firstly necessary to extend ND^c to the more expressive higher-order logics used by interactive proof assistants. Their libraries of formalized mathematics contain proofs of theorems for which shorter contextual natural deduction proofs could be possible.

Acknowledgements. This work was supported by an Stipendium of the Österreichische Akademie der Wissenschaften (APART).

References

1. Bar-Ilan, O., Fuhrmann, O., Hoory, S., Shacham, O., Strichman, O.: Linear-time reductions of resolution proofs. In: Chockler, H., Hu, A.J. (eds.) HVC 2008. LNCS, vol. 5394, pp. 114–128. Springer, Heidelberg (2009)
2. Böhme, S., Nipkow, T.: Sledgehammer: judgement day. In: Giesl, J., Hähnle, R. (eds.) IJCAR 2010. LNCS, vol. 6173, pp. 107–121. Springer, Heidelberg (2010)
3. Boudou, J., Fellner, A., Woltzenlogel Paleo, B.: Skeptik: a proof compression system. In: Demri, S., Kapur, D., Weidenbach, C. (eds.) IJCAR 2014. LNCS, vol. 8562, pp. 374–380. Springer, Heidelberg (2014)
4. Boudou, J., Woltzenlogel Paleo, B.: Compression of propositional resolution proofs by lowering subproofs. In: Galmiche, D., Larchey-Wendling, D. (eds.) TABLEAUX 2013. LNCS, vol. 8123, pp. 59–73. Springer, Heidelberg (2013)
5. Brünnler, K.: Atomic cut elimination for classical logic. In: Baaz, M., Makowsky, J.A. (eds.) CSL 2003. LNCS, vol. 2803, pp. 86–97. Springer, Heidelberg (2003)
6. Brünnler, K., McKinley, R.: An algorithmic interpretation of a deep inference system. In: Cervesato, I., Veith, H., Voronkov, A. (eds.) LPAR 2008. LNCS (LNAI), vol. 5330, pp. 482–496. Springer, Heidelberg (2008)
7. Bruscoli, P., Guglielmi, A.: On the proof complexity of deep inference. ACM Trans. Comput. Logic **10**, 1–34 (2009)

8. Bruscoli, P., Guglielmi, A., Gundersen, T., Parigot, M.: A quasipolynomial cut-elimination procedure in deep inference via atomic flows and threshold formulae. In: Clarke, E.M., Voronkov, A. (eds.) LPAR-16 2010. LNCS, vol. 6355, pp. 136–153. Springer, Heidelberg (2010)

9. Cotton, S.: Two techniques for minimizing resolution proofs. In: Strichman, O., Szeider, S. (eds.) SAT 2010. LNCS, vol. 6175, pp. 306–312. Springer, Heidelberg (2010)

10. Deharbe, D., Fontaine, P., Woltzenlogel Paleo, B.: Quantifier inference rules in the proof format of verit. In: 1st International Workshop on Proof Exchange for Theorem Proving (2011)

11. Delahaye, D., Woltzenlogel Paleo, B. (eds.): All about Proofs, Proofs for All. Mathematical Logic and Foundations, vol. 55. College Publications, London (2015)

12. Fontaine, P., Merz, S., Woltzenlogel Paleo, B.: Compression of propositional resolution proofs via partial regularization. In: Bjørner, N., Sofronie-Stokkermans, V. (eds.) CADE 2011. LNCS, vol. 6803, pp. 237–251. Springer, Heidelberg (2011)

13. Gentzen, G.: Untersuchungen über das logische Schließen. Mathematische Zeitschrift, vol. 39, pp. 176–210, 405–431 (1934–1935)

14. Gorzny, J., Woltzenlogel Paleo, B.: Towards the compression of first-order resolution proofs by lowering unit clauses. In: Felty, A.P., Middeldorp, A. (eds.) CADE-25. LNCS, vol. 9195, pp. 356–366. Springer, Switzerland (2015)

15. Guenot, N.: Nested proof search as reduction in the lambda-calculus. In: Schneider-Kamp, P., Hanus, M. (eds.) PPDP, pp. 183–194. ACM (2011)

16. Guglielmi, A.: A system of interaction and structure. CoRR cs.LO/9910023 (1999)

17. Hetzl, S., Leitsch, A., Weller, D.: Towards algorithmic cut-introduction. In: Bjørner, N., Voronkov, A. (eds.) LPAR-18 2012. LNCS, vol. 7180, pp. 228–242. Springer, Heidelberg (2012)

18. Hetzl, S., Leitsch, A., Weller, D., Woltzenlogel Paleo, B.: Herbrand sequent extraction. In: Autexier, S., Campbell, J., Rubio, J., Sorge, V., Suzuki, M., Wiedijk, F. (eds.) AISC 2008, Calculemus 2008, and MKM 2008. LNCS (LNAI), vol. 5144, pp. 462–477. Springer, Heidelberg (2008)

19. Woltzenlogel Paleo, B.: Herbrand sequent extraction. M.sc. thesis, Technische Universität Dresden; Technische Universität Wien, Dresden, Germany; Wien, Austria (2007)

20. Woltzenlogel Paleo, B.: Herbrand Sequent Extraction. VDM-Verlag, Saarbrücken, Germany (2008)

21. Woltzenlogel Paleo, B.: Contextual natural deduction. In: Artemov, S., Nerode, A. (eds.) LFCS 2013. LNCS, vol. 7734, pp. 372–386. Springer, Heidelberg (2013)

22. Woltzenlogel Paleo, B.: Reducing redundancy in cut-elimination by resolution. J. Logic Comput. (2014). doi:10.1093/logcom/exu075. http://logcom.oxfordjournals.org/content/early/2014/12/13/logcom.exu075.full.pdf?keytype=ref&ijkey=5g54fcql8kBznTf

23. Bruttomesso, R., Sharygina, N., Tsitovich, A.: Resolution proof transformation for compression and interpolation. Formal Methods Syst. Des. 45(1), 1–41 (2014)

24. Tiu, A.F.: A local system for intuitionistic logic. In: Hermann, M., Voronkov, A. (eds.) LPAR 2006. LNCS (LNAI), vol. 4246, pp. 242–256. Springer, Heidelberg (2006)

25. Woltzenlogel Paleo, B.: A general analysis of cut-elimination by CERES. Ph.D. Dissertation, Vienna University of Technology (2009)

26. Woltzenlogel Paleo, B.: Atomic cut introduction by resolution: proof structuring and compression. In: Clarke, E.M., Voronkov, A. (eds.) LPAR-16 2010. LNCS, vol. 6355, pp. 463–480. Springer, Heidelberg (2010)

Hybrid Lustre

Zhenghen Yuan[1], Tingliang Zhou[2(✉)], Jing Liu[1(✉)], Juan Luo[2],
Yi Zhang[2], and Xiaohong Chen[1,3]

[1] Shanghai Key Lab of Trustworthy Computing,
East China Normal University, Shanghai, China
yuanzhengheng@gmail.com, jliu@sei.ecnu.edu.cn
[2] Casco Signal LTD., Shanghai, China
{zhoutingliang,luojuan}@casco.com.cn
[3] National Trustworthy Embedded Software Engineering Research Centre,
Shanghai, China

Abstract. Hybrid Lustre is a formal modeling language for a mixed discrete-continuous system extended from Lustre. Lustre is a data-flow based synchronous language widely used in development of real-time embedded systems. While Luster lacks of a mechanism for modeling continuous behavior of physical processes which are controlled by digital controllers, Hybrid Lustre is proposed as an extension of Lustre to accommodate continuous behaviors in between discrete transitions. The continuous state change can be specified by ordinary differential equations. The syntax and the semantics of Hybrid Lustre are formally described, thus to support verifying the correctness of models of mixed discrete-continuous systems. It is successfully used in development of new generation Communication Based Zone Controller of Casco Signal LTD.

1 Introduction

Synchronous languages including Esterel [1], Lustre [2], Signal [3] have been established as a technology of choice for modeling, specifying, validating, and implementing real-time embedded applications [4] since 1991. As concurrency, simplicity and synchrony have been considered form the beginning of the development of the languages, they have got acceptation by the industries. Lustre may be the most popular one of these three languages. With a commercial tool SCADE (Safety Critical Application Development Environment) developed by Esterel Technologies, many successful systems have been developed and running in Aerospace, Automotive, Rail & Transport and Energy & Nuclear.

Lustre is a dataflow model based language. It can be seen as a diagram where operators are connected by lines which are flows of data. It divides time into discrete instants [4], so that each variable in Lustre is a sequence of values, i.e., variable is a function of time. These features make it easier to ensure synchronous. With a frequency decided by the environment active the Lustre program, variables won't cover their history values so as avoid wrong updates in normal programming languages.

© Springer International Publishing Switzerland 2016
M. Mazzara and A. Voronkov (Eds.): PSI 2015, LNCS 9609, pp. 325–340, 2016.
DOI: 10.1007/978-3-319-41579-6_25

Model checking based approaches are widely used in the verification and validation of embedded systems [5,6]. For the propose of model checking of Lustre programs, the verifier will explore all state space of the program, and declare whether the state follows the property being verified. If there is a negative answer reached, the verifier produces a result with a counter-example to show the state the property gets wrong.

So it's obviously that besides Design model (the system under verification), there should be an Observer which implements the property the system has to keep. As inputs, it receives only the inputs and outputs of Design model which is "black" from the sight of Observer, i.e., what happened in it is not known by Observer. The output of Observer is the answer that whether the state of the system follows the property.

Another model is Environment [7]. Environment should be an abstract of the real outer system. Its main purpose is to give a possible input space of all values the system get from the real environment. However, a node with too much details will increase the complexity of the verification which leads to the opposite side of our springboard. In the solution being used now, a very rough Environment is constructed. It only ensures that the sensors' value are valid and some very simple connections between different variables. The lack of an accurate description and the transition relation of Environment make it possible to produce all correct input state space to the system as well as many unnecessary ones, which increase the state explosion problem.

This makes it important to find a way modeling a more accurate Environment. Now in real-time online social networks, it is getting more important [8,9]. However, for the systems always interact with the physical world, Lustre based on the discrete logic time is not enough. Proposing a language which has the features of Lustre as well as supporting the modeling of physical world is important. To address this, we propose to extend Lustre with the time model of Hybrid Automata. Hybrid Automata is a formal model which combines the discrete systems and continuous dynamics. It is a special kind of finite state machine [10]. In each state, there exists the continuous variables described by Ordinary Differential Equations (ODEs). And among the states, there are the discrete transition processes. Hybrid Lustre is the result language which based on Lustre and extended by the time model of Hybrid Automata, and it supports the description of ODEs.

There are two common ways to describe ODEs. Both of them need to take the initial value and the slope as inputs. The difference is the third input. It can be either the duration time or the final value, and this depends the method how the program transits. Since the real-time embedded systems are activated by logic clock (in Lustre we call it cycles), our method is updating all variables which involved in ODEs. And then the problem rely on the projection of physical time to logic clock. With the terminal value accessible, the system can run in current state without considering the mapping from logic clock to physical time. In fact, this is the time model of hybrid automata. More advantages can be taken by the developers for the only thing they have to do is focusing on the guard actions which leads the transition of system. However, the durations between discrete clocks are often same in Lustre programs (stable cycles), which makes the physical time divided by the stable cycles while waiting for the satisfaction of the transition guard. To get the value of the outputs at the stable cycles, it has to use the initial value, slope and the duration time. That's why we use a combined method to Hybrid Lustre.

This paper presents an extension on Lustre language in order to model hybrid systems. Since the physical world can described by ODEs in most cases, difference between Lustre and Hybrid Lustre is the support of ODEs. Section 2 introduces the Hybrid Dataflow model and the reason why we extend Lustre in such a way. The extended part will be presented in detailed syntax and semantics in Sects. 3 and 4. And an example which is divided from a project verifying Zone Control (ZC) is showed in Sect. 5. Section 6 is the related work and Sect. 7 is conclusions.

2   Hybrid Dataflow Model

Lustre is based on an abstract notion of time. In an informal description, each variable has its own logic clock which ticks when all inputs of the node it belongs to are available. With this definition, each variable has a discrete clock which "ticks" when the node is activated. As a node runs only when the program is activated, and no more than one time at each activation (for the dataflow model), all clocks can be seen as a sub-clock of the one of the program, which is called basic clock of the system. In fact, in Lustre, clock is described as a sequence of Boolean values. The basic clock is a sequence of true values, and other clocks have false values, which means at those instants, the variable has no definition. From the system level, Lustre program is often running with a stable cycle. The developers of synchronous languages consider that if the program's worst running time of each cycle is shorter than the period of the system, we can take the program as running instantaneous. This assumption helps a lot to make Lustre synchrony [4].

Hybrid automata is a classic hybrid model which contains both discrete and continuous behaviors. The transition relations are guarded by Boolean expressions as well as dynamic behaviors are described by location invariants. Discrete event triggers as soon as the guard of it being satisfied. When all guards are not satisfied, location invariants ensure the value of the continuous variables changing.

We take the time model implemented by Hybrid Automata to extend Lustre. This makes the discrete part of Hybrid Lustre almost has no difference with the original. The events are still instantaneous, and [11] proved that this model covers the expressiveness of all models which discrete transitions has none, a constant or a variable time-delay. For Lustre does not have control flows exhibitively, the Sequential Switch operators take the role instead of guarded actions. However, these operators only effect when the logic clock ticks. This makes them not enough to cover the requirements of continuous behaviors. A more precise model is the continuous operators should take a predict at the beginning of the dynamic behaviors. The guards will be established from the correlative Sequential Switch operators of the hybrid variables, and an additional transition will be activated if it is predicted that one of the guards will be satisfied before next discrete cycle comes. A non-negative integer will be specified as the maximum number of the discrete transitions can be triggered during one basic clock duration in order to prevent Zeno.

Definition 1. *A Hybrid Lustre program has a Basic Clock (BC), whose value is a sequence of Real values. These values present the actual time of each discrete cycle. It has two main responsibility:*

First, it defines the universal set of all clocks in the program as well as recording all physical time of all discrete cycles. And secondly, when it is treated as a discrete clock, BC can be seen as a Boolean value which is always true.

Definition 2. *In Hybrid Lustre programs, each discrete variable has a Discrete Clock (DC), whose value is a Boolean sequence. Only when DC's value is true, the value of the variable is updated.*

At any discrete cycle, the number of the values of DC and BC should be same. This is because of that the nodes in the program can be activated only when the system initials a new discrete cycle. If the node is not activated at a cycle, it gets a value false of DCs of the variables in the node.

Definition 3. *When being connected by an operator $\cap$, $DC_1 \cap DC_2$ results in a discrete clock DC_3 which has a cycle at the instants that DC_1 and DC_2 both have a cycle, i.e., the instants $DC_1 = true$ and $DC_2 = true$. And $DC_1 \cap CC$ results in DC_1.*

Definition 4. *When being connected by an operator $\cup$, $DC_1 \cup DC_2$ results in a discrete clock DC_3 which has a cycle at the instants that at least one of DC_1 and DC_2 has a cycle, i.e., the instants $DC_1 = true$ or $DC_2 = true$. And $DC_1 \cup CC$ results in CC.*

3   Syntax of Hybrid Lustre

In this section, the syntax of Hybrid Lustre is formalized. Lustre is extended with two constructs: new type *hybrid* and new operators.

– *hybrid*: *hybrid* is a new type defined in Hybrid Lustre in order to present the continuous variables which does not has a discrete clock, and can be expressed by ODEs.

In order to be known from discrete clocks defined in Hybrid Lustre, we use Continuous Clock (CC) to present the concept of physical time. It can be seen as dense time [12].

Any variables or expressions defined in Lustre denotes an infinite sequence of values. Each value can be seen as a kind of memory of the expression at a certain cycle. Thus the variables and expressions are separated into discrete by the computing cycle. The value between cycles is made no more sense. However, type *hybrid* makes it different that variables defined in this type should have value at any time of the system, or the value of the variable can be known at any instant.

```
e ::= e | uop e1 | e1 bop e2 |
      if e1 then e2 else e3 |
      pre(e) | e1 -> e2 |
      e1 when e2 | e1 current e2|
      ing(e1, e2) | der(e1) |
      e1, ..., en
```

where *bop* is binary language operator and *uop* is unary language operator. These operators can be divided into three kinds showed below.

- boolean operators:
  and, or, not;
- arithmetic operators:
  $+, -, *, /$;
- relational operators:
  $=, <>, >, <, >=, <=$;

Further more, *pre*, $\rightarrow$, *when* and *current* are temporal operators which have definition in Lustre, and *ing* and *der* are newly defined hybrid operators in Hybrid Lustre.

- *pre(e)* represents the last value of e, i.e., the value of e at previous cycle. If e has a *hybrid* type, the previous cycle is read from BC of the program.
- $e_1 \rightarrow e_2$ expresses a sequence whose first value is taken from e_1 and the rest are from e_2.
- e_1 *when* e_2 "projects" e_1 to the clock that the Boolean variable e_2 declares. There are no definition of e_1 when e_2 is false.
- e_1 *current* e_2 returns e_1's value as the last value of e_1 where e_2 is true. For example, if e_1 is a sequence of $(e_0, e_1, e_2, e_3, e_4, ...)$ and e_2 is $(t, f, t, t, f, ...)$, then e_1 *when* e_2 is $(e_0, e_2, e_3, ...)$ with a clock $(t, f, t, t, f, ...)$ and e_1 *current* $e2$ is $(e_0, e_0, e_1, e_2, e_2, ...)$.
- *ing*(e_1, e_2) defines a continuous behavior. The value of the expression is initialized as e_1, and derivative is e_2.
- *der*(e_1) gives an opposite result of *ing*. Its value is the derivative of the expression.

The syntax of the expressions in Hybrid Lustre is introduced above. Expressions are considered as variables that has a certain with it, showing at which cycle the expression has a value. Hybrid Lustre programs are constructed by nodes. It is a package of dataflows with defined inputs and outputs. More detailed syntax on node level can be found in [13]. There is no much difference between Lustre and Hybrid Lustre.

4 Semantics of Hybrid Lustre

4.1 Typing Rules and Semantics

In this section, $discrete\_type$ (dt for short) includes $integer$, $float$ and $boolean$ types. These are all discrete variable types, and their must be defined on a discrete clock. Otherwise, all continuous variables are defined in type $hybrid$, and the clock of them must be continuous clock.

Arithmetic Operators

$$\frac{DC_1 \vdash e_1 : dt \quad DC_2 \vdash e_2 : dt}{DC_1 \cap DC_2 \vdash e_1 \times e_2 : dt}$$

two discrete expressions connected with an arithmetic operator results in a discrete expression. The clock of it is the disjunction of two clocks, i.e., $e_1 \times e_2$ has value only when e_1 and e_2 both have value.

$$\frac{DC \vdash e_1 : dt \quad CC \vdash e_2 : hybrid}{DC \vdash e_1 \times e_2 : dt}$$

with a discrete expression e_1 and a continuous expression e_2 connected with an arithmetic operator, the results should be a discrete expression. The clock it based on is the same as e_1. The operation takes the value of e_2 at current time and compute the result as two discrete expressions.

$$\frac{CC \vdash e_1 : hybrid \quad CC \vdash e_2 : hybrid}{BC \vdash e_1 \times e_2 : float}$$

two continuous expressions can be connected with an arithmetic operator. However the result of it is a discrete variable which based on the basic clock of the program. The operation will first read the value of two continuous expressions at current time, and compute the result as discrete expressions.

Relation Operators

$$\frac{DC_1 \vdash e_1 : dt \quad DC_2 \vdash e_2 : dt}{DC_1 \cap DC_2 \vdash e_1 \times e_2 : boolean}$$

connecting two discrete expressions with a relation operator results in a Boolean sequence. Especially if the clocks of two expressions are different, the Boolean sequence's clock is the disjunction of them.

$$\frac{DC \vdash e_1 : dt \quad CC \vdash e_2 : hybrid}{DC \vdash e_1 \times e_2 : boolean}$$

when a discrete expression compared with a continuous one, the result should be a Boolean sequence with the discrete expression's clock. The comparison will be done with the current value of both expressions.

$$\frac{CC \;\vdash\; e_1 : hybrid \quad CC \;\vdash\; e_2 : hybrid}{BC \;\vdash\; e_1 \times e_2 : boolean}$$

two continuous expressions connected with a relation operator will leads to a Boolean sequence either, but its clock should be constrained to basic clock of the system. Also, before the compare, the value of two continuous expressions will be computed.

Sequential Switch

$$\frac{DC \;\vdash\; e_1 : boolean \quad DC \;\vdash\; e_2 : dt \quad DC \;\vdash\; e_3 : dt}{DC \;\vdash\; if \; e_1 \; then \; e_2 \; else \; e_3 : dt}$$

the expression following if has to be a Boolean expression, and the other two should have a same clock and same type. The result share the same clock of them and the value is decided by the value of e_1.

$$\frac{DC \;\vdash\; e_1 : boolean \quad CC \;\vdash\; e_2 : hybrid \quad CC \;\vdash\; e_3 : hybrid}{DC \;\vdash\; if \; e_1 \; then \; e_2 \; else \; e_3 : dt}$$

even if the expressions after $then$ and $else$ are both continuous, the result is still a discrete expression. The clock of it follows the one of the condition expression. The values of the continuous expressions are still computed by the times stored in basic clock.

followed by ($\rightarrow$)

$$\frac{DC_1 \;\vdash\; e_1 : dt \quad DC_2 \;\vdash\; e_2 : dt}{DC_2 \;\vdash\; e_1 \;\rightarrow\; e_2 : dt}$$

if a discrete expression is followed by another discrete expression, the result should be a discrete expression. Its clock follows the second one.

$$\frac{DC \;\vdash\; e_1 : dt \quad CC \;\vdash\; e_2 : hybrid}{DC \;\vdash\; e_1 \;\rightarrow\; e_2 : float}$$

if a discrete expression is followed by a continuous expression, the result should be a $float$ sequence with the discrete expression's clock.

$$\frac{CC \;\vdash\; e_1 : hybrid \quad DC \;\vdash\; e_2 : dt}{DC \;\vdash\; e_1 \;\rightarrow\; e_2 : float}$$

if a continuous expression is followed by a discrete expression, the first value of the result is the initial value of the continuous one, and the rest is the discrete one's. The clock of the result follows the discrete one and the type is $float$.

$$\frac{CC \;\vdash\; e_1 : hybrid \quad CC \;\vdash\; e_2 : hybrid}{BC \;\vdash\; e_1 \;\rightarrow\; e_2 : float}$$

if a continuous expression is followed by another continuous expression, the result also has a continuous type, with an initial value of the first one and the rest from the second one.

when For *when* operator, the second expression is always a *Boolean* sequence which can be treated as a clock.

$$\frac{DC_1 \vdash e_1 : dt \quad DC_2 \vdash e_2 : boolean}{DC_1 \cap \{e_2 = true\} \vdash e_1 : dt}$$

a discrete expression will be projected to a subset of its values where the new sequence has a clock which is the injection of the discrete one and the *Boolean* sequence.

$$\frac{CC \vdash e_1 : hybrid \quad BC \vdash e_2 : boolean}{\{e_2 = true\} \vdash e_1 : float}$$

a continuous expression can only be connected to a *Boolean* sequence which is defined on a basic clock. The result of the operation is a *float* sequence with a clock where the *Boolean* sequence is true.

current As in *when* operator, the second expression of *current* operator is always a *Boolean* sequence which can be treated as a clock.

$$\frac{DC \vdash e_1 : dt \quad DC \vdash e_2 : boolean}{DC \vdash e_1 \; current \; e_2 : dt}$$

the result sequence won't change its value unless the value of the *Boolean* sequence is true. The clock of the result sequence is same as the discrete sequence.

$$\frac{CC \vdash e_1 : hybrid \quad DC \vdash e_2 : boolean}{DC \vdash e_1 \; current \; e_2 : float}$$

when the expression before the *current* operator is a continuous one, the instants that *Boolean* sequence becomes true can be seen as the change point of the value of the result. It has a discrete type.

ing

$$\frac{DC \vdash e_1 : dt \quad DC \vdash e_2 : dt}{CC \vdash ing(e_1, \; e_2) : hybrid}$$

the parameters of the *ing* operator should be both discrete expressions. And they should have a same clock. The result will become a continuous expression. The first expression is the initial value of the operation in each cycle, and the second one is the derivative.

der

$$\frac{DC \vdash e_1 : dt}{CC \vdash der(e_1) : hybrid}$$

the operator can deal with discrete variables. And the result is a continuous one.

$$\frac{CC \ \vdash \ e_1 : hybrid}{CC \ \vdash \ der(e_1) : hybrid}$$

the operator can deal with continuous variables. And the result is also a continuous one.

4.2   Safe Semantics and Live Semantics

Hybrid Lustre does not have control flows exhibitively. The transition relation between different states can be extract from sequential switch operators (if e_1 then e_2 else e_3). If at a certain cycle, e_1 changes its value from true to false, we consider it is a transfer from state "$X \ = \ e_2$" to state "$X \ = \ e_3$". We can consider e_1 as a transition guard.

However, for Hybrid Lustre, determining the instant at which next transfer may happen is one of the key problem. Discrete expressions will not trigger a transfer between two cycles, but a continuous expression may change the value of transition guard before next discrete instant.

To cross over the gap, a new transition trigger event is introduced here. Generally, in reactive systems, there exists a stable duration time between cycles. In Hybrid Lustre, we assume this stable cycle is known. Then the program can compute the physical time of next cycle by following steps:

1. The program receives necessary resources, so as to activate a new discrete cycle;
2. With the data flow sequence, variables get their current values, i.e., discrete ones have been computed, and continuous one get their initial value as well as the slope between this cycle and the next one. The outputs are computed in this step.
3. Collect all transition guards of the program, and pick out the relative continuous variables. The values of these variables from current cycle to next one will be computed.
4. All transition guards will be judged whether the values of them will change in the coming cycle. If there is any transition will be activated, the exact time should be known and the duration from current cycle to the next one will be divided into two at that instant. Then go to step 2. Otherwise, go to next discrete cycle.

It should be mentioned that the divided cycles between two contiguous discrete cycles should have a maximum number, with which the accuracy can be accepted by the program and ensures the program is nonzeno.

4.3   A Tool

We have implemented a tool which support modeling and simulation of Hybrid Lustre programs. It is based on Ptolemy II [14]. A new director named HL Director has been developed to indicate that the model should follow the syntax and semantic of Hybrid Lustre.

The following operators are developed in HL Director: HLPre, HLFollowedBY, HLWhen, HLCurrent, HLBooleanSelect, HLIng, HLDer.

- HLPre is *pre* operator, which gets the value of the variable in previous discrete cycle.
- HLFollowedBy is *followedby* operator, which changes the initial value of a variable.
- HLWhen is *when* operator, which changes the clock of the variable according to a Boolean sequence.
- HLCurrent is *current* operator, which changes the value of the variable according to a Boolean sequence.
- HLBooleanSelect is *if...then...else...* operator, which returns one of the variable according to the Boolean variable.
- HLIng is *ing* operator, which integrates the value of a variable.
- HLDer is *der* operator, which is derivation.

5   An Application

5.1   Calculation of End of Authority

Communications-Based Train Control (CBTC) system is one kind of typical safety critical systems. Different from the last generation train control system, trains are protected by moving block instead of fixed block. Trackside equipments compute safe sections of each train according to the exact positions. These safe sections are sent to trains again in every compute cycle, and they are called movement authorities (MA). The main part of MA report is a coordinate, shows that the track from the current exact position of a train to MA is safe to pass and any other train can not enter this region. It's blocked.

As MA is an area on the track, it has two coordinates. It always starts from the head of the train, and for ZC, this coordinate is part of Environment which is computed by other systems in CBTC. So the only value ZC should compute is the end point of MA, which called End of Authority (EOA). The computation of EOA relies on the location of the train, the state of signals and points. In the real environment of the node, there are more than 100 sensors. Most of the sensors are numerical value, which decrease the effect of the verification.

5.2   The Environment Node of the Computation of EOA

The Environment of the computation of EOA node (CAL_EOA) focus on showing the constrains of the values of all sensors and the relationship among them. As a detailed example, the following five sensors will be discussed:

- $g\_arrsTrain\_LocMinPoss$
- $g\_arrsTrain\_LocMaxBrchPoss$
- $g\_arrsTrain\_LocMinBrchPoss$
- $g\_arrsTrain\_LocMinOrientations$
- $g\_arrsTrain\_LocMinBrchOrientations$

A train location is decided by four coordinates: $MaxHeadPos$, $MinHeadPos$, $MaxTailPos$, $MinTailPos$. The range $[MinHeadPos, MaxHeadPos]$ shows an imprecise location of train head as well as $[MinTailPos, MaxTailPos]$ is the imprecise location of train tail. $MinHeadPos$ and $MinTailPos$ can be read from $g\_arrsTrain\_LocMinPoss$. However, $MaxHeadPos$ and $MaxTailPos$ are not stored directly in above sensors.

The coordinates have been discussed are based on block-based coordinate system. A point's location can be expressed by a tuple $(Block\_Index, OffsetOnBlock)$. $Block\_Index$ shows on which block the point locates, and $OffsetOnBlock$ gives the exact distance between the point and the start endpoint of the block. Similarly, there is another coordinate system which based on branches. Branch is a connected track consisted by a number of blocks. A branch can not link to another branch, or they should become one branch. The branches may differ at any cycle of the computation, for some equipments can change the connecting relationship among blocks. A branch-based coordinate system is accessible for CAL_EOA node. It has the same structure with block-based coordinate system to locate a point with $(Branch\_Index, OffsetOnBranch)$. Block-based locations are transfered to branch-based locations out of CAL_EOA node, and they are stored in $g\_arrsTrain\_LocMaxBrchPoss$ and $g\_arrsTrain\_LocMinBrchPoss$.

Orientations are directions of the train. The front orientation is the direction from train tail to head, and the other one is on opposite. There also exist a block orientation and a branch one in two sensors: $g\_arrsTrain\_LocMinOrientations$ and $g\_arrsTrain\_LocMinBrchOrientations$.

Totally, there are about one hundred lines of code for the description of five sensors. Among them, eleven lines are "assert"s. These "assert"s are about

- All values should in the valid range.
- Sensors $g\_arrsTrain\_LocMinPoss$ and $g\_arrsTrain\_LocMinBrchPoss$ should be same points on the track.
- Each two directions stored in $g\_arrsTrain\_LocMinOrientations$ or $g\_arrsTrain\_LocMinBrchOrientations$ should be different.

5.3 Realization of Environment with Hybrid Lustre

In this section, a realization of Environment of the CAL_EOA node will be presented. The node will be extended with Hybrid Lustre, and we will show the great difference between the original Lustre and Hybrid Lustre.

```
node LocateTrain() returns ()
let
assert BlkPos2BrchPos(g_arrsTrain_LocMinPoss)
    = g_arrsTrain_LocMinBrchPoss;
assert BlkPos2BrchPos(g_arrsTrain_LocMaxPoss)
    = g_arrsTrain_LocMaxBrchPoss;
```

```
assert g_arrsTrain_LocMinOrientations.Head
   <> g_arrsTrain_LocMinOrientations.Tail;
tel
```

Except the functions mentioned above, Environment can give more constrains about the sensors with Hybrid Lustre. Without an established standard to decided how many constrains will be the best quantity, we take a balance here between the number and the accuracy. Following constrains are modeled in this realization.

Constrains About the Velocity and Acceleration. As a basic physical law, velocity is the derivative of distance the train moved, and acceleration is the derivative of velocity. Apparently, both value have a valid range.

```
LOChCurMinHeadVel = der(g_arrsTrain_LocMinBrchPoss.Head.iAbs);
LOChCurMinHeadAcc = der(LOChCurMinHeadVel);
assert LOChCurMinHeadVel <= MaxVel
   and LOChCurMinHeadVel >= MinVel;
assert LOChCurMinHeadAcc <= MaxAcc
   and LOChCurMinHeadAcc >= MinAcc;
```

Here $MaxVel$, $MinVel$, $MaxAcc$ and $MinAcc$ are predefined constants about the valid range of velocity and acceleration. $LOChPreVel$ and $LOChPreAcc$ are hybrid variables.

Model Some Basic Behaviors with Constrains. In order to give a continuous environment to CAL_EOA node, first we should determine the scope of the node. In this example, Environment should predict the possible location of the train in the following cycle, determine the states that won't be reached in certain situation and decrease the state space which help verification efficiency.

Following is the code of the assertions about $g\_arrsTrain\_LocMinBrchPoss$:

```
LOCbInSafeRng = (LOCiTrainAbs - LOCiEOAAbs >= SafeDist);
LOChMaxAcc = MAX[LOChCurMinHeadAcc, LOChCurMinTailAcc,
              LOChCurMaxHeadAcc, LOChCurMaxTailAcc];
LOChMinAcc = MIN[LOChCurMinHeadAcc, LOChCurMinTailAcc,
              LOChCurMaxHeadAcc, LOChCurMaxTailAcc];
LOChCurMaxAbs = if LOCbInSafeRng
            then ing(g_arrsTrain_LocMinPoss.Head.iAbs,
                    ing(LOChCurVel, LOChMaxAcc))
            else ing(g_arrsTrain_LocMinPoss.Head.iAbs,
                    ing(LOChCurVel, MinAcc));
LOChCurMinAbs = if LOCbInSafeRng
            then ing(g_arrsTrain_LocMinPoss.Head.iAbs,
                    ing(LOChCurVel, LOChMinAcc))
            else ing(g_arrsTrain_LocMinPoss.Head.iAbs,
```

```
                    ing(LOChCurVel, MinAcc));
assert g_arrsTrain_LocMinBrchPoss.Head.iAbs
    >= pre(LOChCurMinAbs);
assert g_arrsTrain_LocMinBrchPoss.Head.iAbs
    <= pre(LOChCurMaxAbs);
```

LOChMaxAcc and *LOChMinAcc* are the maximum value and minimum value of the acceleration. After being integrated twice, they can be considered as the range of the location of the train in next discrete cycle. Furthermore, these code present a basic control logic: if the train is too close to EOA, it should have an emergency break.

The Simulation Result: Figure 1 shows the model described above which is implemented in the tool, it's a part of Environment of *CAL_EOA*. With this model, the most important train control logic can be described. And for these additional constrains about the sensors being used in *CAL_EOA*, the input space can be more precise. As it can be seen in the figure, *g_arrsTrain_LocMaxBrchPoss* and *g_arrsTrain_LocMinBrchPoss* are derivatived twice, reaching the range of the velocity and acceleration of the train. And through some asserts, the values are constrained in valid range. The difference among the values is treated as error value, which leads to a random value of the location of the train in next discrete cycle.

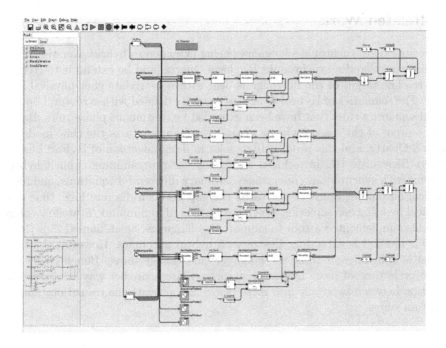

Fig. 1. The Hybrid Lustre tool based on Ptolemy II and the Environment node

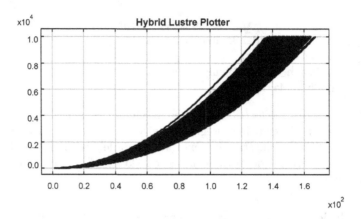

Fig. 2. Simulation result of Environment

Figure 2 is simulation results of the node showed in Fig. 1. The x-axis is time with unit of 100 ms, and the y-axis is the distance the train moved from start with unit of 1 cm. We simulate a train starting from the frontier of ZC. The simulation has been run for 10000 times, and the figure shows that most "distance-time" curves locate in the dark area, so as to each point in it is an input state space of the system.

6   Related Work

There are other synchronous languages being extended to hybrid. Kerstin Bauer [11] has considered a synchronous language Quartz, and he extend it to Hybrid Quartz. The target of the language is deal with non-trivial cyber-physical systems. The semantics of Hybrid Quartz is formally defined with structural operational semantics rules that have been extended by continuous phase rules. Bauer gave a proof of the reason why he chose hybrid automata as the time model of Hybrid Quartz, and this proof help us a lot in design decision of Hybrid Lustre. Albert Benveniste [15] introduced a language for programming explicit hybrid systems with synchronous concurrency, ordinary differential equations, and hierarchical automata. Benveniste crossed the gap between discrete logic time and physical by using zero-crossing which has been used in Simulink/Stateflow. They have also implemented a tool to support this language which named Zlus [16].

Our method is extending Lustre with hybrid automata. However, the time model is still different from the languages mentioned above. Benefited by the static cycle time of most Lustre programs, we use a predict way to divide the duration between two cycle into more pieces and activate the transitions among program states.

7 Conclusions

Real-Time systems have a limitation in dealing with both continuous and discrete data-flows. With increasing calling for formalisms supporting these features, we have constructed an extension of Lustre, namely Hybrid Lustre. Dedicated to the verification of real-time systems, Hybrid Lustre offers formal syntax and semantics to dynamic behaviors. Also the semantics of Hybrid Lustre defines the operations of the operators dealing with hybrid variables.

We have shown an application of Hybrid Lustre from Communications-Based Train Control systems. Focusing on the verification of CAL_EOA node which is one of the most important functions in Zone Controller, the Environment node reaches more constrains with the extended language. This help the verification can be run in a continuous way, opposite from the original cycles which are disconnected with another cycle. And a tool which supports modeling systems with Hybrid Lustre has been developed.

In future work, we will focus on the design method for Environment node, which should contain all situations that the system consider itself running correct.

Acknowledgment. Thanks the reviewers for their valuable comments. This paper is partially supported by the projects funded by the NSFC Trustworthy Software Track 91318301, NSFC Creative Team 61321064, NSFC Key Project 61332008 and NSFC 61170084. The Shanghai Trustworthy Computing Key Lab is supported by Shanghai Knowledge Service Platform ZF 1213. The third author is supported by NSFC 91418203 and Shanghai Project (No. 14511100400).

References

1. Boussinot, F., De Simone, R.: The esterel language. Proc. IEEE **79**(9), 1293–1304 (1991)
2. Halbwachs, N., Caspi, P., Raymond, P., Pilaud, D.: The synchronous data flow programming language lustre. Proc. IEEE **79**(9), 1305–1320 (1991)
3. LeGuernic, P., Gautier, T., Le Borgne, M., Le Maire, C.: Programming real-time applications with signal. Proc. IEEE **79**(9), 1321–1336 (1991)
4. Benveniste, A., Caspi, P., Edwards, S.A., Halbwachs, N., Le Guernic, P., De Simone, R.: The synchronous languages 12 years later. Proc. IEEE **91**(1), 64–83 (2003)
5. Clarke, E.M., Grumberg, O., Peled, D.: Model checking. MIT Press, Cambridge (1999)
6. Chen, M., Qin, X., Koo, H., Mishra, P.: System-Level Validation: High-Level Modeling and Directed Test Generation Techniques. Springer, Heidelberg (2013)
7. Halbwachs, N., Lagnier, F., Ratel, C.: Programming and verifying real-time systems by means of the synchronous data-flow language lustre. IEEE Trans. Softw. Eng. **18**(9), 785–793 (1992)
8. Gu, H., Hang, H., Lv, Q., Grunwald, D.: Fusing text and frienships for location inference in online social networks. In: IEEE/WIC/ACM International Conferences on Web Intelligence and Intelligent Agent Technology (WI-IAT), vol. 1, pp. 158–165. IEEE (2012)

9. Gu, H., Xie, X., Lv, Q., Ruan, Y., Shang, L.: Etree: effective and efficient event modeling for real-time online social media networks. In: 2011 IEEE/WIC/ACM International Conference on Web Intelligence and Intelligent Agent Technology (WI-IAT), vol. 1, pp. 300–307. IEEE (2011)
10. Henzinger, T.A.: The theory of hybrid automata. In: Inan, M.K., Kurshan, R.P. (eds.) Verification of Digital and Hybrid Systems. Springer, Heidelberg (2000)
11. Bauer, K.: A new modelling language for cyber-physical systems. Ph.D. Dissertation, TU Kaiserslautern (2012)
12. André, C., Mallet, F.: Clock constraints in UML/marte CCSL (2008)
13. Halbwachs, N., Raymond, P.: A Tutorial of Lustre. IMAG, Grenoble (1993)
14. Ptolemaeus, C.: System Design, Modeling, and Simulation: Using Ptolemy II. Ptolemy. org, Berkeley (2014)
15. Benveniste, A., Bourkey, T., Caillaud, B., Pouzet, M.: A hybrid synchronous language with hierarchical automata: static typing and translation to synchronous code. In: 2011 Proceedings of the International Conference on Embedded Software (EMSOFT), pp. 137–148. IEEE (2011)
16. Bourke, T., Pouzet, M.: Zélus: a synchronous language with odes. In: Proceedings of the 16th International Conference on Hybrid Systems: Computation and Control, pp. 113–118. ACM (2013)

Author Index

Printed in the United States
By Bookmasters

Printed in the United States
By Bookmasters